ICE CREAM!
The Whole Scoop

ICE CREAM!
The Whole Scoop

GAIL DAMEROW

Glenbridge Publishing Ltd.

Drawings by Patricia Hobbs

Library of Congress Catalog Card Number: 90-80207

International Standard Book Number: 0-944435-09-2

Printed in the U.S.A.

To my ice cream tasting partner, who enjoyed some likely concoctions, and endured many not so likely ones, during the preparation of this book.

Contents

Illustrations

Photographs

Figures

Color Plates

Jacket photograph— Ice Cream Rhapsody

Plate 1. Vanilla Coconut ice cream
Plate 2. Lemon, Orange, and Raspberry sherbet
Plate 3. Pistachio ice cream
Plate 4. Black Cherry ice cream
Plate 5. Vanilla sundae with chocolate sauce
Plate 6. Raspberry Peach ice cream
Plate 7. Ice cream—assorted flavors
Plate 8. Ice cream and fruit

Jacket photograph and plates 1, 7, and 8, courtesy of the American Dairy Association, Rosemont, Illinois.
Plates 2, 3, 4, 5, and 6, courtesy of Taylor Company, Rockton, Illinois.

Foreword

I

Nearly everyone worldwide smiles at the mere mention of ice cream. It is healthy, wholesome, and certainly promotes good feelings—regardless of age or cultural background. It is truly the undisputed champion as America's favorite dessert, and warrants the study of its history, makeup, and uses that are so adequately portrayed in Gail Damerow's book *Ice Cream! The Whole Scoop.*

Often, simple things add much "flavor" to our lives; yet we sometimes fail to appreciate the importance of the details that contribute to the finished product. The variations and artistry in producing a fine dessert or complimentary condiment to a gourmet meal are open to the imagination of everyone. However, a basic knowledge of the ingredients used for the finished product is a *must.*

I firmly believe that this book, *Ice Cream! The Whole Scoop,* should be required reading for those working within the frozen dairy dessert industry and certainly for those of us who merely want to improve our skills and artistry for both professional and home use.

Having dedicated my business life for over thirty years to the ice cream and dessert industry, I felt that my knowledge was nearly complete, but Gail Damerow's book, *Ice Cream! The Whole Scoop,* opened up a vista for exciting new innovations.

I am confident that her excellent contribution will add flavor and fun for the amateur dessert chef, and I truly hope that professionals will use this work to spark their imaginations and provide us all with new and exciting frozen dairy desserts that may well become another form of America's favorite enjoyment.

Kenneth M. Cook
Founder/President of Cook Flavoring Co.
Owner/President, Dreyer's Grand Ice
Cream, Inc., 1963-1981

II

Ice cream around the world takes many tastes, shapes, and even names. There's gelato, ice, sherbet, sorbet, glacé, and on and on. Whether we call them ice cream or something else, all share the quality of being uniquely refreshing.

In a factory at the rate of thousands of gallons per hour, or at home in the one-quart quantities presented in Gail Damerow's book, making ice cream is essentially a two-step process—ingredients are first prepared to form a liquid mix followed by freezing into a finished ice cream product.

One cannot duplicate store-bought ice cream in a kitchen. Small-scale production does not allow for all of the machinery and specialized facilities available to the ice cream manufacturer. Ice cream making at home should be imaginative with lots of creative twists, especially with flavorings. The many flavors offered in Gail Damerow's book assure us that we will never run out. Making ice cream can be the ultimate in creativity, so don't forget to give it your personal touch.

As a food scientist whose professional career spans over three decades of close observation of just about everything that has to do with ice cream, I found *Ice Cream! The Whole Scoop* to be easy and worthwhile reading. I came away with enough new ideas to keep me going for quite some time.

Philip G. Keeney, Ph.D.
Professor Emeritus of Food Science
Pennsylvania State University

Preface

I have never been one to strictly follow a recipe, so it was inevitable that soon after I got my first ice cream maker I started experimenting. In those days I didn't know much about ice cream except that I couldn't get enough of it, so some of my concoctions turned out pretty strange and not so wonderful. I searched in vain for a comprehensive guide to help me avoid the frustrating process of trial and error.

I ended up doing what I invariably do when a subject arouses my passions—I sought out experts and picked their brains. I reasoned that researching ice cream theory would help me better understand its practice. Among the things I learned is that no one knows everything there is to know about ice cream. In fact, some aspects of it have never even been studied.

My own experience shows me that nothing beats ice cream made with honest-to-goodness cream, with its silky smooth texture and its unique ability to blend with any flavoring to create full, rich taste. No wonder the creamy, old-fashioned kind is now called "gourmet" ice cream.

Modern emphasis on a low-fat diet has caused guilt-ridden aficionados like me to seek ways to cut back on the cream in ice cream. My solution has been to perfect techniques for making sherbets, frozen yogurt, and sorbets that let me continue to indulge myself freely. There's no question that gourmet ice cream remains the best, but these days I serve it a little less often.

The ice cream recipes in my personal collection are in a constant state of change, following changes in my family's tastes and dietary needs. Today's diversity of tastes and dietary strictures requires similar creativity on the part of anyone who prepares foods from scratch. That's why I've included in this volume all the little tips and secrets I wish I'd known when I first started out.

This isn't just a recipe book, therefore, but the kind of comprehensive how-to I sought for twenty years. It doesn't pretend to be sensationally innovative. Rather, it sets forth the full range of possibilities so you can do the innovating, creating frozen treats to satisfy your own tastes and dietary needs.

Before we start, let me make one slight confession: I enjoy the incredible luxury of using only prime ingredients—milk, eggs, fruits, and nuts produced in my own backyard. To take full advantage of these natural flavors, I reduce sweetening to a minimum, which happens to fit in with the trend toward more wholesome eating. If your own sweet tooth proves incorrigible, don't hesitate to boost sugar or other sweetening to suit your taste.

An unfortunate note, as this book goes to press, is the renewed threat of salmonella bacteria in eggs, requiring caution when making country ice cream or any other food containing raw eggs. This isn't the first time salmonella has threatened our egg supply. In the 1960s, cases of human salmonellosis from eggs sparked a massive and successful eradication program. In the 1990s, U.S.D.A. researchers are engaged in a similar program to curb the new source of infection.

Like many rural Americans, I produce my own eggs. I have no reason to believe they're infected and therefore have no qualms about using them in ice cream, cooked or raw. Although we're assured that the risk of contracting salmonellosis from eggs is extremely small, if I had to use eggs from an outside source, I would certainly observe the precautions outlined in chapter 13 until eggs become safe once again. I urge you to do likewise.

On a happier subject, I have been asked whether I've made all the recipes in this book, or their variations, and whether I use the brands specifically mentioned in them. Yes and yes. My ice cream makers work overtime whipping up new experiments and old family favorites, keeping our freezer well stocked. Hardly a day goes by that I don't enjoy at least one scoop of homemade ice cream.

Anticipating your next question: My weight hovers around 120 pounds, as it has since I was in sixth grade.

I want to include here a special "thank you" to Jack Melvin Byrne of Vita-Mix Corporation for teaching me how to make food-processor ice cream; to Miles Ezell, Jr. of Purity Dairies for showing me how commercial ice cream is made; and to Duane Poulterer of DDP Corporation for offering helpful tips on molding ice cream.

Thanks also to dairy specialists Philip G. Keeney, Professor Emeritus, The Pennsylvania State University, and Frank Pinkerton of Langston University for reviewing my "ten ton" manuscript and offering helpful suggestions. And a double hot-fudge sundae to all those, too numerous to mention, who contributed to this book on everyone's favorite food—ice cream.

Introduction

The Evolution Of Ice Cream

Ice cream was never really invented. It more or less evolved on its own. Even so, history isn't quite sure of the cold facts surrounding that evolution.

Western historians have long claimed that ice cream originated in biblical times. During the first century A.D., the Roman emperor Nero Claudius Caesar regularly sent his slaves high up into the Apennines for snow to chill wines and fruit juices. One day some bungler spilled saltpeter on the packed snow, supercooling it and freezing the juices into slushy ice—forerunner of today's ice cream.

On the other side of the globe, Eastern historians believe it was the Chinese who first developed the technology for making ices, and there's good evidence to back them up. The adventurer Marco Polo returned to Europe from his thirteenth-century Far East expeditions with recipes for delicious ices flavored with exotic fruits and with tales of their having been enjoyed in Asia for thousands of years.

True Ice Cream

Some say the Chinese were making ice cream from milk and spiced rice over four thousand years ago. Others credit Marco Polo with anticipating true ice cream by adding milk to the ices he discovered in the Orient.

Whatever the case, there is little disagreement that it was Catherine de Medici who introduced an early version of ice cream to the French nobility in 1533 when she married the Duke of Orleans, who later became King Henry II. The story goes that her Italian chefs served a different flavor on each of the thirty-four days of the wedding celebration. Their son, Henry III, became so addicted to the delectable treat that he demanded a daily dose.

Not satisfied with serving the sumptuous sweet by the dish, French chefs began molding it into *bombes glacées* made from concentric spheres of different flavors. This little trick became possible in the 1560s after the Spanish physician, Blasius Villafranca, rediscovered the idea of using ice sprinkled with saltpeter for freezing. His experiments led to the invention of the first home ice cream freezer, consisting of little more than a set of metal bowls with salted ice packed between them.

Frozen desserts eventually found their way to England, where the mid-seventeenth century monarch, Charles I, regarded them so highly that he decreed they be served only at the royal table. The king's hapless chef was threatened with beheading if he dared divulge his delicious secret. By a delightful twist of fate, in 1648 Charles I himself was beheaded, leaving his chef free to reveal the recipes to competitive noblemen.

Until 1670, ices remained the province of the court. In that year, a chef from Palermo established the Café Procope in Paris, where ices were (and still are) served to anyone with the money to buy them. By 1676, the streets were so crowded with copycat shops that an official permit was required for any new enterprise proposing to dispense ices.

During the ensuing French fervor for ices, progressively more cream was added until Parisians were enjoying something very much like today's ice cream. Around 1700, the 84-page *L'Art de Faire des Glacés* came out, the first known book devoted entirely to ice cream recipes.

Upon his first taste of the devastatingly rich confection later in the century, the French novelist Stendhal announced, "What a pity this isn't a sin!"

Elite Treat

It wasn't until recipes reached the colonies that the frozen confection became known as ice cream. Previously it was called "ice," sometimes modified as "milk ice," "cream ice," or "butter ice," depending on the ingredients used. The first written reference to ice cream in the New World is a letter describing a delicious "rarity" served at the residence of Maryland's governor, Thomas Bladen, in 1744.

By 1777 ice cream was being advertised in the *New York Gazette*. In the spring of that Revolutionary War year, the caterer Philip Lenzi published this intriguing ad: "May be had almost every day—ice cream." George Washington purportedly purchased hundreds of dollars worth in a single summer.

Ice cream socials were soon an important part of the American scene, the ice cream either special ordered or homemade. Our first president, with his tremendous appetite for frozen treats, was among those who found it convenient to make them at home. In 1789 he returned from France with a pewter pot freezer. Historic records show that he purchased a second "Cream Machine for Making Ice" in Philadelphia.

Our third president, Thomas Jefferson, was another great aficionado, and so was our fourth president, James Madison. Madison's wife, Dolly, elevated ice cream from a mere confection to a bona fide part of the meal when she served it as dessert at the White House. She created a sensation by combining strawberries from the Madison's garden with fresh cream from their Montpelier dairy to make the strawberry ice cream served at her husband's second inaugural ball.

But ice cream remained a delicacy enjoyed in the New World only by the very wealthy until a New Jersey woman, Nancy Johnson, invented the hand-crank freezer in 1845. Johnson's innovative device both simplified home ice cream making and reduced the cost of producing it commercially. Today, modern connoisseurs with demanding tastes still believe her classic freezer makes the best ice cream.

Necessity of Life

Not long after the invention of the hand-crank freezer, the editor of the influential magazine *Godey's Ladies Book* insisted that ice cream had become "one of the necessities of life. A party without it would be like breakfast without bread or dinner without a roast."

The original hand-crank freezer, and the many improved versions it spawned, made possible the first wholesale ice cream manufacturing plant, established in 1851 by Baltimore milk dealer Jacob Fussell who had been seeking a way to market surplus cream. Ice cream proved so much more profitable than milk that Fussell converted his entire dairy to ice cream production and later opened additional plants in Washington, Boston, and New York. Although Fussell is considered the father of the ice cream industry, his idea didn't really catch on until the centrifugal cream separator was invented in 1867.

In 1906 President Theodore Roosevelt signed the first Food and Drug Act regulating the manufacture of ice cream and other foods. The laws pertaining to frozen desserts are worth looking up if you're interested in knowing what goes into store-bought ice cream. They're published by the United States Government Printing Office as Code of Federal Regulations Title 21, Part 135, and are updated (fittingly enough) every April first.

An Essential Food

To qualify for sugar rations during World War I, industry convinced government to classify ice cream an essential food. Following the war, the height of prohibition found frosty refreshments featured as a fashionable alternative to hard liquor, and the rush was on to convert breweries into ice cream plants.

In those days, commercial ice cream making was a slow process, since only one batch could be frozen at a time. With the invention of the first successful continuous freezer by Clarence Vogt of Louisville, Kentucky, in 1926, it became possible to pour mix in at one end of a machine and have ice cream come out the other. Mass production became a reality and ice cream parlors sprang up everywhere. By 1927 the entire country was singing "I Scream, You Scream, We All Scream for Ice Cream."

But ice cream lost some of its appeal with the repeal of prohibition in 1933. And throughout the Great Depression, many could afford neither ice cream nor the ingredients to make it. World War II, with its quotas on milk and sugar, further dampened ice cream enthusiasm.

When rationing was lifted at the war's end, America went on an ice cream-eating rampage. The emerging affluent society could buy not only fancy foods like ice cream but also new-fangled electric refrigerators with built-in freezer compartments to store it in. At the peak of the 1946 ice cream craze, the latest word was carry-home packages from the neighborhood grocery.

True devotees who still preferred to make their own now had ready access to ice for their hand crank freezers, no longer having to rely on the ice man and his lake ice, cut and stored during winter. In the early 1950s, relief for sore cranking arms came in the form of electric motors offered as an alternative to the hand crank.

Ice Cream for America

Instead of putting the lid back on ice cream, the recession of the 1970s, coupled with the emerging youth cult, nurtured interest in simple pleasures, including a scoop of ice cream. The resulting revolution spilled into the eighties, spurred by the annual "Ice Cream for America Campaign." The brainchild of the International Ice Cream Association, this on-going campaign keeps the fervor for ice cream whipped into a frenzy. The neoprohibitionism of the nineties offers further inducement to indulge in ice cream.

Advancing technology continues to ensure the relevance of homemade ice cream in the modern world. By the early 1980s, both electric and hand-crank devices had been invented to freeze ice cream without ice, and ice cream making accessories for household freezers were pioneered. In addition, improved food processing techniques gave new meaning to the words, "instant ice cream."

Modern presidents maintain the same intimate association with ice cream enjoyed by our founding fathers. Richard Nixon had his favorite flavors flown to the White House from Europe and Hawaii, and Gerald Ford publicly confessed to being an ice creamaholic. In 1984, the importance of ice cream in our lives was reaffirmed when President Ronald Reagan declared July National Ice Cream Month, and the second Sunday in July National Ice Cream Day. And the highlight of the 1988 presidential campaign was the Great Midwestern Presidential Ice Cream Poll.

Trends

Throughout modern times, ice cream has figured big in our quest for faddish foods. During the 1950s and 1960s the mania was for "mellorine," an ice cream imitator developed during World War II, made with vegetable or animal fat instead of cream. In the seventies, frozen yogurt was in, then bided its time to make a come-back in the nineties. The eighties saw a three-way split between gourmet, natural, and nondairy ice creams.

Gourmet or superpremium ice cream satisfied the yuppie craving for rich confections high in cream, cholesterol, and calories. At the other end of the scale, nutrition and fitness followers favored lighter, nondairy desserts. These seemingly opposing forces merged in a mutual appreciation for the old-fashioned, good flavor of all-natural ingredients that continues today.

For all these ups and downs, most of the frosty treats we scoop up remain ice cream in one or another of its various forms, including soft-serve ice milk. We enjoy sherbet, the next runner-up, only five percent as much. Catching up with sherbet in popularity and likely to surpass it during the nineties are French sorbets and Italian sorbetti, thanks in part to heightening health awareness and in part to the enduring allure of European cookery.

Some ice cream experts believe that frozen yogurt and soy ice creams such as Tofutti will attain permanent stature. Others disagree, contending that both will be relegated to the relative obscurity of the once-popular mellorine. Whatever the case, no doubt before long we'll be spooning down something altogether different. Already peeking over the horizon is fiber-rich ice cream made from rice, a treat prophetically enjoyed by the Chinese in the year 2000 . . . B.C.

POPULARITY OF DIFFERENT FREEZES	
Ice cream	63.6%
Ice milk	25.5%
Sherbet	3.8%
Ice	3.6%
Mellorine	0.7%
All others	2.8%

Source: 1988 statistics compiled by the International Ice Cream Association.

Ice Cream Capital

As the twentieth century draws to a close, ice cream parlors are enjoying renewed popularity, ice cream sales are breaking new records, and home ice cream freezers are cranking away like never before. Community service organizations have become partial to old-fashioned ice cream socials, and those oh-so trendy wine tastings of the seventies seem destined for replacement by ice cream tastings of the nineties.

More popular than all other desserts combined, ice cream has become the Great American Dessert. Not only is it our all-time favorite way to end a meal, but many of us have come to regard it as a household staple. Citing the ninety-eight percent who enjoy it on a regular basis, zealots go so far as to name ice cream our nation's number one resource.

On average, each of us spoons down nearly twenty-three quarts per year, making Americans the world's highest per capita consumers and qualifying the United States as the undisputed Ice Cream Capital of the World.

Part One: Freeze It

Technically speaking, the term "ice cream" applies to a specific kind of food. It is, in fact, defined by law. Our everyday usage doesn't always conform with the legal definition, largely because there is no satisfactory generic word for the category of foods that includes not only ice cream but also sherbet, frozen yogurt, Tofutti, sorbet, and the like.

Sometimes we group them all together as "frozen desserts," a term that hardly fits vegetable sorbets, which are served as appetizers or condiments. "Frozen dainties" was an early effort that sounds quaint today, and "frozen refreshments" is cumbersome. We thus tend to call them all "ice cream," much as some of us erroneously call all soft drinks "Coke." But the noun "freeze" handily describes ice cream together with all other frozen treats, and I will use it thus throughout this book.

Formulas

The recipes that follow include every kind of freeze popular today, organized according to basic formula rather than flavor. There are two reasons for this unusual departure from the norm.

First, it's confusing to be confronted with page after page of recipes for vanilla ice cream, for example, with no indication of the significant difference between them. I have therefore introduced each basic freeze in a way that clarifies exactly how it is different from the others. Only after a sound foundation is laid will variations be given.

This method of organization will help you find the answer to the inevitable question, Which recipe is best? Each of us holds our own preferences for the ingredients we use, either because of their contribution to texture and flavor or because of our individual dietary concerns. The second reason for organizing recipes according to category is precisely to help you choose the foundation on which you prefer to build flavoring variations.

Format

Another way recipes in this book depart from the usual is in format. Traditional recipe format requires skipping back and forth between a list of ingredients and separate directions for their use, an unwieldy system making it all too easy to overlook a key ingredient or instruction.

In the recipes that follow, you'll find procedures noted on the left-hand side and ingredients listed at the right. Read each recipe as you would anything else, from left to right, working your way down the page. The narrative explains as you go what's to be done with which ingredients, while a glance down the right-hand column will tell you what ingredients you need to have on hand.

Personal style will strongly influence the way in which you prepare a mix or how you operate your ice cream maker. Two people using the exact same ingredients and seemingly identical freezing methods can easily end up with different results in taste, texture, quality, or quantity. This book gives you all the information you need to adjust your recipes or freezing techniques until you're completely satisfied with the results.

When it comes to frozen treats, anything goes. So be bold. Consider this book a guideline for devising recipes that are distinctly yours. Tasting, evaluating, adjusting, and tasting again—it's all part of the exciting adventure of making your own ice cream!

ABBREVIATIONS	
This symbol	**Means this**
t	teaspoon
T	tablespoon
C	cup
qt	quart
oz	ounce
#	pound
pkg	package
"	inch

MEASUREMENT EQUIVALENTS	
This quantity	**Equals this**
$1\frac{1}{2}$ t	$\frac{1}{2}$ T
3 t	1 T
2 T	$\frac{1}{8}$ C
4 T	$\frac{1}{4}$ C
2 C	1 pint
4 C	1 qt
4 qt	1 gallon

1

Still Freezing

Ever since household freezers became commonplace, people have used them to avoid the need for separate ice cream making appliances. Ice cream made in the freezer cannot be stirred constantly, as it is by the dasher of an ice cream maker. The ice cream is therefore said to be "still frozen" as opposed to "stir frozen."

Smooth Texture

Without stirring, texture tends to be coarse. Smoother texture can be encouraged partly through the procedure you follow and partly through your choice of ingredients. Corn syrup, cornstarch, gelatin, and eggs all interfere with ice crystal formation and encourage incorporation of air. When cream or egg whites are used, they're often whipped before being folded in. Otherwise, the finished mix is whipped after it's frozen firm enough to hold tiny bubbles of air.

Rapid, even freezing keeps ice crystals small. Encourage fast freezing by using shallow containers such as ice trays with the slats removed, loaf pans, cake tins, or anything else that holds a layer no more than two inches deep. Cover filled trays with foil to keep additional ice crystals from forming on the surface as the mix freezes.

You can speed freezing along by placing trays either at the bottom of the freezer compartment or on a shelf with coils. If possible, rest them on already frozen foods rather than directly on the shelf.

Turn the freezer down to its coldest setting, usually around 0° F (–18° C). Most chest and upright freezers normally operate at that low temperature. If you use the freezer compartment of your refrigerator, adjust the setting an hour in advance and return it to normal after the mixture has frozen.

Even the best still-frozen desserts are never quite as smooth as stir-frozen ones. Since ice crystals continue to grow during storage, causing constant deterioration of texture, plan to serve still-frozen creations within a day or so.

On Ice

The great thing about still freezing is that it lets you make ice cream without electricity. You can, for example, freeze ice cream on outings to surprise family and friends. You'll need a picnic chest or other large, insulated container loaded with cracked ice. In winter you can use lake ice or hard-packed snow.

Pour your mix into a freezer-safe tray with a snap-on lid that won't let brine seep in. Ideal containers include Tupperware or Rubbermaid ones designed for storing cupcakes or pies. With the lid securely in place, bed the filled container in cracked ice combined three-to-one with rock salt.

Pack at least three inches of ice around the sides, top, and bottom of the container. In really hot weather, you may need to drain off brine and add more ice and salt before freezing is complete, usually in four to six hours.

Mousse

The quintessential still-frozen dessert, so rich it's served in mini-portions, is mousse made from sweetened, flavored whipped cream. For a basic frozen mousse, mix heavy cream with one-quarter cup sugar per cup. Whip the cream into soft peaks (never stiff ones or the texture will be unpleasantly buttery).

Gently fold in the flavoring of your choice, including any of those suggested in appendix A. It's common practice, though not essential, to add an equal portion of softened ice cream of complementary flavor.

After the mousse is partially frozen, a little liqueur or some finely chopped nuts or fruit may be added. Candied fruit and dried dates work best, but fresh, frozen, or canned fruit are okay, provided they're well drained (to prevent excess juice from spoiling texture).

For elegant individual servings, freeze mousse in pleated cupcake papers, in fluted nut cups, in paper soufflé cups (if you can find them), or in scallop shells coated with nonstick cooking spray. Or, if you prefer, shape it in a large, decorative gelatin mold and bring it to the table for slicing and serving. Complete directions for successful molding are given in Chapter 26, "Bombes and Other Molds."

CLOUD NINE

This airy, basic mousse goes well with fresh sliced fruit or sugared berries. For a variation that's firmer in texture and has a custardlike flavor, beat 2 egg yolks until light, add the honey, heat in a double boiler until thick, then chill before folding in remaining ingredients.

Beat stiff	**2 egg whites.**
Fold in	**¹/₂ C honey.**
Whip and fold in	**1¹/₂ C heavy cream** **¹/₄ t almond extract.**

Freeze firm, 3 to 4 hours.

yield: about 1 quart

FRENCH MOUSSE

The absolute ultimate in rich, creamy perfection is this classic French mousse made with egg yolks, mounds of gently whipped cream, and boiled sugar-water syrup. You'll need either a candy thermometer or an eye for judging the soft ball stage—when a small amount of syrup forms a flattened ball in a glass of cold water. For flavoring variations, substitute sherry for the vanilla, or fold in ¹/₂ C finely chopped nuts or shaved chocolate.

In small saucepan combine	**³/₄ C sugar** **¹/₃ C hot water.**
Boil to soft ball stage, 235° F (114° C).	
In double boiler combine	**5 egg yolks** **2 T warm water.**
Gradually beat in hot syrup.	
Stirring, cook until thick, 6 to 8 minutes.	
Remove from heat and stir until cool.	
Add	**1 T vanilla.**
Whip and fold in	**2 C heavy cream.**

Freeze firm, 3 to 4 hours.

yield: about 1 quart

CHOCOLATE MOUSSE

This chocolate version of traditional French mousse calls for light corn syrup in place of sugar-water syrup. For a Continental flair, include 2 T orange or almond liqueur. To create a double chocolate treat, fold in $1/2$ C coarsely grated, semisweet chocolate. Unmold onto spoonfuls of sundae sauce (recipes in Chapter 24, "Sundaes, Parfaits, and Splits") or freeze and serve in chocolate cups (described in Chapter 22, "Edible Cups").

In double boiler melt	**6-oz semisweet chocolate.**
In medium bowl beat	**6 egg yolks.**
Stir in	**1 C white corn syrup.**
Add melted chocolate.	
Stirring, heat in double boiler until thickened.	
Cool.	
Whip and fold in	**$1^1/_2$ C heavy cream 1 t vanilla.**
Freeze firm.	

yield: about 1 quart

BERRY MOUSSE

Gelatin lends firmness to the texture of this berry mousse. Strain blackberries or raspberries to remove the seeds, an unnecessary step with strawberries. If you substitute sweetened frozen berries, reduce the sugar by half. Garnish with whole fresh sugared berries, or purée additional sweetened berries as an accompanying sauce.

Crush	**2 C fresh berries.**
Cover with	**$1/_2$ C sugar.**
Let stand 1 hour.	
Purée.	
In small saucepan soften	**1 pkg plain gelatin**
in	**$1/_4$ C cold water.**
Heat until gelatin dissolves.	
Remove from heat and stir in berries.	
Chill until slightly thickened.	
Whip and fold in	**1 C heavy cream.**
Freeze firm, 3 to 4 hours.	

yield: about 1 quart

BISCUIT TORTONI

In 1798, a Neapolitan named Velloni opened an ice cream shop on the *Boulevard des Italiens* in Paris. It was so successful that he established a chain, overextending himself and ending in bankruptcy. His head waiter, a fellow named Tortoni, took over the original shop and did so well that the composer Offenbach extolled him in one of his operettas. This mousse was created by Tortoni's son and remains a favorite to this day. Some versions call for sherry in place of rum, others omit the spirits entirely.

Combine

> **1 C heavy cream**
> **1 C crumbled macaroons**
> **$^1/_2$ C sifted powdered sugar.**

Chill 30 minutes.

Stir in

> **$^1/_4$ C rum.**

Beat into soft peaks

> **1 C heavy cream**
> **1 t vanilla.**

Fold in crumb mixture.

Spoon into 12 fluted cupcake liners.

Sprinkle with

> **$^1/_4$ C chopped toasted almonds.**

Top with

> **12 maraschino cherries.**

Cover and freeze firm, 3 hours or overnight.

yield: 12 servings

Fruit Salad

A popular variation of mousse is fruit salad, in which the sweetened whipped cream is flavored to taste with mayonnaise. One to two tablespoons of mayonnaise per cup of whipped cream is about right.

A simple fruit salad consists of three parts mayonnaised whipped cream combined with two parts well-drained bits of pineapple, apricot, peach, pear, prune, maraschino cherry, or any combination of these.

Fruit salad is usually frozen in a flat container, sliced into squares, and served on a bed of grape or lettuce leaves. It may also be molded in individual ornamental gelatin molds. Perhaps the prettiest composition is a large molded ring, arranged on a platter and the center heaped with sliced fruit or whole berries—the perfect accompaniment to a light, summery meal.

AMBROSIA FRUIT SALAD

Ambrosia, the food of Greek and Roman gods, confers everlasting life on any mortal who tastes it. You may not believe in the old mythology, but you'll think you're in seventh heaven when you taste this ambrosia.

Dissolve

in

1 small pkg orange gelatin

1 C boiling water.

Reserving liquid, drain

11-oz can mandarin oranges
8-oz can crushed pineapple.

Add enough water to make 1 C and add to gelatin.

Chill until thick.

Fold in fruit and

1 C whipped cream
1 C flaked coconut
1/4 C finely chopped walnuts
2 T mayonnaise.

Pour into freezer tray.

Freeze firm.

yield: about 1 quart

CRANBERRY SWIRL

This fruit salad looks pretty as a picture when served on lettuce leaves and garnished with whole cranberries and orange twists. For equal appeal, spoon it into hollowed-out orange cups (directions in Chapter 22, "Edible Cups").

Finely chop	**2 C cranberries.**
In large mixer combine with	**1 C sugar.**
Let stand 5 minutes.	
Add	**3 egg whites** **1 T orange juice** **1 t grated orange rind** **1 t vanilla.**
Beat at low speed until frothy.	
On high speed, beat into stiff peaks (8 to 10 min).	
In small bowl, whip into soft peaks	**1 C heavy cream.**
Combine 1 C whipped cream with	**1 C chopped celery.**
Fold in cranberries.	
Spread in 12" x 7" x 2" pan.	
Into remaining cream fold	**⅓ C mayonnaise** **1 t grated orange rind.**
Spoon on top of cranberry mixture and swirl gently with a knife.	
Sprinkle with	**½ C finely chopped nuts.**
Cover and freeze firm, about 6 hours.	

yield: about 1 quart

Ice Cream, Sherbet, and Ice

Because mousse contains mostly airy whipped cream, it freezes nicely without additional stirring or beating. To achieve similar smoothness in less rich desserts, stir occasionally to incorporate air and break down ice crystals. Stir ice creams, sherbets, and ices as soon as they freeze slushy, repeating every half hour until freezing is complete.

For increased smoothness, whirl the partially frozen mix in a powerful blender or food processor; or use an electric or hand beater and a bowl large enough to prevent icy chunks from jumping out. If necessary, break up unwieldy lumps with a fork. Start beaters at slow speed and gradually increase to high as the mixture nears velvety smoothness. Repeat once or twice while freezing progresses.

To minimize melting during beating, prechill the bowl or blender carafe and return the mixture to the freezer as quickly as possible. The timing is touchy here—if you beat the mixture too soon, it will melt back down and you'll have to start freezing all over again. Begin beating when the edges are quite solid but the center remains fairly slushy, which usually takes one and a half hours.

Freeze and Serve

Complete freezing takes three to five hours, depending on the depth of your freezer trays, your freezer setting, and the combination of ingredients you use. Freezing time will be less if you retain the same shallow trays after the final stirring, rather than packing the ice cream into cartons. If you prefer to serve slices from a brick, finish freezing in a loaf pan or other blocky container, allowing plenty of room for expansion. A third alternative that nets an especially luxurious dessert is to spread the nearly frozen mixture into a prefrozen pie shell (recipes in Chapter 29, "Ice Cream Pies").

Because still-frozen ice cream is harder than its stir-frozen counterpart, it requires a longer tempering period before slicing or scooping (for details, see Chapter 18, "Hardening and Storing"). Partial thawing and refreezing ruins texture, so pack only as much into each container as you plan to serve at one time.

VANILLA ICE CREAM

Gelatin gives this ice cream extra body, letting you get by with less stirring. If you're among those who feel that the flavor of gelatin overpowers delicate vanilla, omit the gelatin and substitute light cream for the milk.

In saucepan soften	**1 t plain gelatin**
in	**½ C milk.**
Heat until gelatin dissolves.	
Stir in	**½ C sugar.**
Cool.	

VANILLA ICE CREAM, cont'd.

Pour into freezer tray.

Chill until slushy.

Whip into soft peaks   **1¹/₂ C heavy cream.**

Add   **2 t vanilla.**

Beat frozen mixture.

Fold in whipped cream.

Pour into freezer tray or mold.

Freeze firm.

yield: about 1 quart

FRENCH VANILLA ICE CREAM

French vanilla gets its richness and smooth texture from a custard base. It's the perfect thing to serve on warm stewed fruit, fruit dumplings, or hot pie. For flavor variation, add 1 T brandy, sherry, or any liqueur in place of vanilla.

Beat   **3 egg yolks.**

Beat in   **1 C confectioner's sugar**
²/₃ C cream.

Cook in double boiler until slightly thickened.

Cool and add   **2 t vanilla.**

Whip into soft peaks   **1¹/₃ C heavy cream.**

Beat stiff but not dry   **3 egg whites.**

Fold cream and whites into cooled custard.

Freeze firm.

yield: about 1 quart

CREAMY CARAMEL ICE CREAM

This recipe takes advantage of two characteristics of evaporated milk— its slightly caramelized flavor and its ability to whip up light and fluffy. For a delightful coffee undertone, dissolve 1 t instant coffee in the ¹/₄ C evaporated milk. To make *caramel nut* ice cream, fold in ¹/₂ C finely chopped pecans with the whipped milk.

In small saucepan melt	¹/₂ **T butter.**
Add	¹/₃ **C brown sugar** **2 T water.**
Stir until sugar dissolves.	
Bring to boil, boil 3 minutes.	
Stir in	¹/₄ **C evaporated milk.**
Cool and add	**1 t vanilla.**
Chill.	
Chill well, then whip	³/₄ **C evaporated milk.**
Fold in sugar mixture.	
Freeze firm, 3 to 4 hours.	

yield: about 1 quart

CHERRY ICE CREAM

Fresh cherries add crunchy bits of tasty fruit to this confection. Canned cherries are already pitted, but they're neither as crunchy nor as easy to chop. Whether you use fresh or canned, select sour cherries such as Queen Anne, which are more flavorful than sweet ones like Bing. This recipe will also make *peach* or *apricot* ice cream with the simple substitution of the appropriate fruit.

Pit and chop	**2 C sour cherries.**
Add	**1 C sugar.**
Let stand 20 minutes.	
Stir in	**1 C heavy cream.**
Pour into freezer tray.	
Freeze slushy.	
Turn into large bowl and beat smooth.	

CHERRY ICE CREAM, cont'd.

Whip into soft peaks and add   **1 C heavy cream.**

Freeze firm, 3 to 4 hours.

yield: about 1 quart

BREAKFAST ICE CREAM

Fussy little eaters don't take much coaxing to chow down on a breakfast of fortified cereal topped with egg-rich French vanilla, garnished with fresh strawberries or sliced bananas. Or serve up a scoop of this specially formulated breakfast ice cream with the raisins, honey, eggs, and high protein cereal already incorporated.

Lightly beat   **1 egg yolk.**

Add   **¹/₄ C sugar**
    ¹/₄ C honey
    ¹/₂ T flour.

In double boiler heat   **1 C milk.**

Pour a little milk over yolk mixture, stir mixture into remaining milk.

Stirring, heat until mixture coats a metal spoon.

Strain and chill.

Add   **1 t vanilla**
    2 C half and half.

Pour into freezer tray.

Freeze slushy.

In large bowl, beat smooth.

Stir in   **¹/₂ C chopped raisins**
    ³/₄ C high protein cereal.

Freeze firm, 3 to 4 hours.

yield: about 1 quart

ORANGE FROZEN YOGURT

This tangy frozen yogurt retains its soft-serve texture, even after hours in the freezer. Experiment with fruit juices and yogurt flavors to create your own winning combinations.

Mix thoroughly	1¹/₃ C orange yogurt
	1¹/₃ C orange juice
	¹/₂ C light corn syrup
	2 t lemon juice.
Pour into freezer tray.	
Freeze slushy.	
Whip smooth.	
Beat foamy	3 egg whites.
Add	2 T powdered sugar.
Beat stiff.	
Fold into yogurt mixture.	
Freeze firm, 4 to 5 hours.	

yield: about 1 quart

CAFÉ AU LAIT SHERBET

Here's a delightful dessert that doubles as after-dinner coffee—scooped into a cup, heaped with whipped cream, and topped with a single chocolate curl. For a sensational frozen pie, freeze sherbet firm in a chocolate crumb or brownie crust (recipes in Chapter 29), spread with a layer of French mousse, and sprinkle with grated semisweet chocolate and chopped toasted almonds.

In saucepan soften	1 pkg plain gelatin
in	2¹/₂ C milk.
Combine and add	¹/₂ C sugar
	2 T instant coffee crystals.
Stirring, heat until coffee and sugar dissolve.	
Cool.	
Freeze almost firm, about 2 hours.	

CAFÉ AU LAIT SHERBET,
cont'd.

Beat into soft peaks	**2 egg whites.**
Gradually add	**2 T sugar.**
Beat frozen mixture smooth.	
Fold in egg whites.	
Freeze firm, 3 to 4 hours.	

yield: about 1 quart

WATERMELON ICE

There's nothing more refreshing on a summer day than a slice of chilled watermelon, unless it's a glorious pink scoop of watermelon ice. Garnish with blueberries or tiny balls of fresh cantaloupe and honeydew. Adjust sugar as required by the melon's sweetness.

In small saucepan soften	**1 pkg plain gelatin**
in	**¼ C cold water.**
Heat until dissolved.	
Remove seeds and rind from	**3# watermelon.**
Purée for 3 cups pulp.	
Stir in gelatin and	**3-oz thawed lemonade concentrate** **⅛ t salt** **¼ C sugar.**
Pour into freezer tray.	
Freeze slushy.	
Turn into large bowl, beat smooth.	
Freeze firm, 3 to 4 hours.	

yield: about 1 quart

PERSIMMON SORBET

An all too often overlooked autumn fruit that makes an easy yet delightful sorbet is the sweet, mild flavored persimmon. Its orange-red fruit is fully ripe when the skin turns soft and glossy. Separate the pulp from fibrous threads by pressing through a sieve with the back of a spoon. Serve this delicacy California style, on a bed of fresh grape leaves.

Blend

4 C persimmon purée
¹/₂ C sugar
2 T lemon or lime juice.

Freeze, stirring once or twice until firm.

yield: about 1 quart

CRANBERRY SPOOM

Winter holidays wouldn't be the same without cranberry sauce. For a change of pace, serve this spunky sorbet as an appetizer, heaped into orange tulip cups made according to directions in Chapter 22, "Edible Cups." Or layer it with orange sherbet and vanilla ice cream in a colorful holiday bombe, following instructions in Chapter 26.

Beat smooth

1# jellied cran-berry sauce.

Add

1 orange rind, grated
²/₃ C orange juice.

Pour into freezer tray.

Freeze almost firm.

Beat into soft peaks

3 egg whites.

Gradually add

¹/₃ C sugar.

In large cold bowl, beat mixture smooth.

Fold in egg whites.

Freeze firm, 3 to 4 hours.

yield: about 1 quart

JAMAICAN LIME SPOOM

End a heavy meal or begin a light one with this fluffy sorbet. For *gin rickey* spoom, substitute gin for rum. Or, if you prefer, leave the spirits out altogether. You'll need two large limes or three small ones. (See Chapter 3 for a full discussion of spooms.)

In medium saucepan, soften	**1 pkg plain gelatin**
in	**2 C milk.**
Add	**1 C sugar.**
Bring just to boil.	
Cool.	
Stir in	**¹/₃ C lime juice** **2 t grated lime** **rind** **2 T rum.**
Pour into freezer tray.	
Freeze almost firm.	
In chilled bowl, combine with	**2 egg whites.**
Beat smooth.	
Freeze firm, about 4 hours.	

yield: about 1 quart

Frozen Suckers

The invention of frozen ice on a stick is credited to two Americans named Ross and Robbins who, in the 1870s, marketed their frozen fruit concoctions as Hokey-Pokeys. The term was derived from the prototype of the Good Humor Man, the hokey-pokey man—a schoolchild's corruption of the cry of Italian ice cream vendors, "Ecco un poco," or, "Here's a little." The dictionary still defines hokey-pokey as cheap ice cream sold by street vendors.

The Popsicle as we know it now didn't come about until 1923 when an Oakland, California, amusement park lemonade concessionaire named Frank Epperson left a glass of lemonade on a windowsill one wintry night while visiting friends in New Jersey. By the next morning the juice had frozen in the glass, firmly trapping the stirring spoon.

To extract the frozen lemonade, Epperson ran warm water over the outside of the glass. The contents slipped out easily, but the spoon remained firmly stuck. Epperson patented this "invention" as the Epsicle, later registered under the trade name Popsicle.

Hokey-pokeys, Popsicles, fruitsicles, ice pops, frozen suckers—whatever you call them, they're classified as kids' stuff despite the refreshing simplicity that endears them equally to adults. Few can resist a frozen sucker as a quick and cooling snack on a busy summer day. It's also just the thing to sooth itchy gums when allergy season rolls around.

Molding

Ice pops are generally frozen without any stirring whatever, but you can successfully mold nearly any soft ice cream, sherbet, or ice. Molds are designed expressly for making frozen suckers, or you can use ice cube trays or cupcake papers set in muffin tins. By far the most convenient size and shape is the ordinary three-ounce paper cup.

Add sticks after the mixture freezes slushy enough to hold them upright. Proper sticks are hard to find. A good starting place is a craft or hobby shop. Tongue depressors, candy apple sticks, and wooden spoons make passable substitutes.

Suckers require three to six hours to freeze, depending on size, combination of ingredients, and freezer setting. When they feel solid to your squeeze, they're ready to eat. Molds will release after being held for a moment in warm water. A paper mold may simply be torn away.

FROZEN FRUIT SUCKERS

Orange reigns as the all-time favorite ice pop flavor, but you can use any beverage—flavored milk, soft drinks, Kool-Aid, fruit punch, lemonade, or any other juice. Crushed fruit adds nutritional value. Mashed strawberries and crushed pineapple are both delicious.

Mix and divide among 6 molds

1³/₄ C juice
¹/₂ C sugar.

Divide and spoon in

¹/₂ C mashed fruit.

Freeze firm.

yield: 6 3-oz suckers

SUGARLESS SUCKERS

During summer weather when the calories from sugar increase body heat and add to discomfort, let frozen apple juice concentrate supply all the sweetness an ice pop needs. This recipe is especially good made with raspberries, pressed through a sieve to remove the seeds.

Mix well

1 C fruit purée
²/₃ C thawed apple juice concentrate
²/₃ C water.

Mold and freeze.

yield: 6 3-oz suckers

FROZEN YOGURT SUCKERS

Yogurt adds refreshing tang and increases the nutritional value of an ice pop. Simply stir up and mold any flavored, sweetened yogurt, or try this sherbet-like formula containing plain yogurt and fruit juice or purée.

Mix well

1¼ **C juice or**
 purée
1 C plain yogurt
¼ **C honey.**

Mold and freeze firm.

yield: 6 3-oz suckers

Granita

Granita is an Italian original, one of the two kinds of ice served at a typical Italian *gelateria*, or ice cream shop. (The other is *sorbetto*, discussed in Chapter 3, "Ice and Sorbet.") Its name comes from the Italian word for "grainy," which aptly describes the coarse texture resulting from freezing without beating. Because it contains less air, a granita is much stronger in flavor than a stir-frozen ice.

A traditional granita is grated or shaved, making it incredibly light and powdery. Sometimes it's chipped, instead, into icy shards. The American trick of freezing it in ice cube trays to process in a blender is nothing short of heretical.

Technique

You can easily make a proper granita with a fine, snowy texture by freezing it in trays and periodically raking it with a fork. The idea is to break apart the ice crystals without destroying their characteristic shape. For the sake of convenience, the mix may be made up a day in advance and kept refrigerated in a covered container. A few hours before serving, stir the mix well and pour it into freezer trays.

Using a fork, gently crush icy lumps two or three times during freezing. Depending on your freezer setting, in two to three hours the granita will be ready to serve. Rake it once more with a fork to lighten up the texture and serve it in prechilled bowls or glasses to reduce melting.

A serving of granita looks remarkably like a dish of sparkling edible sequins. Lemon and coffee are the most popular flavors, but chocolate and strawberry don't lag far behind. For a decidedly American variation, purée six cups cubed watermelon together with three tablespoons lemon juice and three-quarters cup sugar. Freeze for about an hour and rake with a fork before serving.

LEMON GRANITA

The best lemon granita is made from fresh juice squeezed from six or seven lemons for each quart. Reserve the shells to make serving cups following directions in Chapter 22, "Edible Cups." Top each serving with whipped cream flavored with grated rind, or garnish the granita with a lemon twist. To make *mint* granita, add ¼ C crushed mint leaves to the boiled syrup, cool, strain, and add the lemon juice.

| In saucepan bring to boil | 1⅓ C sugar |
| | 2⅔ C water. |

Stir until sugar dissolves.

Continue cooking 5 minutes.

Cool to room temperature.

| Stir in | 1⅓ C lemon juice. |

Cover and chill 1 to 2 hours.

Stir and pour into freezer tray.

Freeze firm, about 2 hours, scraping with a fork every 30 minutes.

Scrape once more before serving.

yield: about 1 quart

STRAWBERRY GRANITA

You can use sweetened frozen strawberries in this recipe if you reduce the sugar to ⅓ cup. Garnish with fresh whole strawberries or serve on a bed of sliced kiwi. For *kiwi* granita, simply substitute kiwi purée for strawberries.

| In saucepan bring to boil | ⅔ C sugar |
| | 1⅓ C water. |

Stir until sugar dissolves.

Continue cooking 5 minutes.

Cool to room temperature.

| Purée and stir in | 2⅔ C fresh strawberries |
| | 2 T lemon juice. |

STRAWBERRY GRANITA, cont'd.

Cover and chill 1 to 2 hours.

Stir and pour into freezer tray.

Freeze firm, about 2 hours, scraping with a fork every 30 minutes.

Scrape once more before serving.

yield: about 1 quart

COFFEE GRANITA

Served Sicilian style—folded into an equal portion of whipped cream—coffee granita is purely addictive. Sicilians have even been known to serve it for breakfast. If you prefer, reserve the whipped cream as topping and garnish with a chocolate curl or a twist of candied lemon. Or hold the whipped cream and instead add a splash of anisette, grappa, or Sambuca.

In saucepan combine

$^1/_2$ **C sugar**
3" strip lemon rind
1 C water.

Bring to boil, stirring until sugar dissolves.

Remove from heat and add

$^1/_3$ **C instant coffee.**

Cool and stir in

2$^1/_2$ C cold water.

Strain.

Cover and chill 1 to 2 hours.

Stir and pour into freezer tray.

Freeze firm, about 2 hours, scraping with a fork every 30 minutes.

Scrape once more before serving.

yield: about 1 quart

CHOCOLATE GRANITA

Those of us brought up on milk chocolate experience an entirely new taste sensation in this perky chocolate granita. To achieve milk chocolate richness, fold in an equal portion of slightly sweetened whipped cream, perhaps flavored with liqueur, rum, or brandy.

Sift together	²/₃ **C cocoa** ²/₃ **C sugar.**
In saucepan bring to a simmer	1¹/₃ **C water.**
Gradually whisk in cocoa mixture.	
Stir until sugar dissolves.	
Remove from heat and add	**1 t vanilla** **pinch salt.**
Cool, then stir in	**1 C cold water.**
Cover and chill 1 to 2 hours.	
Stir and pour into freezer tray.	
Freeze firm, about 2 hours, scraping with a fork every 30 minutes.	
Scrape once more before serving.	

yield: about 1 quart

Snow Cones

Some chroniclers liken granita to a snow cone, a comparison that's not at all apt. Snow cones consist of plain ice, shaved and doused with fruit syrup. Store-bought ones are typically flavored artificially.

Snow cones are easy to make at home by scooping icy slush into water-fountain paper cones and drizzling on fruit-flavored pancake syrup or thinned-down sundae sauce (recipes in Chapter 24, "Sundaes, Parfaits, and Splits"). For a decidedly adult version, splash shaved ice with your favorite liqueur and call it a "frappé."

Prepare the slush by processing ice cubes in an ice crusher or food processor; or whirl cubes in a blender with a little water, then drain away the water before packing the "snow" into cones; or use a table-top ice shaver designed expressly for the purpose (a source is listed in Appendix C, "Supplies"). Another option is to take a tip from the treat's name and use clean, freshly fallen snow, as did the legendary Aztec emperor Montezuma, who is said to have enjoyed his snow cones doused with warm chocolate.

Snow Cream

Before electricity and refrigeration made ice a household commodity, rural ice cream lovers had to wait until the first snowfall to enjoy their favorite frosty treat. Since rural electrification was completed just over fifty years ago, snow cream remains traditional in many areas, where folks still swear it's the best ice cream ever.

It's been said that snow cream recipes are like snowflakes—no two are alike. Each version starts with a large, prechilled bowl and a generous amount of fresh, fluffy snow, harvested after at least a six-inch fall and gathered well away from roadsides, heavy industry, and other potential sources of pollutants.

Since snow varies so much in density and texture, it's hard to say exactly how much you'll need. Gather plenty so your snow-cream-in-progress won't start melting if you have to dash out for more. Take care not to pack down the snow as you gather it up.

Back in the house, gradually stir in fruit juice or sweetened cream until you achieve ice cream consistency. Pour the snow cream into a covered container and bury it deep in a snow drift to harden for an hour or two, or serve it freshly made in prechilled bowls to retard melting.

Old-timers insist snow cream tastes best when eaten in front of a warm crackling fire, participants spooning the delicacy from a communal bowl. This tradition is as practical as it is cozy since the large serving bowl retards melting while the snow cream is being eaten.

SNOW CREAM

Some variation of this basic recipe is found throughout snow cream country. Sometimes a well-beaten egg is added, sometimes brown sugar replaces the granulated sugar, and sometimes whole milk or chocolate milk is used instead of cream.

In large bowl gather **2-qts fresh, clean snow.**

Combine and stir in **1 C cream**
¹/₂ C sugar
1 t vanilla
dash salt.

yield: about 1 quart

CHOCOLATE SNOW CREAM

This version from Ontario, Canada, has quite a different texture from traditional American snow cream. The flavor can easily be varied by using different kinds of pudding.

Beat at high speed until fluffy

2-qts lightly packed snow
1 can evaporated milk
1 C milk powder
³/₄ C sugar
1 pkg instant chocolate pudding mix
1 T vanilla.

Freeze firm, 2 to 4 hours.

yield: about 1¹/₂ quarts

2

Selecting an Ice Cream Freezer

In the days before electricity, ice cream was made in a set of metal bowls, together called an "ice cream pot," "French pot," or "pot freezer." The smaller bowl was filled with mix and nestled into a larger bowl packed with ice and salt.

You swirled the small bowl in a bed of ice to keep it in motion so your ice cream froze evenly. At the same time, you scraped the mixture from the side of the bowl and worked it smooth with a wooden paddle. It took great skill and patience to keep brine from seeping over the edge, ruining the ice cream.

In 1845, New England housewife Nancy Johnson got the bright idea of replacing the smaller bowl with a lidded cream can fitted with a rotary dasher turned by a crank. In place of the larger bowl, she used a bucket to hold the ice.

With minor improvements, Johnson's invention remained pretty much as she designed it until around 1950, when some clever soul thought of replacing the cranking handle with an electric motor. Since then, modern ice cream freezers have been continually modified to keep up with changing technology.

Freezer Features

No matter how up-to-date their design, ice cream freezers all have the same main features: a source of power, a covered canister, a dasher with scraper blades, and a container of coolant.

In hand-crank models, the power source is you. Purists claim that hand cranking is the only way to achieve superior texture because it lets you control the speed of agitation. Electrically controlled freezers turn at a steady rate from start to finish. Originally the motor was mounted above the cream can. Now freezers come with the motor housed beneath the canister or beside it, letting you lift the lid without removing the motor assembly.

Some canisters have an add-ingredient opening in the lid so you can easily add nuts, chocolate chips, and other flavorings as freezing nears completion. Others have transparent lids so you can gauge progress as the ice cream freezes and select just the right moment for last-minute additions.

Canisters range in size from one cup to twenty quarts. Both the canister's size and its shape affect freezing. The greater the surface area in relation to volume, the more contact ice cream has with the cold walls and the faster it will freeze. Consequently, tall, thin cans work faster than short, blocky ones. All canisters are made of metal because it's such a good conductor of heat.

The dasher suspended at the center of a canister may be metal, plastic, or wood. In some freezers the dasher rotates. In others, the canister revolves while the dasher remains stationary. In either case, during freezing the sharp-edged blades continuously remove frozen mix from the canister walls and move it toward the center, pushing new mix into contact with the canister walls.

The dasher ensures uniform consistency by preventing ingredients from settling out during freezing. It controls texture by beating in air and by scraping away ice crystals as they form, keeping them from growing large and lumpy. Compared to still freezing, stir freezing is faster. The resulting ice cream is smoother, letting you cut back on rich ingredients without sacrificing creamy texture.

The canister is set into a larger container of coolant consisting of either ice and salt or one of several kinds of antifreeze. When antifreeze is used, the canister, coolant, and outer container are permanently sealed together. Regardless of the coolant and container, the principle remains the same—ice cream freezes by giving up its warmth to frozen coolant. The potentially bewildering selection of modern freezers can be divided into six main groups, according to the kind of coolant they use.

Crushed Ice

Old-style freezers that work with crushed ice and rock salt vary in capacity from two to twenty quarts and come in both hand-crank and electric models. They're the most economical choice for freezing lots of ice cream at once. Because hand cranking allows full control of dasher speed, and because varying the amount of salt sprinkled into the ice controls temperature, hand-crank, crushed-ice freezers are preferred by connoisseurs.

Depending on the model and on the mix to be frozen, hand cranking takes twenty to forty-five minutes, of which only

True connoisseurs feel that the best ice cream comes from an old-fashioned hand-crank freezer. (Photo courtesy of Nasco, Fort Atkinson, Wisconsin.)

Ice Cream Freezer Parts:
All ice cream makers consist
of the same basic parts—

1. Source of power
   a. electric

b. hand-crank

2. Canister lid

3. Dasher

4. Canister or cream can

5. Container to
   hold coolant

the last five minutes are truly hard work. Electric models require about the same amount of time but involve less work and more noise. The chief disadvantage here is not in the power source, however, but in the effort expended to crush ice, which can deter you from making ice cream as often as you'd like.

The ice bucket is traditionally made of wood, since wood is a poor conductor of heat and thus protects the ice from melting fast in warm weather. Because wood is heavy, it lends stability to hand-crank models, making them easier for one person to operate. Some of the cheaper buckets made of plastic require a team of two—one to hold down the ice bucket while the other cranks away. Hand cranking is fun at parties where everyone takes a turn, but an electric unit is more convenient for everyday use.

Ice Cubes

A step up from freezers operated on crushed ice and rock salt are those calling for ordinary ice cubes and table salt. These compact units are designed to look like any other kitchen appliance, with the canister sitting atop the power unit in the fashion of a blender. Some models come as accessories to food processors.

Unfortunately, these tidy countertop appliances don't hold up well under steady use, making them suitable only for the occasional ice cream bash. They also tend to stall while the ice cream is still fairly soupy.

Their chief appeal is that they work on whole ice cubes, although if your cubes are too large to pack into the tub, you may end up having to crush them anyway. On the plus side, you need only four to six trays of ice (or about half an automatic ice-maker basketful) to freeze two quarts in fifteen to thirty minutes.

Tidy counter-top ice cream makers work with ordinary ice cubes. (Photo courtesy of Nasco, Fort Atkinson, Wisconsin.)

Sealed-in Coolant

Donvier revolutionized home ice cream making in the early 1980s with sealed-in coolant freezers. Since the chemical coolant is permanently sealed inside a cylinder, these units are sometimes called "cylinder" freezers.

Easy to use and perfect for kids, sealed-in coolant freezers work in twenty to thirty minutes after being stored in the household freezer for several hours. If you immediately clean and refreeze the canister, you won't have to wait quite as long to make a second batch.

These units work on the principle that antifreeze freezes at a lower temperature than ice and therefore takes longer to thaw. Adequately freezing the coolant requires a freezer setting of 0° F (–18° C) or lower. During cool weather, you can freeze the ice cream and leave it to harden in the ice cream maker for up to an hour. Conversely, during very hot weather, air temperature may thaw the coolant before the ice cream becomes completely frozen.

Because the canister is an integral part of the coolant assembly, you have to pour mix in quickly and immediately start cranking before the dasher freezes tight to the canister wall. Here's where the better electric models have the advantage—just start it up and pour the mix in through a slot in the lid while the dasher turns. Instructions for hand operated models suggest only occasional cranking, but constant turning speeds up freezing for smoother ice cream. In addition, if you wait too long between cranks, the dasher will freeze in place and may snap when you try to force it.

Sizes range from one and a half quarts down to a tiny one cup, just right for experimenting with new flavors or bagging for lunch.

The sealed-in coolant ice cream maker, pioneered by Donvier, is perfect for kids. (Photo courtesy of Krups North America, Closter, New Jersey.)

Self Cooling

Decidedly the most high-tech ice cream makers, and among the most expensive, are the internally cooled models. Essentially miniature freezers that rely on compression instead of ice, these ice cream makers produce one and one-half quarts in fifteen to thirty-five minutes after a short precooling period. When one batch is done, you can freeze another almost immediately.

Some models have permanently mounted canisters, some have removable ones, and some have both. To speed up freezing and facilitate canister removal, pour a little brine or alcohol into the permanent canister before mounting the removable one. Vodka works best for this—you'll never notice if a drop accidentally gets into your ice cream.

These appliances are heavy and bulky, requiring a good bit of open counter space to let the air vents function properly. Even though one of these takes up lots of room, it should be permanently kept on the countertop where it will be used, since tipping one while moving it can damage the condenser.

Operated according to instruction, internally cooled freezers incorporate very little air, making ice cream as dense and smooth as the best superpremiums. These are the easiest of all ice cream makers to use. They're also fairly quiet—just the thing for making dessert in the kitchen without disturbing guests at the table in the dining room.

Top-of-the-line self-contained ice cream makers, like the Gaggia pictured here, are imported from Italy. (Photo courtesy of Liberty/Richter, Carlstadt, New Jersey.)

Batch Freezers

Batch freezers are internally-cooled machines designed for commercial use. Countertop models are cooled either by air or by water. The latter works more consistently, but requires permanent hook-up to a waterline and drain so may be restricted by local building codes.

Batch freezers are considerably more complex to install and operate than freezers designed strictly for home use. They are also more expensive and take up more space. But they allow greater control of incorporated air and final ice cream temperature, they make at least twice as much ice cream at a time, and they'll freeze batch after batch, nonstop. One is worth your consideration if you have a big family or give lots of parties.

Household Freezer

The latest innovation in ice cream makers uses the cold air in your household freezer as a coolant. Such units come either as a separate appliance that plugs into an outside outlet or as an accessory that fits into the ice-making mechanism of specifically designated freezers.

The primary advantage to these models is ease of use—simply slip one into the freezer, plug it in, and leave it to do its work. Because sound is muffled by the freezer, these units are among the quietest. On the down side, because they give up

Commercial batch freezers like this three-quart Taylor require permanent installation. (Photo courtesy of Taylor Co., Rockton, Illinois.)

heat to the inside of the freezer, these units reduce freezer efficiency. In addition, they take up lots of space; you may have to remove some frozen food or even take out a shelf to fit one in.

Processing time depends on the freezer's food load, frost conditions, and how often you open the door while ice cream making is in progress. Under ideal conditions, it takes one and a half to two hours to make one quart, a relatively long freezing time that results in ice cream as light and smooth as marshmallow fluff.

Accessory units require no special assembly, but the individual appliances can be somewhat awkward to put together. On the other hand, in some freezers you can permanently install the motor so you need only slide in the canister when you crave ice cream.

Mix as Coolant

The idea of using frozen ingredients as the coolant was pioneered and perfected by the folks at Vita-Mix and is now promoted for other brands of food processors as well. Instead of making your mix and freezing it under agitation, here you freeze some of the ingredients and combine them under agitation, getting things started with a half cup of milk, cream, yogurt, or other liquid per cup of frozen ingredients.

You can make ice cream in mere minutes using any food processor fitted with a stainless steel blade. Ice cream made this way has very little air and is best served fresh or after a very short hardening period. If you store it in the freezer for more than an hour or two, it gets too hard to scoop. You'll have to cut it into chunks and reprocess.

Making ice cream that's neither lumpy nor soupy takes a bit of experience. Once you get the hang of it, though, there's no quicker way to whip up such tasty treats as fresh fruit or vegetable sorbets and savory ice creams from whole roasted nuts ground right in the food processor before you toss in remaining ingredients.

Freezer Care

No matter which ice cream maker you choose, giving it proper care will ensure your continuing satisfaction. Start out by reading the instruction manual carefully, taking note of which parts are or are not washable or dishwasher safe.

Wooden ice buckets should be rinsed in plain water and toweled dry. If the bucket dries out and becomes leaky between uses, simply fill it with water and allow it to soak several hours until the staves swell and become watertight once more.

Always use a plastic, rubber, or wooden scraper when emptying the canister. Metal utensils leave scratches, which not only interfere with freezing but also provide hiding places for bacteria. Ice cream is so sensitive to bacteria that in the early 1800s both children and elderly were warned about upset stomachs from eating ice cream. With today's improved sanitation practices, ice cream stomach ache is virtually unheard of.

Properly cleaning the canister after each use not only eliminates bacteria but also prevents the accumulation of an unsanitary, grayish, chalky deposit called "milkstone," which develops from the milk protein, milkfat (cream), and minerals in dairy products. Milkstone occurs more often in canisters rinsed in hard water and can be avoided by using soft water.

Immediately after emptying the canister, rinse it, the lid, and the dasher in lukewarm water of about 100° F (38° C), warm enough to melt milkfat but not hot enough to harden milk protein. If dairy residue has been allowed to dry in the cream can, loosen

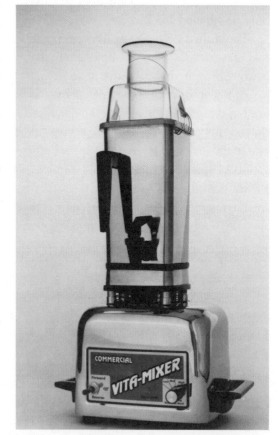

Vita-Mix pioneered the idea of food processors as ice cream makers. (Photo courtesy of Vita-Mix Corporation, Cleveland, Ohio.)

it by soaking the canister in warm water. Using a stiff brush, never a scratchy scouring pad, scrub the canister and dasher with water and a little Clorox bleach (one tablespoon per gallon) as a sanitizer. Rinse the canister and dasher in hot water and dry thoroughly.

Lightly coat a tinned canister with cooking oil so it won't rust. Thoroughly wipe all other parts and dry them well, taking care to remove brine from all metal parts to prevent rusting. Oil the motor assembly as needed and store all parts in a dust-free place.

These simple steps will prolong the life of your ice cream maker, and in turn it will reward you with batch after batch of your favorite ice cream.

3

Ice and Sorbet

Ices and sorbets may be low on the ice cream evolutionary scale, but they're high in versatility. Besides making delicious desserts, they're dandy as substitutes for dressing on refreshing luncheon salads, as side dishes to lighten up a heavy meal, or as unusual, perky appetizers. And because they contain fewer calories, they cool you down more quickly than ice cream does.

Ices, the simplest of all freezes, are made of sugar, water, and fruit juice or purée. They were once called "water ices" to distinguish them from "milk ices" (today's sherbets) and "cream ices" (today's ice creams).

By government decree, commercially made ices cannot contain dairy products or egg yolks. But they may include gelatin or egg whites, both of which give them the creamy consistency of sherbet. Since most of us expect an ice to be coarse rather than creamy, not everyone goes along with the government's definition.

There's also no consensus on what a *sorbet* is. In France, where the word originated, it refers to either an ice or a sherbet. In this country, the word has been used to designate all manner of frozen concoctions, including ones containing yogurt, creamed vegetables, and even sautéed onions. Most Americans consider "sorbet" to be an upscale word for "ice."

Ices

During formal Victorian dinners, famous for lasting two or three hours, as many as three of the courses were ices. Most were based on lemon ice with other flavorings added, a fine trick you can use today to invent nearly any flavor. Ices are usually made with fresh or cooked fruit juice or purée. Rarely are extracts used.

An ice is supposed to be tart, but its puckering quality is offset by sweetness. High sugar content is also responsible for the characteristic texture, preventing the ice from becoming too coarse or freezing too firm. But too much sugar will keep the ice from freezing at all.

The best ices contain no more than one part sugar to four parts juice or purée and water. When the sugar and water are boiled into a light syrup and then cooled before adding juice or puree, the resulting ice has a slightly smoother texture. Americans often omit this step for the sake of simplicity.

Substituting corn syrup for up to one-third of the sugar prevents crystallization on the surface of an ice destined for storage in the freezer. Corn syrup also raises the melting point, making the ice feel less cold in your mouth.

Reducing Sweetness

Before it's frozen, the mix for an ice should taste too strong and too sweet. If the ice is still too sweet after freezing, next time add two to four tablespoons of lemon juice. Lemon juice tones down sweetness without destroying texture and also enhances other fruity flavorings. Substantially reducing the amount of sugar, or substituting diet sweetener, adversely affects texture.

It's possible to eliminate sweetening altogether by using apple juice or apple juice concentrate in place of all or part of the water. A 100-percent natural, sugar-free ice might, for example, be made from equal parts of apple, pineapple, and orange juice with an optional fourth part of crushed fruit thrown in for extra flavor. This sort of ice does not harden well but tastes great fresh.

If you plan to store a low-sugar or no-sugar ice in the freezer rather than serve it freshly frozen, you'll need a stabilizer to keep it from getting too firm or unpleasantly coarse. You might add one-half tablespoon plain gelatin, softened in one-quarter cup water, per quart. Commercially packaged flavored gelatins, by the way, make handy instant mixes—just freeze the prepared gelatin in your ice cream maker after it cools but before it sets.

If you're among those who object to the flavor or texture of gelatin as a stabilizer, you can stir in one or two whipped egg whites just before freezing a mix. The result will be a fluffy "spoom," that delightful treat deserving of fuller discussion later in this chapter.

Serving

Properly made ices have the approximate consistency of densely packed snow. In most cases, both texture and flavor are finest at soft-serve consistency. Upon hardening, many ices become either too firm or too crumbly to scoop, and they are too cold to impart their fullest flavor. You can partially overcome these obstacles by softening the ice for twenty to thirty minutes in the refrigerator or by whirling it in a food processor just before serving.

When you make more ice than you can serve fresh, consider molding it as frozen suckers, as described in Chapter 1, "Still Freezing." Or harden it by the scoop on a prechilled baking sheet to float in tall glasses of cold juice or ginger ale. You'll find more on prescooping in Chapter 21, "By the Scoop."

BASIC FRUIT ICE

This easy recipe makes terrific *blackberry, blueberry, cranberry, papaya, peach,* and *raspberry* ice. When using berries with gritty seeds, strain the purée to remove them. For particularly tart fruits, increase sugar to 1 cup.

Dissolve	²/₃ C sugar
in	2²/₃ C boiling water.
Cool.	
Add	1¹/₃ C purée 1 T lemon juice.
Chill and stir freeze.	
	yield: about 1 quart

FRUIT ICE

This ice is fluffier than basic ice because gelatin allows more air to be whipped in during freezing. This recipe is particularly good with strong flavors like *strawberry* or *pineapple*. If you use purée instead of juice, the flavor will be even fruitier.

In	1¹/₃ C boiling water
dissolve	1 t plain gelatin ¹/₃ C sugar 3 T corn syrup.
Chill and add	²/₃ C fruit juice or purée 2 t lemon juice.
Stir freeze.	
	yield: about 1 quart

LEMON ICE

Enjoy this ice plain or use it as a foundation for other flavors. For example, make *mint* ice by steeping ¹/₂ C freshly chopped mint leaves in the hot syrup, or simply add a few drops of mint extract just before freezing. Serve the resulting ice as a substitute for mint jelly with lamb or chevon.

In saucepan combine	1²/₃ C sugar 2 t grated lemon rind. 3¹/₃ C water.
Boil 5 minutes.	
Cool, strain, and add	²/₃ C lemon juice.
Chill and stir freeze.	
	yield: about 1 quart

ORANGE ICE

Essentially a version of lemon ice, orange ice is super refreshing as is, but becomes something extraordinary when splashed with rum or orange liqueur and topped with warmed marmalade. Like lemon ice, it can also be used as a springboard for other flavors. Make *passion fruit* ice, for example, by substituting puréed passion fruit for as much as one-half the orange juice.

In saucepan, combine

1¹/₃ C sugar
2 t grated orange rind
2²/₃ C water.

Boil 5 minutes.

Cool, strain and add

1¹/₃ C orange juice
3 T lemon juice.

Chill and stir freeze.

yield: about 1 quart

GRAPEFRUIT ICE

There's nothing simpler than this spunky ice made with fresh grapefruit juice. Use pink grapefruit for a delicate rosy color and best flavor. If you prefer yellow fruit, taste the mix for sweetness and add sugar as needed. Include 2 T crème de menthe or orange liqueur to further enhance the flavor. Or add ¹/₄ C Campari for a trendy treat.

Strain

3¹/₂ C grapefruit juice.

Stir in until dissolved

³/₄ C sugar.

Chill and stir freeze.

yield: about 1 quart

ROSE PETAL ICE

Rose petals were used as a flavoring as far back as the second century A.D., when rosewater was mentioned in the works of the Greek poet, Nicander. Floral flavorings were particularly popular in seventeenth-century England, where this recipe likely originated. Many of our modern hybrid roses have little flavor, so look for a fragrant old-time variety, grown without sprays, and gather up some petals for this delicate ice—itself pure poetry.

Cover

¹/₂# rose petals

with

3¹/₂ C boiling water.

Stir in until dissolved

2 C sugar.

Cover and steep until cool.

Strain and chill.

Stir freeze.

yield: about 1 quart

COCONUT ICE

Serve this ice with slices of tropical fruit and sprinkle a little freshly grated coconut on top. To substitute dried coconut for fresh, combine 4 C grated coconut and 4 C water (or 5 C flaked coconut and 5 C water), simmer 5 minutes, and cool. Press out and re-serve the liquid to add to the sugar and vanilla.

Reserving water, crack open	**1 large coconut.**
Scrape out meat with metal spoon, stopping short of brown rind.	
Whirl in blender with	**1¹/₂ C boiling water.**
Repeat with	**1 large coconut 1¹/₂ C boiling water.**
Combine and set aside to cool.	
Strain, press out and reserve liquid.	
To liquid add	**1 C reserved coconut water 1 C sugar 1 t vanilla.**
Chill and stir freeze.	

yield: about 1 quart

APRICOT ICE

Making this flavorful ice is a cinch when you use canned fruit. To sub-stitute fresh apricots, peel, pit, and halve 1¹/₂# fruit, and stew in lightly sugared water until soft. Whether you use fresh or canned fruit, you'll deepen the flavor by adding 2 T kirsch.

Drain and purée	**2¹/₄ C canned apricots.**
Add	**1¹/₂ C orange juice 4 T lemon juice.**
Stir in until dissolved	**²/₃ C sugar.**
Chill and stir freeze.	

yield: about 1 quart

KIWI ICE

The tart-sweet kiwi makes a subtle, pale green ice. It's terrific scooped over a pineapple ring and garnished with whole fresh strawberries. If you prefer smooth ice without gritty seeds, strain the purée through a fine sieve.

Combine

3 C kiwi purée
1 t lemon juice
$^1/_2$ C water
$^1/_2$ C sugar.

Chill and stir freeze.

yield: about 1 quart

THREE FRUIT ICE

This smooth-textured, delicious ice keeps quite well, suggesting one great way to store over-ripe bargain bananas. For variety, substitute crushed pineapple or puréed strawberries.

In a saucepan, combine

1 C water
$^1/_2$ C sugar.

Stirring, heat until sugar dissolves.

Add

$^3/_4$ C orange juice
$^1/_4$ C lemon juice.

Chill.

Peel, mash and add

2 ripe bananas
($1^1/_4$ C).

Stir freeze.

yield: about 1 quart

GATORADE BANANA ICE

On steamy summer days when nothing you drink seems to cool you down, whip up a batch of this potassium-rich ice. Serve it freshly frozen, since it gets very crumbly on hardening.

Combine

3 C Gatorade
1 large ripe
  banana
$^1/_2$ C sugar
2 T lemon juice.

Stir freeze.

yield: about 1 quart

APPLE ICE

This gently spiced ice makes a nutritious and cooling afternoon snack and also goes well with cottage cheese on a luncheon plate. Although the recipe calls for fresh apples, you may substitute 1³/₄ C puréed apple sauce and omit the first addition of water.

Peel and dice

³/₄# apples (2 medium).

Cook over medium heat, uncovered, 15 minutes with

**1³/₄ C water
¹/₄ t grated lemon rind
¹/₈ t cinnamon
¹/₃ C sugar.**

Purée for 1³/₄ C and add

**1³/₄ C water
¹/₃ C sugar
2 T lemon juice.**

Chill and stir freeze.

yield: about 1 quart

PINEAPPLE ICE

Thanks to its inherent sweetness, pineapple juice may be frozen without additional ingredients and served soft straight from the ice cream maker. The ice won't hold up well, however, if kept any length of time. Here's a fruitier-flavored, finer-textured ice you can make ahead and store until serving time.

Boil 5 minutes

**³/₄ C sugar
3 C water.**

Chill.

Liquefy in blender

**³/₄ C crushed pineapple
¹/₄ C lemon juice.**

Combine with syrup.

Chill and stir freeze.

yield: about 1 quart

CRANBERRY ICE

During winter holidays when fresh cranberries are plentiful, serve this brightly colored ice as a decidedly different side dish or use it to perk up turkey leftovers. It stores quite well and may be frozen in advance to reduce hectic, last-minute holiday preparations. For a spicy version, add $1/2$ t cinnamon, $1/8$ t allspice, and $1/8$ t nutmeg, and substitute orange juice for water.

Combine

2 C cranberries
1 C sugar
2 C water.

Simmer until cranberries pop.

Mash.

Cool and strain.

Chill and stir freeze.

yield: about 1 quart

Spooms

The U.S. government, in its infinite wisdom, says that an ice fluffed up with egg whites is just another ice, since it contains no dairy products. But adding whipped egg white lends a creamy consistency that's highly reminiscent of sherbet. Many people refer to this kind of freeze as "ice sherbet" to distinguish it from "milk sherbet," which contains dairy products.

The British aren't bothered by this categorizing dilemma. They've given the freeze a name all its own—"spoom"—an airy sort of word that aptly conveys the idea of light, puffy texture.

The simplest spoom is made by beating two egg whites and folding in three cups of sweetened fruit juice such as lemonade or limeade. Any ice can be turned into spoom merely by adding one or two beaten whites just before freezing. You'll get the lightest possible texture by warming the eggs to room temperature before whipping them. In place of raw egg whites (review the caution in Chapter 13), you can make spooms with pasteurized egg white powder sold as a cake decorating supply.

BASIC FRUIT SPOOM

Berry, *melon*, *pineapple*, and *purple plum* are just some of the delicious variations you can make from this basic spoom recipe. If you purée canned fruit, reduce the sugar slightly to compensate for the sweetened syrup from the can.

Blend together	**1¹/₃ C fruit purée** **1¹/₃ C cold water.**
Whip into soft peaks	**3 egg whites.**
Gradually add	**²/₃ C sugar.**
Fold into purée.	
Chill and stir freeze.	

yield: about 1 quart

CHERRY SPOOM

This bit of summer is best served freshly frozen, since it turns very crumbly on hardening. Although the recipe calls for fresh, tart red cherries, a one-pound can of pitted cherries may be substituted.

Chop	**2 C cherries.**
Combine with	**¹/₂ C sugar.**
Let stand 1 hour.	
Strain juice and combine with	**¹/₂ pkg plain gelatin.**
Heat together with	**2 T orange juice** **¹/₂ T lemon juice.**
Add cherries and chill.	
Beat into soft peaks	**1 egg white.**
Fold into cherry mixture.	
Stir freeze.	

yield: about 1 quart

TANGERINE SPOOM

The extra steps required to make this fine-textured spoom give it qualities that let you prepare it well ahead of serving. It's the perfect choice to layer in one of the molds described in Chapter 26, "Bombes and Other Molds." Substitute 8 limes for *lime* spoom or 2 grapefruits for *grapefruit* spoom.

Strain juice from **5 tangerines.**

Blanch rinds 1 minute in boiling water.

Rinse in cold water.

In saucepan, combine rinds with **1½ C sugar**
1½ C water.

Boil 5 minutes.

Strain and cool.

Combine syrup with juice and **2 T orange**
liqueur.

Chill.

In saucepan, combine **½ C sugar**
¼ C water.

Without stirring, simmer
8 to 10 minutes until foamy.

Whip into soft peaks **2 egg whites**
pinch salt.

Slowly beat in hot syrup.

Beat 5 minutes more
until stiff and glossy.

Chill.

Fold mixtures together and stir freeze.

yield: about 1 quart

AVOCADO PINEAPPLE SPOOM

The most flavorful avocado freezes are made from the dark green to purplish Hass, available from early spring through summer. Green-skinned winter avocados, of which Fuerte is the most common, aren't nearly as tasty. Serve this spoom on a green salad, garnished with additional sliced avocados, or surround it with pineapple chunks and fresh whole strawberries for a colorful dessert.

Combine and boil 5 minutes

2 C nonsweetened pineapple juice
1 C sugar
¹/₂ C lemon juice
¹/₂ t salt.

Chill, and add

2 C avocado purée.

Beat into stiff peaks

4 egg whites.

Gradually add

¹/₂ C sugar.

Fold into avocado mixture.

Stir freeze.

yield: about 1 quart

Frappés and Slushes

"Frappé," French for "beaten," sometimes refers to a snowcone made with a strong-flavored liqueur. More often it refers to a combination of fruit juices, frozen slushy and served in a tall glass as a drink or dessert. A slush is similar to a fruit frappé, but contains only one kind of juice. Frozen firm, frappés and slushes are essentially like any other ice.

You can make both in either an ice cream maker or a blender. In an ice cream maker, simply freeze lemonade, fruit punch, or any other sweetened drink, or try puréed water-melon, peaches, strawberries, or other ripe, juicy fruit combined with a little sugar or apple juice concentrate.

In a blender, combine puréed fruit or fruit juice concentrate with crushed or cracked ice, adding a little at a time until the blades whirl freely and the drink is smooth. A six ounce can of concentrate combined with five or six cups of crushed ice nets three tall servings or six short ones.

FRUIT FRAPPÉ

The traditional frappé is made with grape juice, but you can successfully substitute apple or any other fruit juice of choice.

Combine

2 t lemon juice
¹/₄ C orange juice
¹/₂ C fruit juice

¹/₄ C sugar

3 C water.

Chill and stir freeze just until slushy.

yield: about 1 quart

ORANGE SLUSH

Make a flavorful slush from any of your favorite juicy, sweet fruits by substituting purée for orange juice in this recipe. Especially savory are *strawberry* and *watermelon* slush.

Combine

3¹/₂ C orange juice
¹/₃ C light corn syrup.

Chill and stir freeze just until slushy.

yield: about 1 quart

Sorbetti

The classic ices served at a typical Italian ice cream shop, or *gelateria,* are more strongly flavored than the traditional American ices. They're made with more fruit juice or purée and less water, and remain softer even after hardening.

Called "sorbetti," these ices consist of one-part sugar and one-part water, boiled five minutes (or microwaved on high for two to three minutes), cooled, and added to two-parts juice or puréed fruit. When made with juice instead of purée, they fluff up more than usual, which explains why a one-quart recipe sometimes overflows a one-quart ice cream maker.

In place of granulated sugar, some sorbetto aficionados prefer fructose, a flavorless fruit-derived powdered sugar that dissolves readily without heating. The resulting texture is a cross between a traditional sorbetto and a granita. Fructose is available at most health food stores.

The best sorbetti are made from fresh, ripe fruit. With the exception of apples, pears, and cranberries, the fruit is seldom cooked on the theory that sorbetto should taste more like fresh fruit and less like jam. To further enhance flavor, liqueurs are often added. So are spices, especially cinnamon.

Like other ices, sorbetti are best when fresh, but unlike other ices, when hardened they don't usually require tempering before scooping. Whether served as dessert or as a prelude to the meat course of a major meal, sorbetti are traditionally spooned into tall-stemmed glasses and garnished with a single slice of fruit.

SORBETTO

A sorbetto almost always contains lemon juice for proper tartness, but you can do without it if you like yours sweeter. Common fruits like *apricot*, *black cherry*, and *peach* make tasty sorbetti, but don't be shy about experimenting with exotic fruits like *papaya* or *mango*.

Boil 5 minutes

1 C sugar
1 C water.

Cool.

Add

2 C fruit purée or
** juice**
¹⁄₄ C lemon juice.

Chill and stir freeze.

yield: about 1 quart

BERRY SORBETTO

A little orange juice increases depth of flavor for most fruits and berries. This recipe, which is equally terrific as *raspberry*, *blackberry*, or *strawberry* sorbetto, takes about 1 quart of berries. Remove gritty seeds, if you wish, by pressing the purée through a fine sieve.

Boil 5 minutes

1 C sugar
1 C water
grated rind of 1
** lemon.**

Cool.

Add

1¹⁄₂ C berries
¹⁄₄ C orange juice
¹⁄₄ C lemon juice.

Strain and chill.

Stir freeze.

yield: about 1 quart

Vegetable Sorbets

Vegetable ices, nearly always called sorbets, add a light and colorful touch to lunches, brunches, and heavy holiday meals. Serve them as refreshing appetizers, as between-course palate cleansers, or as a gentle transition to dessert.

One of the simplest and most popular vegetable sorbets is made by spicing chilled tomato juice with a touch of Tabasco, a dash of Worcestershire, or a splash of vodka. You can invent any number of interesting sorbets based on your favorite cooked vegetables or raw vegetable salads, puréed with a little juice or water and spiced with dill, mint, wintergreen, or rosemary. Or start the meal with a scoop of soup, made by puréeing and freezing gazpacho, borscht, vichyssoise, chlodnik, or your own favorite cold soup.

Like most ices, vegetable sorbets are at their best when freshly frozen. Although they may be held in the freezer for a short time, most become extremely crumbly on hardening and must be softened and whipped or whirled in a food processor before serving.

Appropriate garnishes include a single cherry tomato, a sprig of celery, a few mint leaves, a broccoli spear, or a carrot stick. In contrast to the half-cup serving usual for most other freezes, allow one-quarter to one-third cup per serving of vegetable sorbet.

BEET SORBET

Scoop crimson beet sorbet onto a plate of cold cuts, use it as dressing for a green salad, or mound it into scraped-out halves of orange rind to accompany pork, duck, or goose. Beets turn starchy and lose their sweetness during storage, so if yours don't come straight from the garden, compensate by adding as much as ¹/₂ C sugar.

Cook until tender **3# (8-10 medium) beets.**

Peel, cool, and chop.

Purée with **²/₃ C orange juice concentrate**
2 T lemon juice
¹/₂ t allspice
¹/₂ t cinnamon
1 t salt.

Chill and stir freeze.

yield: about 1 quart

CELERY SORBET

Served in small, hollowed-out tomatoes, this sorbet makes an outstanding between-course refresher. Surround the tomato with a ring of boiled shrimp or crab and you've got an eye-appealing appetizer. If you aren't crazy about cilantro, a popular West Coast herb variously called fresh coriander or Chinese parsley, substitute curly parsley.

Rinse, trim, and purée	**3# celery**
with	**³/₄ C cilantro** **6 T lime juice** **2 T sugar.**
Strain and discard fiber.	
Chill and stir freeze.	
	yield: about 1 quart

CARROT PINEAPPLE SORBET

This variation on a classic salad goes well with sliced turkey or cold chicken. For variety, soak 2 T chopped golden raisins in 1 T dark rum (or plump the raisins in boiling water) and stir them in before freezing. For added crunch, add 2 T chopped pecans, or reserve the nuts to sprinkle on top.

In saucepan, soften	**¹/₂ pkg unflavored gelatin**
in	**¹/₃ C orange juice.**
Heat until gelatin dissolves.	
Purée, and add	**1 C orange juice** **2 medium carrots, chopped** **¹/₃ C pineapple chunks** **¹/₃ C sugar.**
Stir freeze.	
	yield: about 1 quart

Punch

Any ice in which an alcoholic beverage replaces or supplements fruit juices is traditionally called "punch," although today it's more likely to be called "sorbet." At least one of the ices served during those fabulous Victorian dinners was a punch. It usually came mid-meal, as a contrast to the hot soup the dinner opened with, and often consisted of lemon ice fortified with one-third cup dark rum per quart.

To make a punch, substitute wine or champagne for all or part of the juice in any ice, or add one to two tablespoons of an appropriately flavored liquor or liqueur per quart. This addition reduces the perception of sweetness, keeps the ice from getting too firm on hardening, and strengthens flavor. Sorbetti are especially likely to contain liqueur as a flavor strengthener.

Any ice made with less than fully ripe, flavorful fruit will benefit from the addition of a matching liqueur—kirsch with cherry, for instance, or peach schnapps with peach. For a more exotic touch, try contrast—orange liqueur with strawberry, brandy with apricot, rum with banana.

Alcohol slows freezing, so speed things by adding it only after the ice is nearly frozen. Too much alcohol inhibits freezing altogether, so don't use as much liquor or liqueur as you would a less alcoholic wine, champagne, or beer.

That's right, beer. One punch recipe calls for only slightly sweetened, flat beer. Try it at your own peril. On the other hand, if you're the adventuresome sort, combine one and one-half cups each of beer and cranberry juice with one-third cup sugar to make a pretty pink sorbet that's delicately flavored and decidedly refreshing.

SPIRITED SORBET

Make this tart punch with a fruity liqueur such as *black currant*, *blackberry*, or *black raspberry*. Serve it in wine glasses, garnished with a thin curl of lemon peel.

Boil 5 minutes	**3 C water** **6 T sugar.**
Chill, and add	**²/₃ C liqueur** **¹/₄ C lemon juice** **¹/₄ t salt.**
Stir freeze.	

yield: about 1 quart

SAUVIGNON SORBET

Wine punch is a terrific palate refresher or *le trou de milieu* (literally, "hole in the middle") served before the meat dish of a multicourse meal. It also doubles as a unique afternoon cocktail on a lazy summer day. Nearly any full-bodied red wine will work in this recipe. If you're a white wine buff, a simple substitution will net you *chardonnay* sorbet.

In	¹/₄ **C cold water**
soften	¹/₂ **T plain gelatin.**
Heat	**1 C water** ¹/₂ **C sugar.**
Add gelatin and stir until dissolved.	
Add	**1 t grated lemon rind.**
Cool and strain.	
Stir in	**2¹/₂ C Cabernet Sauvignon.**
Stir freeze.	

yield: about 1 quart

ROSÉ SORBET

Use fresh or thawed blueberries, strawberries, blackberries, or raspberries with the seeds strained out to make this pastel punch. Serve it in wine glasses with a splash of additional rosé, or scoop it into chilled dishes and top with fresh berries.

Whirl in blender	**2 C berries** **2²/₃ C rosé wine.**
In saucepan, combine with	²/₃ **C sugar** ¹/₄ **t cinnamon.**
Stirring, bring to boil until sugar dissolves, then simmer 2 minutes.	
In	**2 T water**
dissolve	¹/₄ **C cornstarch.**
Stir into hot mixture and heat until thick and bubbly.	
Stirring, cook 2 minutes more.	
Chill and stir freeze.	

yield: about 1 quart

DAIQUIRI SORBET

Creating mixed-drink flavored punches is a breeze. Simply select an ice recipe and add appropriate spirits—$^1/_4$ C Southern Comfort plus 1 T lime juice per quart cranberry ice for *Scarlet O'Hara* sorbet, for example, or 1/3 C bourbon per quart mint ice for *mint julep* sorbet. To make *margarita* sorbet, substitute limes for lemons in lemon ice and add $^1/_4$ C tequila. Make *lime daiquiri* sorbet the same way, using $^1/_3$ C light rum for the spirits. Or try this shortcut, which easily converts to *strawberry daiquiri* sorbet with the addition of $^1/_2$ C puréed strawberries, or *banana daiquiri* sorbet with the inclusion of 1 ripe mashed banana.

Mix

12-oz limeade concentrate
1$^1/_2$ C cold water
$^1/_4$ C powdered sugar
$^1/_2$ C light rum.

Chill and stir freeze.

yield: about 1 quart

PUNCHED APRICOTS

Muscatel lends distinct flavor to this apricot punch, but you can substitute lighter tokay or dark, fortified Malaga. Although the recipe calls for canned apricots, you can use 1$^1/_2$# peeled, pitted, fresh apricots steamed until soft in lightly sugared syrup.

In

1 C boiling water

dissolve

$^3/_4$ C sugar.

Cool.

Purée

2 C apricots with juice.

Add cooled syrup and

$^1/_2$ C cold water
$^1/_2$ C muscatel
juice of 1 lemon
$^1/_8$ t salt.

Stir freeze.

yield: about 1 quart

SPICY CHAMPAGNE SPOOM

Make this punch with any sweet or dry champagne combined with the spice of your choice—¹/₂ t whole allspice or ground nutmeg, 1 t whole cloves, 1 T grated ginger, or a 2" cinnamon stick. Serve in champagne glasses with additional champagne or wine splashed on top. Garnish with a thin curl of lemon peel, a piece of cinnamon stick, or a dash of nutmeg.

Boil 5 minutes	¹/₄ C sugar ¹/₂ C water **spice of your choice.**
Remove from heat and add	**1 C champagne 1 T grated lemon peel.**
Chill, and strain.	
Boil 5 minutes	¹/₂ C sugar ¹/₄ C water.
Whip into soft peaks	**2 egg whites.**
Slowly beat in hot syrup.	
Beat 5 minutes more until stiff and glossy.	
Chill.	
Fold mixtures together.	
Stir freeze.	
	yield: about 1 quart

PEAR PUNCH

Select a large, very ripe, juicy variety such as the Chinese pear for this delicately flavored ice. For *gingered-pear* punch, add 2 t grated ginger to the boiling syrup and strain after chilling.

Boil 5 minutes	³/₄ C sugar ¹/₂ C water.
Chill.	
Peel, core, and purée	**5 pears.**
Add chilled syrup and	**¹/₂ C white wine juice of 1 lemon.**
Stir freeze.	
	yield: about 1 quart

4

Sherbet and Ice Milk

A sherbet essentially is an ice with milk replacing some of the juice or water. Some people believe a proper sherbet should be very sweet and not too smooth. Others feel it should be very much like ice cream in body and texture.

The first commercial sherbets appeared in this country in 1932 as an alternative to ice cream, which was scarce during the Depression and, later, during World War II. Because it contains less fat than ice cream, sherbet remains a popular alternative.

Commercially made sherbet can officially be no more than fifty percent dairy product or it technically becomes ice milk, but the distinction between sherbet, ice milk, and ice cream blurs when they are homemade. The smoothest and richest sherbets are made with light cream, half and half, or whipping cream instead of milk.

Regardless which dairy product you use, stir in the lemon juice and other acidic fruits or juices just before freezing. Otherwise the mix may curdle, a problem affecting aesthetics more than taste or texture. If curdling does result (and it happens occasionally to the most experienced home ice cream maker), allow the mix to cool, then whip it or whirl it in a food processor for a minute or two until the ingredients are fully blended.

ORANGE SHERBET

The gentle flavor of this sherbet may be intensified by adding one of the following: $^1/_4$ t orange extract, the puréed fruit of up to 6 fresh oranges, or 2 small cans of mandarin oranges, drained well. Texture and flavor are both enhanced with the addition of $^1/_4$ C vodka, tequila, or orange brandy as freezing nears completion.

Combine

$^2/_3$ **C orange juice**
  concentrate
1 C sugar
2 T lemon juice
$^1/_2$ **t orange rind.**

Slowly pour in

$2^1/_2$ **C milk.**

Stir freeze.

yield: about 1 quart

CREAMY ORANGE SHERBET

This sherbet requires extra steps, but is so creamy smooth you'll have a hard time telling it from full-fledged ice cream. For a reduced-calorie, less creamy version, substitute milk for the cream. Natural orange sherbet lacks the gaudy color of the commercial kind. If you wish, add a drop or two of orange food dye.

Simmer 10 minutes	²/₃ **C water** **1 C sugar.**
Grate and add	**rind of 1 orange.**
Cook 5 minutes more.	
Cool, then chill.	
In large bowl beat foamy	**3 egg whites.**
Combine and stir in	**1³/₄ C orange juice** **1 T lemon juice.**
Add cooled syrup and	**¹/₂ C heavy cream.**
Stir freeze.	

yield: about 1 quart

LIME SHERBET

Like orange sherbet, lime sherbet has a very pale color that may be brightened with a few drops of green food dye. To make *lemon* sherbet, refreshing in itself but also a fine foundation for other fruit flavors, substitute lemon juice and rind for lime.

Heat	**3 C milk.**
Stir in until dissolved	**1 C sugar.**
Chill.	
Add	²/₃ **C lime juice** **1 t grated lime rind.**
Stir freeze.	

yield: about 1 quart

RASPBERRY SHERBET

Raspberry sherbet makes a first-rate dressing for a fruit salad arranged on a bed of lettuce and accompanied by a scoop of cottage cheese. Or serve it as dessert with fresh or thawed raspberries tossed together with a little kirsch or raspberry liqueur.

Thaw, purée, and strain	**2 pkg frozen raspberries.**
Heat	**²/₃ C sugar** **2 T light corn syrup** **2 C milk.**
Stir until sugar dissolves.	
Cool.	
Add purée and	**2 T lemon juice.**
Stir freeze.	

yield: about 1 quart

FRUIT SHERBET

Nearly any fruit juice or purée is tasty in a sherbet. One of the top ten favorite sherbets, *pineapple*, can be made from either pineapple juice or pureed crushed pineapple.

Heat until bubbles form	**2¹/₂ C milk.**
Stir in until dissolved	**²/₃ C sugar.**
Chill.	
Add	**1 C fruit juice or purée** **1 T lemon juice.**
Stir freeze.	

yield: about 1 quart

CRANBERRY ORANGE SHERBET

Here's another ultra-creamy sherbet with the consistency of a richer ice cream, but not the calories. It stores nicely, and the flavor continues to improve on hardening, so make plenty. You can use either fresh or frozen cranberries.

In medium saucepan, combine

1 C sugar
¹/₂ T plain gelatin
¹/₂ t grated orange rind.

Stir in

1¹/₂ C milk.

Stir over low heat until gelatin and sugar dissolve.

Cool.

Purée almost smooth

1 C cranberries

with

¹/₂ C orange juice.

Stir into milk mixture.

Stir freeze.

yield: about 1 quart

CHAMPAGNE SHERBET

This sherbet can be made with champagne or white wine. Either way, it's perfect for sprucing up fruit compote. Or scoop it into elegant stemmed glasses partially filled with additional chilled champagne or wine.

Whisk

3 egg whites
²/₃ C sugar.

Blend in

1¹/₃ C heavy cream
²/₃ C cold water
²/₃ C champagne.

Stir freeze.

yield: about 1 quart

PIÑA COLADA SHERBET

This recipe is based on a tropical drink popularized in the 1970s. Serve it in a goblet garnished with one-quarter of a pineapple ring, or scoop it onto a whole pineapple ring and garnish with mango slices. Include one mashed ripe banana for *banana colada* sherbet or ¹/₂ C puréed strawberries for *strawberry colada* sherbet. If you prefer to do without the spirits, include ¹/₄ C sugar for the sake of texture.

Combine

8³/₄-oz cream of coconut
1¹/₂ C milk
1 C pineapple juice
¹/₄ C dark rum.

Stir freeze.

yield: about 1 quart

Soufflé

A soufflé is a light-textured freeze made by adding one or two beaten whole eggs to a quart of sherbet or ice mix. Whether or not they contain dairy products, all soufflés are officially included in the "sherbet" category.

Even soufflés made without dairy products are so creamy smooth that most people have trouble distinguishing them from milk-based sherbets. When milk or cream is included, the soufflé has slightly greater depth of flavor and won't harden quite as firm.

In preparing the following recipes you might, for safety's sake (see Chapter 13), prefer to use an egg substitute such as Egg Beaters. Alternatively, combine raw eggs with sugar and water or milk or cream and cook them, following the custard-making directions in chapter 6.

BASIC SOUFFLÉ

Pineapple makes an exceptionally tasty soufflé. Also outstanding is *two-fruit* soufflé made from such combinations as ¹/₄ C pineapple and ¹/₄ C sliced strawberries, or ¹/₄ C blueberries and ¹/₄ C puréed orange sections, or ¹/₄ C apricots and ¹/₄ C flavorful peaches or nectarines.

Whirl in blender

1¹/₂ C water or milk
1 egg
²/₃ C sugar
¹/₂ C puréed fruit
1¹/₂ T lemon juice.

Stir freeze.

yield: about 1 quart

CREAMY SOUFFLÉ

This creamy soufflé borders on true ice cream in both flavor and texture. For a*pricot*, *strawberry*, or *peach* soufflé, add ¼ t almond extract. For *pineapple* soufflé, omit the vanilla.

Beat thick

2 eggs
⅔ C sugar.

Whirl in blender

2 C berries or
  chopped fruit
1½ C cream or
  milk
½ t vanilla.

Blend with eggs.

Chill and freeze.

yield: about 1 quart

Ice Milk

Ice milk is simply ice cream containing so little cream that its fat content falls to between two and seven percent. Because it's so low in fat, ice milk seems colder than regular ice cream when hardened. It is popular among the diet conscious since it has about half the calories of gourmet ice cream, provided you don't increase the sweetener to enrich flavor or improve hardening consistency.

Because it contains little fat, ice milk turns coarse and icy and becomes difficult to scoop when hardened. To minimize this, use whole milk rather than low-fat or skim milk. You can further boost the solid content by substituting undiluted evaporated milk for all or part of the whole milk called for. If you aren't fond of the caramelized taste of evaporated milk, flavor the mix with cocoa, coffee, butterscotch, or any other strong, compatible ingredient.

A second way to improve the texture of ice milk destined for hardening is to add milk powder at the rate of no more than one-third cup per cup liquid milk. But don't plan to store the resulting ice milk for long since the extra lactose will eventually crystallize and turn gritty.

The easiest way to avoid these problems is to serve ice milk straight from the ice cream freezer, when its taste and texture are at their peaks. Seventy-five percent of the soft-serve ice cream sold commercially is actually ice milk, and half the ice milk made commercially is served soft. Commercial soft-serve, which first appeared on the Atlanta boardwalk many years ago, is especially popular in the South and West.

VANILLA ICE MILK

Vanilla ice milk, made with whole or skim milk, is a refreshing treat when served soft, but tastes bland when hardened. Flavor it in the same ways you would flavor regular ice cream, as described in Chapters 14 and 15 and Appendix A.

Heat just until bubbles form	**3¹/₂ C milk.**
Stir in until dissolved	**²/₃ C sugar.**
Cool.	
Add	**¹/₂ T vanilla** **¹/₈ t salt.**
Chill and stir freeze.	

yield: about 1 quart

HONEY ICE MILK

Honey adds flavor and contributes to the fine texture of this easy-to-make ice milk. Add ¹/₂ C mashed banana for *banana honey* ice milk. Serve it with sliced bananas or other fresh fruit for a nutritious snack.

Combine	**3¹/₂ C whole or** **skim milk** **¹/₂ C honey** **¹/₈ t salt.**
Chill and stir freeze.	

yield: about 1 quart

CHOCOLATE ICE MILK

Cocoa and cinnamon combine to create the impression of greater richness in this delectable dessert, which hardens nicely and keeps quite well for ice milk. To make *rocky road*, omit the cinnamon and stir in ¹/₂ C miniature marshmallows and ¹/₂ C chopped walnuts.

Combine	**6 T cocoa** **1 C sugar.**
Add	**3¹/₂ C milk** **1 t vanilla** **pinch ground** **cinnamon.**
Stir until sugar dissolves.	
Chill and stir freeze.	

yield: about 1 quart

MANDARIN CHOCOLATE ICE MILK

The classic combination of orange and chocolate lends extra dimension to this delicious ice milk. If you squeeze the juice fresh, you'll need two to three oranges.

Stir together	**1 C sugar**
	6 T cocoa.
Add	**1 C orange juice**
	2¹/₂ C milk
	¹/₂ t vanilla
	¹/₂ t orange rind.

Stir until sugar dissolves.

Chill.

Strain and stir freeze.

yield: about 1 quart

COUNTRY ICE MILK

Country ice milk contains whole eggs for extra richness, making it a good base for fruit flavors created by substituting up to 1 C fruit juice or sweetened purée for an equal amount of milk. If you're watching the fats in your diet, or you have suspicions about the safety of raw eggs, use egg substitute in this recipe and the following one.

Beat thoroughly	**2 eggs.**
Gradually add	**²/₃ C sugar.**
Beat stiff.	
Stir in	**3 C milk**
	2 t vanilla.
Chill and stir freeze.	

yield: about 1 quart

SMOOTH-AS-SILK ICE MILK

This country ice milk has exceptionally smooth texture and hardens quite nicely. It originated as a way for home dairy operators to approximate rich, scoopable ice cream without the bother of extracting extra cream from home produced milk.

In small saucepan soften	**¹/₂ pkg plain gelatin**
in	**2¹/₂ C milk.**
Heat to dissolve gelatin.	
Stir in until dissolved	**¹/₄ C sugar.**
Cool and add	**¹/₂ T vanilla** **¹/₈ t salt.**
Chill.	
Beat	**2 eggs.**
Add and beat stiff	**¹/₄ C sugar.**
Beat in gelatin mixture.	
Stir freeze.	

yield: about 1 quart

5

Ice Cream

Ice cream is richer and smoother than sherbet because it contains more cream. It is also less tart, about half as sweet, and has a higher melting point so it doesn't feel as cold in your mouth.

The ingredient that varies most from one ice cream to another (aside from flavoring, of course) is cream. The amount of cream you use determines an ice cream's richness, which is measured according to fat content. Milkfat ranges from twenty percent or more in gourmet ice cream down to two percent in ice milk. Balancing cream and other dairy products to control ice cream quality is the subject of Chapter 11, "The Cream in Ice Cream."

Homemade versus Store-Bought

In contrast to the commercial kind, most homemade ice cream is made with fresh cream rather than condensed or powdered milk. It usually has less air and more flavoring goodies such as pieces of fruit, crumbled cookies, or chocolate bits. Because a serving of equal size weighs more, homemade ice cream has more calories. Because it is considerably denser, it's harder to scoop unless you allow it to soften to dipping consistency.

STORE-BOUGHT ICE CREAM	
Economy	Meets legal minimum requirements; usually artificially flavored; 10% fat.
Trade brand	Above minimum requirements; may be artificially flavored; 10-12% fat.
Premium	High in fat and other solids; less air; often contains natural flavorings; 12-14% fat.
Superpremium	Very high in fat and other solids; very little air; usually contains natural flavorings; 14-20% fat.

Gourmet, superpremium, or so-called "designer" ice cream is perhaps closest to homemade because it has so little air beaten in and includes lots of flavoring solids. Superpremium and premium together account for 35 percent of all ice cream sold.

Flavor

Vanilla is nearly everyone's favorite flavor, but, as any ice cream aficionado will tell you, there's vanilla and then there's vanilla. Vanilla ice cream can be dense and rich, light and smooth, or anything in between; it all depends on the ingredients and how they're put together.

All other flavors evolve from one of the basic forms of vanilla, whether Philadelphia, American, French, or some other variation. The trick to inventing flavors of your own is to select the most appropriate foundation as a springboard. Not only should you like the taste and texture, but the ingredients must be compatible with the flavoring you wish to use. Experienced ice cream makers tend to favor a particular foundation for one flavoring group, such as fruit, and some other base for flavors like nut or bisque.

Philadelphia Ice Cream

According to *The Whitehouse Cook Book* of 1887, "genuine" ice cream contains only pure, sweet cream combined with sugar in proportions of two quarts cream to one pound (two and one-fourth cups) sugar. "Beat up," add flavoring, and freeze.

This is a perfect description of Philadelphia ice cream, a favorite to this day. Modern cooks are likely to heat the cream and stir in the sugar until it dissolves, an optional step that makes the texture smoother and more velvety. The cream need be warmed only until bubbles begin to form around the edges. To keep the cream from sticking to the bottom, rinse the saucepan first in cold water, or heat the cream in a microwave set on high for one to two minutes.

Some Philadelphia recipes call for whipping all or part of the cream, a step you can take any time you wish to increase volume and lighten texture. To reduce richness, substitute light cream or milk for a portion of the heavy cream.

PHILADELPHIA VANILLA ICE CREAM

During the nineteenth century, Philadelphia was home to nearly fifty ice cream manufacturers, making that city the nation's ice cream capital. Although Pennsylvania is still a major ice cream producer, it is now second to California. Despite this drop in production stature, Philadelphia ice cream remains "number one."

Heat just until bubbles form	**3 C cream.**
Stir in until dissolved	**²/₃ C sugar.**
Cool and add	**¹/₂ T vanilla.**
Chill and stir freeze.	

yield: about 1 quart

TRADITIONAL PHILADELPHIA VANILLA ICE CREAM

Traditional Philadelphia vanilla is shot through with tiny black flecks that are ground up vanilla beans or seeds scraped from the pod—you know it's real vanilla because you can actually see it. Beyond Philadelphia, these specks are viewed with suspicion, so most recipes include a step for straining them out or circumvent the issue by calling for vanilla extract. On behalf of Philadelphia vanilla purists, here's the real thing. Use light or heavy cream, depending on desired richness.

Split and scrape seeds from	**3" vanilla bean.**
Add to	**3 C cream.**
Heat just until bubbles form.	
Stir in until dissolved	**²/₃ C sugar.**
Chill and stir freeze.	

yield: about 1 quart

SPIRITED COFFEE ICE CREAM

When using strong flavorings such as coffee or chocolate, it's necessary to increase the sweetening, as this recipe demonstrates. To make *spirited chocolate,* substitute ¹/₄ C cocoa for the instant coffee. Or try *spirited*

Heat just until bubbles form	**3 C cream.**
Stir in until dissolved	**3 T instant coffee** **1 C sugar.**
Chill.	

SPIRITED COFFEE ICE CREAM, cont'd.

mocha by including half of each. For the alcoholic spirits (which are optional) try quality brandy, Irish whiskey, or Bristol cream sherry.

Stir freeze until slushy.

Add   ¹/₄ **C alcoholic spirits.**

Complete freezing.

yield: about 1 quart

PHILADELPHIA FRUIT ICE CREAM

Fruit flavors are created simply by substituting juice or sweetened purée for a portion of the cream, usually at the rate of one cup per quart. For the remainder use heavy cream to preserve richness, lighter cream to reduce calories. Adjust sugar according to the sweetness of the fruit, using up to ³/₄ C for tart flavors like *pink grapefruit*.

Mix and chill   **2 C cream**
                                     ¹/₄ **C sugar.**

Mix and chill   **1 C fruit juice or purée**
                                     ¹/₄ **C sugar**
                                     ¹/₂ **T lemon juice.**

Combine and stir freeze.

yield: about 1 quart

AVOCADO ICE CREAM

To enhance the satisfying, nutty flavor of this ultra-smooth, pastel ice cream, stir in ¹/₂ C coarsely ground hazelnuts and create *avocado hazelnut*. Or chop the nuts and sprinkle them atop each scoop. For a wildly different appetizer or chip dip, stir 1 T grated onion into the avocado purée, substitute ¹/₃ C mayonnaise or plain yogurt for an equal amount of cream, and add ¹/₈ t salt plus a pinch of black pepper. Scoop this *zippy avocado* ice cream into avocado shells or hollowed-out tomatoes and pass the tortilla chips.

Dissolve   ²/₃ **C sugar**

in   **2 C cream.**

Purée   **2 large avocados**
                                     2 T lemon juice.

Combine with a little cream and beat smooth.

Add remaining cream and beat smooth.

Stir freeze.

yield: about 1 quart

HOLIDAY AMBROSIA ICE CREAM

Combining different kinds of fruit creates an exotic medley that's usually given an otherworldly name like ambrosia or heavenly hash. Nuts increase textural variety. This fantastic Philadelphia ice cream calls for fruit and nuts. It reaches perfection when the flavors are allowed to blend for a brief hardening period. Serve this ice cream as a delightful alternative to traditional holiday cakes and pies.

Whirl in blender

$^{1}/_{2}$ C cranberries
$^{1}/_{2}$ C sugar
$^{1}/_{2}$ C crushed pineapple.

Chill.

Combine

2 C cream
$^{1}/_{4}$ C sugar
$^{1}/_{2}$ t vanilla.

Stir freeze until slushy.

Add chilled fruit and

$^{1}/_{4}$ C chopped walnuts.

Complete freezing.

yield: about 1 quart

HONEYED FRUIT 'N' NUT ICE CREAM

Using honey as a sweetener offers extra flavoring dimension. Make it even more special by coordinating fruit and nuts. Toasted almonds are super with *apricot* or *peach*, for example, and walnuts are great with *pineapple* or *prune*. Combine freshly pressed carrot juice and chopped pecans for deliciously different *honeyed carrot nut* ice cream. Omit the nuts, if you prefer, for *honeyed fruit* ice cream. If you don't care for the way honey affects taste and texture, substitute $^{1}/_{2}$ C sugar and make *fruit 'n' nut* ice cream.

Combine and chill

1 C juice or purée
$^{1}/_{3}$ C honey.

Blend in

$2^{1}/_{2}$ C heavy cream.

Stir freeze until slushy.

Chop and stir in

$^{1}/_{3}$ C nuts.

Complete freezing.

yield: about 1 quart

JAMMER JELLY ICE CREAM

This Philadelphia ice cream derives both sweetness and flavor from jam, jelly, or preserves. Use a single flavor, or be creative and combine $^1/_2$ C each of two complementary kinds like currant and raspberry or apricot and marmalade. The spirits, which are optional, enhance flavor and reduce the impression of sweetness. Use kirsch for all flavors, or coordinate flavored brandies or liqueurs. Try ginger brandy with ginger preserves for *ginger* ice cream, or crème de menthe with mint jelly for *mint* ice cream. If desired, perk up color with a few drops of food dye.

Heat just until bubbles form	**2$^1/_2$ C cream.**
In small saucepan, melt	**1 C jam.**
Stir smooth and add to warm cream.	
Cool and strain.	
Stir in	**$^1/_8$ t almond extract.**
Chill and add	**2 T spirits.**
Stir freeze.	

yield: about 1 quart

PEPPERMINT CRUNCH ICE CREAM

This old-timey recipe surely originated as an ingenious way to use up Christmas candy canes. Crush the canes by whirling them in a food processor, or wrap them in a plastic bag and bash it with a rolling pin. If you prefer smooth texture, omit the final addition of crushed candy. You'll need $^1/_4$# of canes for smooth ice cream, $^1/_3$# for this version, and $^1/_2$# if you make it extra crunchy by doubling the final candy addition. You can also use this recipe to make *candy stick* ice cream from crushed candy sticks of any flavor—cinnamon, wintergreen, licorice or your favorite.

Heat just until bubbles form	**1$^1/_3$ C milk.**
Remove from heat and add	**$^2/_3$ C crushed canes.**
Stir until dissolved.	
Chill.	
Whip into soft peaks	**1$^1/_3$ C heavy cream.**
Fold into milk mixture.	
Chill.	
Stir freeze, and add	**$^1/_3$ C crushed canes.**

yield: about 1 quart

Country Ice Cream

When light cream or milk is used in Philadelphia ice cream, eggs are sometimes added to preserve creamy texture and the semblance of richness. Then, of course, you've no longer got Philadelphia but American or country ice cream.

For ultra-rich country ice cream, use *both* heavy cream and eggs. For exceptionally light texture, whether or not the cream is reduced, whip the yolks and whites separately (each with half the sugar) and fold in the whites at the last minute.

Before adding raw eggs to ice cream, read about them in Chapter 13, "Emulsifiers and Stabilizers." If safety dictates, either use egg substitute or cook the mix and turn it into frozen custard, the subject of the next chapter.

COUNTRY VANILLA ICE CREAM

Country ice cream doubtless derives its name from the country fresh milk, cream, and eggs that go into it. There seem to be at least as many versions as there are people who make it. Each differs in its proportion of milk to cream and in the number of eggs added to achieve the desired texture and richness.

Combine	1½ C milk
	1½ C cream
	1½ t vanilla.
Chill.	
Beat	2 eggs.
Add	½ C sugar.
Whip stiff.	
Fold into milk mixture.	
Stir freeze.	

yield: about 1 quart

COUNTRY STRAWBERRY ICE CREAM

Like Philadelphia ice cream, country ice cream can be flavored with fruit by substituting juice or sweetened purée for some of the milk or cream. According to your preference, use only

Purée	2 C fresh strawberries.
Combine with	1 T lemon juice
	½ C sugar.

COUNTRY STRAWBERRY ICE CREAM, cont'd.

one egg and all cream, as in this recipe, or include up to three eggs and substitute milk for some of the cream. This strawberry version, or any other fruit flavor, can be made even fruitier by adding 2 T orange liqueur.

Let stand several hours.

Heat just until bubbles form	**2 C cream.**
Stir in until dissolved	**¼ C sugar.**
Cool.	
Beat and stir in	**1 egg.**
Add purée and	**1 t vanilla.**
Stir freeze.	

yield: about 1 quart

PISTACHIO ICE CREAM

Nut flavors are easy—simply add chopped nuts and a bit of extract, as in this pistachio recipe. Include a few drops of green tint, if you wish, for traditional color. Make *maple nut* by substituting maple flavoring (Mapeline) for almond extract and English walnuts or black walnuts for pistachios. Or use Grape-nuts cereal in place of nuts for yummy *Grape-nuts* ice cream, which is technically a bisque since it's made with baked goods instead of true nuts.

Combine	**1 C milk** **1½ C cream** **1 t vanilla** **½ t almond** **extract.**
Chill.	
Beat	**2 eggs**
Add	**½ C sugar.**
Whip stiff and fold into milk mixture.	
Stir freeze until slushy.	
Chop and stir in	**⅓ C pistachio** **nuts.**
Complete freezing.	

yield: about 1 quart

ORANGE CHOCOLATE CHIP ICE CREAM

You can turn any flavor into "chip" ice cream by stirring in 1/2 C miniature chocolate bits per quart. Or start with basic vanilla and use additional extract, as in this orange-flavored country chip ice cream. For *mint chip*, substitute mint extract for orange. Add an extra wallop of flavoring with minted chocolate chips, and you'll have *double mint chip* ice cream.

Combine

**1 C milk
1 1/2 C cream
1/2 t vanilla
1 t orange
extract.**

Chill.

Beat

2 eggs.

Add and beat stiff

1/2 C sugar.

Fold into milk mixture.

Stir freeze until slushy.

Add

**1/2 C chocolate
bits.**

Complete freezing.

yield: about 1 quart

PUMPKIN PIE À LA MODE

This country ice cream captures all the best flavors of a slice of spicy pumpkin pie topped with a scoop of ice cream. For *Western pumpkin*, add 2 T rum. For *New England pumpkin*, add 1 t maple flavoring. If you're nuts about nuts, make *pumpkin nut* by stirring in 1/3 C chopped walnuts or pecans. For all versions, 1/2 T pumpkin pie spice may be used in place of all other spices. Pumpkin ice cream is pretty dense when it hardens, so allow plenty of time for tempering.

Beat thick

3 eggs.

Stir in

**2 C cream
1 C pumpkin
purée
1/2 C brown
sugar
1/3 C sugar
1 t cinnamon
1/4 t nutmeg
1/4 t ginger.**

Chill and stir freeze.

yield: about 1 quart

INDIAN ICE CREAM

Here's an up-dated version of that roadside refreshment savored by the Indians of central Mexico, who discovered corn milk as an innovative ice cream ingredient. Vary the flavor by including a tablespoon or two of molasses or maple syrup, or substitute mild-flavored honey for some or all of the sugar. Surprise your guests by serving this ice cream next Thanksgiving, perhaps topped with a spoonful of warmed whole cranberry sauce.

Purée	**17-oz can creamed corn.**
Strain for 1½ C purée.	
Beat thick	**3 egg yolks.**
Gradually add	**²⁄₃ C sugar.**
Beat stiff.	
Stir in corn cream and	**1 C heavy cream** **1 T lemon juice** **½ t vanilla** **¼ t nutmeg.**
Stir freeze.	
	yield: about 1 quart

RUM RAISIN ICE CREAM

This Northeastern favorite gets its superbly smooth texture from corn syrup and rum. If you prefer a non-alcoholic version, substitute ½ T rum extract for the spirits. For *chocolate rum raisin*, heat the cream and corn syrup together and add 2 squares semisweet chocolate, stirring until melted. Cool, omit lemon juice, and increase vanilla to 1 t.

Chop	**½ C dark raisins.**
Soak several hours in	**¼ C dark rum.**
Beat thick	**2 eggs** **²⁄₃ C sugar.**
Combine, and beat in	**2 C cream** **¼ C light corn syrup** **1 t lemon juice** **½ t vanilla.**
Stir freeze until slushy.	
Add marinated raisins.	
Complete freezing.	
	yield: about 1 quart

HONEY COUNTRY ICE CREAM

In addition to its role as a sweetener, honey stands on its own as a fine flavoring, as shown in this recipe. To make *banana honey* ice cream, add 1 ripe mashed banana and $1/2$ t lemon juice. For *date honey* add $1/2$ C chopped dates. Or include $1/2$ C each chopped dates and either walnuts or pecans for *date honey nut*. Make popular *carob honey* by thoroughly blending $1/3$ C nonsweetened carob powder with the honey and light cream.

Combine and mix well	$1/3$ C honey 1 C light cream.
Beat in	1 C light cream 1 egg 2 t vanilla.
Stir in	1 C heavy cream.
Chill and stir freeze.	

yield: about 1 quart

───────⟋⟍───────

CREAMY COUNTRY ICE CREAM

This incredibly rich country ice cream has a delicate, mousse-like texture, thanks to the French trick of adding sugar-water syrup plus the combination of heavy cream and egg yolks. Turn it into a rich bisque such as *cookies 'n' cream* by stirring in $1/2$ C (about six) crushed chocolate sandwich cookies, crumbled brownies, or other bakery favorite, as freezing nears completion.

In small saucepan, combine	$1/4$ C water $1/2$ C sugar.
Stirring, boil 2 minutes.	
At high speed, beat	6 egg yolks.
Continue beating eggs while drizzling with hot syrup.	
Beat until cool, about 5 minutes.	
Whip into soft peaks	2 C heavy cream.
Fold into egg mixture.	
Add	2 t vanilla.
Chill and stir freeze.	

yield: about 1 quart

CHOCOLATE VELVET ICE CREAM

Also reminiscent of frozen mousse, but requiring fewer steps than the previous recipe, is this decadently rich chocolate ice cream. The addition of grated chocolate provides extra bursts of flavor, but you may omit it if you prefer smoother, unbroken texture. For a triple chocolate treat, leave in the extra chocolate and splash each serving with crème de cacao.

Stir together	$^2/_3$ **C sugar** $^1/_3$ **C cocoa.**
Beat in	**3 egg yolks.**
Gradually beat in	$2^2/_3$ **C cream.**
Chill and stir freeze.	
Grate and stir in	$^1/_3$ **C semisweet chocolate.**

yield: about 1 quart

Instant Ice Cream

Ice cream has the official endorsement of the U.S. Army as a morale food, something anyone can relate to who has ever felt blue. The smallest scoop can cheer you up and bolster your resolve quicker than almost anything else in the world.

It's such an effective morale booster that the Navy commissioned a floating ice cream parlor in the western Pacific during World War II, and instant mix was developed as a nonperishable way to supply ice cream to our troops overseas.

Instant ice cream isn't quite as good as ice cream made from scratch, but it does have exceptionally smooth consistency and isn't half bad if you customize it with fruit, berries, chocolate chips, nuts, cookie crumbs, or other goodies.

There are several different brands of ice cream mix. Some can be found at the supermarket. Others are packaged together with new ice cream freezers to get you started and can be reordered by mail. The chief advantage to packaged mixes is that they let you whip up a batch of ice cream at a moment's notice without having a lot of ingredients on hand.

Instant pudding makes a handy mix and comes in a broad assortment of flavors. Let the pudding stand on its own, or customize it with any of the add-ins you would use for regular ice cream. Pudding mix suggests one way to make fast ice cream in a food processor. Simply whirl instant pudding with the required amount of milk and toss in enough frozen fruit to achieve soft-serve consistency.

Another form of instant mix is flavored gelatin, made according to directions but dissolved in milk or cream instead of water. When using either pudding or gelatin to make ice cream, prepare the mix as usual and let it cool but not set before pouring it into your ice cream maker for freezing.

You can use flavored gelatin in another way to add color, flavor, and textural variety to ice cream. Mix up a package with only half the water called for and let it set up in a one-quarter-inch-thick layer. After it firms, cut it into tiny cubes (or mash into flakes with a fork) and stir it into freshly frozen ice cream. Orange gelatin is pretty, and tastes terrific, in vanilla ice cream. Raspberry adds an interesting touch to chocolate. Mix and match according to your taste, with an eye toward appealing color combinations.

TWO-TONE ICE CREAM

Make this stunning two-tone treat, picture perfect and great for parties, with any fruit-flavored gelatin. Substitute orange rind when using orange gelatin, lime rind with lime. For *confetti* ice cream, combine two contrasting flavors, taking care not to clash colors. Raspberry goes well with orange, for example, but isn't visually appealing with lime. For a less rich, more sherbet-like freeze, substitute milk for the cream.

Dissolve **3-oz flavored gelatin**

in **1 C boiling water.**

Mold in a thin layer in flat-bottomed container.

Chill.

Combine **3-oz same flavor gelatin**
$^1\!/_2$ C sugar
1 C boiling water.

Cool, stir in **$2^1\!/_2$ C cream**
2 T lemon juice
grated rind $^1\!/_2$ lemon.

Stir freeze.

Dice gelatin and fold in.

yield: about 1 quart

ALMOND PISTACHIO ICE CREAM

In this recipe, light or heavy cream is combined with milk to increase richness, but you can use all milk instead. To lighten up the texture, retain the heavy cream, whipping it into soft peaks and folding it in just before freezing. This is a step you should definitely take for any pudding ice cream you wish to harden.

Combine

2 4-oz instant pistachio pudding mix
2 C milk
2 C cream
$^1/_2$ t almond extract
$^1/_4$ C chopped toasted almonds.

Chill and freeze.

yield: about 1 quart

FUDGY ICE CREAM

This ice cream comes as close as you can get to the taste of a store-bought Fudgsicle, especially if you use Jello chocolate fudge instant pudding mix. If your ice cream maker won't hold the whole batch, divide it in half and freeze in two portions, or mold the excess as frozen suckers, described in Chapter 1, Still Freezing.

Mix well

14-oz condensed milk
4-oz instant pudding mix
4 C milk.

Stir freeze.

yield: about 2 quarts

CREAMY PUDDING ICE CREAM

If you're among those who can taste the "instant" in instant pudding, try this recipe calling for regular pudding mix. To microwave, heat the mix on high for 6 minutes, stirring occasionally during the last 3 minutes.

Combine

4-oz regular pudding mix
2 C milk
$^1/_2$ C sugar.

Cook as directed.

Chill.

Whip and fold in

2 C heavy cream.

Stir freeze.

yield: about 1 quart

6

Frozen Custard

Frozen custard, also known as parfait, French ice cream, New York ice cream, or sometimes Neapolitan ice cream, is made from eggs cooked into a thickened custard. Although frozen custard is usually very rich, there are ways you can vary it to retain smooth texture and the semblance of richness yet create an ice cream that's somewhat kinder to your waistline.

Custard

Most recipes call for a double boiler to prevent the scorching and lumps that occur when custard firms up around the edges of a hot pan. You can achieve nearly the same results with a heavy saucepan over low heat. Rinse the pan in cold water before you start.

Heat the milk or cream until bubbles form around the edges. Add the sugar and stir until it dissolves. Lightly beat the eggs and temper them by stirring in a small amount of warm milk. Slowly pour the egg mixture into the remainder of the heated milk, stirring constantly. Although the two-step procedure of pouring heated ingredients into the eggs, then pouring it back into the mix might seem like so much rigmarole, it keeps the eggs from getting too hot too fast and poaching in the milk. The result is smoother ice cream. You can avoid the extra step by using only yolks, since the whites are the culprits in causing curdling.

Thickening

Continue cooking the custard, stirring constantly so it will heat uniformly and neither stick nor get lumpy. The custard will begin to thicken around 175° F (80° C), well before the boiling point is reached. Don't allow it to boil or it will curdle.

To guard against overheating, have a large bowl or basin of cold water handy. If the mixture thickens too quickly or appears on the brink of boiling, quickly nestle the hot pan in the cold water and stir like mad to cool the custard down. With practice, you'll learn to see the custard begin to thicken and feel the resistance as you stir, which takes about ten minutes.

A microwave helps eliminate some of the guesswork. Heat milk on high for three to four minutes, or cream on medium-high one to two minutes. Combine the milk or cream with eggs as before and heat on medium-high one to two minutes more, stirring once or twice. If you use yolks only, heat the mixture on high two to three minutes, stirring occasionally.

Whether or not you use a microwave, the custard is done when a thin filmy layer coats a clean wooden or metal spoon, dipped in and lifted out at a slant. If you draw your finger across the back of the spoon, a clear trail should remain. Cool the custard in a metal bowl set into a larger bowl or basin of ice, stirring occasionally to ensure smoothness.

Straining the custard speeds cooling and breaks up or removes lumps that otherwise disrupt texture. This step is important if the mixture managed to boil and curdle. Cool the custard to room temperature before adding flavoring and other ingredients, then chill before freezing it in an ice cream maker.

Strong flavorings like chocolate, coffee, and nut work best in frozen custard. Many ice cream aficionados feel that the taste of custard overwhelms the delicate flavors of fresh fruit, but don't be reluctant to try any flavoring that appeals to your taste buds.

FRENCH VANILLA ICE CREAM

The creamy richness of this ice cream is influenced by the number of egg yolks you use and the proportion of milk to cream. For super rich ice cream, include up to six egg yolks and use heavy cream in place of all the milk and cream.

Heat | **1 C milk**
$^1/_2$ C sugar.

Beat thick | **4 egg yolks.**

Stir into milk mixture.

Continue stirring over low heat until mixture coats a metal spoon, about 10 minutes.

Cool.

Add | **$1^1/_2$ C cream**
2 t vanilla.

Chill and stir freeze.

yield: about 1 quart

HONEY ALMOND ICE CREAM

The flavor of this scrumptious ice cream will depend on the kind of honey you choose. Experiment with exotic ones, using up to $^2/_3$ C honey, depending on strength of flavor and your own sweet tooth. For delectable *cherry almond* ice cream, stir in $^1/_2$ C chopped maraschino cherries.

Heat	**3 C heavy cream.**
Beat until thick	**6 egg yolks** **$^1/_2$ C honey.**
Stir into warm cream.	
Continue stirring over low heat until mixture coats a metal spoon, about 10 minutes.	
Cool.	
Add	**$^1/_8$ t almond extract.**
Chill, stir freeze, and add	**$^1/_2$ C toasted almonds.**

yield: about 1 quart

HONEY BLOSSOM ICE CREAM

The delicate flavor of jasmine, camomile, rose, lavender, or orange blossoms makes this old-fashioned ice cream a special treat. For a different taste, substitute loose tea leaves, from conservative English breakfast to zippy orange spice tea, reducing the amount of tea to $^1/_4$ C, if desired, for milder flavor. Choose honey that blends well with the main flavoring, such as orange blossom honey with orange petals, or substitute sugar and let the flavor of the blossoms or tea predominate. You'll find dried flower petals and a variety of honeys at any natural food store.

Heat	**3 C milk.**
Pour onto	**$^1/_2$ C dried flower petals.**
Steep 15 minutes and strain.	
Lightly beat	**2 eggs.**
Beat in	**$^1/_2$ C honey.**
Add flavored milk.	
Stirring, heat until thickened.	
Cool, strain, and add to	**1 C heavy cream.**
Chill and stir freeze.	

yield: about 1 quart

MOLASSES PRALINE ICE CREAM

Here's another old-time recipe, this one reminiscent of traditional molasses taffy, cooled in winter's first snow. Molasses tastes quite strong, so don't hesitate to replace a portion with sugar if you wish to tone it down.

Heat	**1 C milk.**
Beat together	**5 egg yolks** **²/₃ C light molasses.**
Stir into milk mixture.	
Continue stirring over low heat until mixture coats a metal spoon, about 10 minutes.	
Cool.	
Add	**1¹/₂ C heavy cream.**
Chill, stir freeze, and add	**¹/₄ C chopped pecans.**

yield: about 1 quart

NOT QUITE FRENCH VANILLA ICE CREAM

If you love French ice cream but consider eggs forbidden fruit, here's a passable version thickened with flour instead. True connoisseurs who prefer arrowroot instead of flour (for reasons described in Chapter 13) can substitute 1 t arrowroot per 1 T flour. To reduce calories, use milk in place of cream.

In large saucepan, combine	**¹/₂ C sugar** **1 T flour.**
Stir in	**2 C milk.**
Stirring, heat until sugar dissolves.	
Cool.	
Add	**2 C cream** **1 T vanilla.**
Chill and stir freeze.	

yield: about 1 quart

GINGERBREAD ICE CREAM

The spicy gingerbread flavor of this rum raisin variation is sure to carry you back to Grandma's kitchen. Serve it during the winter holidays as an alternative to calorie-packed pies and cakes.

Chop	$^1/_4$ **C golden raisins.**
Toss with	**2 T dark rum.**
Set aside.	
Heat	$^2/_3$ **C milk** $^1/_3$ **C sugar.**
Beat	**2 eggs** $^1/_2$ **T light molasses.**

Stir in a little hot milk, then add eggs to milk.

Stir over low heat until mixture thickens, 2 to 3 minutes.

Cover and chill.

Add	**1 C heavy cream** **l/2 T vanilla.**

Stir freeze.

Stir in raisin mixture and	$^1/_3$ **C crushed gingersnaps.**

yield: about 1 quart

BUTTER PECAN ICE CREAM

This ice cream takes its color from caramelized sugar. If the liquified sugar turns lumpy when you pour it into the milk, just keep stirring until it dissolves. You can simplify things by using brown sugar for similar color but a slightly different flavor. Leave out the pecans, and you'll have *caramel* ice cream. If you add ¹/₄ C coarsely grated chocolate after freezing, you'll have *caramel chocolate* ice cream.

In small skillet, melt	¹/₂ **T butter.**
Add and toast lightly	¹/₃ **C chopped pecans.**
Sprinkle with	**dash salt.**
Set aside until well cooled.	
Heat	**1¹/₂ C light cream** **1 C milk.**
Set aside.	
In small skillet, melt	¹/₄ **C sugar.**
Stir until golden.	
Over low heat, gradually stir into hot milk and cream.	
Lightly beat	**2 eggs** ¹/₃ **C sugar.**
Stir in a little hot milk, then add eggs to milk.	
Stir over low heat until mixture thickens, about 3 minutes.	
Strain, cool, and stir in	¹/₂ **T vanilla.**
Chill and stir freeze.	
Add cooled pecans.	

yield: about 1 quart

BUTTERSCOTCH ICE CREAM

Any vanilla ice cream can easily be turned into butterscotch by adding as much as ³/₄ C butterscotch sauce or by melting 1 C (6 oz) butterscotch bits in the heated milk or cream. This recipe starts from scratch and includes evaporated milk to strengthen the butterscotch flavor. Enhance flavor further by adding 1 to 2 t instant coffee, ¹/₄ C cognac, or 2 T almond liqueur.

In skillet, heat	³/₄ **C dark brown sugar** **3 T butter.**
Stir until sugar melts.	
Slowly add	²/₃ **C water.**
Stirring, simmer 5 minutes.	
Beat	**1 egg yolk.**
Stir into hot mixture.	
Continue stirring over low heat until mixture thickens.	
Cool and add	1¹/₄ **C cream** ³/₄ **C evaporated milk** 1¹/₂ **t vanilla.**
Chill and stir freeze.	

yield: about 1 quart

MEXICAN CHOCOLATE ICE CREAM

Modern Mexican chocolate gets its characteristic flavor from cinnamon and almonds, but it wasn't always so. Early south-of-the-border concoctions got their zip from chili peppers and were tinted a gaudy orange. This more conservative, very smooth ice cream is made with sweetened condensed milk for that delicious caramel undertone so typical of Mexican sweets.

In double boiler, melt	**2-oz nonsweetened chocolate.**
Slowly stir in	**1 can condensed milk.**
Add	¹/₄ **t cinnamon** ¹/₃ **C sugar.**
Stirring, heat until thick and glossy, about 10 minutes.	
Beat	**2 egg yolks.**
Stir into milk mixture.	

MEXICAN CHOCOLATE ICE CREAM, cont'd.

Continue stirring over low heat 2 minutes more.

Remove from heat and beat cool, about 5 minutes.

Whip into soft peaks   **2 C heavy cream.**

Fold in   **1 t vanilla**
         $^1/_8$ t almond.

Fold into chocolate mixture.

Chill and stir freeze.

yield: about 1 quart

FRENCH CHOCOLATE ICE CREAM

Flour is sometimes added to increase smoothness and body, as in this chocolate version, which you might try with $^1/_4$ C nonsweetened cocoa in place of chocolate to see which you like best. If you don't care for chocolate's bitter edge, increase the sugar to no more than one cup. For *Belgian chocolate*, stir in $^1/_4$ C rum or 1 t rum extract and $^1/_2$ C chopped hazelnuts. To make *mandarin chocolate*, add 1 T grated orange rind and $^1/_2$ t orange extract or 2 T orange liqueur.

Heat   **$1^1/_4$ C milk.**

Stir in until melted   **2-oz nonsweetened chocolate.**

Combine   **$^1/_2$ C sugar**
         1 T flour.

Add and beat well   **1 lightly beaten egg.**

Stir in a little hot milk, then add egg to milk.

Stir over low heat until mixture thickens, about 3 minutes.

Cool.

Stir in   **$1^1/_4$ C cream**
         $^1/_2$ t vanilla.

Chill and stir freeze.

yield: about 1 quart

WHITE CHOCOLATE ICE CREAM

In true French tradition, this extra smooth ice cream is sweetened with a "simple syrup" made by boiling sugar and water to the soft-ball stage. Use a candy thermometer or test the boiled syrup by dripping some into a glass of cold water to see if it forms a flattened ball. For *white chocolate nut* ice cream, include ¹/₄ C coarsely chopped almonds or hazelnuts, with or without the addition of 2 T almond or hazelnut liqueur.

In small saucepan, combine	**²/₃ C sugar** **²/₃ C water.**
On high heat, boil to 234° F (114° C).	
Beat until thick	**4 egg yolks.**
Beating, gradually pour in hot syrup and beat until cool, about 5 minutes.	
In small saucepan, melt	**8-oz white chocolate.**
Stir into egg mixture.	
Chill.	
Beat in	**1¹/₂ C heavy cream.**
Stir freeze.	

yield: about 1 quart

PEACHES 'N' CREAM ICE CREAM

Some folks feel the flavors of fruit and frozen custard don't mix. You be the judge. Try not only peaches, but strawberries for *berries 'n' cream*, and apricots for *'cots 'n' cream*. Give your creations an extra boost by adding 2 T orange liqueur.

Combine and set aside	**1¹/₂ C mashed peaches** **¹/₄ C sugar.**
Beat frothy	**1 egg.**
Combine and add to egg	**¹/₃ C sugar** **¹/₂ T flour.**
Beat thick.	
Add and mix well	**1 C milk.**

PEACHES 'N' CREAM ICE CREAM, cont'd.

In large saucepan, cook over low heat until mixture coats a metal spoon (about 15 minutes).

Cool.

Stir in

$^1/_2$ **C heavy cream**
1 t vanilla
$^1/_4$ **t almond**
  extract.

Chill, add peaches, and stir freeze.

yield: about 1 quart

PIE À LA MODE ICE CREAM

The flavoring here is half a 10$^1/_2$-ounce can of pie filling. If you prefer homemade filling, mix up enough for an 8-inch pie and use half, reserving the remainder as topping. Or, if your ice cream maker can handle it, double the recipe. With cherry or peach filling, add $^1/_4$ t almond extract. With apple or peach, add $^1/_4$ t cinnamon. For a new twist in pie à la mode, spoon this ice cream into one of the pie shells described in Chapter 29, "Ice Cream Pies."

In large saucepan, combine

$^1/_4$ **C sugar**
1 T flour.

Stir in

1$^1/_4$ C milk.

Stirring, heat until thickened.

Beat

1 egg.

Stir in a little hot milk, then add egg to milk.

Stir over low heat 2 minutes more.

Cool, then chill.

Combine with

1 C whipping
  cream
$^1/_2$ **can pie filling**
2 t vanilla.

Stir freeze.

yield: about 1 quart

COFFEE ICE CREAM

When the main flavoring is mostly water, as it is in brewed coffee ice cream, flour adds needed solids. Rather than brewing fresh coffee, you can substitute 2 T instant and double the milk to 1 C. To make *mocha almond fudge*, stir ¼ C chopped toasted almonds and ½ C crumbled fudge into the finished ice cream. For *almond mocha*, stir in ¼ C each grated semisweet chocolate and chopped toasted almonds. Enhance the flavor of any variation with 2 T coffee liqueur.

In saucepan, combine	½ C sugar 1 T flour.
Stir in	½ C milk ½ C strong coffee.
Heat until thickened.	
Beat	2 egg yolks.
Stir into coffee mixture.	
Continue stirring over low heat 1 minute more.	
Cool.	
Add	2 C cream 1 t vanilla.
Chill and stir freeze.	

yield: about 1 quart

PEANUT BUTTER 'N' JELLY ICE CREAM

For this chilly twist on a schoolyard sandwich, purists insist on grape jelly, but whose business is it if you slip in strawberry or currant jelly instead? The choice of smooth or chunky peanut butter is also yours. Gelatin is added here to offset the effect of peanut butter, keeping the ice cream from turning crumbly on hardening.

In medium saucepan, combine	½ C sugar 4-oz plain gelatin.
Stir in	1 C cream.
Stir over medium heat until sugar and gelatin dissolve.	
Beat	1 egg.
Stir in a little hot cream, then add egg to cream.	
Stir over low heat 2 minutes more.	
Remove from heat and stir in until melted	½ C peanut butter.

**PEANUT BUTTER 'N' JELLY
ICE CREAM, cont'd.**

Cool.

Add   **2 C cream
                                              1 t vanilla.**

Chill and stir freeze.

Swirl in   **¹/₂ C jelly.**

yield: about 1 quart

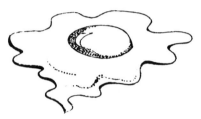

VANILLA CUSTARD ICE
CREAM

Here's a smooth frozen custard you
can make even when you're short on
cream. It has all the flavor of French
vanilla but not the calories. To make
chocolate, add ¹/₄ C nonsweetened
cocoa to the heating milk.

Heat   **2 C milk.**

Combine   **1 egg
                                              ¹/₂ C sugar
                                              1 T flour.**

Stir in a little hot milk, then
add egg mixture to milk.

Stir over low heat until
thickened, about 3 minutes.

Cool.

Add   **1¹/₂ C milk
                                              1 t vanilla.**

Chill and stir freeze.

yield: about 1 quart

LUSCIOUS LEMON ICE CREAM

If you've never had a lick of lemon ice cream, deny yourself no longer! This not-so-French version calls for zesty bits of lemon rind, but you may prefer the smoother texture achieved by straining the mix or omitting the rind and substituting ¼ t lemon extract or lemon oil. If you're among those who like the natural tartness of lemon, cut back a bit on the sugar. A little different, but no less delicious, is *lime* ice cream. Lime rinds are quite thin, so take care not to grate in any of the bitter white membrane.

In double boiler, blend	**1 C sugar** **1 T flour.**
Slowly stir in	**1 C milk.**
Stirring, cook until thickened.	
Cool.	
Add	**2 C cream.**
Chill.	
Add	**½ T grated lemon rind** **¼ C lemon juice.**
Stir freeze.	
	yield: about 1 quart

Frozen Pudding

Frozen pudding is an especially rich custard-based ice cream containing nuts, sometimes spices, and lots of dried or candied fruit, usually soaked in liqueur, brandy, or rum. Frozen puddings are particularly popular around the winter holidays, when they're made with candied fruits and peels, mincemeat, and nuts, and served with a spoonful of chilled vanilla or custard sauce (see Chapter 24 for sauce recipes).

Nesselrode is a variation of frozen pudding created by a nineteenth-century French chef who named it after his master, a Russian count. The classic version calls for finely chopped candied fruits, raisins, chestnut purée, and maraschino liqueur. An American adaptation often includes crushed pineapple, maraschino cherries, walnuts, almonds, pecans, and rum or brandy. The British, who call their version "plum pudding," use figs, dates, mincemeat, and spices, including cinnamon, ginger, allspice, and cloves, as well as nuts and candied fruits and peels.

The fruit mix is usually stabilized with sugar-water syrup and is added to a rich frozen custard in proportions of not more than one part fruit to five parts ice cream mix. While most variations are based on vanilla ice cream, many Britons prefer chocolate.

NESSELRODE ICE CREAM

Ready-made nesselrode mix used to be sold in grocery stores and is perhaps still available in some areas. Just in case, here's a variation you can mix yourself. Feel free to substitute other fruits and nuts to suit your taste.

Nesselrode mix:

Simmer 5 minutes

> 3 T chopped maraschino cherries
> 2 T crushed pineapple
> 2 T chopped cooked chestnuts
> ¼ C sugar
> ⅓ C water.

Cool.

Stir in

> 2 T rum.

Set aside.

Ice Cream:

Heat

> 1½ C milk
> ¼ C sugar
> ¼ C seedless raisins.

Beat

> 2 egg yolks.

Stir into warm milk.

Continue stirring over low heat until mixture thickens.

Chill, and add

> 1½ C heavy cream
> ½ t vanilla.

Stir freeze.

Stir in nesselrode mix.

yield: about 1 quart

Gelato

Italian gelatos differ from French ice creams in having more powerful flavor and denser texture, thanks to the inclusion of more solids and less air. Although they're usually made with milk instead of cream, they often contain more eggs than French ice creams and thus taste equally rich, if not richer.

Technically speaking, gelato is any kind of freeze served at an Italian ice cream shop, or *gelateria*, including gelato itself as well as granita (discussed in Chapter 1), sorbetto (Chapter 3), and a very light-textured ice cream, *semifreddo,* made with whipped cream or beaten egg whites. To give any of the following gelatos a lighter, more semifreddo-like texture, reduce the eggs to two or three, include the yolks as usual, but whip the whites with a little sugar and fold them in just before freezing.

The best known gelato flavors are vanilla, a very rich vanilla called *crèma,* and chocolate, often combined with hazelnuts (*gianduia*). Liqueur flavors are also popular, and so is espresso coffee. Chocolate chip is a modern hit among younger Italians, perhaps because it's so very American. Make it by adding a handful of miniature chips or coarsely chopped chocolate to any basic chocolate or vanilla gelato.

VANILLA GELATO

Subtle flavoring variations here include adding to the warming milk a slice of fresh lemon peel, up to ten fresh roasted coffee beans, or a one-inch piece of cinnamon stick, which you then strain out. For *nut* gelato, stir in ¹/₄ C coarsely chopped nuts of your choice. For spirited flavors, include up to ¹/₄ C liquor, liqueur, or a combination thereof, such as 2 T each brandy and amaretto. For *coffee* gelato, add ¹/₂ T instant coffee and ¹/₂ t cocoa. To make gelato *di crèma,* substitute light or heavy cream for the milk. You can then make *banana* gelato by adding four medium mashed bananas, or *chestnut* gelato by adding ¹/₄# finely chopped marrons glacés.

In heavy saucepan, heat	**2¹/₂ C milk.**
Stir in until dissolved	**¹/₂ C sugar.**
Beat thick	**6 egg yolks.**
Stir into milk mixture.	
Over low heat, stir until mixture coats a metal spoon, about 10 minutes.	
Cool, strain, and add	**¹/₂ T vanilla.**
Chill and stir freeze.	
	yield: about 1 quart

ESPRESSO GELATO

The classic continental combination of citrus and coffee gives this gelato its outstanding flavor. Use either lemon or orange rind, taking care not to include any of the bitter white membrane. Serve coffee gelato plain or with a splash of coffee liqueur or Sambuca, and sprinkle with chopped toasted almonds. For *cappuccino* gelato, add ¹/₄ t cinnamon and ¹/₈ t nutmeg. If you have trouble finding instant espresso, a mail-order source is listed in Appendix C, "Supplies."

In heavy saucepan, heat	**2¹/₂ C milk** **¹/₂ t grated rind.**
Stir in until dissolved	**³/₄ C sugar.**
Beat thick	**6 egg yolks.**
Stir into milk mixture.	
Over low heat, stir until mixture coats a metal spoon, about 10 minutes.	
Cool, strain, and add	**¹/₂ T vanilla** **2 T instant espresso.**
Chill and stir freeze.	

yield: about 1 quart

CHOCOLATE GELATO

Vary the richness of this chocolate gelato by substituting cream for a portion of the milk, or increase the number of egg yolks to five or six. If you prefer to do without the rum, add ¹/₂ t vanilla or almond extract instead. For *chocolate hazelnut* gelato, add ¹/₄ C coarsely ground hazelnuts and substitute 2 T hazelnut liqueur for the rum.

In heavy saucepan, heat	**2¹/₂ C milk.**
Add and stir until melted	**3-oz nonsweetened chocolate.**
Stir in until dissolved	**³/₄ C sugar.**
Beat thick	**3 egg yolks.**
Stir into milk mixture.	
Over low heat, stir until mixture coats a metal spoon, about 10 minutes.	
Remove from heat and add	**¹/₄ C dark rum.**
Chill and stir freeze.	

yield: about 1 quart

CHOCOLATE CAPPUCCINO GELATO

This intensely chocolate-coffee gelato is so chewy it's a bit like frozen fudge. If you wish to harden it before serving, mold it in a loaf pan and serve it in slices. Garnish with mandarin oranges and a bit of orange liqueur, or top with whipped cream and warmed orange marmalade.

In heavy saucepan, heat	**2¹/₂ C milk.**
Stir in until dissolved	**³/₄ C sugar.**
Beat thick	**3 egg yolks.**
Stir into milk mixture.	
Over low heat, stir until mixture coats a metal spoon, about 10 minutes.	
Stir in	**3-oz nonsweetened chocolate.** **¹/₄ C nonsweetened cocoa** **2 T instant espresso.**
Strain and add	**2 t grated orange rind.**
Beat until cool.	
Chill and stir freeze.	

yield: about 1 quart

APRICOT GELATO

True Italian fruit gelato (*gelato alla frutta*) contains mostly sweetened fruit purée and little cream or milk, making it something of a sherbet. This version can be made with any kind of preserves including marmalade. Intensify fruit flavor by adding 2 T of an appropriately flavored brandy, in this case apricot.

In heavy saucepan, heat	**2¹/₂ C milk** **2 thin slices lemon rind.**
Stir in until dissolved	**¹/₄ C sugar.**
Beat thick	**8 egg yolks.**
Stir into milk mixture.	
Over low heat, stir until mixture coats a metal spoon, about 10 minutes.	

APRICOT GELATO, cont'd.

Strain and cool.

In small saucepan, heat
until melted, about 3 minutes, **12-oz apricot
preserves.**

Purée and thoroughly stir into
cooled cream mixture.

Chill and stir freeze.

yield: about 1 quart

MARZIPAN GELATO

This gelato is so decadent you may as
well indulge yourself fully and serve
it in pools of warm fudge or cherry
sauce (recipes in Chapter 24). In place
of almond paste, you can substitute
³/₄ C coarsely ground blanched almonds plus 6 T granulated sugar,
stirred into the milk mixture after
straining.

In heavy saucepan, heat **2¹/₂ C milk.**

Stir in until dissolved **1 C sugar.**

Beat together **8 egg yolks
8-oz almond paste.**

Stir into milk mixture.

Over low heat, stir until
mixture coats a metal
spoon, about 10 minutes.

Strain, chill, and stir freeze.

yield: about 1 quart

ZABAIONE GELATO

Zabaione, a traditional Italian dessert made of egg yolks and marsala wine, becomes a classic semifreddo when fluffed up with whipped egg whites. For the semifreddo version of this zabaione gelato, whip two or three egg whites with a bit of sugar and fold them in along with the cream and wine. If you wish, use Madeira, port, or sherry in place of Marsala. Serve zabaione with fruit or almond macaroons.

In heavy saucepan, heat	**2 C milk.**
Stir in until dissolved	**¹/₂ C sugar.**
Beat thick	**6 egg yolks.**
Stir into milk mixture.	
Over low heat, stir until mixture coats a metal spoon, about 10 minutes.	
Cool, strain, and chill.	
Freeze slushy and fold in	**¹/₂ C whipped cream** **¹/₄ C dry Marsala.**

yield: about 1 quart

7

Frozen Yogurt

Yogurt gets its tang and depth of flavor from cultured milk—pure milk to which beneficial bacteria have been added. As the bacteria multiply, they produce a mild acid that coagulates the milk into the semi-solid known as yogurt.

Like its cultured cousins, buttermilk and sour cream, yogurt contains lactase enzymes that consume milk sugar (lactose) as a source of energy. If you're among the many people who are allergic to lactose and can't handle regular ice cream, you may find frozen yogurt easier to digest.

There are as yet no federal regulations standardizing frozen yogurt, which allows considerable variation in the amount of yogurt actually included in different brands. Some contain no active culture at all—a good enough reason to make your own frozen yogurt. If you like to work from scratch, you might start by making your own yogurt.

Homemade Yogurt

Plain homemade yogurt is a real treat compared to the sour, sometimes bitter yogurt sold in grocery stores. It's also cheaper than store-bought. If you're lucky enough to produce your own milk, the cost is practically negligible.

When you make your own yogurt, you have full control over flavor and texture as well as the kind of milk you use, whether whole or low-fat from cows, sheep, goats, or soy beans—important considerations for dieters and for those who suffer from a milk allergy. (For more information on goat and sheep milk, see Chapter 9, "Dairy Alternatives." Soy milk is discussed in Chapter 10, "Soy Ice Cream.")

You probably already have on hand all the yogurt-making equipment you'll need: an enamel or stainless steel saucepan, a candy-making or dairy thermometer, a covered casserole or glass jars with lids, and a warm place for incubation. A commercially made electric or nonelectric yogurt maker conveniently combines covered container and warm place.

Incubating

Heat the milk to 110° F (43° C), or until it feels hot to the wrist but does not burn. If you're using home-produced milk, your yogurt will be a bit firmer and also more consistent from one time to the next if you pasteurize the milk and let it cool to the required temperature before you start.

Add one-fourth cup nonsweetened, unflavored, store-bought yogurt per quart of milk. Stir thoroughly, pour into a yogurt maker, glass jars, or casserole, cover, and incubate in a warm place where the temperature remains as close as possible to 110° F (43° C).

Commercially sold yogurt makers are designed to provide the ideal incubating environment. Good places to incubate yogurt in jars or a casserole dish might be inside a gas oven warmed by a pilot light, in a preheated electric oven with the heat turned off, or near a hot water heater. You can also place jars in a covered crock pot, pressure canner, or insulated picnic carrier partially filled with warm water and wrapped in towels to retain the heat.

Exactly how much heat is needed for fermentation depends on the strain of culture you use. The most common cultures become relatively inactive below 100° F (38° C), although some of the freeze dried ones ferment well at 70° F (21° C). All cultures die at temperatures above 120° F (49° C).

Fermentation takes between three and seven hours, sometimes as much as ten, depending on the strain and the exact incubation temperature. Up to a point, the warmer the temperature, the shorter the incubation period. You'll know the yogurt is ready when you press the surface with back of a spoon and it retains the impression. If you use jars, slightly tilt one of the jars, and the finished yogurt will separate cleanly from the side.

Refrigerate the yogurt as soon as it's ready. Left out too long, homemade yogurt separates into the curds and whey of Little Miss Muffet fame.

Taste

The longer yogurt takes to ferment, the tangier it will be. If it takes too long, it turns downright sour. Degree of tanginess is also influenced by the fat content of the milk. Creamier milk is less acidic and makes sweeter yogurt.

Just how your homemade yogurt tastes also depends on the kind of starter you choose. You can't go too far wrong using plain store-bought yogurt, provided the label specifies active yogurt culture. Oddly, the yogurt you make usually tastes better than the brand you start out with. Natural food stores and dairy supply outlets carry a variety of easy-to-store, freeze-dried cultures. Each produces a slightly different flavor, requiring experimentation until you find the one that most appeals to you.

Whether you use a commercial brand or a freeze dried culture, if you try to stretch it by saving a little yogurt to start the next batch, your culture will quickly fizzle out. Instead, prepare a "mother culture" to use as the starter for several successive batches.

A mother culture is simply fresh yogurt refrigerated immediately after it coagulates and before the bacteria play themselves out. Refrigeration slows the progress of bacteria through their life cycle, but even a mother culture loses flavor and vigor after a while and has to be replaced. If you don't wait too long, you can usually make a fresh mother culture from the old one. Under optimum conditions, the longest you can keep a culture going is about a month.

Cutting Calories

Whole milk yogurt is sweet and smooth textured and makes smooth, creamy ice cream. Nonetheless, many people favor low-fat or no-fat yogurt made from two percent or skim milk.

To make low-fat yogurt from home produced milk, refrigerate the fresh milk overnight in a wide-mouthed container. The cream will rise to the surface, where you can easily skim it off with a large slotted ladle. The resulting skim milk will contain around one percent milkfat. You'll need a centrifugal cream separator if you want to do better than that.

Whether made from commercial or home-produced milk, lo-cal yogurt will be thicker, more nutritious, and less likely to separate into whey (liquid) and curds (the remaining solid portion) if you add one-third cup milk powder to each quart of liquid milk. For pleasantly creamy frozen yogurt, include a little gelatin in the yogurt as an additional thickener.

To make tasty, low-calorie yogurt from non-fat dry milk, soften one-half packet (one-half tablespoon) plain gelatin in one-half cup water, heat until the gelatin dissolves, add two cups non-fat milk powder plus enough warm water to make one quart, stir in the culture, and incubate. With this yogurt, you can dispense with any additional gelatin called for in a frozen yogurt recipe.

Frozen Yogurt

Frozen yogurt is one of the easiest freezes to make. Simply blend in two-thirds to three-quarters cup sugar or honey per quart and add the flavoring of your choice. For fruit flavors, combine one cup puréed fruit with three cups plain sweetened yogurt. If you prefer sherbet, combine two cups puréed fruit with two cups plain sweetened yogurt. For a thicker mix and creamier freeze, strain the yogurt in a yogurt strainer or a square of cheesecloth. (Use the whey in place of water for tasty, high-protein sorbets.)

You can also freeze any brand of flavored yogurt, with or without adding one cup drained, mashed fruit per quart. Be aware, though, that most commercial yogurt contains artificial flavoring and color, as well as preservatives to increase shelf life.

Almost all commercial frozen yogurt is low in fat, calories, cholesterol and sodium, but is high in sugar. Homemade frozen yogurt often contains cream, so it may be lower in sugar, since the cream reduces tanginess and lets you cut back on sweetening, but it's higher in fat. Yet adding cream gives you the best of two worlds—the tang of yogurt combined with the creamy richness of ice cream.

In place of cream, you can use undiluted evaporated milk, which contains less fat than cream but contributes less water than regular milk. You can also use powdered milk, diluted with only half the usual amount of water.

There's no secret to inventing new frozen yogurt flavors. Simply substitute yogurt for some or all of the milk or cream in any of your favorite ice cream or sherbet recipes and increase sweetening to taste.

VANILLA FROZEN YOGURT

In this basic recipe, use heavy cream for greater richness, light cream for a lighter touch; or substitute evaporated milk for reduced calories and extra flavor. If you're among those who feel that vanilla and yogurt don't mix but that yogurt and honey were meant to be, substitute ¹/₂ C honey for the sugar and ¹/₂ t almond extract for the vanilla and make *honey almond* frozen yogurt.

Beat smooth

Chill and stir freeze.

2 C plain yogurt
1 C cream
²/₃ C sugar
2 t vanilla.

yield: about 1 quart

FRUITY FROZEN YOGURT

From vanilla to fruit-flavored frozen yogurt is an easy step. Simply omit vanilla and, in place of cream, add puréed blueberries, strawberries, banana, or papaya sprinkled with 2 T lemon or lime juice. If you use sweetened canned or thawed frozen fruit, reduce the sugar accordingly.

Combine

Beat smooth and blend in

Chill and stir freeze.

1 C coarsely
   puréed fruit
²/₃ C sugar.

2¹/₂ C plain yogurt.

yield: about 1 quart

RASPBERRY PINEAPPLE
FROZEN YOGURT

A combination of fruits results in full-flavored frozen yogurt. With suitable substitutions this recipe makes equally delicious *strawberry pineapple* or *apricot pineapple* frozen yogurt.

Purée and strain seeds from

Purée and add

Chill.

1 C raspberries.

¹/₂ C crushed
   pineapple
¹/₄ C sugar.

**RASPBERRY PINEAPPLE
FROZEN YOGURT, cont'd.**

Beat smooth and add

1 C orange juice
$^1/_4$ C corn syrup
$1^1/_2$ C plain yogurt.

Stir freeze.

yield: about 1 quart

**SPICY PEACH FROZEN
YOGURT**

This old-fashioned combination of peaches and spice is sure to remind you of Grandma's country cooking. When you can't wait until peaches are in season, use canned ones and reduce the sugar to $^1/_2$ C. This recipe makes terrific pie filling (pie shell recipes appear in Chapter 29), garnished with toasted sliced almonds.

Peel and chop

$^1/_2$ C peaches.

Add

$^2/_3$ C sugar.

Set aside for several hours.

Beat smooth and stir in

3 C yogurt.

Stir in

$^1/_8$ t ground
   nutmeg
$^1/_4$ t ground
   cinnamon
$^1/_8$ t cloves
1 t vanilla.

Chill and stir freeze.

yield: about 1 quart

ORANGE FROZEN YOGURT

Juices also make fine flavorings, as demonstrated by this savory treat with lemon added to increase its refreshing appeal. You can make *pineapple* frozen yogurt by substituting non-sweetened pineapple juice for the orange juice, and grated lemon rind for the orange rind.

Combine

$^2/_3$ C orange juice
$^2/_3$ C sugar
2 T lemon juice
$^1/_2$ T grated
   orange rind.

Beat smooth and stir in

$2^1/_2$ C plain yogurt.

Stir freeze.

yield: about 1 quart

LEMON FROZEN YOGURT

Lemon is arguably the tastiest, most refreshing frozen yogurt of all. It's especially terrific with fresh blueberries, but goes quite well with any berry or fruit in season. Served fresh from the ice cream maker, its texture is velvety smooth.

Beat smooth

2 C yogurt
1 C cream
1 C sugar
$^1/_3$ C lemon juice
1 t grated lemon rind
$^1/_2$ t lemon extract.

Chill and stir freeze.

yield: about 1 quart

CAROB HONEY FROZEN YOGURT

Often touted as a chocolate substitute, carob actually has a unique and pleasing flavor of its own. If you feel that honey overpowers the delicate flavor, substitute $^1/_3$ C corn syrup for half the honey or use $^1/_2$ C granulated sugar instead.

In saucepan, combine

$^1/_2$ C carob powder
$^1/_2$ C milk.

Blend in

$^2/_3$ C honey.

Stirring, heat until smooth, about 3 minutes.

Cool.

Beat smooth and stir in

2$^1/_2$ C plain yogurt
1 t vanilla.

Chill and stir freeze.

yield: about 1 quart

CUCUMBER COOLER

Served in scooped-out cucumber boats, made according to directions in Chapter 22, this frozen yogurt is a terrific summer appetizer. Or scoop it over a rosette of avocado slices or tomato wedges as a cool dressing for a summery salad plate. The texture is creamy when freshly frozen but turns quite crumbly after hardening.

Peel, seed, and purée — **2# cucumbers.**

Beat smooth and stir in

1¹/₂ T lemon juice
³/₄ C plain yogurt
³/₄ C fresh dill
¹/₂ T sugar
¹/₄ t salt.

Stir freeze.

yield: about 1 quart

ORANGE BEET FROZEN YOGURT

This pretty treat with a perky taste doubles nicely as a luncheon side dish or icy dressing for a green salad of shredded lettuce and sliced cucumber. You'll need four to five medium beets, preferably garden fresh.

Cook until tender — **1¹/₂# beets.**

Peel and cool.

Purée with

¹/₃ C orange juice concentrate
2 T lemon juice
¹/₄ t allspice
¹/₄ t cinnamon
¹/₂ t salt
2 C plain yogurt.

Stir freeze.

yield: about 1 quart

TOMATO CELERY FROZEN YOGURT

Here's an easy frozen yogurt to surround with cut vegetables and serve as a dip, sprinkled with chopped fresh dill or garnished with sprigs of fresh parsley. For extra zing, include a dash of Tabasco sauce.

Purée

1 C chopped celery
1¹/₂ C tomato juice
1¹/₂ C plain yogurt
1 t lemon juice
dash pepper.

Chill and stir freeze.

yield: about 1 quart

SMOOTH FROZEN YOGURT

Gelatin contributes extra body and smooth texture to this and the following variation, allowing them to harden nicely. As for any basic frozen yogurt, you can substitute 1/2 C honey and 1/2 t almond extract in place of sugar and vanilla.

In saucepan, soften	**1 pkg plain gelatin**
in	**3/4 C milk.**
Heat milk and add	**2/3 C sugar.**
Stir until smooth.	
Cool.	
Blend in	**2 1/2 C plain yogurt** **1 T vanilla.**
Beat smooth.	
Chill and stir freeze.	
	yield: about 1 quart

DATE DELIGHT

Here, dates contribute sweetness, letting you cut back on other sweetening if you wish. For added flavor, include 1/2 t grated orange or lemon rind. For *date nut delight*, stir in 1/3 C chopped walnuts or pecans. Or switch gears and use stewed prunes for *prune nut delight*.

In saucepan, soften	**1 pkg plain gelatin**
in	**1/4 C milk.**
Heat milk and add	**1/2 C cream.**
Add	**2/3 C minced dates** **1/2 C honey.**
Stirring, cook until smooth.	
Blend in	**2 C plain yogurt.**
Beat smooth.	
Chill and stir freeze.	
	yield: about 1 quart

COUNTRY FROZEN YOGURT

Egg yolks contribute the same richness to frozen yogurt as they do to country ice cream. As for any ice cream, when in doubt about the safety of raw eggs, combine them with the milk and cook into a custard. The beaten white is added to lighten texture, but you can leave it out if you prefer.

Combine

1 C milk
²/₃ C sugar.

Heat until sugar dissolves.

Lightly beat

1 egg yolk.

Slowly stir in warm milk.

Cool.

Beat smooth

2 C plain yogurt
¹/₂ T vanilla.

Fold into milk mixture.

Chill.

Beat into soft peaks

1 egg white.

Gradually add

1 T sugar.

Beat stiff and fold into mix.

Stir freeze.

yield: about 1 quart

COUNTRY FROZEN FRUIT YOGURT

Substitute fresh fruit for the milk in country frozen yogurt, and you can make all manner of mouth-watering fruit flavors. Try apricot, peach, blackberry, blueberry, raspberry, strawberry, or any fruit or berry of your choice, adjusting sugar according to the sweetness of the fruit.

In saucepan, combine — **1 C fruit**
²/₃ C sugar.

Stirring constantly, bring to boil over high heat.

Reduce heat to medium.

Cook until fruit falls apart, 1 to 4 minutes.

Remove from heat and purée.

Lightly beat — **1 egg yolk**
¹/₂ T lemon juice.

Slowly stir in fruit mixture.

Heat 3 minutes more.

Cool.

Beat smooth — **2 C yogurt.**

Fold in fruit mixture.

Chill.

Beat into soft peaks — **1 egg white.**

Gradually add 1 T sugar.

Beat into stiff peaks.

Gently fold in fruit mixture.

Stir freeze.

yield: about 1 quart

FRENCH VANILLA FROZEN YOGURT

This yogurt version of French ice cream uses several egg yolks to carry flavor and contribute richness. To add body and improve hardening qualities, soften 1 pkg plain gelatin in the milk before warming it. Fruit sauce makes a tasty accompaniment (recipes in Chapter 24).

In a double boiler, heat	$^2/_3$ **C milk.**
Add	$^2/_3$ **C sugar.**
Gradually stir warm milk into	**4 beaten egg yolks.**
Stirring constantly, heat until slightly thickened.	
Cool.	
Beat smooth and stir in	**2 C plain yogurt** **1 T vanilla.**
Chill and stir freeze.	

yield: about 1 quart

LEMON HONEY FROZEN YOGURT

The sweet and sour combination of honey and lemon is one of the most popular frozen yogurt flavors. Here, egg yolks are added for richer color as well as texture and flavor. Try different kinds of honey and see which you like best.

In saucepan, combine	$^2/_3$ **C honey** **2 T lemon juice** **1 t grated lemon rind** **2 egg yolks.**
Stir over medium heat until smooth and well blended.	
Cool.	
Beat smooth and add	**2$^1/_2$ C plain yogurt.**
Chill.	
Beat stiff and fold in	**2 egg whites.**
Stir freeze.	

yield: about 1 quart

COFFEE FROZEN YOGURT

This taste-tingling treat is doubly scrumptious with the addition of 2 T coffee liqueur, stirred in as freezing nears completion. For added crunch, include ¹/₂ C finely chopped toasted almonds.

In double boiler, combine	**³/₄ C sugar** **1 T instant coffee.**
Add	**2 C milk.**
Stirring, heat until sugar dissolves.	
Pour a little warm milk into	**2 beaten eggs.**
Stir eggs into milk.	
Stirring, heat until slightly thickened.	
Cool.	
Beat smooth and stir in	**1 C plain yogurt** **¹/₂ t vanilla.**
Chill and stir freeze.	

yield: about 1 quart

PEACHY FROZEN YOGURT SHERBET

A simple syrup of boiled sugar-water lends extra smoothness to this frozen yogurt sherbet. You'll need 5 to 7 pitted, peeled peaches, depending on their size. For deeper flavor, use nectarines or apricots for a portion of the peaches. To make *cherry* frozen yogurt sherbet, substitute fresh pitted cherries.

In saucepan, bring to boil	**2 C water** **1 C sugar.**
Simmer 5 minutes.	
Cool.	
Add	**1¹/₃ C peach purée** **¹/₄ C lemon juice** **¹/₄ t almond** **extract.**
Chill.	
Beat smooth and stir in	**1 C plain yogurt.**
Stir freeze.	

yield: about 1 quart

Buttermilk

Until yogurt was introduced to the United States through Middle Eastern cuisine, buttermilk was used to make refreshingly tart sherbets. These delicious sherbets are often passed over in the craze for frozen yogurt, but they're slowly coming back as old recipes are being rediscovered.

The buttermilk that results from churning sweet cream into butter makes especially good ice cream, with a richness of flavor out of all proportion to its fat content. This factor is of particular significance to those who favor low fat ice creams. Buttermilk contains more natural lecithin than whole milk and is similar to egg yolk in contributing to the smoothness of ice cream.

The buttermilk used in sherbet today is rarely the liquid left from butter making, which has become as scarce as hand paddled butter. Instead, it's a cultured fermentation of skim milk—essentially a kind of liquid yogurt. It tastes different from yogurt because a different culture strain is used for fermentation. Just as you can keep a home yogurt-making culture going, you can also make your own buttermilk.

Bring one quart skim milk to room temperature, add $^1/_2$ cup cultured buttermilk (either store-bought or from your mother culture), and incubate at 80° to 85° F (26.5° to 29.5° C). The buttermilk is done when it has thickened and tastes the way you like it, which takes anywhere from five to twenty-four hours. Stir and refrigerate.

Cultured buttermilk can be purchased in powdered form, handy for those who don't use enough to keep fresh buttermilk on hand. Although powdered buttermilk adds the same tang as fresh, its active culture has been destroyed during drying and does not reactivate when reconstituted.

While you can substitute fresh or reconstituted buttermilk for sweet milk in any ice cream or sherbet, the following recipes take special advantage of buttermilk's distinctive characteristics. Even if you don't care for it as a drink, you may be delighted with the ice cream it makes.

BUTTERMILK SHERBET

This fruit sherbet is especially good with fresh apricots, peaches, or strawberries. When substituting canned or thawed frozen fruit, reduce the sugar and eliminate the stabilizing period. For extra zip in peach or nectarine sherbet, add 1 t fresh grated ginger.

Combine

$1^1/_2$ **C fruit purée**
$^1/_4$ **C lemon juice**
1 C sugar.

Set aside for several hours.

Beat smooth and add

2 C buttermilk.

Chill and stir freeze.

yield: about 1 quart

BUTTERMILK FUDGE ICE CREAM

Cultured milk and chocolate make a delightfully distinctive combination, which should come as no surprise if you've ever tasted old-fashioned buttermilk fudge. For variety, add $^1/_2$ t grated orange rind and/or 2 T crème de cacao.

In saucepan, combine	$^3/_4$ C sugar $^1/_3$ C nonsweetened cocoa.
Add and heat	$^3/_4$ C milk.
Stir until sugar dissolves.	
Cool.	
Beat smooth	$2^2/_3$ C buttermilk $^1/_2$ t vanilla.
Combine with chocolate milk.	
Chill and stir freeze.	

yield: about 1 quart

WHITE CHOCOLATE BUTTERMILK ICE CREAM

If you substitute light cream or milk for the cream in this rich recipe, the resulting ice cream won't harden as well, so serve it freshly frozen. In place of lemon juice, you might try 2 T apricot brandy.

In saucepan, combine	1 C heavy cream 1 C milk $^1/_2$ C sugar 4 egg yolks.
Stir over low heat until mixture coats back of spoon, about 10 minutes.	
Remove from heat.	
Coarsely grate	5-oz white chocolate.
Add to mixture, along with	2 t vanilla.
Stir until chocolate melts.	
Cool and chill.	

WHITE CHOCOLATE BUTTERMILK ICE CREAM, cont'd.

Blend in   **1 C buttermilk**
1 T lemon juice.

Stir freeze.

yield: about 1 quart

BUTTERMILK FRUIT ICE CREAM

Grape juice was once a popular flavoring in this old-time ice cream. Pineapple is also good. Feel free to experiment with any of your own favorite full-flavored juices. (Before using raw eggs in ice cream, read about them in Chapter 13.)

Beat smooth   **2$^{1}/_{2}$ C buttermilk**
1 C sugar.

Beat and add   **1 egg yolk.**

Add   **2 T lemon juice**
$^{1}/_{2}$ C fruit juice.

Chill.

Whip to soft peaks and fold in   **1 egg white.**

Stir freeze.

yield: about 1 quart

AVOCADO BUTTERMILK SHERBET

Besides making a delightfully different, light dessert, this sweet-tart sherbet provides terrific accompaniment for turkey or roast beef. For a hearty West Coast-style snack, serve Japanese rice cakes on the side.

Purée   **2 avocados.**

Beat smooth and blend in   **2 C buttermilk**
$^{1}/_{2}$ C sugar
$^{1}/_{4}$ C honey
$^{1}/_{4}$ C light corn syrup
$^{1}/_{4}$ C lemon juice.

Chill and stir freeze.

yield: about 1 quart

Sour Cream

Sour cream is a cultured dairy product often used in European ice cream to give it a tangy twist. If you use it often enough, it's worth making your own from heavy cream and a little buttermilk.

In a clean, warm jar, combine one tablespoon buttermilk per cup cream. Tighten the lid and shake the jar gently until the mixture is thoroughly blended. Incubate at 80° to 85° F (26.5° to 29.5° C) until thick, between twenty-four and forty-eight hours. Stir well and refrigerate.

Substitute sour cream for sweet cream in any ice cream to which you'd like to add a touch of sophistication; or enjoy the following tried-and-true recipes.

BERRY EASY ICE CREAM

In fine European tradition, this ice cream gets its unique flavor from cultured sour cream. Make it with blueberries, strawberries, or raspberries with the seeds strained out; or substitute peaches or apricots.

Purée

1¹/₂ C berries
1 C sugar
2 C sour cream.

Whip and fold in

¹/₂ C heavy cream.

Stir freeze.

yield: about 1 quart

MANGO CREAM

This delectable dessert takes 4 fresh ripe mangoes, or substitute juicy peaches if you wish. Serve with sliced bananas dipped in orange or banana liqueur.

Blend

1³/₄ C mango purée
1 T lime juice
1 C sugar.

Chill.

Beat smooth and blend in

1³/₄ C sour cream.

Stir freeze.

yield: about 1 quart

BLUEBERRY CHEESECAKE ICE CREAM

Serve this new version of an old favorite with heaps of fresh blueberries. Or combine it with lemon sherbet in a molded bombe (directions in Chapter 26), or use it to fill an ice cream cake (directions in Chapter 27).

Beat	**2 eggs.**
Add	**³/₄ C sugar.**
Beat stiff.	
Beat smooth and add	**1 C sour cream** **1 C light cream** **1 t vanilla** **¹/₂ t grated lemon rind.**
Chill and stir freeze.	
Stir in	**1 C blueberries.**

yield: about 1 quart

BANANA PINEAPPLE CREAM

Scoop this luscious ice cream over lettuce leaves and serve it as a fruit salad, or garnish with pineapple chunks and mandarin oranges and serve it as dessert.

Mash or purée	**2 bananas.**
Add, undrained,	**8-oz crushed pineapple.**
Stir in	**¹/₄ C flaked coconut.**
Beat smooth and blend in	**2 C sour cream** **³/₄ C sugar.**
Chill and stir freeze.	
Stir in	**¹/₄ C chopped pecans.**

yield: about 1 quart

OLD WORLD BISQUE

Make this rich European dessert with miniature chocolate chips or coarsely grated milk chocolate. Serve in goblets, garnished with a single chocolate leaf (directions in Chapter 28), or scoop over rum-soaked macaroons and sprinkle with chopped toasted almonds.

Beat smooth

3 C sour cream
1 C sugar
2 T dark rum
1 t vanilla.

Stir freeze.

Stir in

$^1/_2$ C chocolate chips
$^1/_2$ C crumbled macaroons.

yield: about 1 quart

8

Ice Cream for Restrictive Diets

Given a choice, most people would select the richest ice creams, even if it meant eating less of them. But not everyone has such strong will power, and some cannot tolerate even the tiniest amounts of gourmet ice cream.

Of all the foods forbidden in restrictive diets, ice cream is the one most often craved for. All manner of substitutes have been invented to satisfy this craving without breaching dietary restrictions.

Dietetic Considerations

Ice cream suffers notoriously bad press as a fattening food, which it can be when included in a diet already loaded with calories. But nearly anyone who enjoys a well-balanced diet can occasionally eat ice cream without putting on weight. At 150 to 250 calories, an average half-cup serving is among the least caloric of desserts, if you consider that a slice of cheese cake contains 300 calories, a serving of frosted chocolate cake, 313, or a piece of apple pie, 330.

It's possible to actually lose weight while regularly enjoying a scoop of ice cream. An important part of the famous Hollywood diet is a daily scoop of low-calorie ice cream as both a source of carbohydrates and an appetite depressant.

Whether lo-cal or not, the many nutrients in ice cream can be counted toward satisfying daily dietary requirements, making it possible to cut back on other foods. Perhaps most important of all is ice cream's significant psychological effect—including something in your diet so tasty you feel it ought to be forbidden helps prevent serious cheating.

Counting Calories

One way to keep off pounds without denying yourself the pleasures is to gravitate toward ice milk, frozen yogurt, sherbet, and ices at the lower end of the caloric scale and only occasionally dip into a superpremium. In general, freezes that are lower in fat contain fewer calories, even though they may be higher in sugar. The amount of incorporated air is, of course, a factor—a dense sherbet may contain just as many calories as an airy ice cream.

If it's ice cream itself you crave, you can convert your favorite recipes to dietetic versions in three different ways—cut back on cream, reduce sweetening, and incorporate air. Provided you aren't tempted to eat more because the calories are fewer, the resulting ice cream should keep you slim while satisfying your sweet tooth.

Some commercially made dietetic ice creams contain cream substitutes that somewhat fairly imitate the flavor and texture of cream. These cream clones tend to be controversial and, in any case, are not yet available for home use. To reduce the cream content in your own favorite recipes, substitute nondairy creamer for heavy cream, evaporated milk for light cream or half and half, and skim milk, reconstituted nonfat dry milk, buttermilk, or nonfat yogurt for whole milk.

Alternatively, make your own mock cream by combining low fat milk with an equal amount of low fat cottage cheese, cream cheese or *neufchâtel* and whirl smooth in a blender. For ersatz sour cream, whirl equal parts nonfat cottage cheese and nonfat yogurt. Since fat carries flavor, don't expect reduced-fat ice cream to taste quite as good as the real thing.

A second way to cut back on calories is to reduce sweetening. In most recipes, you can reduce the sugar or honey by twenty percent (about three tablespoons per cup) without noticing much difference in taste. Substituting non-nutritive sweeteners, discussed more fully in Chapter 12, is another alternative.

Using puréed prunes, dates or raisins, or any sweet, ripe fruit as the primary flavoring also lets you cut back on calories. Sun-ripened fruits and their juices are considerably sweeter than those harvested unripe and then stored for weeks on a grocery shelf. The same is true of dairy fresh cream compared to overly aged cream. Seeking out sources for these superior products lets you take advantage of their natural sweetness to cut down on less healthful forms of sugar. Sugar, like cream, contributes to texture as well as flavor, so cutting back creates ice cream that is less smooth and that hardens to a much firmer consistency.

A third way to lower calories is to introduce more air. It stands to reason that the more puffed up ice cream is, the fewer calories each serving contains. You can add air by folding whipped egg whites into a mix or by including unflavored gelatin, which fluffs up as it's whipped by the ice cream maker. In some cases, you can further encourage the introduction of air, called "overrun," by changing the way you operate your ice cream maker (for details, see Chapter 17, "Stir Freezing").

To estimate the number of calories in a half-cup serving of any recipe, look up each of the ingredients on a calorie counter. Add up total calories from all ingredients, divide by the number of quarts the recipe makes, then divide by eight. If you're not happy with the result, zero in on the culprit contributing the most calories and substitute something similar but less caloric.

CALORIC RANGE OF COMMERCIAL PRODUCTS (per half-cup serving)	
Ice cream, superpremium	240-360
Ice cream, premium	155-300
Ice cream, regular	130-250
Soy-based, hard	130-230
Ice cream, soft serve	175-190
Lemon ice	130-165
Frozen yogurt, hard	110-160
Soy-based, soft serve	95-160
Economy ice cream	120-150
Sherbet	95-140
Ice milk, soft serve	110-135
Ice cream, dietetic	80-135
Ice (except lemon)	105-130
Frozen yogurt, soft serve	100-120
Ice milk, hard	90-110

LEMON WHIP

This creamy smooth, sweet-tart ice cream has 154 calories per half-cup serving. For added flavor without added calories, include a little freshly grated lemon or orange rind. If you substitute noncaloric sweetener for half the sugar, you'll knock the calories down to 106. Or use all noncaloric sweetener for 58 calories.

Beat until light and fluffy **4 egg whites.**

Add and beat stiff **1 C sugar.**

Fold in **2 C evaporated milk**
½ C lemon juice.

Stir freeze.

yield: about 1 quart

DIETER'S DELIGHT

This lo-cal treat contains about 145 calories per half-cup serving. Make *chocolate* delight by adding 4 T nonsweetened cocoa, and the calorie count goes up to 161. Or add 2 medium bananas for *banana* delight, and you've got 167 calories. Substitute 3 T apple juice concentrate for the sugar and the calorie count plummets to 115.

Combine	**2 C evaporated milk.** **1¹/₃ C milk** **¹/₃ C sugar** **1 t vanilla.**
Chill and stir freeze.	
	yield: about 1 quart

SLIM STRAWBERRY SHERBET

This fluffed-up sherbet has only 89 calories per half-cup serving thanks to all the air beaten in with the egg white. If you substitute noncaloric sweetener for half the sugar, the calories drop to 70 per serving. Reconstituted powdered milk may be used in place of fresh skim milk without changing the calorie count.

Purée and chill	**2 C strawberries** **¹/₄ C sugar** **¹/₃ C lemonade concentrate.**
Beat into soft peaks	**3 egg whites.**
Gradually beat in	**2 T sugar.**
Fold in	**1¹/₂ C skimmed milk.**
Fold in fruit.	
Stir freeze.	
	yield: about 1 quart

GINGER ALE SPOOM

For a very lo-cal ice, combine one part fruit purée with two parts water and sweeten to taste with sugar substitute. The calorie count will lie between 14 and 17, depending on the kind of fruit you use. The following ice, an imitation champagne spoom, contains 60 calories per serving. Make it with noncaloric sweetener, and calories drop to a mere 23.

Soften	**¹/₂ pkg plain gelatin**
in	**4 T lemon juice** **3 T pineapple juice.**
Heat and stir to dissolve	**¹/₃ C sugar.**

GINGER ALE SPOOM, cont'd.

Cool and add	**3 T orange juice** **2²/₃ C diet ginger ale.**

Chill.

Beat into soft peaks	**1 egg white.**
Gradually add	**1 T sugar.**

Fold into ginger ale mixture.

Stir freeze.

yield: about 1 quart

LO-CAL WHIPPED CREAM

When you crave a luxurious dessert topped with heaps of whipped cream, crown a scoop of diet ice cream with lo-cal whipped cream. Compared to 58 calories in the real thing, this version has only 9 calories per tablespoon (6, if you replace the sugar with noncaloric sweetener). Lo-cal whipped cream goes flat in about an hour, but it freezes beautifully. Shape extra into puffs on a chilled baking sheet, freeze firm, wrap, and keep frozen until needed.

In chilled bowl, combine	**3 T nonfat milk powder** **3 T ice water.**

Using chilled beater, beat into soft peaks at medium-high, about 3 minutes.

Add	**2 t lemon juice.**

Whip 5 minutes more.

Add	**1 T sugar.**

Whip 1 more minute.

yield: about 1 cup

Diabetic Considerations

During normal digestion, most of the food we eat, including ice cream, is converted to glucose, a kind of sugar the body uses as fuel. The hormone insulin helps glucose enter individual body cells. When the body produces too little insulin to keep up with its own needs, blood sugar rises too much or too fast, creating the imbalance known as diabetes.

In contrast to dietetic ice cream, in which the emphasis is on reducing fat, in diabetic ice cream the idea is to reduce or eliminate sugars, or simple carbohydrates, since they are absorbed into the bloodstream too rapidly for a diabetic to handle.

Average ice cream contains as much as twenty percent sugar. All but the lactose (milk sugar component) can be replaced by substituting alternative sweeteners (discussed more fully in chapter 12). Many diabetics are overweight and must therefore also cut back on fat.

In 1950, when the American Diabetes Association first published its food exchange lists to help diabetics formulate suitable diets, ice cream was included in the bread category. In the 1976 revision, however, ice cream was banished on the grounds that it is too high in both sugar and fat.

Subsequent studies at the University of Toronto measured ice cream and other foods for their glycemic impact—the body's reaction to these foods compared to glucose, which yields the highest response. Ice cream came out fairly low on the scale, yet diabetics were still cautioned that it contains too much fat to be enjoyed often.

A group of Massachusetts medical professionals also showed that a normal serving of ice cream, eaten as part of a regular meal, causes only a modest increase in blood glucose levels. They held that the fat in ice cream slows absorption of sugar, minimizing impact. These researchers cautiously concluded that some diabetics may enjoy ice cream, provided dietary adjustments are made to accommodate the extra fat.

The American Diabetes Association capitulated by reinstating ice cream in its 1986 revision of the exchange lists. Ice cream is now recommended for occasional use only, to be eaten in small portions by those with good blood-glucose control. The revision committee hastened to explain that "occasional use" does not mean diabetics are encouraged to eat ice cream, rather that it isn't realistic to expect anyone to avoid this seductive treat.

The inclusion of ice cream in a diabetic diet requires both determining the number of calories per serving and working the serving into the food exchange schedule. Consult *Exchange List for Meal Planning,* 1986 edition, to determine exchange equivalents for ice cream, ice milk, frozen yogurt, and sherbet. Since background diet and the degree to which it is conscientiously followed also figure in, diabetics should discuss the question of ice cream with a physician or dietician.

SUGAR-FREE VANILLA

This ice cream counts for $\frac{1}{2}$ whole milk plus $\frac{1}{2}$ lean meat exchange and 85 calories per half-cup serving.

Combine	**1$\frac{1}{2}$ C evaporated milk** **1$\frac{1}{2}$ C milk** **1 T vanilla.**
Beat egg substitute equal to	**4 eggs.**
Fold into milk mixture.	
Add sugar substitute equal to	**$\frac{1}{2}$ C sugar.**
Chill and stir freeze.	

yield: about 1 quart

SUGAR-FREE CHOCOLATE

This chocolate ice cream counts as 1 skim milk exchange and 68 calories per half-cup serving.

In	**3 C skim milk**
soften	**1 pkg plain gelatin.**
Heat until gelatin dissolves.	
Stir in	**4-oz sugar-free cocoa** **$\frac{1}{8}$ t cinnamon.**
Cool and add	**1 t vanilla.**
Chill and stir freeze.	

yield: about 1 quart

SUGAR-FREE DATE DELIGHT

Date delight, which can also be made with prunes or raisins, counts for ¹/₂ starch plus ¹/₂ low-fat milk exchange and 91 calories per half-cup serving. For *spicy* date delight, add ¹/₂ t cinnamon plus ¹/₄ t each ground cloves and nutmeg.

In medium saucepan, blend	**1¹/₃ C whole milk** **1 T cornstarch** **¹/₈ t salt.**
Add	**²/₃ C chopped dates.**
Over medium heat, stir until mixture thickens.	
Beat egg substitute equal to	**4 eggs.**
Gradually beat in warm milk.	
Cool.	
Add sugar substitute equal to	**¹/₄ C sugar** **1 t vanilla.**
Chill.	
Chill and whip	**1 C evaporated milk.**
Fold into date mixture.	
Stir freeze.	

yield: about 1 quart

SUGAR-FREE FROZEN YOGURT

Made with blackberries, blueberries, mandarin oranges, peaches, or pineapple, this frozen yogurt counts for ½ skim milk exchange and 76 calories per half-cup serving. If you prefer less tartness, increase sweetening to equal ⅔ C sugar.

In **¼ C water**

soften **1 pkg plain gelatin.**

Heat until gelatin dissolves.

Stir in sugar substitute equal to **½ C sugar**
2 C fruit
2 C plain low-fat yogurt.

Stir freeze.

yield: about 1 quart

SUGAR-FREE BUTTERMILK SHERBET

This sherbet counts for ½ fruit exchange and 33 calories per half-cup serving. Substitute crushed pineapple, and you've got ½ skim milk exchange and 50 calories. If you prefer less tartness, increase sweetening to equal ⅔ C sugar.

In **2 C buttermilk**

soften **½ pkg plain gelatin.**

Heat until gelatin dissolves.

Add sugar substitute equal to **½ C sugar**
1 C sliced strawberries
1 t vanilla.

Chill.

Beat stiff and fold in **2 egg whites.**

Stir freeze.

yield: about 1 quart

SUGAR-FREE FRUIT SPOOM

Made with apricots, peaches, or cherries mixed or matched with apple, grapefruit, orange, or pineapple juice, this spoom counts for 1 fruit exchange and 52 calories per half-cup serving. Increase sweetening slightly if the fruit is on the tart side.

Purée sugar substitute equal to

¹/₄ C sugar
2²/₃ C chopped fruit
¹/₃ C fruit juice
1 T lemon juice.

Chill.

Beat stiff **3 egg whites.**

Fold into fruit mixture.

Stir freeze.

yield: about 1 quart

SUGAR-FREE SUNDAE SAUCE

Diabetics needn't deny themselves the occasional sundae, thanks to dietetic pudding. Count this sauce as ¹/₂ fat exchange and 35 calories per quarter-cup serving. When making hot fudge or warm butterscotch sauce, use a sugar substitute that retains its sweetness even when heated, and stir it in along with the margarine.

In small saucepan, combine

1 envelope diet pudding
³/₄ C water.

Stirring, bring to boil over low heat.

Remove from heat and stir in **1 T margarine.**

Cool.

Add sugar substitute equal to **¹/₄ C sugar.**

yield: about ³/₄ cup

SUGAR-FREE PINEAPPLE SUNDAE SAUCE

For this sauce, use crushed pineapple in its own juice, draining the fruit through a sieve and reserving the juice to measure separately. Count ¹/₄ cup as ¹/₂ starch exchange and 41 calories.

In small saucepan, bring to boil

¹/₃ C crushed pineapple
¹/₄ C pineapple juice
¹/₄ C plain diet syrup
1 T water.

Cool.

yield: about 1 cup

Low Cholesterol

Contrary to popular belief, ice cream contains little cholesterol unless it's made with whole eggs or egg yolks. It is considered a high-cholesterol food because, in addition to the meager 0.3 percent cholesterol in cream, ice cream usually contains a whole load of saturated fats that are worse, by some accounts, than dietary cholesterol.

Cholesterol is a wax-like fatty substance found only in foods of animal origin. It promotes good health as long as it remains balanced in the body. When the balancing mechanism breaks down, the body converts saturated fats into excess cholesterol, which builds up in the arteries and causes those dire consequences reported on in the media.

By the time the cholesterol hysteria peaked, we were left with the certain knowledge that some of us suffer from high blood cholesterol. As a result, the American Heart Association recommends avoiding ice cream in favor of sherbets, ices, and ice milks. But there are ways to make fairly decent low-cholesterol ice cream, provided you know a little about fats.

There are two kinds of fat—saturated and unsaturated. Saturated fats, found in meat, palm oil, coconut oil, and high-fat dairy products, are the prime suspects in high blood cholesterol. You can minimize saturated fats in ice cream by substituting skim or low-fat milk, buttermilk, or low-fat yogurt for whole milk and cream, as previously described for dietetic ice cream.

Low-fat ice cream isn't nearly as creamy smooth as the gourmet kind. It's not as tasty, either, since one of the functions of fat is to carry flavor. To improve both the texture and flavor of low-fat ice cream, add one-quarter cup vegetable oil per quart of mix. If the recipe calls for heating the mix, you can melt in some margarine instead.

Unsaturated fats, the kind found in most vegetable oils, are thought not to raise blood cholesterol. In fact, they may even help reduce it. Oils all contain the same amount of calories (120 per tablespoon) and fat (14 grams per tablespoon), but that fat may be either saturated or unsaturated.

Good oils that are high in unsaturated fats are corn, cottonseed, peanut, safflower, sesame, soybean, sunflower, and walnut. Best of all is canola oil. For ice cream making, select the oil that tastes best to you, avoiding coconut oil, which is higher in saturated fats than even butter.

The yolks of eggs are relatively high in fat (5 grams per egg) *and* cholesterol (250 milligrams), but not all authorities agree on the harmfulness of dietary cholesterol. Some recommend avoiding egg yolks entirely, which means no frozen custards, country ice creams, or soufflés unless they're made with egg substitute. Spooms are fine, since they contain only fat-free egg whites. The following "cholesterol-free" recipes are based on recommendations by the American Heart Association.

COMPARISON OF DIETARY FATS			
	Saturated	**Polyunsaturated**	**Monounsaturated**
Butter, regular*	66%	4%	30%
Canola oil	6%	32%	62%
Coconut oil	87%	2%	11%
Corn oil	13%	62%	25%
Cottonseed oil	26%	52%	22%
Margarine, regular	17%	34%	49%
Palm oil	49%	9%	42%
Peanut oil	18%	33%	49%
Safflower oil	10%	77%	13%
Sesame oil	14%	42%	44%
Soybean oil	15%	61%	24%
Sunflower oil	10%	66%	24%
Walnut oil	9%	63%	28%

*Butterfat also contains 33 percent cholesterol. (The butterfat content of cream varies from 10.5 percent in half and half to 36 percent or more in heavy cream, as specified on the label.)

CHOLESTEROL-FREE VANILLA ICE CREAM

This basic recipe can be flavored the same as any foundation ice cream. For ideas, consult Appendix A, "Mix-ins."

In saucepan, stir together

²/₃ **C nonfat milk powder**
¹/₂ **C sugar**
1¹/₂ **T flour**
¹/₈ **t salt.**

Blend in

2²/₃ **C water.**

Bring to simmer and add

¹/₃ **C margarine.**

Stirring, simmer 3 minutes.

Cool.

Stir in

1 **T vanilla.**

**CHOLESTEROL-FREE
VANILLA ICE CREAM, cont'd.**

Beat frothy.   **3 egg whites.**

Fold into mixture.

Chill and stir freeze.

yield: about 1 quart

CHOLESTEROL-FREE
CHOCOLATE ICE CREAM

If you aren't fond of bittersweet fla-   Soften   **¹/₂ pkg plain
vors, increase the sugar in this recipe   gelatin**
to ³/₄ C. For cholesterol-free *mocha*
ice cream, stir in 1 T decaffeinated   in   **2 T cold water.**
instant coffee along with the cocoa.
                                            In saucepan, combine   **¹/₂ C sugar
                                                                      ¹/₄ C nonsweetened
                                                                         cocoa
                                                                      ³/₄ C nonfat milk
                                                                         powder.**

                                            Blend in   **2¹/₄ C water.**

                                            Bring to simmer and add   **¹/₃ C margarine.**

                                            Stirring, simmer 3 minutes.

                                            Stir in softened gelatin.

                                            Cool.

                                            Add   **1 T vanilla extract
                                                                      ¹/₂ t almond
                                                                         extract.**

                                            Chill and stir freeze.

                                            yield: about 1 quart

CHOLESTEROL-FREE FRUIT ICE CREAM

Make this ice cream with peaches, apricots, or pineapple. If you prefer strawberry or orange, omit the almond extract.

Stir together	**2 C nonfat milk powder** **$^1/_3$ C sugar.**
Blend in	**$^1/_3$ C water** **3 T lemon juice.**
Gradually beat in	**3 T oil.**
Add	**$1^1/_3$ C purée or juice** **$^1/_4$ t almond extract.**

yield: about 1 quart

High Fiber

Farmers have always known that animals need plenty of roughage to keep them healthy, so it seems ironic that it took so long for us to recognize the human need for fiber. Fiber aids digestion and slows the absorption of fats and sugars, preventing them from turning into unwanted weight. Fiber is especially beneficial to diabetics since, in slowing the absorption of carbohydrates, it minimizes fluctuations in blood glucose.

Experts say we need twenty-five to thirty-five grams of fiber each day, yet many of the highly touted fiber-rich foods taste like sawdust. Not so of fruits and vegetables, and the ices and sorbets made from them according to the recipes offered in Chapter 3. Other tasty sources of fiber are nut ice creams and the rice-based ice creams described in the next chapter.

HIGH-FIBER FREEZE

If you freeze a ripe, medium-sized banana and whirl it in the blender with a drop of lemon juice, vanilla, or almond extract, you'll have a single serving of a tasty freeze with about 3 grams of fiber. You'll get approximately 2 grams from a half-cup serving of the following recipe when you make it with fresh or canned, puréed apples (applesauce), apricots, blueberries, cherries, peaches, pears, or raspberries. Adjust sugar according to the sweetness of the fruit. This freeze doesn't store well, so plan to serve it fresh from the ice cream maker, or freeze it in cubes and whirl them in a food processor at serving time.

Combine and chill

3^1/$_2$ C fruit purée
^{1}/$_2$ C sugar
1 T lemon juice.

Stir freeze.

yield: about 1 quart

9

Dairy Alternatives

Millions of Americans are allergic to milk, thus allergic to ice cream as well. Depending on the nature of the allergy, it may still be possible for some of these folks to enjoy homemade ice cream, either by altering the milk and cream or by using substitutes.

If your digestive system absolutely cannot handle milk of any kind, you'll have to be content with ice cream imitations. Spooms, nondairy soufflés, and creamy, banana-based ices like three-fruit freeze offer reasonable substitutes. Recipes for these appear in Chapters 3 and 4. Perhaps you'll also enjoy the rice-based ice creams described later in this chapter, or the soy-based ones in the next.

Lactose Intolerance

Milk tastes sweet because about five percent of it consists of the complex sugar lactose. Before lactose can be digested, it must be broken down into two simple sugars, glucose and galactose. The process uses an enzyme called lactase.

Like other mammals, most humans are born with the ability to produce lactase within our bodies. Most of us (like other mammalian infants) gradually lose that ability, becoming lactase deficient by age three. For about twenty-five percent of us, however, lactase production persists into adulthood. Thus, throughout their lives most descendants of Northern Europeans, African pastoralists and Northwest Indians may consume milk and ice cream without discomfort.

Lactase deficiency affects the remaining seventy-five percent of the world's adult population, including a great percentage of American Indians, Asians, Blacks, Mediterraneans, Ashkenazic Jews, Southern and Central Europeans, and Central and South Americans. In the United States, twelve percent of the population, or 30 million, suffer some degree of lactose intolerance. Even if you're not genetically predisposed, you can become temporarily or permanently lactose intolerant due to health conditions or the use of medications, especially antibiotics and arthritis anti-inflammatory drugs.

Without the lactase enzyme to break it down, lactose remains undigested in the intestine, drawing water from surrounding tissue in the reverse of what's supposed to happen during digestion. The result is bloating, cramps, gas, nausea, and diarrhea. This discomfort understandably causes anyone who suffers lactase deficiency to avoid milk products, including ice cream and sherbet.

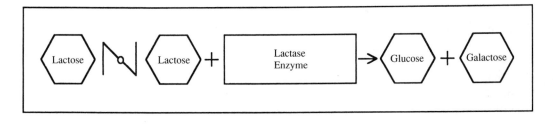

Liquid lactase enzyme breaks down the complex milk sugar, lactose, into the easy-to-digest simple sugars, glucose and galactose, enhancing both the flavor and texture of ice cream as well as giving it a sweeter taste.

Low-Lactose Ice Cream

Cornell University researchers discovered that when ice cream is enjoyed as part of a meal, it is less likely to trigger a reaction than when eaten as a between-meal snack. Yet the fact remains that some people can't tolerate any lactose at all. Since dairy-based freezes are the most palatable source of dietary calcium for many adults and for some finicky children, the inability to eat them poses a somewhat serious problem.

Fortunately, lactase concentrate has entered the picture, a substitute made from the extract of a dairy yeast and essentially the same as the enzyme produced within the human body. Taken in tablet form just before dairy products are consumed, it converts lactose into easily digested simple sugars.

Lactase also comes in liquid form and can be added directly to milk, cream, or an ice cream mix. Only a few drops, stirred into milk or mix, is needed. After twenty-four hours under refrigeration, seventy to seventy-five percent of the lactose in the milk or ice cream mix will be broken down. Most people can tolerate what little remains. For the rest, a longer aging period converts one-hundred percent of the lactose. Since an ice cream mix is thicker than milk, it should be stirred periodically during aging to ensure even circulation of the lactase enzyme.

Lactase becomes inactive at a low pH, so certain precautions are needed when using it in acidic mixes such as fruit sherbet or frozen yogurt. For low-lactose sherbet, either treat the milk first or age liquid lactase in the mix before adding fruit. Because yogurt is highly acidic, any milk or cream combined with it should be treated beforehand. To ensure complete conversion of lactose in homemade yogurt, stir in a little lactase at the same time you add the yogurt culture.

Lactase does not affect the nutritional value of ice cream, but it does improve calcium absorption. As a food rather than a drug, it may be safely and conveniently used even in households where not all members are lactose intolerant. In the event you can't find lactase at a local pharmacy or natural food store, a source is listed in Appendix C, "Supplies."

Protein Allergies

Not all sensitivity to milk is caused by lactose deficiency. Five percent of all Americans are allergic to milk protein. Reaction to milk protein is one of the four most common kinds of allergy. Symptoms in children include eczema and digestive problems such as diarrhea, vomiting, and colic. Adults feel bloated and gassy within minutes or sometimes hours after drinking milk or eating ice cream.

If you are allergic to cow milk, you may not react similarly to goat or sheep milk since their protein make-up is not quite the same. In addition, both contain a greater proportion of small fat globules, making them easier to digest. Less undigested residue is left in the colon to ferment and cause gas or cramps.

Goat and Sheep Milk

Dairy goats have been steadily gaining in popularity ever since the first registered doe was imported earlier this century. Sheep dairying is relatively new here, interest first sparked at the 1982 World Sheep Festival in Missouri. Female sheep, or ewes, give the most highly concentrated milk of all, and on a worldwide basis are kept more often as dairy animals than cows and goats combined.

America's growing interest in goats and sheep as dairy animals is due in large part to the realization that many illnesses can be traced to cow milk allergies. In addition, natural food buffs appreciate goat and sheep milk, produced without feed additives or production stimulants. Further increasing their appeal, these animals are small, relatively inexpensive, and easy to handle, making them ideal for home dairies.

Like cow milk, goat milk and sheep milk vary in composition according to individual, breed, stage of lactation, diet, time of year, weather, and other environmental considerations. Under proper management, milk from goats and sheep tastes remarkably similar to cow milk, except that most goat milk and all sheep milk is perceptibly sweeter because it contains more milkfat.

While ewe milk is still scarce in this country, fresh goat milk is widely available through small dairies and natural food stores. Evaporated and powdered goat milk are carried by many supermarkets, drugstores, and natural food stores. If you can't find a source locally, one is listed in Appendix C.

Like powdered and evaporated cow milk, goat milk in the same forms doesn't taste like fresh milk. Unlike powdered and evaporated cow milk, which is skim, the goat milk versions are equivalent to whole milk. In addition, goat milk powder tastes a bit bitter. If you use it to make yogurt, you can improve both flavor and texture by bringing the reconstituted milk to a boil, then cooling it down before adding the yogurt culture. Pure goat milk yogurt culture, containing no cow milk proteins, is now available. A source is listed in Appendix C.

COMPARISON OF MILK SOLIDS (average values)			
	Cow	**Goat**	**Sheep**
Water	87.3%	86.7%	80.7%
Lactose	4.6	4.3	5.4
Protein	3.3	3.6	6.0
Minerals			
Calcium	.12	.13	.19
Phosphorus	.09	.11	.16
Sodium	.05	.05	.04
Magnesium	.01	.01	.02
Potassium	.15	.20	.14
Fat	3.9	4.5	7.0
Cholesterol	.01	.01	unknown
Calories per cup	156	166	245

Ice Cream

Make ice cream, sherbet, or frozen yogurt from goat and sheep milk just as you would from cow milk, taking into account the higher fat content. Goat milk may contain 6.5 percent milkfat or more and ewe milk as much as 10 percent, so it takes less cream to make equally rich ice cream. In fact, those involved in sheep dairying enjoy creamy ice creams without adding any cream at all.

Compared to the slightly yellow-tinged ice cream made from cow milk, vanilla ice cream made from goat and sheep milk looks pure white. This is because goats and sheep utilize the carotene in their feed more efficiently. Instead of transmitting this vitamin A precursor into their milk, as cows do, they transmit already converted, virtually colorless vitamin A. You can, if you wish, compensate for the resulting lack of color by adding one or two egg yolks or a drop of yellow food dye.

Incidentally, unless the label specifies otherwise, commercial brands of ice cream contain only cow milk. Even with labeling, no commercial ice cream may be made from different kinds of milk mixed together, so that customers know what they're getting. Of course, there's no reason you can't combine, for example, cream from cows and milk from sheep or goats in your homemade ice cream, except that doing so will defeat your purpose if you're trying to avoid a cow milk allergy.

Nondairy Alternatives

Even if you're allergic to all kinds of milk, you still needn't deprive yourself of ice cream. Some experts believe nondairy ice cream is the wave of the future. You can make a simple homemade mix by substituting reconstituted, nondairy creamer for milk in any of the ice milk recipes in Chapter 4. Technically, the term "ice cream" refers only to dairy ice cream. The nondairy kind is called "parevine." Some people call it "pseudo ice cream" or "imitation ice cream," emphasizing the challenge of simulating the taste and texture of true ice cream. Since the idea is to make the nondairy kind as close as possible to the real thing, most of us call it ice cream and let it go at that.

Although nondairy ice cream is still pretty much in the experimental stages, those based on soy or rice appear the most promising. Soy-based ice cream rates a chapter all its own, so here we'll look at rice-based ice cream, also called "rice cream."

Rice Cream

The ancient Chinese are said to have made ice cream from rice and milk flavored with camphor. Although camphor isn't likely to become one of our top ten favorite flavors, we seem to be heading back toward rice cream, thanks to dietary trends favoring carbohydrates and fiber.

Because modern rice cream is made without dairy products, it contains neither saturated fats nor lactose. And since rice is high in natural sugars compared to soy beans, rice cream doesn't need the extra sweetening required by its competitor, soy ice cream. As an additional point in its favor, rice cream is so satisfying that you can easily stop at one scoop, no matter how tasty the flavor.

Rice Milk

The "rice milk" used in rice cream is nothing more than soft-cooked rice, thinned down and whipped smooth. It can be made from any kind of rice, white or brown, although brown varieties provide more total nutrients and fiber. The flavor and texture of your rice cream will vary with the kind of rice you use and the thickness of its grains. As with all good things, you'll have to experiment to learn which rice makes the kind of rice cream you like best.

Different kinds of rice cook up to different amounts. Some kinds double; others may quadruple. Soft cooking requires using twice the normal amount of water, resulting in twice the normal amount of rice. You'll need three cups of soft-cooked rice to make one quart (four cups) rice milk. Omit the salt if you wish, or include the usual amount to enhance the flavor of your rice cream.

Soft-cooked rice takes approximately twice the usual cooking time. After all the water has absorbed, cool and whirl in a blender, adding one part water per two parts rice or as much as you need for milky consistency. To make extra creamy rice cream with smoother texture, add soy milk or nondairy creamer instead of water. Further increase creaminess by including up to one-quarter cup vegetable oil per quart, or by melting in one-quarter cup margarine while the rice is still warm.

Use rice milk in place of milk in any ice milk or sherbet recipe or in the scoopless shakes described in Chapter 23, "Soda Fountain Drinks." Allow at least twenty minutes of tempering before scooping hardened rice cream.

VANILLA RICE CREAM

To this basic recipe add 1 t lemon zest for *lemon* rice cream. Or substitute $^1/_2$ C honey and 1 t almond extract for the sugar and vanilla for *almond honey* rice cream of slightly different texture. To make *cinnamon raisin* rice cream, add $^1/_4$ t cinnamon and $^1/_2$ C chopped raisins. For *blueberry* rice cream, add 1 C fresh blueberries and $^1/_2$ t lemon zest. If you prefer not to use sugar, substitute an equal amount of rice syrup.

Combine and blend well

$3^3/_4$ C rice milk
$^3/_4$ C sugar
2 t vanilla.

Chill and stir freeze.

yield: about 1 quart

SOY 'N' RICE CREAM

This recipe starts from scratch with uncooked rice and combines the best of both rice- and soy-based ice creams. You may, if you wish, substitute whole or skim milk for soy milk. The best flavors here are *pineapple*, *strawberry* or any tart, full-flavored fruit.

Steam until milk is fully absorbed, about 30 minutes,

$^1/_4$ C rice
2 C soy milk.

Stir in and cook 5 minutes more

1 beaten egg.

Wrap saucepan in towel and let set until cool.

Whirl in blender with

1 C soy milk
$^1/_2$ C crushed fruit
$^1/_2$ C sugar
$^1/_2$ t almond extract.

Chill and stir freeze.

yield: about 1 quart

RICE SHERBET

Flavor this sherbet with blueberries, strawberries, apricots, or your own favorite fruit or fruit juice. Rice sherbet is at its best served straight from the ice cream maker. If you prefer to make it ahead, run it through a blender or food processor before serving.

Whirl smooth in a blender

$1^{1}/_{3}$ **C soft-cooked rice**
$2^{2}/_{3}$ **C juice or purée**
$^{1}/_{3}$ **C orange juice**
$^{1}/_{4}$ **C sugar or honey**
$^{1}/_{8}$ **t almond extract**
$^{1}/_{8}$ **t vanilla.**

Chill and stir freeze.

yield: about 1 quart

RICE TOPPING

Rice cream may be topped with any compatible sundae sauce made from the recipes in Chapter 24. Or pair it with this rice-based fruit topping. Stir in a dash of nutmeg or cinnamon, if you wish, or sprinkle a little spice on top, and garnish with whole berries or sliced fresh fruit.

Blend well

$^{2}/_{3}$ **C rice milk**
2 T C honey
$^{1}/_{3}$ **C fruit or berries.**

yield: about 1 cup

Amasaki

Just as yogurt is made by culturing milk, the sweet concentrate called "amasaki" is made by culturing cooked rice with "koji." Koji is a special form of grain inoculated with the gentle mold *Aspergillus oryzae,* which ferments the rice and converts its starches into sugars. Rice Dream, a brand of rice cream first marketed in 1984, is made with amasaki.

Amasaki is sometimes recommended for diabetics and cancer patients to satisfy their craving for sweets. In addition to being high in natural sugars, it is also abundant in digestion-aiding enzymes. It is sometimes combined with soy milk and fruit to make thick, healthful shakes. You can find it at natural food stores and some delicatessens. It is also available at most Oriental markets, although the brands you'll find there are apt to have sugar added.

Each brand of amasaki has its own distinctive flavor. Textures also vary, ranging from sticky and taffy-like to the consistency of syrupy. It may take shopping around to find one you like. There is a thinned-down beverage also called amasaki, so take care you get the concentrated pudding form needed to make ice cream. Better yet, make your own, experimenting with technique until you're satisfied with the results.

Fermentation

Traditional Japanese amasaki is made from glutinous brown rice, a uniquely sweet and flavorful sort of rice offering the most consistent results. Any kind of rice, or in fact many other grain, can be substituted with varying degrees of success.

Begin by washing and draining two cups of rice and soaking it overnight in four cups of water. Then cook the rice until all the water is absorbed. Sweet brown rice is generally pressure cooked for forty-five minutes.

While the rice is still warm, thoroughly stir in about one-quarter cup koji, the exact amount depending on how sweet you want your amasaki to be. Transfer the rice to a glass bowl or yogurt maker, cover with a damp towel, and set in a warm place to incubate. Stir occasionally to ensure complete blending of the koji.

Amasaki incubates in four to ten hours. The longer it ferments, the sweeter it will be, up to a point—fermented too long, it becomes bitter. When the amasaki tastes right to you, turn it into a saucepan and bring it just to a boil. Immediately spoon it into a jar with a tight-fitting lid and chill. Amasaki keeps well in the refrigerator for up to a week.

Don't expect your homemade amasaki to have the same consistent quality as the commercial kind. Besides having stricter control over the wide range of variables affecting fermentation, commercial producers use a secret centrifugal process to control the amount and kind of enzymes in their koji.

Whether commercially purchased or homemade, amasaki used at the rate of one and one-half cups per quart makes rice cream of excellent texture, even after hardening. In the event you have trouble finding Oriental products locally, mail-order sources for amasaki, koji, and sweet rice are listed in Appendix C.

AMASAKI SHERBET

The combination of amasaki and pineapple in this sherbet is a natural, but you can make other flavors by substituting apple juice for the pineapple juice and adding blueberries, raspberries, or strawberries in place of the fruit. If you prefer greater sweetness, add sugar or honey to taste, or use apple juice concentrate for the juice. For smoother texture and stronger flavor, use soy milk instead of juice. This recipe was formulated with Eden brand amasaki. Other brands, or homemade, may require minor flavoring adjustments.

In saucepan, blend

$^1/_2$ T cornstarch
1 C pineapple juice.

Cook until clear and add

$1^1/_2$ C amasaki.

Stirring, heat until smooth, 3 to 5 minutes.

Cool.

Whirl in blender with

$1^1/_2$ C pineapple
1 t vanilla
$^1/_4$ t salt.

Chill and stir freeze.

yield: about 1 quart

Eskimo Ice Cream

The average Alaskan eats twice as much ice cream as most of the rest of us, perhaps because the fat and calories help keep them warm during those long, dark Alaskan winters. Well before their territory was overrun by whalers, trappers, and missionaries, the Eskimos were enjoying their own brand of nondairy ice cream, *aqutaq*. As with any ice cream, there are as many different versions as there are aqutaq makers.

Like today's superpremium ice creams, traditional aqutaq relies on fat for its smooth texture. It's made by slowly stirring seal oil and water or fresh snow into reindeer, caribou, or moose tallow. The mixture is beaten by hand until it turns fluffy, stiff, and white. At this point, before flavoring is added, it tastes like a mild cheese spread.

Aqutaq is flavored and sweetened with fresh or dried native berries, favorites being salmonberries, cloudberries, blueberries, blackberries, crowberries, and lingonberries. Sometimes bits of meat or fish are included along with the berries, creating a concentrated food similar to the pemmican enjoyed by some Indian tribes. (If fish-flavored ice cream sounds a bit strange, consider the smoked salmon ice cream served in Great Britain.)

Modern aqutaq is likely to be made from beef tallow, vegetable shortening, butter, or even mashed potatoes. It is sweetened with sugar and flavored with fruit, often imported from the lower forty-eight, and may be served chilled or frozen. Like any plain dairy ice cream or sherbet, a little unflavored aqutaq makes a good dressing for fruit salad.

20TH-CENTURY AQUTAQ

Aqutaq was traditionally stirred by hand, but there's no reason you can't beat it with a wire whisk or an electric mixer. To avoid grittiness, use super fine or powdered sugar. For authentic flavor, add lingonberries (mountain cranberries) and shredded boiled whitefish. Or stir in blackberries, blueberries, or salmonberries and serve with strips of smoked salmon.

Cream until fluffy

$^1/_2$ **C shortening**
1 C sugar
$^1/_4$ **C ice water.**

Gently fold in

3 C berries.

yield: about 1 quart

IDA'S AQUTAQ

In Alaska, Ida is famous for her exceptional aqutaq. To keep her family of eight in ice cream for two days, she mixes up eight quarts at a time, adding ingredients in small increments to keep the texture light. This is a scaled-down version of Ida's recipe, which she flavors with grapes, fresh apples, cooked dried apples, raisins, raspberries, or "any fruit that tastes good."

Combine

2 T instant mashed
  potatoes
2 T water.

Cream

$^1/_4$ **C shortening.**

Combine and beat in

3 T sugar
2 T icy cold water.

Add potatoes and beat well.

Fold in

3 C fruit or
  berries.

yield: about 1 quart

10

Soy Ice Cream

Billed as a guilt-free, nondairy frozen dessert, soy ice cream exploded on the scene as "Tofutti" in the early 1980s. Some people claim they can't tell it apart from dairy ice cream. Others fancy it as a flavor cross between ice cream and frozen yogurt. Still others dislike it altogether. Because it's low in saturated fats, soy ice cream needn't be excluded from cholesterol-lowering diets. As a nondairy dessert, it presents no problems for those sensitive to lactose or milk proteins.

Tofutti

Acceptance in the United States of soybean products as dairy substitutes has been slow in coming, although the bean itself is one of our oldest cultivated crops. It was introduced here in 1804, and production has steadily increased ever since. Soybeans are grown primarily to feed livestock, yet they rank among the top five high-protein foods, right along with meat, fish, eggs, and milk.

The first ice cream in the United States made from soybeans was patented in 1922 by a Chinese-American named Lee Len Thuey. His simple recipe called for a quart of soybean curd, called "tofu," combined with three-quarters to one cup of sugar and a little flavoring. The concoction failed to catch on. It would be another sixty years before Americans were ready for Tofutti.

Meantime, auto magnate Henry Ford was attempting to develop soybean plastics. He was among the first Americans to recognize the importance of soybeans to human nutrition. In 1931 his laboratories in Dearborn, Michigan, developed soy-based ice creams and sherbets, which were served in the Ford cafeteria during the cream shortages of World War II. Unfortunately, economics eventually forced Ford to discontinue his soy research.

Over in China, American Seventh-Day Adventist missionary-physician Harry Miller was concerned about undernourishment among Chinese infants. Recognizing that soybeans were a widely accepted local food, while dairy products were not, Miller set about to develop a palatable, soy-based infant formula that was both easy to digest and easy to store. The logical next step for his formula was ice cream, first made at Miller's soy dairy in

Shanghai in 1936. In the mid-1950s, this ice cream was introduced to patients at the Seventh-Day Tokyo Sanitarium in Japan.

Soon thereafter, Seventh-Day Adventist communities in California and Tennessee were making and selling Ice Bean, the first commercial soy ice cream in this country. Despite increasing evidence that many illnesses result from dairy milk allergies, soy ice cream was still not taken seriously in dairyland USA.

Then, in the early 1970s, a Brooklyn caterer named David Mintz decided it was high time someone solved a knotty problem presented by Jewish dietary strictures. It seems that Orthodox Jews may not enjoy dairy ice cream as dessert after a meal containing meat. Mintz ordered up a supply of tofu and, after nine years of testing and tasting, in 1982 came up with Tofutti.

Although he can't take full credit for inventing the idea of soy ice cream, Mintz is certainly responsible for bringing it to the attention of a nation that was finally ready for it. By the end of the decade, thirty brands of soy ice cream had appeared on the market. At last count, we were scooping up 22 million quarts per year.

Soy Protein

Few brands of soy ice cream contain soy milk or tofu. Most are made from isolated soy proteins, which are not only cheaper but yield more dairylike flavor and texture. Isolated soy protein, a fine white powder that is ninety to ninety-two percent pure protein, tastes the least beany of all soy products and is lowest in gas-causing sugars. Since it is dry and nonperishable and therefore easy to transport and store, it is particularly well suited for commercial use.

Isolated soy proteins are obtained by soaking crushed beans in a petroleum solvent until their oil floats away, then immersing the remaining meal in solutions of sodium hydroxide and hydrochloric acid from which the proteins are extracted. Many people are justifiably concerned about the use of all these chemicals.

In 1987, an alternative method of extraction was introduced by INTSOY, the International Soybean Program at the University of Illinois. The new concept involves dry heat extrusion followed by mechanical extraction, a relatively inexpensive process that, in contrast to solvent extraction, is feasible on a small scale. It seems only a matter of time before some entrepreneur takes up this new procedure.

Meanwhile, whether naturally produced or not, isolated soy proteins remain unavailable for home ice cream making. Happily, soy milk is sold widely and makes quite tasty ice cream. Although some brands contain soy protein isolate, others are naturally extracted from the bean.

Soy Milk

The idea of making milk from beans was the brainchild of the pre-Christian Chinese philosopher Whi Nain Tze, who accurately believed it would become an important food in the Orient. It is made by soaking, grinding, cooking, and straining dried soybeans.

The resulting milk is richer in protein than dairy milk and lower in both fat and carbohydrates. The milk is also alkaline, whereas dairy milk is acidic. Although soy milk resembles dairy milk in both appearance and consistency, it doesn't taste much like it. Orientals prefer it that way. Unlike most Americans, they don't expect soy milk and soy ice cream to taste like dairy products. They enjoy the somewhat beany flavor and object to the idea of eliminating or masking it. For this reason, ready-to-serve soy milk varies considerably from one brand to the next, ranging in flavor from bland to somewhat malty. Most brands contain added sweeteners, emulsifiers, and salt to round out their flavor, and most are adjusted to be nutritionally equivalent to dairy milk.

Soy milk comes in the same basic forms as dairy milk—liquid, concentrated (evaporated), and powdered. Some brands are intended for adult use, others are formulated for infants. All can be used in ice cream. Powdered and concentrated soy milk, packaged in cans, are equivalent to whole milk, in contrast to powdered and evaporated dairy milk, which are skim. Ready-to-serve soy milk comes in vacuum-sealed cartons that keep well without refrigeration, although flavor may deteriorate somewhat with age.

Soy milk in all its forms is now carried by most major grocery chains and natural food stores. If you have trouble finding it locally, check with the sources in Appendix C, "Supplies."

COMPARISON OF SOY MILK AND COW MILK		
	Soy* (%)	**Cow (%)**
Water	93	87
Fat	1.5	3.9
Protein	3.4	3.3
Sugars	2.0	4.6
Minerals	0.5	.7
Calcium	.02	.12
Phosphorous	.05	.09
Calories per cup	79	156

*Values are for plain, unadjusted soy milk before sugar or minerals are added to make it equivalent to cow milk. For information on specific brands, consult packaging labels.

Milking the Bean

Although you can buy soy milk that tastes homemade, some people still make their own to reduce cost and ensure purity. The milk resulting from the process developed by INTSOY is relatively free of beany flavor, has nearly three percent protein and, like all naturally extracted soy milk, contains no vitamins or minerals.

For one and two-thirds quarts of milk, clean two-thirds cup whole raw soy beans. Add two cups boiling water and one-eighth teaspoon baking soda. Boil ten minutes to inactivate the lipoxidase enzyme responsible for beany flavor, then drain, discarding the water. Add one-quarter teaspoon baking soda plus four cups fresh boiling water. You can increase or decrease the consistency of the final milk by adjusting the proportion of beans and water here.

Boil five minutes. In small batches, whirl beans and cooking water in a blender at high speed for one minute. Strain the purée through six layers of finely woven, moistened cheesecloth, squeezing out as much liquid as you can. Bring the extracted liquid to a boil, watching that it doesn't foam over. In contrast to dairy milk, you needn't worry about soy milk scorching. Simmer twenty minutes, no longer or you'll start losing protein.

According to taste, add one tablespoon or more sugar or honey and one-half teaspoon or more salt. For creamy, whole-milk texture, add one tablespoon soy oil or one teaspoon lecithin (available at natural food stores). Stir thoroughly, pour into heated jars, and seal.

The quicker soy milk is cooled, the longer it will keep. Stored in tightly covered jars in the refrigerator, it should last four or five days.

Soy Ice Cream

Use soy milk in ice cream essentially as you would dairy milk. Some brands contain enough oil and other additives to make them equivalent to whole milk. Some, notably Edensoy, are fortified with emulsifiers that lend creamier texture.

When you use homemade soy milk or an equivalent commercial brand, you'll improve ice cream texture by adding one-quarter cup vegetable oil per quart of mix. The kind of oil you use will influence the flavor of the ice cream. Many people favor soy, sesame, or coconut oil, but beware—the latter is very high in saturated fats and should be avoided if you're concerned about cholesterol. (The saturated fat content of various oils is listed in Chapter 8.) When a recipe calls for heating the mix, you can use margarine instead of oil.

Occasionally, an ice cream recipe calls for soy cream. Make this by whirling soy milk in a blender with an equal amount of soy oil (or as much as you need to achieve desired consistency). With the blender running, gradually add the oil in a steady stream until the cream is thoroughly homogenized. Use soy cream as you would dairy cream. You can also substitute soy milk concentrate for cream.

Including dairy products in soy ice cream seems to defeat its whole purpose. Nonetheless, many people add dairy milk, cream, yogurt, or buttermilk, particularly when using homemade soy milk. Besides smoothing out flavor and increasing richness, dairy products add extra food value, especially calcium, which soy is decidedly short on.

Flavor

Since soy milk lacks the natural sweetness of dairy milk, soy ice cream usually requires more sugar or honey than dairy ice cream. Again, the amount of sweetener you need depends on the kind of soy milk you use. Some brands contain much more sweetening than others.

Soy milk also lacks the natural sodium of dairy milk, so adding a little salt enhances ice cream flavor. In place of salt, some soy enthusiasts prefer *miso*, a brown or almost black paste made from crushed soybeans fermented with the same koji described in the previous chapter. Miso is available at most natural food stores.

Commercial soy milk comes in a number of subtle flavors, none strong enough to carry through into ice cream without additional flavoring. Among the flavors that blend best with soy are banana, coffee, and malt. Carob is, perhaps, the most successful flavoring since it not only blends well with the taste of soy but contributes natural emulsifiers that improve ice cream texture. Most of us find chocolate disappointing in soy ice cream because it lacks that characteristic milk chocolate flavor we've learned to expect. And many feel vanilla is unsuccessful with stronger tasting soy milks whose beaniness overwhelms vanilla's delicate flavor.

Four out of five aficionados prefer soy ice cream hardened rather than served soft. Hardening lowers the temperature, giving ice cream a somewhat milder taste. Hardened soy ice cream needs about twenty minutes of tempering before it can be successfully scooped.

SOY ICE CREAM

This basic recipe was formulated with Edensoy. Other brands may require increasing honey to ²/₃ C and/or adding ¹/₄ C vegetable oil. This ice cream is tasty plain and also makes a good foundation for other flavorings.

In medium saucepan, combine

1 C soy milk
¹/₂ C honey
¹/₈ t salt.

Over low heat, stir until well blended.

Chill.

Add

2 C soy milk
¹/₂ t almond extract.

Stir freeze.

yield: about 1 quart

HONEY SOY ICE CREAM

This recipe is designed for basic soy milks, akin to homemade, and is a favorite among true aficionados of soy. Others prefer stronger flavorings such as *coffee* (add 2 T instant) or *carob* (add 1/4 C). For *malted* or *malted carob* ice cream, substitute 1/3 C barley malt syrup and 1/2 C sugar (or 1/3 C corn syrup) for the honey.

In medium saucepan, combine

1 C soy milk
2/3 C honey
1/4 C oil
1/8 t salt.

Over low heat, stir until well blended.

Chill.

Add

1 3/4 C soy milk
2 t vanilla
1 t liquid lecithin.

Stir freeze.

yield: about 1 quart

BERRY SOY ICE CREAM

Adjust the sweetening and oil in this and the following recipes according to the kind of soy milk you use, following the previous two formulas as examples. The best flavors here are *strawberry, blackberry,* and *raspberry* (with the seeds strained out), or any full-flavor berry or fruit.

Blend well

2 C soy milk
1/2 C sugar
1/4 C oil
1/8 t salt.

Stir in

1 1/2 C purée.

Chill and stir freeze.

yield: about 1 quart

INSTANT SOY ICE CREAM

Although ready-to-serve soy milk is now widely available, some people still prefer the convenience of soy milk powder. Here's a basic recipe for fine textured, creamy ice cream. The strong underlying soybean taste calls for equally strong flavorings.

Whirl in blender

1 C soy milk powder
3 C water
2/3 C honey
1/4 C oil
1 t vanilla
1/8 t salt.

Stir freeze.

yield: about 1 quart

BANANA PECAN SOY ICE CREAM

This ice cream has many popular variations including *banana date, banana pineapple*, and *banana coconut*, made by substituting chopped pitted dates, drained crushed pineapple, or shredded coconut for the pecans. Or be adventuresome and toss in a combination of all four.

In medium saucepan, combine	**2¹/₂ C soy milk** **¹/₂ C honey** **¹/₄ C oil** **¹/₈ t salt.**
Over low heat, stir until well blended.	
Chill.	
Mash and add	**2 ripe bananas.**
Stir freeze and add	**¹/₂ C chopped pecans.**

yield: about 1 quart

MAPLE NUT SOY ICE CREAM

Make this tasty ice cream with English walnuts, black walnuts, or pecans, and serve it with fresh blueberries. Or stir in ¹/₂ C blueberries instead of nuts for delicious *blueberry maple* soy ice cream.

Combine and blend well	**3 C soy milk** **¹/₃ C maple syrup** **¹/₄ C sugar** **¹/₄ C oil** **1 T vanilla** **¹/₂ T maple flavoring** **¹/₈ t salt.**
Chill.	
Stir freeze and add	**¹/₂ C chopped nuts.**

yield: about 1 quart

CAROB MINT SOY ICE CREAM

Like chocolate, carob lends itself to numerous combination flavors. For *carob orange* use orange extract in place of mint. For *carob cinnamon*, substitute ground cinnamon. For plain *carob*, substitute vanilla extract. To

In medium saucepan, combine	**1 C soy milk** **¹/₂ C honey** **¹/₄ C carob powder** **2 T sesame purée** **1 T sesame oil** **¹/₈ t salt.**

CAROB MINT SOY ICE CREAM, cont'd.

make *chocolate*, use nonsweetened cocoa in place of carob. Veteran soy ice cream makers find that a little sesame purée, or tahini, along with a touch of sesame oil adds depth to both flavor and texture.

Over low heat, stir until well blended.

Chill.

Add

2 C soy milk
¹/₄ t mint extract
or oil.

Stir freeze.

yield: about 1 quart

SOY SHERBET

Flavor this fun mix-and-match sherbet with *banana, mango, peach, pineapple, strawberry,* or *avocado* purée combined with pineapple juice. Or make *orange* sherbet by using half orange juice and half pineapple juice plus the pulp from one large orange and a bit of grated rind. Other tasty combinations include *apricot, blackberry, cherry,* or *purple plum* combined with apple or orange juice. If you don't care for coconut, substitute chopped cashews or peanuts.

In

soften

1 C soy milk

1 pkg plain gelatin.

Heat until gelatin dissolves.

Cool.

Whirl in blender with

1¹/₂ C fruit juice
¹/₂ C fruit purée
¹/₂ C shredded
  coconut
¹/₂ C sugar
¹/₄ C oil
1 t lemon juice
¹/₈ t salt.

Chill and stir freeze.

yield: about 1 quart

Soy Yogurt

Frozen yogurt can be made from cultured soy milk, just like it's made from cultured dairy milk according to the directions in Chapter 7, "Frozen Yogurt." The same frozen yogurt recipes hold, with the same minor recipe changes as needed for making ice cream from soy milk—add a little salt, add oil, and increase sweetening according to the nature of the soy milk in the yogurt.

Unlike dairy milk, which is standardized from one brand to the next, soy milk varies a great deal. Not all brands make equally good yogurt. It pays to shop around until you find just the taste you like. You can't go far wrong with Edensoy, one of the oldest brands on the market. Yogurt made from it tastes very much like dairy yogurt, except for a pleasantly maltlike undertone.

Yogurt made from powdered soy milk, on the other hand, is significantly different from dairy yogurt. The surface is dull rather than shiny, and the texture is quite grainy. The flavor is sweet and somewhat bland, but will be tangier if you stir in one or two tablespoons of fructose along with the yogurt culture.

In general, soy yogurt tends to be thinner than dairy yogurt. To thicken it, add a little soy milk powder or gelatin, the same as you would thicken dairy milk yogurt; or simmer the soy milk for up to forty-five minutes in an uncovered saucepan to evaporate some of the water. The higher concentration of soy protein will produce tangier as well as thicker yogurt. If your yogurt develops watery separation, drain away the excess liquid for firmer frozen yogurt.

Two brands of starter are sold specifically for culturing soy milk—Soyadophilus and Theradophilus. Plain dairy yogurt or freeze-dried culture from a dairy supplier also work. If dietary strictures require an absolutely nondairy product, use soy yogurt cultured with dairy yogurt as your mother culture. Your second-generation yogurt will be virtually dairy free.

Flavor frozen soy yogurt with the same flavorings you would use in frozen dairy yogurt, unless the yogurt was made from soy milk powder. In that case, you'll find flavors like caramel and coffee more successful than fruit.

BASIC FROZEN SOY YOGURT

This recipe offers a foundation for nearly any flavor you can think of. For *coffee,* add 1 T instant coffee. For *carob honey,* substitute honey for the sugar, add $^1/_2$ C carob powder, heat both with the soy milk, and cool before stirring in remaining ingredients. For fruit and berry flavors, substitute purée for soy milk. With sweetened frozen or canned fruit, decrease sugar to $^3/_4$ C or honey to $^1/_2$ C. If the milk you make the yogurt from contains emulsifiers (as does Edensoy), you can omit the oil.

Blend together

2$^1/_2$ C soy yogurt
1 C soy milk
1 C sugar (or
 $^2/_3$ C honey)
$^1/_4$ C oil
$^1/_8$ t salt.

Stir freeze.

yield: about 1 quart

CARAMEL FROZEN SOY YOGURT

Caramel-flavored frozen yogurt can be made from the previous recipe by substituting brown sugar for the white sugar and using margarine instead of oil, heating both with the soy milk until the margarine melts and the sugar dissolves. Or make real caramel from burnt sugar, following this recipe. If the liquefied sugar turns lumpy when the milk is added, keep stirring until it dissolves. For *coffee caramel,* add 1 T instant coffee.

Heat **1 C soy milk.**

Set aside.

In small skillet, melt **¼ C sugar.**

Stir until golden.

Over low heat, gradually stir into warm milk.

Remove from heat and stir in **2 T margarine.**

Cool.

Beat until stiff **2 eggs**
½ C sugar.

Stir into milk mixture.

Chill.

Beat together and add **2 C soy yogurt**
½ T vanilla.

Stir freeze.

yield: about 1 quart

Tofu

Infinitely adaptable tofu was introduced to the United States from Asia, where it has long been an important source of protein. Called "meat without a bone" in the Orient, it is essentially curdled soy milk with the watery separation, or whey, drained off. The solid part, or curds, are then pressed into soft, custardy tofu. Like other soy products, tofu varies considerably from one brand to the next. Some brands are mild tasting, others have a strongly soybean flavor or leave a powdery aftertaste and therefore make less successful ice cream.

Tofu is available fresh, canned, and (when you can find it) powdered. The canned version, called "soy food," "vegetable cheese," or "soy curd," is sold at natural food outlets and has the texture of cottage cheese. Brands with pungent herbs blended in aren't suitable for ice cream, but the plain kind is, if you whip it smooth with a little soy milk.

Fresh tofu, sometimes called "bean curd" or "bean cake," is carried in the produce section of most supermarkets and comes in solid, though fragile, blocks. It is packaged either in vacuum sealed containers that keep for as long as two months under refrigeration or in small, water-filled plastic tubs that last about a week under the best conditions. When tofu tastes sour, it's losing freshness.

Tofu comes in four classes. "Regular" or "traditional" is made from whole soybeans. "Silken" comes from soy milk. "Derivative" tofu contains isolated soy proteins or other derivatives. "Combination" includes a mixture of whole soybeans and soy protein derivatives. All are supposed to be nutritionally equal, and the label need not specify which you're getting.

What the label does specify, usually, is the consistency of the tofu, whether soft, regular, firm or extra firm. Soft tofu contains 5 to 6.4 percent protein. It is moist with a smooth, silky texture, and is the kind to use if you don't want to add soy milk or other liquid to your ice cream mix.

Regular or medium-firm tofu contains 6.5 to 9.9 percent protein and is what you get when the label doesn't specify consistency. Here you'll probably want to add a little soy milk to thin down your mix. Firm (10 to 13.9 percent protein) and extra-firm (14 percent protein) are very dense and require the addition of soy milk to keep ice cream from getting overly stiff.

Any kind of tofu makes a nutritious, delicious nondairy shake. Just toss some in a blender with chunks of frozen fruit, a little sugar or honey, perhaps an egg or a spoonful of wheat germ, and enough soy milk or fruit juice to thin to milkshake consistency.

Tofu Ice Cream

Despite the sometimes misleading brand names, most commercial soy ice cream contains very little tofu, if any, because of its relatively high cost and dense texture. Some people within the ice cream industry consider the addition of tofu to be little more than a marketing gimmick.

But quality tofu does have a few advantages over soy milk for home ice cream making. It contains approximately twice the protein, it contributes smooth texture, and, like dairy cream, it readily absorbs flavorings. As with soy milk and soy yogurt, the most successful tofu ice cream is made with relatively strong flavorings such as malt and carob or full-flavored fruits like pineapple and strawberry.

Because it's so high in solids, tofu ice cream freezes faster and harder than most dairy ice cream. A short period of hardening is beneficial, but fully hardened tofu ice cream needs thirty minutes of tempering in the refrigerator before it can be scooped. Tofu ice cream is so filling that you'll likely feel satisfied with smaller than usual portions.

SOFT TOFU ICE CREAM

Use this basic recipe as the foundation for *coffee* by adding 3 T instant coffee, for *chocolate* by including $^{1}/_{4}$ C cocoa, or for *carob* by adding $^{1}/_{2}$ C carob powder. For dairylike creaminess, include up to three egg yolks or $^{1}/_{2}$ C vegetable oil. If you wish, use 1 C sugar in place of honey.

Whirl in blender

3 C soft tofu
  (1$^{1}/_{2}$#)
$^{2}/_{3}$ C honey
1 T vanilla
$^{1}/_{8}$ t salt.

Chill and stir freeze.

yield: about 1 quart

REGULAR TOFU ICE CREAM

Soy milk is added here to lighten texture. When using firm or extra-firm tofu, increase soy milk proportionately. Use the same flavorings as for soft tofu ice cream or consult Appendix A, "Mix-ins," for ideas.

Blend smooth

2 C regular tofu
  (1#)
$^{2}/_{3}$ C honey
$^{1}/_{2}$ C soy milk
$^{1}/_{2}$ C vegetable oil
1 T vanilla
$^{1}/_{8}$ t salt.

Chill and stir freeze.

yield: about 1 quart

TOFRUITY

Strongly flavored fruits such as strawberries, raspberries, and crushed pineapple generally work best in tofu ice cream, but feel free to try apricot, cranberry, grapefruit, or any of your other favorites. For extra fruit flavor, substitute orange, pineapple, or other fruit juice for soy milk.

Blend until smooth

1$^{1}/_{3}$ C soft tofu
  ($^{2}/_{3}$#)
1$^{1}/_{3}$ C fruit purée
$^{2}/_{3}$ C soy milk
1 C sugar
$^{1}/_{3}$ C oil
1 T lemon juice
$^{1}/_{4}$ t salt.

Chill and stir freeze.

yield: about 1 quart

CREAMY BANANA HONEY TOFU ICE CREAM

Banana honey is one of the most popular flavors in homemade tofu ice cream. This and the following recipe are offered to demonstrate two different ways of making it. Try both and decide which you like best. The principles demonstrated here hold true for any flavor.

Whirl in blender	**1 C tofu ($^1/_2$#)** **1 C soy milk** **$^2/_3$ C honey** **$^1/_3$ C oil** **$^1/_2$ T vanilla** **$^1/_8$ t salt.**
Chill.	
Mash and add	**3 medium bananas.**
Stir freeze.	

yield: about 1 quart

SMOOTH BANANA HONEY TOFU ICE CREAM

If you choose not to add oil, you may prefer this recipe, which uses gelatin to enhance body. Vary this, or the preceding recipe, by stirring in $^1/_2$ C chopped walnuts, pecans, or toasted almonds for *banana honey nut* tofu ice cream. Or make *banana honey coconut* by adding $^1/_2$ C shredded coconut.

In small saucepan, soften	**1 t plain gelatin**
in	**1 C soy milk.**
Heat until gelatin dissolves.	
Whirl in blender with	**1 C tofu ($^1/_2$#)** **$^2/_3$ C honey** **$^1/_8$ t salt.**
Chill.	
Mash and add	**3 medium bananas** **$^1/_2$ T vanilla.**
Stir freeze.	

yield: about 1 quart

TOFU SHERBET

Use your imagination when combining fruits and juices in this delightful sherbet. To get you started, try strawberries with orange juice, puréed and strained raspberries with red currant or cranberry juice, peaches with apricot nectar, or pineapple with coconut milk. If you wish, substitute ½ C honey for the sugar.

Whirl in blender

1 C tofu (½#)
1 C soy milk
1 C fruit purée
⅔ C sugar
⅓ C fruit juice
2 T oil
1 T lemon juice
⅛ t salt.

Chill and stir freeze.

yield: about 1 quart

Soy Sundaes

Not only can you make ice cream from soy, you can make entire soy sundaes and banana splits, complete with gobs of gooey caramel or fudge toppings, heaped with commercial nondairy whipped cream or homemade whipped tofu cream, and lots of chopped roasted soy nuts sprinkled on top.

Let's start with the nuts. Crunchy, roasted soy nuts look a lot like salted peanuts and have a pleasant, decidedly nutty flavor. They're delicious chopped and sprinkled on any scoop of ice cream, soy or not. You can buy them at natural food outlets or roast your own.

First, soak whole dried beans overnight to render them digestible. Drain well and spread one-layer deep on a well-oiled baking sheet. Roast in the oven at 350° F (177° C), stirring often, until nicely browned. Salt to taste. Store soy nuts in an airtight container to keep them crisp.

HOT HONEY FUDGE SUNDAE SAUCE

Convert sundae sauces from Chapter 24 into nondairy toppings by substituting soy milk for milk, soy milk concentrate for evaporated milk or cream, and margarine for butter. Or try any of the following three sundae sauces. This one, which can be made with either carob or cocoa powder, is thick and fudgy.

In small saucepan, combine

3 T margarine
6 T honey.

Remove from heat and add

6 T cocoa powder.

Stir in

6 T soy milk.

Serve warm.

yield: about 1 cup

CAROB SUNDAE SAUCE

This sauce is good cold or warm. For delicious *malted chocolate* sundae sauce, substitute cocoa for carob and barley malt syrup for corn syrup.

In small saucepan, combine	**1 C sugar**
	¼ C carob powder
	pinch salt.
Stir in	**½ C soy milk.**
Add and bring to boil	**2 t corn syrup.**
Remove from heat and stir in	**1 T margarine.**
Cool.	
Beat in	**2 t vanilla.**

yield: about 1 cup

CARAMEL NUT SUNDAE SAUCE

Walnuts, pecans, or roasted soy nuts add crunch to this caramel sauce. Serve it warm or cooled, topped with a generous gob of whipped tofu cream.

In small saucepan, combine	**¾ C brown sugar**
	2 T corn syrup
	2 T soy milk
	pinch salt.
Bring to boil.	
Remove from heat and add	**2 T soy milk.**
Beat smooth and stir in	**¼ C chopped nuts.**

yield: about 1 cup

WHIPPED TOFU CREAM

Serve this nondairy whipped cream plain, or flavor it with 2 T cocoa or carob powder, 2 t instant coffee, or $^1/_8$ t orange or lemon extract. Kids love to snack on whipped tofu cream ice pops, frozen according to the directions in Chapter 1, "Still Freezing."

Whirl in blender — $^3/_4$ **C tofu** ($^1/_3$**#**).

With blender running, drizzle in — **1$^1/_2$ T oil.**

Add — **3 T sugar**
1 t vanilla
$^1/_8$ **t salt.**

If mixture stops turning
in blender, add up to — **1$^1/_2$ T soy milk.**

Chill.

Whip and serve.

yield: about 1 cup

Part Two: Perfect It

The more ice cream you make, the more you'll look for that one perfect recipe. But clearly, each of us has a different idea of what constitutes perfection. One of the nicest things about making your own ice cream is that you can alter its characteristics to suit yourself.

Ice cream is a complex combination of physical properties that are not yet thoroughly understood. Some ingredients are in true solution, others remain in suspension, still others are in coarse dispersion. This, plus the process of crystal development during freezing, makes ice cream a fun and fascinating thing to study.

You don't have to be a science whiz to satisfy your sweet tooth. But if you want to go beyond someone else's idea of perfection and make ice cream that represents your own ideal, you must recognize the factors that determine its quality. The kinds of ingredients you use, the way you put them together, and the influence your equipment has on the outcome are all significant and interrelated factors. These technical details, in simplified form, are discussed in the following section, which is designed to take the mystery out of ice cream making, but not the magic.

Here you'll find guidelines for selecting and handling ingredients to make exactly the texture and flavor you like best. You'll learn how ingredients interact with one another so you can better balance flavors or invent new ones of your own. You'll discover how to modify freezing techniques to adjust ice cream texture, and how to preserve that texture through proper storage.

Finally, these chapters will help you broaden your ice cream knowledge to become a true connoisseur, ready to evaluate your creations like a pro or show them off at ice cream tastings.

11

The Cream in Ice Cream

At least ninety-five percent of all frozen treats contain milk or other dairy products, using up some twenty percent of the nation's milk supply. Perfecting existing recipes or devising new ones requires understanding the role of dairy products, which can be divided into three main groups:

— Whole and skim milk as sources of liquid bulk
— Condensed, evaporated, and powdered milk as sources of nonfat milk solids
— Cream and butter as sources of fat

The dairy industry standardizes all its products, so you can count on consistent results from those you find at the grocery store. However, at their source, dairy products vary somewhat in composition. If you use home-produced milk and cream, don't be surprised if your recipes turn out slightly different each time.

Milk

On average, whole milk contains about eighty-seven percent water. The remainder consists of proteins, lactose (milk sugar), vitamins, minerals, trace minerals, and fat. The nonwater portions, as distinct from the water portion, are called "solids." Solids are further broken down into fat and nonfat solids. Industry, with its penchant for convoluted language, calls the latter "milk-solids-not-fat."

Technically speaking, the fat solids should be called "milkfat" until made into butter. Then they become "butterfat." For practical purposes, the two are one and the same. Whole milk contains about four percent milkfat and nine percent nonfat solids. Skim milk contains only a fraction of the fat found in whole milk. The primary role of whole or skim milk is to provide enough bulk for a recipe to yield the right amount. Their secondary function is to contribute milk solids.

The more milk a recipe calls for, the snowier or icier will be the result. Examples are sherbet and ice milk. Recipes calling for less milk and more cream produce smoother, more velvety ice cream, with superpremium or gourmet ice cream at the top of the list.

COMPOSITION OF SOLIDS IN VARIOUS DAIRY PRODUCTS			
	Fat	**Nonfat Milk Solids**	**Total Solids**
Milk, whole	4.00%	8.79%	12.79%
Milk, skim	0.00	8.60	8.60
Milk, powdered	.00	97.00	97.00
Milk, condensed	8.00	23.00	73.00
Milk, evaporated	8.00	20.00	28.00
Cream, light	18.00	7.31	25.31
Cream, whipping	30.00	6.24	36.24
Cream, heavy	40.00	5.35	45.35
Butter, unsalted	82.50	0.50	83.00

Adapted from: W. W. Arbuckle, *Ice Cream*, AVI Publishing Company, Inc., Westport, CT, 1986.

Nonfat Milk Solids

When all the fat and water are removed from whole milk, only nonfat solids remain. Concentrated sources are powdered, evaporated, and condensed milk. Any of these can be used to reduce the richness of ice cream yet preserve its smoothness, while avoiding snowy or flaky texture.

The lactose contributed by nonfat solids increases the sweetness of a mix, letting you cut back a little on other sweeteners. The minerals add a slight saltiness that rounds out ice cream flavor. Milk proteins improve whipping and contribute to smooth texture. On the whole, nonfat milk solids increase nutritional value as well as promote smoother texture and firmer body.

NONFAT MILK SOLIDS	
Protein	36.7%
Lactose	55.5%
Minerals	7.8%

Nonfat Dry Milk

Nonfat dry milk, commonly known as "powdered milk," is the most concentrated form of nonfat milk solids. It's made from pasteurized skim milk, air dried to remove ninety-five percent of the moisture. Although whole dry milk is used in commercial ice cream, only the nonfat variety is widely available for home use.

Good quality powdered milk has a fresh, sweet taste. Never should it be yellowish, lumpy or caked, or fail to dissolve properly. The fresher the powder, the better the flavor it will impart to ice cream. Stored too long, milk powder absorbs moisture from the air, making it taste stale, turn lumpy, and become difficult to dissolve.

Whenever you open a new box, pour the milk powder into an airtight container or wrap and seal it in plastic bags. Store it in a cool, dry place. For best ice cream flavor, reconstitute the milk at least two hours before using it, or age your mixture after blending the milk powder with other ingredients.

Powdered milk is relatively high in calcium, offering an inexpensive and painless way to increase your dietary intake of this necessary mineral. Simply add a tablespoon or two of milk powder to any ice cream recipe. Each tablespoon adds fifty-two milligrams of calcium, but only fifteen calories.

Evaporated Milk

Evaporated milk, either whole or light (skim), has had about half its water removed. Evaporated milk comes in cans of two sizes—five ounces, equal to a little less than two-thirds of a cup, and twelve ounces, equal to one and one-half cups.

Evaporated whole milk has approximately the same consistency as light cream but only half the calories. It's often used in diet ice cream and frozen yogurt, adding extra solids to improve texture without increasing saturated fat and calories. To lighten the texture of still-frozen ice creams, chill evaporated milk in the freezer for fifteen minutes and whip it like cream. There's no point in whipping evaporated milk if you're stir freezing—the dasher beats the air right back out.

Evaporated milk gets its strong caramelized flavor while being sterilized in the can. Use this characteristic taste to enhance flavorings like butterscotch, caramel, coffee, and chocolate, or mask it with heftier flavorings like peppermint and lemon. Evaporated milk overwhelms more delicate flavors, but you can tone it down by combining it with an equal portion of powdered milk, diluted with only half the usual amount of water.

Avoid evaporated milk that's overly brown, a sign that it was sterilized at too high a temperature, or any that has turned yellow, an indication of old age. Avoid, too, lesser-quality brands that taste bitter or burnt.

Condensed Milk

Condensed milk is sweetened whole milk with its water reduced sixty percent. It comes in 14.5-ounce cans (about one and one-third cup), containing the equivalent of two and one-half cups of milk plus one-half cup of sugar. Condensed milk is widely used in the ice cream industry, which has access to more versions than are available for home use, including whole or skim, sweetened or nonsweetened.

Like evaporated milk, condensed milk whips well and tastes a bit like caramel. By some accounts, it's the best thing that ever happened to ice cream.

Balance

For successful ice cream, you need to strike a delicate balance between nonfat solids and milkfat. The less cream you use, the more nonfat solids you can add. But there's a limit—too many nonfat solids cause ice cream to become heavy or pasty. They may also result in lactose crystallization, making the ice cream feel gritty or sandy in your mouth. At the other end of the scale, the more cream you use, the fewer nonfat solids you need. There's a limit here, too—ice cream that's very high in fat may feel unpleasantly buttery in your mouth.

Many people prefer high-solids, low-fat ice cream, which is slightly chewy, less rich, and melts less smoothly than other ice creams. Historically, this kind of ice cream has been a favorite in the western states. It is also preferred where fresh milk and cream are scarce, such as remote portions of Alaska. Southerners similarly favor ice cream at the lower end of the milkfat scale, but without the extra solids. New Englanders prefer extra rich ice cream. The gourmet ice cream frenzy of the 1980s simply followed this trend to its extreme.

Cream

For the true connoisseur, cream is the most important ingredient in ice cream. Cream contributes mellow richness and smooth texture that's difficult to get from any other source. It imparts a subtle flavor of its own and is responsible for carrying other flavorings. It increases melting resistance and improves stability, reducing the need for additional stabilizers.

Cream consists primarily of milkfat. Because it is lighter than water, it naturally rises to the top of milk, a process called "creaming out." In the days when milkmen still delivered, kids raced each other to the back door on cold winter mornings, hoping the cream that had risen into the neck of the bottle had frozen and popped up like a cork, creating ice cream in its purest form.

To prevent this creaming out, whole milk is now homogenized to break up fat particles and keep them in suspension. Skim milk is obtained by pumping whole milk through a centrifugal separator, which spurts milkfat out one spout and defatted milk out another. Since milkfat solidifies at temperatures below 92° F (33° C), in small backyard dairies, fresh milk is simply chilled until the cream rises to the surface to be skimmed off with a slotted ladle.

Cream is essentially milkfat combined with some milk. It is classified according to its percentage of milkfat, ranging from half and half containing no less than 10.5 percent milkfat, to heavy cream with 40 percent or more. In each category, commercial dairies usually include only the minimum milkfat required by law, which varies from state to state. So it pays to read labels and compare brands.

Knowing the milkfat content of the dairy products you use lets you maintain consistency as you experiment with different flavors. For example, if your vanilla ice cream contains three cups of whole milk at 3.5 percent fat and one cup of cream at 30 percent, your ice cream will be about 10 percent fat (3 times 3.5 plus 1 times 30, divided by 4). If you wish to maintain similar richness in ice cream flavored with one cup of strawberries (zero fat), you'll need one cup of milk and two cups of 18 percent cream (1 times 0 plus 1 times 3.5 plus 2 times 18, divided by 4).

MILKFAT RANGES*		
	Milkfat	
Dairy Product	**at least** **%**	**less than** **%**
Milk, nonfat dry	—	1
Milk, skim	—	0.1
Milk, low-fat	0.5	2
Milk, whole	3.25	—
Evaporated, whole	7.9	—
Evaporated, light	—	0.5
Cream, half and half	10.5	18
Cream, sour	18	—
Cream, light (coffee cream) (table cream)	18	30
Cream, whipping (light whipping)	30	36
Cream, heavy (heavy whipping)	36	—
*According to Code of Federal Regulations. Some states have higher standards.		

Too Much of a Good Thing

In ice cream, milkfat is the ingredient that varies most, ranging from ten to twenty-four percent, with twelve about average. Gourmet or superpremium is highest in fat, accounting for its characteristic denseness. All that fat inhibits whipping, allowing the introduction of little air during freezing. High fat in a homemade mix makes it less stable. Occasionally the milkfat will start churning into butterfat before freezing is complete, causing texture to be disrupted by unpleasant lumps of butter.

Commercially made vanilla ice cream often contains more cream than other flavors of the same brand. Manufacturers make up for the extra cost of some flavorings by reducing milkfat to keep all flavors the same price. In homemade ice cream, calories tend to be more important than cost. The more cream an ice cream contains, the more caloric it becomes. Luckily, creamy ice cream is also more satisfying, so you can be happy with a smaller portion.

At the same time, the more cream an ice cream contains, the less nutritionally balanced it is, with more energy from fat and sugar and less protein from nonfat solids. But fat carries flavor, so richer ice creams invariably taste better. Except for patients temporarily dependent on ice cream for nutrition, most of us go for flavor, food value be hanged.

Whipping

Some recipes call for whipping the cream before folding it into the mix. This step is essential for still-frozen ice creams, and it helps lighten the texture of stir-frozen ones in the high fat range. If you're fortunate enough to produce fresh cream at home, you'll get better results if you let it age in the refrigerator for at least a day before whipping it.

You can whip cream with a rotary beater or, if you have a strong wrist, a wire whisk. With an electric beater, you run the risk of churning the cream into butter. It helps to first chill the bowl, beaters, and cream for at least two hours, especially on hot days when cream churns more readily.

If you do use an electric beater, start on medium and switch to low as soon as the cream starts to thicken. The cream is whipped if it holds soft peaks when the beater is lifted out, but the cream still has a glossy sheen. If the sheen is lost, you've gone too far. You can save the day by whipping in two tablespoons of light cream or evaporated milk per cup liquid cream.

Properly whipped heavy cream should double in volume, one cup whipping into about two cups. After whipping, the cream will keep in the refrigerator up to two hours. To keep it from going flat in an ice cream mix, fold it in just before freezing.

Freezing Cream

Those who produce their own milk in small backyard dairies often find it convenient to freeze fresh cream until they've saved enough to make a big batch of ice cream. To prevent off flavors from developing, only pasteurized cream should be stored. Even so, frozen cream is never quite as tasty as fresh cream, although the slight sacrifice in flavor is not an unreasonable compromise.

Freezing destroys the normal emulsion of milkfat, as evidenced by the clear, buttery oil that sometimes floats to the surface. To prevent this, as well as to preserve flavor, add granulated sugar at the rate of ten percent by weight or about one and one-half tablespoons per cup of cream. Remember to deduct this added sugar from the amount specified in the ice cream recipe.

Frozen cream keeps well at $-10°$ F ($-23°$ C) for up to six months. Thaw it rapidly, crushing frozen lumps to hasten the process. To perk up flavor, combine two parts fresh cream per three parts frozen cream. Since freezing and thawing cream, then refreezing it in ice cream, causes some loss in quality, it's best to store surplus cream as ice cream right from the start.

Cream Alternatives

The best ice cream is made from fresh, high quality cream, but evaporated milk and unsalted butter are often used as substitutes, primarily because they keep so well. Butter is nothing more than concentrated milkfat molded into a convenient shape. But butter doesn't have quite the same desirable freezing properties since it lacks the emulsifier, lecithin, that occurs naturally in cream. This can be overcome by adding egg yolks or a small amount of lecithin to the ice cream mix. (For more on this, see Chapter 13, "Emulsifiers and Stabilizers.")

You don't necessarily have to use another form of milkfat as a substitute for cream. An alternative now used in the ice cream industry, but not yet available for home use, is a low-calorie fat substitute derived from the protein of milk and egg whites. Until it comes on the market, you can imitate milkfat's creamy richness with any kind of oil. Vegetable oils are commonly used by those who shun saturated fats and by those who prefer nondairy ice creams. Frozen nondairy creamer also makes a reasonable cream substitute. Read more about these and other alternatives in Chapter 8, "Ice Cream for Restrictive Diets," and Chapter 10, "Soy Ice Cream."

| SUBSTITUTING UNSALTED BUTTER AND MILK FOR CREAM ||
This	Equals
$^7/_8$ C milk + 3 T butter	1 C light cream
$^3/_4$ C milk + $^1/_3$ C butter	1 C heavy cream

Dairy Flavor

The delicate flavor of dairy products is important to quality ice cream. Prove this to yourself by freezing a batch made only from four cups of light cream combined with one-half cup of sugar. Serve it fresh from the ice cream maker. Savor its pleasing dairy taste and keep it in mind as you move on to more exotic but nonetheless complementary flavors.

12

How Sweet It Is

After cream, sweeteners are the second most important ingredient in ice cream. Sugar contributes more than sweetness. It supplies a source of energy, intensifies delicate flavors, and improves texture by increasing total solids.

Boosting the solids in a mix lowers its freezing point. Each five percent increase in sugar, for example, reduces the freezing point 1° F (0.56° C). Ice cream with a lower freezing point takes longer to freeze, giving the dasher more time to whip it smooth. It also remains more scoopable, even when hardened.

A nonsweetened mix freezes so fast that the dasher gets trapped against the canister wall, unable to turn. The resulting ice cream, if you could call it that, tastes flat and becomes very hard when frozen completely.

Too much sugar, on the other hand, overwhelms flavor, actually decreasing the intensity of strong flavorings like coffee and chocolate. Excessive sugar can lower the freezing point so much that the mix never freezes quite solid but remains slushy and sticky.

The amount of sweetening needed in sherbets and ices depends only partly on the relative sweetness of the fruit or juices used. Because these freezes contain no fat and few solids, they rely on sugar for their fine texture. Like ice creams, sherbets and ices made with too much sugar are soft and syrupy. Too little sugar makes them hard, crumbly, or overly coarse.

Just how sweet ice cream or any other freeze should be is partly dictated by habit, and preferences vary from one region to the next. Southerners and Easterners like ice cream sweeter than do Midwesterners and Westerners. Most children and young adults prefer sweeter ice creams, a trend that reverses as they grow older. Seasonally, we all favor less sweet ice cream when the weather turns warm. If you gradually reduce the amount of sweetener you used in homemade ice cream, you'll find that most commercial varieties begin tasting excessively sweet.

How Much Is Enough

Educating your palate to enjoy minimum sweetness improves your appreciation of the more subtle ice cream flavors. Exactly how much sweetening is enough depends on the flavorings you use and on the type of mix you're freezing. Strong flavors usually require a bit more sugar than milder ones. Nondairy freezes like ices and soy based ice creams need more than those containing dairy products. Since different kinds of sweetener have different intensities, combining two or more often increases the perception of sweetness, allowing the total amount to be reduced.

Despite published charts comparing various sweeteners, including the one in this chapter, no objective test has yet been devised to measure sweetness. You can do your own subjective evaluations using the tea test. Brew up a pot of tea and pour equal amounts into two cups. Sweeten one to taste with a measured amount of table sugar. Into the second cup, measure the sweetener you wish to evaluate, adding as much as it takes to make the tea taste as sweet as the first cup. To avoid confusing your taste buds, taste the tea only with the tip of your tongue, where your sweetness sensors are. Use in ice cream the same relative amount of the second sweetener you needed to sweeten the tea to taste.

Granulated Sugar

Most ice cream makers prefer plain old table sugar, or sucrose, because it produces the most familiar texture and flavor. Sucrose is derived from beets or from sugar cane, the two sugars being identical in composition. Both are nearly one-hundred percent total solids.

Unless sugar contributes most of the solids, as it does in an ice, you can use the minimum amount that tastes sweet enough to you. A good starting place is one-half cup sugar, or its equivalent, per quart ice cream, two-thirds cup per quart sherbet, frozen yogurt, or soy ice cream, and three-quarters to one cup per quart ice or sorbetti. Remember, a mix should always taste too sweet, since apparent sweetness is reduced by freezing.

Sugar is usually the sole source of sweetening in ice cream. In ices and sherbets it is often combined with a little honey, corn sugar, corn syrup, or some form of stabilizer to prevent crystallization on the surface during storage.

Brown and Maple Sugar

Brown sugar comes from sugar cane and is nearly as sweet as granulated sugar. Due to its characteristic strong flavor, it is rarely used for ice creams except in butterscotch flavors and in toppings. When measuring, pack light or dark brown sugar firmly into the cup to eliminate air pockets.

Maple sugar, made by boiling down sap collected from maple trees, contains about eighty-six percent sucrose as well as traces of other sweeteners. Use it for specialty flavors like maple nut and blueberry maple ice cream. Since maple sugar is quite solid and dissolves very slowly, speed things along by grating it before combining it with other ingredients. Maple flavoring, used in combination with granulated sugar, is a poor but common substitute.

Corn Sugar

Occasionally a recipe calls for refined corn sugar, or dextrose, which is derived by heating corn starch in the presence of acid. It is less sweet than granulated sugar, less readily soluble, and crystallizes more slowly. It is available at any beer-making supply outlet.

Corn sugar is used primarily to inhibit sugary crystallization on the surface of stored sherbets and ices and to prevent crumbliness in hardened, super-rich gourmet ice creams. It also depresses the freezing point, keeping ice cream soft and scoopable, even after hardening. To prevent excessive softness, use no more than one part corn sugar per three parts granulated sugar.

Honey

Honey contains some twenty-five different sugars including fructose, sucrose and dextrose. It is used as both a sweetener and a flavoring. It creates smooth texture but the ice cream takes longer to freeze. Use too much, and your ice cream will never harden properly.

Although honey isn't as sweet as granulated sugar, it is normally used in lesser amounts because it contributes its own strong flavor. You'll get good results by substituting two-thirds to three-quarters cup of honey for each cup of sugar, but you can use up to one and one-third cups, depending on personal taste. For more subtle flavor, replace only half the sugar. If the honey has begun to crystallize in the jar, heat the uncovered jar in a pan of warm water until the crystals dissolve.

Honey is classified according to its flavor, as determined by the predominating blossom from which it comes. In general, the lighter the color, the milder its flavor. Many ice cream makers favor alfalfa, clover, orange, and tupelo. Because honey imparts a delicious flavor of its own, it can be used without additional flavoring.

When you use it in combination with other flavorings, take care to avoid clashes. Many ice cream lovers feel that honey doesn't go at all well with coffee or vanilla, for example. Almond extract, on the other hand, brings out honey's more delicate undertones. Honey also complements the snappy tartness of lemon to create a special favorite among frozen yogurt fans.

COMPOSITION OF HONEY	
Invert sugar (glucose & fructose)	74.5%
Moisture	17.5%
Sucrose	02.0%
Dextrin	02.0%
Miscellaneous*	03.8%
*Includes organic acids and traces of vitamins and minerals.	

Syrups

Except in very rich ice creams or sorbets containing mostly fruit purée, syrups do not make good primary sweeteners because they contribute too much extra moisture. Light corn syrup, used in conjunction with sugar, gives smoother texture and firmer body to low-solids, low-fat freezes such as diet ice cream, ice milk, and sherbet. A small amount prevents sugar separation in ices and sherbets to be stored before serving. Otherwise, corn syrup is usually reserved for hot fudge and other chewy sundae toppings (Chapter 24).

Marshmallow, which is essentially corn syrup with gelatin added to absorb excess moisture, contributes a nougat-like quality to ice creams flavored with bits of candy or candied fruit. For each quart of ice cream, warm one cup of the milk or cream called for in the recipe, blend in a seven ounce jar of marshmallow, and omit the recipe's sugar. For any flavor, up to a dozen and a half marshmallows melted into a quart of mix enhances body.

Maple syrup is so delicately flavored, contains so little sweetening, and has so much moisture that it makes a better topping than a sweetener. Since every rule needs exceptions, here's one: ice made with one cup maple syrup per three cups puréed blueberries or soft-cooked apples. Here's another: Philadelphia ice cream made from one and one-half cups maple syrup per two and one-half cups heavy cream. Most other freezes are more successful when maple sugar or its less subtle substitute, maple flavoring, is used.

Rice Syrup

Rice syrup was introduced from Japan in the early 1970s and is now sold by most natural food stores and beer-making suppliers. It contains three percent glucose, forty-five percent maltose, and fifty percent complex carbohydrates. It is a favorite with natural food buffs and with those who watch their blood sugar levels, since it is believed to raise blood sugar more gradually than either sugar or honey. It's expected to become more widely accepted when a granulated version comes out.

Rice syrup is made from cooked rice combined with dried sprouted barley, or malt, which contributes enzymes that convert rice starches into sugars. The mixture is then strained and cooked to the desired consistency, which varies from brand to brand. Traditional (imported) Japanese rice syrup, called rice malt syrup, is more expensive and has a stronger, earthier flavor than the milder, sweeter American kind.

Straight barley malt syrup is stronger in flavor than any rice syrup, but is virtually interchangeable with it. Both barley malt and rice syrup tend to ferment in the jar. If you see bubbles moving to the surface, take a taste before adding it to ice cream, to avoid an off flavor.

Just as rice syrup varies in consistency from one brand to another, it also varies in sweetness. Most brands can be substituted for sugar, one to one. Since it makes ice cream denser and less sweet, rice syrup is best used in combination with another form of sugar, at least until a granulated version becomes available. Ice cream sweetened with rice syrup is very smooth and has a somewhat malty taste that makes a terrific foundation for nut flavors.

Fructose

Fructose, also called levulose, is a natural sweetener derived from fruit and other plants, and from enzyme conversion of corn starch. It is available in granular form at most grocery and natural food stores. An alternative source of fructose is nonsweetened apple juice concentrate, which can be substituted for sugar at the rate of one-half cup per cup sugar. Ice cream sweetened with fructose tastes a touch bland compared to ice cream sweetened with granulated sugar.

Although it has the same number of calories as table sugar (eighteen per teaspoon), pure fructose is one-hundred fifty times sweeter. The amount needed for equivalent sweetness therefore contains only two-thirds the calories. Unlike table sugar, fructose does not require insulin to metabolize and so may be used with caution by some diabetics.

Non-Nutritive Sweeteners

Compared to sweeteners that contribute calories as well as sweetness, non-nutritive sweeteners do not wreak havoc with your waistline because they contain few if any calories. In addition, they do not upset the body's glucose-insulin balance, making them of particular importance to diabetics.

Because they are so sweet, they're used in such small amounts that they don't contribute their fair share of solids to an ice cream mix. The result is therefore similar in texture to nonsweetened ice cream, and is best soft-served straight from the ice cream maker.

Saccharin, a petroleum product, was the first non-nutritive sweetener used commercially. It leaves a bitter aftertaste, especially when it's been heated. Although studies indicate it may cause cancer, it remains on the market due to pressure from the diabetic lobby.

Aspartame, marketed under the trade name NutraSweet, is a synthetic protein compound containing two amino acids (L-aspartic and L-phenylalanine) not normally found together in nature. It technically contains calories but is so sweet that it's essentially noncaloric in the amounts normally used. Aspartame doesn't have the unpleasant aftertaste of saccharin, but it breaks down and loses its sweetness when heated. Despite evidence that it may be associated with behavioral problems and brain damage, the FDA has described aspartame as one of the safest food additives we'll ever see.

Cyclamate, an organic compound that increases in sweetness when heated and has no bitter aftertaste, is banned in the United States due to evidence that it may cause cancer. It is still available in many other countries, and reconsideration of the ban has been strongly urged here.

New on the non-nutritive sweetener scene are biospherics, indigestible sugars occurring naturally in flaxseed gum, red algae, and mountain ash berries. Biospherics are nearly as sweet as sucrose, equally bulky and have the advantage that they are not damaged by heat.

New studies are constantly popping up regarding alternative sweeteners. Many have been linked with cancer, behavioral changes, and brain damage, causing the American Academy of Pediatricians to question their safety for pregnant women and young children. Since their status keeps changing, experts advise using noncaloric sweeteners only according to a doctor's directions.

The manufacturer's directions should also be scrupulously followed. Information on how much non-nutritive sweetener should be used to replace the amount of sugar in a given recipe can be found on the label of each brand. The label should also tell you if the sweetener can be added while a mix is being heated or if it shouldn't be added until after the mix has cooled. Adjust your recipes accordingly.

SWEETENING EFFECTS COMPARED TO TABLE SUGAR	
Sweetener	**Sweetening Effect (%)**
Saccharin	30,000
Aspartame	18,000
Cyclamate	3,000
Fructose	150
Granulated sugar (sucrose)	100
Maple sugar	98
Brown sugar	96
Corn sugar (dextrose)	82
Corn sugar (glucose)	80
Honey (dextrose, fructose, sucrose)	75
Maple syrup	59
Corn syrup (dextrose & maltose)	54
Rice syrup (maltose, glucose)	50
Galactose	32
Maltose	32
Lactose	20

Salt

Salt, or sodium, increases perception of sweetness by rounding out overall flavor. It is an important part of our diets, but most of us consume far more than our bodies need and are constantly being urged to cut back.

Since sodium is a natural constituent of milk—one cup of whole milk contains 120 milligrams—you needn't add salt to most ice creams, sherbets, or frozen yogurts. Exceptions, some feel, are frozen custards and nut ice creams. A little salt also helps bring out the flavor of vegetable sorbets and soy ice creams. In any case, never use so much that you can actually taste it.

13

Emulsifiers and Stabilizers

Emulsifiers and stabilizers suffer bad press because few people understand their true nature and purpose. An emulsifier is simply any ingredient that allows you to reduce the fat in an ice cream mix. It does so by blending two ingredients that don't naturally mix, bonding their molecular particles together and serving as a bridge between them. Emulsifiers improve whipping qualities, thereby increasing smoothness. Stabilizers perform a similar function and are also used as thickening agents to prevent separation or curdling. Stabilizers thus help preserve the texture, body or flavor of ice cream.

Eggs

If you've ever made mayonnaise, you already know how effective egg yolks are as an emulsifier, allowing oil and vinegar to combine readily while being whipped. Egg yolks do the same for the fat and water components of an ice cream mix. Egg yolks are not as strong emulsifying agents as the obscure substances with complicated names found in commercial ice creams, but they're more readily available for home use.

Milk contains tiny particles of fat suspended in liquid, making it a natural emulsion. When you beat in cream and an additional emulsifying ingredient such as eggs, the milkfat in the cream is broken up into evenly distributed droplets, resulting in smoother texture. This is the idea behind American or country ice cream, which contains relatively small amounts of cream, highly emulsified to create the impression of greater richness.

Besides making smoother textured ice cream with firmer body, eggs increase nutritional value and help blend the flavors of other ingredients. They help in whipping up low-solids mixes and those containing fat from sources other than cream. Some people don't care to use eggs, claiming they can detect eggy flavor in ice cream and a strong meringue taste in sherbet and spoom. It is true that too many eggs, or combining them with the wrong ingredients, can lead to an undesirable strong flavor or cause ice cream to melt into an uncharacteristic foamy mess.

Ice creams made with whole eggs rely on the yolks to make up for the fat lost by using less rich cream and on the whites to lighten body. Add only one egg at a time and carefully beat it in before adding the next. When the eggs are beaten before being added, warm them to room temperature and they'll whip up fluffier.

If just the yolks are called for, use the leftover whites in an airy spoom (Chapter 3), a festive baked Alaska (Chapter 30), or meringue cups (Chapter 22) to serve your frozen creations in. If you need only the whites, use the yolks to make custard-based ice cream (Chapter 6) or frozen yogurt (Chapter 7). Refrigerate separated whites or yolks in tightly covered containers and use them within four days. Yolks keep best if you cover them with cold water. When you're ready to use them, pour the water off.

Egg whites alone don't do much for most ice creams, but for sherbets, sorbets, frozen yogurts, and diet ice creams they lighten texture if you whip them just to the soft peak stage, then fold them in. Soft peaks curl when you lift out the beater; stiff peaks stand straight up when the beater is removed. Overbeaten whites, which resemble bunched-up clouds, tend to separate out.

Caution

Despite the usefulness of eggs in ice cream, adding them raw offers the potential for salmonella infection. Salmonella occurs primarily when cracked-shell eggs are used or when a mix containing raw eggs is left too long at room temperature. Although freezing prevents the multiplication of bacteria and reduces the risk of salmonella in ice cream, commercial products never contain raw eggs. All commercial mixes are pasteurized. Heating a mix to 160° F (71° C) destroys any salmonella bacteria that might be present.

In the 1980s, a previously unknown and especially virulent form of salmonella was traced to raw eggs. Until the problem is under control, take the precaution of heating eggs in milk or cream according to the custard-making directions in Chapter 6. Alternatively, use a pasteurized egg substitute such as Egg Beaters. And, until it's ascertained that the bacteria are lodged in the yolks and not in the whites (as is suspected) avoid soft meringues as well as spooms and other freezes containing uncooked whites. Alternatively, use pasteurized egg white powder, sold as a cake-decorating ingredient (some mail-order sources are listed in Appendix C). For up-to-date information on the status of salmonella in eggs, call the USDA meat and poultry hotline, toll-free: 1-800-535-4555.

Even where eggs are safe when delivered to the store, they may be several weeks old by the time you bring them home. Therefore, eggs used in ice cream are best obtained fresh from the source.

Lecithin

Given the whipping properties of egg whites, surprisingly it's not the whites but the yolks that improve the whipping qualities of ice cream—by creating a permanent emulsion. Yolks are also responsible for stabilizing a mix and enriching its flavor.

While high-fat and chocolate ice creams benefit highly from these properties, ultra-rich French ice creams and Italian gelati would be nothing without egg yolks. These and other ice creams depend on yolks to create a finely dispersed and stable emulsion, made possible because yolks contain a relatively large amount of lecithin.

Lecithin is a natural emulsifier found in milk, eggs and some vegetables. Isolated lecithin, derived from soybeans and available at natural food shops, provides an alternative for those who choose not to use eggs. You need only one-quarter teaspoon per quart of mix to increase smoothness and stability. Too much lecithin wreaks havoc with texture and with flavor. To dissolve lecithin granules, combine them with milk or other liquid and beat for two minutes or whirl in a blender one minute.

An alternative to lecithin from egg yolks or soybeans is buttermilk, which contains more lecithin than whole milk and has a similar effect to egg yolk when used in ice cream. You may replace all or part of the milk in any recipe with buttermilk.

Most emulsifiers also serve as stabilizers, minimizing the need for additional stabilizing ingredients.

Stabilizers

The use of stabilizers in ice cream dates back to the eighteenth century, when many recipes called for the stabilizer arrowroot. Stabilizers soak up water like a sponge, preventing it from freezing into large crystals. They also reduce heat shock when ice cream is stored for any length of time, especially in a self-defrosting freezer. The importance of stabilizers to a particular recipe depends on how much water it contains.

High-fat and chocolate ice creams have little free water and therefore little need for stabilizing. Ice milk, diet ice cream, sherbet, and other freezes containing fewer solids have a higher proportion of water and so benefit from a stabilizer, which prevents the formation of large ice crystals and thereby increases smoothness, keeps sugar from separating out, and inhibits melting in warm weather. Most stabilizers double as thickening agents, contributing to firmer body.

Because milk, cream, and other dairy products contain natural stabilizers, ice creams in general benefit less from additional stabilizers than do ices and sherbets. The latter have a tendency toward crumbliness or settling out of sugary syrups, a phenomenon called "bleeding." When corn syrup or other sweeteners are added to sherbets and ices to prevent sugar crystals from forming on the surface, as described in the preceding chapter, these sweeteners double as stabilizers.

Stabilizers are used in such small quantities that they contribute little in the way of food value or flavor, but they indirectly influence flavor by improving texture. Using too much inhibits whipping, subdues delicate flavoring undertones, causes gumminess, and makes a freeze unnaturally retain its shape after melting.

Most stabilizers, including those with formidable names like agar-agar and carrageenan, are natural in origin. Some of the ones used commercially are chemically modified, leading to consumer prejudice against them. Stabilizers used in homemade recipes include such common ingredients as flour and gelatin.

Thickeners

Use flour, cornstarch, or arrowroot to stabilize and thicken ice creams containing fruit juices, percolated coffee, and other high-moisture flavorings. When the flavoring is acidic, such as lemon juice, add the acidic ingredient only after the mix has cooled. Stirring in high-acid ingredients while a mix is still warm may cause the stabilizer to lose its thickening effect.

Use flour at the rate of one tablespoon per quart. To prevent lumping, blend the flour with sugar before stirring it into a warming mix. Continue stirring and heating until the mix begins to thicken, then heat it three minutes more to smooth out the taste by ensuring that the flour is fully cooked. Alternatively, microwave the mix on high for three minutes.

Cornstarch is less likely than flour to lose its thickening ability when combined with acidic ingredients. It is the preferred thickening agent for those who are allergic to wheat. Use it at the rate of one-half tablespoon per quart. To prevent lumping, blend the cornstarch with sugar and dissolve both in cold liquid before adding it to a warming mix. Stir gently, bring the mix to the boiling point, and heat one minute longer. Or microwave on full power for five minutes. Don't overcook, or the cornstarch will lose its thickening ability. Thickening power may also be lost if the mix contains an excessive amount of sugar.

With either flour and cornstarch, use a double boiler to prevent scorching. Straining the mix before chilling it removes any lumps that may have formed.

Arrowroot, a popular ingredient in ice creams of the Victorian era and still widely used in England, remains virtually unknown to American cooks. It comes from the tubers of several different species of tropical plants and may be found in the spice section of larger grocery stores. A similar product sold in natural food stores is root starch derived from the kudzu vine.

Arrowroot does not have the same raw taste as flour and cornstarch, does not lump as readily, is easier to digest, and provides an alternative for those allergic to both wheat and corn. It thickens at a lower temperature and requires a shorter cooking time than cornstarch, making it ideal for use in mixes containing eggs, which curdle at the higher temperatures required to thicken flour and cornstarch.

Use arrowroot at the rate of one teaspoon per quart, blending it with sugar before stirring it into the mix. Tart fruit sorbets will be smoother in texture and have less tendency to crumble if you use arrowroot in combination with gelatin.

Gelatin

Plain gelatin is used as a stabilizer in ices and sherbets and to a lesser extent in ice creams. Some people object to its detectable flavor, others don't care for the way it puffs up texture. To minimize these problems, use just enough for a thin gel to form at room temperature. Usually one teaspoon per quart is plenty. Each quarter-ounce packet holds three teaspoons, or one tablespoon.

INGREDIENT RECAP		
Ingredient	**Advantages**	**Using too much**
Milkfat	increases richness smoothes texture improves body	hinders whipping increases calories high saturated fats
Nonfat milk solids	improve texture improve body increase overrun	causes sandiness tastes "cooked" may taste salty
Sweeteners	improve texture enhance flavor increase total solids	overpower flavor hinder whipping increase freezing time
Egg yolks	aid whipping smoother texture richer flavor	foamy melting eggy flavor cholesterol
Emulsifier	smoother texture stiffer body	undesirable texture affects flavor
Stabilizer	smoother texture better body	undesirable stiffness increases melting resistance
Total solids	smoother texture better body more nutrition less cold	heavy body reduces cooling ability

Based on W. W. Arbuckle, *Ice Cream*, AVI Publishing Company, Inc., Westport, Connecticut, 1986.

Adding gelatin directly to a warm mix may cause it to turn into a stringy mass. For this reason, recipes call for softening gelatin in a bit of cold liquid, which is then heated and stirred once or twice until the gelatin dissolves. Use either a small saucepan over low heat or a microwave set on high for one minute. Age a mix containing gelatin for at least four hours to allow its stabilizing properties to develop fully.

Although gelatin is of animal origin, vegetable imitations are available through natural food outlets. Agar-agar, for instance, is a popular mineral-rich vegetarian gelatin derived from seaweed. In general, vegetable gelatins dissolve less readily and are more likely to cause crumbliness.

An alternative to gelatin is powdered pectin, a carbohydrate from apples and citrus that is found in the home canning section of most grocery stores. For each quart of ice or sorbet mix, dissolve one teaspoon pectin in a little water or fruit juice and, stirring, bring it to a boil. Remove from heat and add the remaining fruit or juices. Stir two minutes until the pectin is completely dissolved and thoroughly mixed.

Many makers of ices prefer pectin because it lacks gelatin's flavor and high whipping qualities. To get the best of both, use one-half teaspoon of each.

Preservatives

Preservatives aren't necessary in commercial or homemade ice creams because freezing itself is a terrific preservative.

14

Unlimited Flavors

That famous grump Andy Rooney believes "ice cream was just as good when they only had three flavors: vanilla, chocolate, and strawberry." Yet one of the reasons for ice cream's universal appeal is precisely the terrific number of flavors it comes in.

Maryland ice cream maker Manuel Hendler was the first to expand beyond the Big Three in 1905. Compared with today's exotic flavors, the original three now seem rather quaint. The International Ice Cream Association once kept track of flavors, but stopped counting at 247. Baskin Robbins alone develops a new one every month and now has over six hundred. Nevertheless, Rooney's old stand-bys remain among today's top ten favorites, accounting for sixty-one percent of all frozen desserts consumed in the United States.

TOP TEN ICE CREAM FLAVOR FAVORITES	
Vanilla	29.0%
Chocolate	8.9%
Butter Pecan	5.3%
Strawberry	5.3%
Neapolitan	4.2%
Chocolate Chip	3.9%
French Vanilla	3.8%
Cookies 'n' Cream	3.6%
Vanilla Fudge	2.6%
All other	33.4%

Source: *The Latest Scoop*, International Ice Cream Association, Washington, DC, 1989.

Choices, Choices

The popularity of each flavor varies from one region to the next. Ginger, saffron, and various tea flavors are often featured in ethnic communities. Rocky road goes over big in the Midwest. Blueberry, coffee, Grape-Nuts, and maple are favored in New England and eastern Canada. Date, avocado, persimmon, and prune are frequent West Coast choices. Peanut and crushed candy are Southern favorites, while Texans love any flavor as long as it's pecan.

Even within regions there are distinct flavoring differences. The coffee ice cream you enjoy in New York, for example, is likely to be stronger than the same flavor served in Boston. Nationwide trends include blending bits of cookie or crushed candy into vanilla and, bucking a general drift away from alcohol consumption, spiking various flavors with liquor for such tempting treats as rum raisin, banana daiquiri, and eggnog ice cream.

Commercial manufacturers are necessarily restricted to producing only best-selling flavors, since flavoring is among the costliest ingredients. Flavoring choices for homemade ice creams, on the other hand, are limited only by imagination and personal taste.

Sources

The flavor of any ice cream results from the blend of ingredients, some of which (like sugar) make a significant contribution without having much flavor of their own. The most interesting flavors consist of a combination of two or more flavorings. Many new flavors are merely takeoffs on time-tested combinations.

It isn't always easy to tell what a new combination will taste like, especially since the flavor balance of a mix changes during aging and freezing. Dreaming up successful new flavors therefore requires a bit of intuition and a bit of experimentation. Even experienced ice cream makers don't always get palate-pleasing perfection the first time around.

In addition to various liquors and liqueurs, the main sources of ice cream flavorings are vanilla, chocolate, extracts, spices, fruits, and nuts. These can be divided into three groups, according to whether they are natural, artificial, or a combination of the two.

Most natural flavorings taste pleasant, even in fairly high concentrations. They consist of fruits, nuts, and the ground-up stems, roots, and bark that make up our various spices. Many extracts and oils are also naturally derived from fruits, nuts, leaves, and stems. These extracts and oils may be found in greater variety in pharmacies than in most grocery stores.

Artificial or synthetic flavorings began appearing as natural ones became more expensive. An artificial flavoring may or may not be chemically the same as the flavor it attempts to imitate. Too many times we're fooled by the smell, while the taste bears little resemblance to the real thing.

Although we differ in our choices, we all judge ice cream by its flavor, and most of us agree that natural flavorings taste best. Yet natural flavorings tend to be fairly delicate and easily damaged by careless handling.

Vanilla

Vanilla ice cream is more than three times as popular as the next runner-up. In no other food is the quality of this flavoring as important as it is in ice cream.

There are over fifty different species of vanilla orchid producing four- to twelve-inch long, bean-shaped pods, golden yellow when ripe but turning dark brown to black when dried. These pods were among the strange and wonderful things brought back by Hernando Cortez to Spain, where "vanilla" got its name from the Spanish word "vaina," meaning pod. Vanilla soon became prized as a powerful aphrodisiac. By the mid-sixteenth century, it was being enjoyed in all the royal courts of Europe. Ice cream-loving President Thomas Jefferson discovered vanilla in France while on a diplomatic visit and introduced it to the colonies.

Which of the fifty species produces the finest flavor is a matter for serious debate. For years the favorite has been *Vanilla planifolia*, native to the rain forests of southeastern Mexico and Central America, where it was highly prized by the Aztecs as a flavoring in chocolate. The same climbing perennial, commonly called "the orchid of commerce," is now grown in other tropical areas, where differences in climate result in differences in flavor. Most of the vanilla imported today is from Madagascar. Inferior varieties, including vanilla from Tahiti, are harsher in taste.

The exact taste of vanilla depends on species, where it is grown, and how it is cured. All of this may soon become moot—California researchers are experimenting with cellular reproduction under highly controlled laboratory conditions. Vanilla clones are expected to become commercially available by the mid-1990s.

Traditional vanilla ice cream, which connoisseurs still consider best, is delicately flavored with the tiny black seeds scraped from inside a vanilla pod. Philadelphians are suspicious of any other kind, but elsewhere only elite ice cream is shot through with telltale black specks.

Use a one and one-half- to three-inch piece of pod per quart, according to taste. Unlike extract, which evaporates if heated, the vanilla bean imparts its flavor best in a warming mix. Some ice cream makers don't strip away the seeds, preferring instead to rinse and freeze the expensive pod and reuse it several times more.

Vanilla Extract

Despite the superiority of the bean, most ice cream makers find it convenient to use vanilla as an extract. "Pure vanilla extract" is made by percolating finely chopped beans in a thirty-five percent solution of ethyl alcohol. As with coffee, the exact manner of percolation determines final flavor. "Pure vanilla flavor" is made much the same way, except that less than thirty-five percent alcohol, or propylene glycol, is used as a solvent.

How much vanilla extract you need depends on how strong you want the flavor to be and on the balance of other ingredients in the recipe. Add more to high-fat ice creams, to those containing less sweetener, and to vanilla ice creams rather than to flavors in which vanilla's role is to bring out other flavors.

As a rule of thumb, add two teaspoons per quart vanilla ice cream, one teaspoon per quart any other flavor, but one tablespoon per quart low-fat, low-sugar ice cream or ice milk. When a recipe calls for heating, add extract only after the mix has cooled so its volatile essence won't evaporate away.

Imitation Vanilla

Pure vanilla is fairly expensive, tempting people to seek cheaper alternatives. Don't fall for big bargain jars of so-called vanilla extract sold in Mexico. This cheap but dangerous flavoring is derived from the tonka bean, which smells and tastes remarkably like vanilla but is chemically quite different and is poisonous.

Another inexpensive alternative is artificial vanilla. During World War II, American cooks had to turn to this more available substitute. Due to its lower price, it is still being used, sometimes with a little real vanilla included to improve the taste.

The flavor of vanilla comes ultimately from the fragrant, white crystalline substance, vanillin, which develops when the bean is cured. Synthetic vanillin, derived from wood pulp or from oil of cloves, is chemically the same but lacks the other substances that naturally accompany true vanillin and contribute to its depth of flavor. Synthetic vanillin is considerably harsher, with an unpleasant aftertaste. Another disadvantage is that it has no set standard for strength, as does real vanilla. Yet, when reference is made to vanillin on the label of commercial ice cream, you can be certain it's the synthetic sort.

Chocolate

The second most popular ice cream flavor is chocolate, named after a variation of the Aztec word, "chocolatl." Chocolate comes from the almond-sized seeds of the evergreen *Theobroma cacao*, or "Food of the Gods," a tropical tree growing in Central and South America, Africa, and the East and West Indies. The best beans are from cultivated trees. Inferior ones are gathered from wild trees growing under less favorable climatic and soil conditions.

Cocoa beans vary considerably in quality, some being more bitter and having a stronger acidic bite than others. Most chocolate contains a blend of three distinct bean varieties, Criollo, Forastero, and Trinitario. Quite a complex process is required to turn these beans into chocolate. Exactly how it's done influences the quality of the resulting chocolate. Inferior products, which are usually cheaper, taste unnatural and bitter. The best way to judge the quality of any chocolate is to taste it in a cup of hot chocolate, using exactly the same amount of milk and sugar with each kind of chocolate or cocoa being compared.

Chocolate flavoring is not a reasonable alternative to chocolate, which it resembles in color only. Carob (or St. John's Bread) is sometimes considered a chocolate substitute, although it really holds its own as an entirely separate flavoring. It comes from the beans of the locust tree and is naturally sweet, containing up to forty-six percent sugar, so you don't need to add as much sugar as you do for chocolate. Carob is sold both raw and roasted, the latter being mellower and lighter in flavor. Both are favorites among fans of natural foods.

Chocolate Forms

The kind of chocolate you use determines the ultimate flavor of your ice cream as well as the mix of other ingredients you'll need for good balance. The foundation of all forms of chocolate is chocolate liquor, made from the nibs or meat of cocoa beans. The beans are roasted, their outer shells removed, and the nibs ground up until friction reduces them to a liquid. This chocolate liquor is fifty percent fat, or cocoa butter, which allows chocolate to turn fluid when heated.

Nonsweetened baking chocolate, or bitter chocolate, is simply chocolate liquor cooled in molds. If a little sugar is added before the liquor is molded, bittersweet chocolate is the result. If a lot of sugar is added, sweet cooking chocolate results.

Semisweet chocolate contains extra cocoa butter. Sweet dark chocolate has vanilla added. Milk chocolate is essentially sweet dark chocolate combined with milk solids. The very best chocolate for ice cream is nonsweetened chocolate containing only chocolate liquor.

When cocoa butter is extracted from chocolate liquor and combined with milk powder, sugar, and flavoring, the result is that delicately flavored treat known in Europe as "white chocolate." The United States government does not like us to call this confection "chocolate," claiming that chocolate must contain entire chocolate liquor. It is consequently packaged in this country as "white cocoa butter coating" and other similar circumlocutions. Because it contains extra milk solids, white chocolate must be stirred constantly during melting for good blending.

Many white chocolate aficionados feel the flavor comes out best when it is combined with buttermilk, sour cream or yogurt. Others like to flavor it with peppermint, although that seems a waste considering its naturally delicate taste. Mint goes much better with a fuller-bodied, darker chocolate. Since white chocolate has such gentle flavor, rather than being melted as a flavoring, it is much more successful grated into a bisque.

After the cocoa butter has been extracted from chocolate liquor, the remaining solids are ground into cocoa powder, the most highly concentrated form of chocolate flavoring. To prevent lumping when using cocoa, blend it with sugar before stirring in liquid ingredients. Pre-melted chocolate, measured into one-ounce packets, is cocoa that's been reconstituted with vegetable oil instead of cocoa butter. Although it is handy to use, it lacks the full flavor of regular chocolate.

The color of both cocoa and chocolate is influenced by the blend of beans, their fat content, and the way they're processed. Chocolate color is also affected by temperature. At temperatures higher than 78° F (26° C), chocolate develops a grayish "bloom" caused by fat rising to the surface. This is an appearance problem only, not affecting flavor. Flavor may, however, be affected by storing chocolate in the refrigerator, where it easily picks up undesirable odors from other foods.

American or Dutched

Cocoa is processed either by the American (or natural) method or by the Dutch method. Hershey's and Nestlés are American. Droste, Fry's, Poulain and Saco are blended from American and Dutched. The American process uses high pressure to remove most of the cocoa butter from chocolate liquor. In the Dutch process, alkali is added to break up the remaining solids into finer powder.

Dutched cocoa dissolves more readily than natural cocoa, has a richer flavor, and lacks lingering bitterness. These differences are due in part to the neutralizing effects of alkali retained from the processing and in part to the greater amount of cocoa butter remaining in Dutched cocoa. The cocoa butter itself has little flavor, but like all fats, it carries and intensifies other flavors.

A dark, rich, reddish color characterizes ice cream made with Dutch process cocoa. It's also very smooth, since Dutched cocoa makes the mix more whipable. For equal smoothness in ice cream made with natural cocoa, cut back a bit on sugar, add a few egg yolks, and toss in a scant pinch of baking soda.

COCOA COMPARED TO CHOCOLATE		
	Flavor	**Fat**
Cocoa, American	90%	10%
Cocoa, Dutched	76%	24%
Chocolate, baking	48%	52%

Chocolate Ice Cream

If you're among those who do not enjoy the characteristic bitterness of chocolate, you can take off the edge by adding extra sugar equal to the weight of the chocolate, or roughly half its volume. This ratio comes out to about one tablespoon for each ounce of nonsweetened chocolate, or one-half tablespoon per tablespoon cocoa.

For uniform distribution of chocolate flavor, warm the mix over low heat and then chill it before freezing it. Since squares melt rather slowly, it's tempting to increase the heat to speed things up, but if you do you'll run the risk of scorching. Instead, hasten melting by chilling the squares and grating them into a bowl large enough to catch fly-away shavings.

Several techniques have been developed to avoid scorching chocolate when it's used to coat ice cream (Chapter 21) or trim cakes and bombes (Chapter 28). (1) Leave the squares in their paper wrappers and set them in a warm place on the range (or in a microwave on high) until melted. (2) Unwrap the chocolate and place it in a measuring cup set in hot water. (3) Melt chocolate in a double boiler over hot, not boiling, water that doesn't touch the underside of the pan. (4) Place chocolate in a dish and microwave on medium for one to two minutes until melted, stirring once or twice. (5) Opt for chocolate shell coating.

Because chocolate contains more fat and less flavoring than cocoa, it takes more to obtain equally strong chocolate taste. For good flavor in ice cream, soy ice cream, or frozen yogurt, use at least two ounces baking chocolate or one-quarter cup (one-half ounce) cocoa per quart. Don't overlook the possibility of blending in a little of each—a sinfully delicious extravagance.

CHOCOLATE EQUIVALENTS	
This	**Equals**
1 square chocolate	1-oz chocolate
1-oz cocoa	4 T cocoa
1-oz baking chocolate	3 T cocoa + 1 T fat*
1-oz semisweet chocolate	1 T cocoa + 2 t fat + 2 t sugar
or	²/₃-oz baking chocolate + 2¹/₂ t sugar
1-oz German sweet chocolate	1 T cocoa + 2¹/₄ t fat + 1¹/₄ t sugar
*butter, margarine, shortening, or oil	

Chocolate Syrup

Some ice cream makers prefer the taste and uniform texture achieved with chocolate syrup. You can use store-bought chocolate syrup or make your own. Blend one-half cup cocoa with four and one-half tablespoons sugar in a small saucepan. Measure out one cup water and stir enough into the mixture to make a paste. Heat the mixture and gradually stir in the remaining water. Bring nearly to a boil, simmer fifteen minutes, then cool.

You'll actually have a syrup of sorts as soon as the boiling point is reached, but longer heating makes it thicker and smoother and dissolves the cocoa more thoroughly for fuller flavor. To a quart of your favorite vanilla ice cream mix, add about one-half cup syrup, according to your taste.

Chocolate Enhancers

Chocolate has long been equated with fun, and it can be lots of fun to combine other flavorings with chocolate to enhance or vary its flavor. So-called flavored cocoa is now available in a variety of blends, but most tend to be too heavy-handed in ice cream. So reward your taste buds by creating your own house specials. Vanilla and almond extracts, for example, bring out chocolate's delicate undertones. Mint gives it a delightfully different twist. Malt combined with chocolate is a classic.

Liquors and liqueurs lend a certain sophistication that's popular during holidays and other festive occasions. Besides adding flavor of their own, spirits strengthen any flavor by raising the melting point of ice cream. Rum and brandy both go well with chocolate. Orange and coffee liqueurs are also favorites.

Delicate-tasting white chocolate requires a light touch. Almond, hazelnut, and chocolate are all suitable liqueurs. Additional mix-ins include finely chopped almonds or hazelnuts and bits of candied or dried fruit. Maraschino cherries and chopped apricots are two winners.

Fruits that add sparkle to dark chocolate ice cream include cherries, raspberries, strawberries, and oranges. Pieces of baked goods such as Grape-Nuts or bits of brownie contribute textural as well as taste variety. So do coarsely chopped nutmeats, chocolate chips, and miniature marshmallows. The latter will be chewier if you set them out to dry a bit before using them.

Although the trend in baking is toward larger chocolate chunks, in ice cream, smaller is better. Use miniature chips or chop up regular-sized ones with a knife or whirl them briefly in a food processor. For more subtle bursts of flavor that's less disruptive to texture, shave or grate semisweet or bittersweet chocolate.

Coffee

Perhaps the ultimate chocolate enhancer is coffee, which also stands on its own as one of the best ice cream flavorings. Most coffee comes from Brazil. Since Brazilian beans have a milder, less distinct flavor than those grown elsewhere, they're often blended with beans from other areas such as Jamaica, Colombia or Hawaii.

Coffee flavor is affected not only by place of origin, but also by the way the beans are roasted. They are heated at a higher temperature for a longer time to make espresso than to make American roast, resulting in darker coffee with richer flavor. Within the two categories, espresso and American, there are many variations resulting in different flavors.

Pungent espresso is traditionally made under steam pressure, requiring a special machine. Today it is often brewed in a drip pot, or made from instant espresso crystals. Either makes a fine ice cream flavoring, although the former requires the addition of a thickener such as arrowroot (see Chapter 13) to make up for the extra water. Instant coffee, on the other hand, can be dissolved right in the milk or cream of any basic mix. (A source for instant espresso is listed in Appendix C, "Supplies.") Whether you're flavoring ice cream or frozen yogurt, the coffee will taste immensely richer if it's combined with a little Tia Maria.

Flavored coffees, instant or brewed, make interesting ice creams. With the instant kind you'll have to adjust your recipe to compensate for the extra sugar. Not all brands are blended with the same masterful hand, so shop with ice cream flavor in mind. (A source for the original, and still tastiest, instant flavored coffee is listed in Appendix C.) One of the best uses for flavored coffees is topping, made by adding a little water or cream and heating just until bubbly.

Spices

Spice flavors range from the merely unusual to the bizarre—mustard ice cream, anyone? Although sometimes used as primary flavorings, spices are more often added to enhance other flavors. They not only add spunk but also fool your taste buds into sensing greater richness, allowing you to cut back on more caloric ingredients. Spices should be used sparingly in this role so no distinct spicy taste is detectable.

Spices are so pungent you need only a small amount, especially of those stored in jars or tins, which stay fresh longer than when packed in cardboard boxes. The most common spices in ice cream are ginger, cinnamon, nutmeg, and cloves, all products of the tropics. Ginger is derived from the root of a bush, cinnamon from the bark of a tree, nutmeg and cloves from dried fruits or berries.

The hottest, most flavorful ginger is grown in Jamaica and is light in color. In the form of either ground spice or ginger preserves, it makes tantalizing, taste-tingling ice cream. Don't overlook its special affinity for apricot.

The best cinnamon is from China, the finest nutmeg, from the West Indies, and the darkest, most pungent cloves, from the Spice Islands. In ground cloves look for rich color as an assurance that aromatic oils have not been extracted for some other purpose, such as synthesizing vanillin.

Nutmeg is a natural in eggnog ice cream and in malted vanilla or chocolate. In fact, it was once customary to pass a nutmeg shaker when serving malted milkshakes. Use minute amounts of nutmeg, cinnamon, or cloves to enhance chocolate and coffee ice creams, or add a pinch to perk up peach and apple—which brings us around to the fruit flavors.

15

From Fruit to Nuts

An amazingly large percentage of fruit grown across the United States finds its way into ice cream. Strawberry ranks as the top fruit flavor, followed by cherry, raspberry, and peach. Orange is the most popular sherbet. Lemon, lime, pineapple, and banana follow close behind.

Apricots make tasty, tangy sorbets. Apples and Bartlett pears make intriguingly delicate ones. Currants, plums, and rhubarb are terrific in sorbets and sherbets but lend an unappetizing dishwater hue to ice creams. Versatile cranberries, with their bright color and distinctive, tart flavor, go great in any freeze.

Fruit can be used as flavoring in all its various forms—fresh, frozen, canned, juiced, preserved, candied, and dried.

MOST POPULAR FRUIT ICE CREAMS	
Strawberry	66.9%
Cherry	23.8%
Raspberry	4.4%
Peach	3.8%
All other	1.1%
Source: *The Latest Scoop,* IICA, 1985.	

Fruit

Soft, fully ripe fresh fruit, deep in color and rich in flavor, makes the tastiest ice cream. Select red- or pink-cored strawberries and sour rather than sweet varieties of cherry. Choose yellow-fleshed peaches and nectarines, which have a stronger flavor and firmer texture than white ones. Look for yellow-skinned, darkly speckled bananas.

Avoid the hard, tasteless, crunchy fruit often found in grocery stores—it doesn't get any better frozen into ice cream. If unripe or out-of-season fruit is all you can find, you can improve the flavor somewhat by chopping and soaking the fruit in liqueur of the same flavor, or in orange liqueur. Flavor can also be enhanced by adding one-quarter teaspoon fruit-flavored extract per quart. (A source for some of the less common extracts is listed in Appendix C, "Supplies.") In general, if you can't find sun-ripened fruit, you'll get better flavor from frozen fruit.

Canned fruit rarely imparts the same rich, natural flavor as fresh or frozen fruit, partly because the high temperature required for canning destroys flavor, primarily because most fruit is canned unripe so it will remain firm. Strawberries suffer the most flavor loss through canning. Apricots, peaches, and pears fare a bit better. The flavor intensities of stable fruits like cherries, figs, and pineapple may actually increase.

Dried fruits impart an entirely different flavor from fresh, frozen, or canned ones. Although they're sometimes substituted during the off season or used in combination with other fruits for variety, they're most often enjoyed in holiday puddings. Especially suitable are apricots, dates, figs, prunes, and raisins. With the exception of strawberries, freeze-dried fruits do not plump easily and are therefore unsuccessful in ice cream.

Successful juice flavorings include apple, grape, lemon, lime, orange, pineapple, and apricot nectar. Freshly extracted juices and nectars have the best flavor. Frozen ones run a close second. Frozen juice concentrates, especially mild-flavored apple, can be used as a partial substitute for more caloric sweeteners. The extra water and sugar in fruit juice drinks makes them less suitable as flavorings. The more intensely flavored ones, however, may be poured into an ice cream freezer right out of the can or bottle as a complete sorbet mix.

Jams and preserves may be used to flavor sorbets and French ice creams, but they're more often reserved for ripples and aufaits (Chapter 25) or as sundae toppings (Chapter 24). It takes so much jam to get strong fruit flavor that the excess sugar lowers the freezing point and keeps ice cream from freezing properly.

Candied fruits, including cherries, pineapple, citron, and citrus peel, make tempting trimmings for holiday bombes (Chapter 26). They also add taste and textural variety to rich mousses and frozen puddings. The best known ice creams flavored with candied fruit are spumoni and tutti frutti.

Vegetables

Vegetable sorbets date back to at least the nineteenth century, when cucumber and spinach ices were enjoyed in London. Not until fairly recently, though, have vegetable sorbets been taken seriously in this country as refreshing appetizers and relishes. Among the flavors most often served today are beet, cucumber, tomato, pepper, and savory herb.

A little slower to catch on, but still nothing new, are vegetable ice creams. The Indians of Mexico have long had a sweet tooth for sweet corn ice cream, and the taste for it follows American tourists home. Pumpkin in the Northeast and avocado on the West Coast are two vegetable flavors that have withstood the test of time. Imaginative gardeners across the country are beginning to freeze bountiful summer harvests into such exotic confections as zucchini or jalapeño pepper ice cream and sauerkraut sherbet.

New Yorkers remain in the vanguard in exploring the potential of vegetable flavors. Beet-potato ice cream was served at the 1964 New York World's Fair, asparagus ice cream appeared on the menu at Wall Street's once-famous Delmonico's restaurant, and garlic ice cream was featured at the 1986 Garlic Festival in Ithaca.

Not to be outdone, the Maryland Sweet Potato Grower's Association commissioned ice cream expert emeritus Wendell Arbuckle to concoct a recipe for sweet potato ice cream. And the citizens of Eaton Rapids, Michigan, celebrate the area's two most important industries, ice cream and pickles, in an annual festival featuring—what else?—pickle ice cream.

Vegetable flavors have even been blessed from above. Reverend C. L. Kennedy of Tampa, Florida, had a heavenly vision in 1984 commanding him to "put vegetables into ice cream." Thereafter, his Glorious Church of God in Christ made and sold ice creams flavored with spinach, celery, carrots, and beets.

Vegetables, like fruit, should be fresh and fully ripe to impart maximum flavor. The distinction between the two is actually not that great, being primarily one of perception. Technically speaking, avocados, cucumbers, peas, peppers, pumpkins, tomatoes, and zucchini are all fruits.

Preparation

The amount of fruit or vegetable needed to flavor ice cream depends on the richness of the mix and intensity of the flavoring. A general rule is one cup per quart of very rich ice cream or frozen yogurt. Three-quarters of a cup may be plenty for less rich mixes or when flavor is strong, while one and one-half cups may be more suitable in extra-rich ice creams or when flavor is on the delicate side. Sherbet contains at least fifty percent fruit, or two cups per quart. Fruit sorbet may be made solely from sweetened fruit purée and a little lemon juice.

Puréed fruit and vegetables impart more intense color to ice cream than finely chopped ones, but you'll need more for good flavor. For the best flavor and appearance, as well as for textural variety, coarsely purée a portion and chop the rest into small bits.

Insert the grating blade when using a food processor for chopping. In a blender, chop small batches at a time with short bursts of power to avoid liquefying. You want to end up with recognizable shreds; on the other hand, you don't want chunks large enough to become unpleasantly icy when frozen.

Fruit and fresh vegetables prepared for sorbets are nearly always puréed completely. So are seedy berries, persimmons, and kiwi, which must be run through a sieve to remove their seeds. Some fruit ice cream fans like to leave in a small portion of crunchy kiwi or berry seeds for the sake of authenticity.

A potato peeler may be used to peel apples, pears, and many vegetables. As an alternative to peeling apples and pears, cut them into chunks and steam them until slightly soft, adding just enough water to prevent scorching. Cool the fruit and press it through a coarse sieve. Most of the tough skin will be left behind.

To peel apricots, nectarines, peaches, and tomatoes, dip them in boiling water for one-half to one minute until the skins split. Cool in icy water, then slip off the skins with your fingers. The flavor of apricots, peaches, and nectarines will be stronger if you include up to one-third of the skins, liquefied and stirred into the puréed pulp.

When preparing bananas ahead, toss them with lemon, orange or pineapple juice to prevent darkening. Broiling eliminates the need to coat bananas with juice and also intensifies their flavor. Peel them and cut them in half lengthwise. Broil, cut side up, four inches from the heat for four minutes or until they turn bubbly and brown.

Although most fruit is used raw, most vegetables are cooked. Exceptions are avocados, carrots, cucumbers, tomatoes, and zucchini, which are used raw, and apples, pears, and bananas, which are often cooked. To preserve the greatest amount of flavor in cooked fruit and vegetables, steam or simmer them just until they're cooked through, then cool quickly before puréeing.

Add purée to your mix before freezing starts. Hold back chopped fruit or vegetables to add when the mix is nearly frozen. Including these larger bits too soon may cause them to become puréed by the dasher or to stick to the dasher and slow the freezing process.

Stabilizing

Most raw fruit, when exposed to air, loses flavor and aroma through oxidation. This loss can be prevented by stabilizing the fruit with sugar. With few exceptions, nonstabilized fruit becomes cardboard-tasting in ice cream and frozen yogurt. The same doesn't occur in ices and sorbets because, right from the start, the fruit is incorporated into a highly sweetened mix.

Most brands of ice cream are made from one basic recipe to which different flavorings are added. Because the prepared fruit contains extra sugar, commercial fruit ice cream is usually sweeter than other flavors. This needn't be true for homemade. Instead of adding more sugar to the fruit, use half the amount desired in the ice cream and stir the rest into the milk or cream. Increase sweetening only as necessary to compensate for tarter fruits.

Sprinkle the sugar over the prepared fruit and gently stir until the sugar dissolves and juice begins to flow. Age sweetened fruit in a covered container in the refrigerator overnight, allowing time for the juice and sugar to blend into a flavorful syrup and for some of this syrup to be absorbed by the fruit so it won't freeze icy hard. If you haven't got all night, you can hasten the aging of sweetened apricots, cherries, peaches, blackberries, or figs by bringing them just to a boil and continue heating three to five minutes. Cool, then chill.

If you grow your own fruit or obtain it in bulk in season, prepare it for year-round ice cream making. Peel and purée as usual and add sugar according the proportions in the accompanying chart. Freeze sweetened purée in containers that hold just enough for one batch.

When flavoring with frozen fruit, whether your own or from the store, let it thaw and age overnight in the refrigerator to smooth out rough, icy texture. Unless the fruit was frozen without sugar, you needn't sprinkle on more. Remember to reduce sweetening in the mix to keep your ice cream from becoming overly sweet. Reduce sweetening, too, when adding fruit canned in syrup. Canned fruit, incidentally, has been aged in the can and does not require an additional aging period.

If you make food processor ice cream, don't thaw your frozen fruit but process it while it's still frozen. For smoothest texture, instead of freezing fruit in chunks, purée it as for other ice creams and freeze the purée in cubes or in thin slabs you can easily break apart.

When using apples, pears, peaches, nectarines, bananas, and other fruits that darken on exposure to air, preserve color by coating the fruit with lemon, orange, or pineapple juice

RATIOS FOR STABILIZING FRUIT WITH SUGAR (by weight*)	
Apple	7:1
Apricot	4:1
Avocado	4:1
Banana	4:1
Banana (very ripe)	1:0**
Blackberry	3:1
Blueberry	4:1
Cherry (sour)	3:1
Cherry (sweet)	5:1
Cranberry	3:1
Fig	4:1
Fruit, mixed	3:1
Lemon	1:1
Lime	1:1
Melon	3:1
Orange	5:1
Peach	4:1
Pear	4:1
Persimmon	4:1
Pineapple	4:1
Plum	4:1
Prune	6:1
Raspberry	3:1
Rhubarb	3:1
Strawberry (sour)	3:1
Strawberry (sweet)	4:1

*One pound of sugar equals about two and one-quarter cups.
**Coat with lemon juice instead.

or ascorbic acid (vitamin C powder). One-quarter teaspoon dissolved ascorbic acid in one tablespoon water is enough to coat one pound of fruit. In addition to stabilizing color, ascorbic acid increases food value and contributes a slight but pleasant tang. It is sold by most pharmacies and natural food shops.

Citrus

Citrus is a bit different from other fruit since most of its flavor is in the oily peel rather than in the pulp or juice. Use only the colored portion. The white part, or albedo, responsible for holding together peel and pulp, is bitter. In tribute to its zippy tang, citrus rind is called "zest" by gourmet cooks. Finely grated, it is used in combination with nearly every other fruit flavor.

Some ice cream makers object to the way zest disrupts the smooth texture of ice cream and so prefer to extract the flavoring and discard the peel. One way to do this is to stir coarsely grated rind into a warm mix, let it stand thirty minutes, then strain. Another way is to combine coarsely grated rind with the required amount of sugar, let stand overnight while the sugar absorbs citrus oil, then sift out the rind.

Many pharmacies carry commercially prepared citrus oils. The best are imported— lemon from Sicily, orange from Spain, grapefruit from Mexico, lime from Mexico and the West Indies, and mandarin orange from Italy. Extracts are also available, containing five percent citrus oil combined with alcohol. Because they're so diluted, extracts don't con- tribute the same zesty magic as pure oils.

Some ice cream and sherbet recipes, and most sorbet recipes, call for citrus juice. As you might expect, fresh juice tastes better than the bottled kind. Lemon juice strengthens the flavor of other fruits, particularly bananas and persimmons. The best lemons are yellow with no hint of green.

The tastiest limes are dark green, but don't pay a premium just for the juice—lemon juice tastes nearly the same, the flavor difference being mostly in the peel. Tree-sweetened grapefruits have clearly visible gray scars. Flavorful oranges are bright in color. Properly ripened ones of the navel variety shamelessly display bulging belly buttons.

Extract the maximum amount of juice from any of these by rolling the whole fruit between your palms or against a counter top before juicing or by first dropping the whole fruit into hot water for a few minutes. Alternatively, microwave lemons or limes for twenty

APPROXIMATE CITRUS FLAVORING EQUIVALENTS
1 t freshly grated peel
1 t dried peel
2 t grated candied peel
2 T fresh juice
$^{1}/_{2}$ t extract
1 drop oil

seconds on high, turn, microwave twenty seconds more, and let them set one minute before juicing.

To prevent curdling of dairy-based mixes, add citrus pulp or juice only to well chilled dairy products, preferably just before the mix is frozen. Alternatively, pour citrus into the ice cream maker after ice crystals begin to develop. Curdling is aesthetically unpleasant but affects neither flavor nor texture.

Plumping Dried Fruit

With the exception of dates and coconut, dried fruit should be softened, or plumped, before being added to ice cream. Plump raisins by soaking them in a little rum or brandy. You can also cover them with water, bring it nearly to a boil, continue heating a few minutes, then let it stand one hour until the raisins swell.

Many ice cream makers prefer chopped raisins. For variety, leave one-third whole and chop the rest. Chopping is easier if the raisins have been spread on a baking sheet and popped into the freezer for half an hour. Allow one-third to one-half cup per quart of mix.

Plump apricots and figs by covering them with water and letting them soak six to ten hours, or overnight. Add one part sugar to two parts fruit by weight. If desired, then simmer until tender, about one hour. Nonsulfured apricots and Calimyrna figs are best in ice cream.

Stew prunes in just enough water to prevent scorching, adding one part sugar to six parts prunes by weight. Continue heating until tender, adding more water if necessary. Cool and purée. Allow three-quarters to one cup plumped apricots, figs, or prunes per quart of mix.

Coconut

When autumn coconuts appear, think about flavoring ice creams and sorbets with fresh grated coconut meat or extracted milk. Alone, coconut is a delicate flavoring, but it does something incredible to ice cream containing coffee, nuts, or tropical fruit. Select coconuts that feel heavy and that slosh when you shake them. Skip any whose three little eyes are moist or moldy.

Cracking open a coconut requires a hammer and a hard surface, such as a garage floor. If you wish to save the delicately delicious liquid inside, drill out two of the eyes or poke them in with a stout nail, ice pick, or screwdriver and drain the coconut water into a glass.

This tasty liquid is not the same as coconut milk, which is the juice squeezed from the white meat scraped out of the shell with a sturdy metal spoon. Wrap the scrapings in several layers of cheesecloth, squeeze out the flavorful milk, then discard the dry pulp. If the milk is a bit thick, thin it with a little coconut liquid.

How much milk you'll get depends entirely on the size of the coconut and how fresh it is. For a surer measure, or if you're in a hurry, you can extract coconut milk from a can, shelved in the mixed drink department at most grocery stores.

To enjoy the finer flavor of freshly grated coconut, in contrast to the dry kind packaged in plastic bags, poke out two eyes and drain away the liquid, then loosen the meat from the shell by baking the whole coconut in a 400° F (204° C) oven for fifteen minutes. Tap the coconut all over with a hammer and crack it open with one good whack. Use a pointed knife to pry the meat loose. Peel away the brown skin with a potato peeler and cut the meat into chunks. Grate it by hand or whirl it in a blender. One medium coconut will give you about four cups of finely grated meat.

Toasted coconut adds a delicious taste and pleasing crunch to freshly made ice cream but turns soggy and loses its appeal in ice cream stored for any length of time. If the ice cream won't be served fresh, reserve toasted coconut to sprinkle on top at serving time.

To toast fresh coconut, spread grated meat thinly on a baking sheet and brown lightly in a 350° F (180° C) oven for fifteen minutes, stirring frequently. Toast store-bought flaked or shredded coconut at 325° F (165° C) for ten minutes, stirring until browned. To microwave, spread the coconut on a plate and heat it on medium-high, stirring once every minute, until it is lightly browned, which will take three to four minutes depending on whether the coconut is fresh or dried.

Nuts

Nuts are often used in combination with coconut or fruit, or both, but they also stand on their own as outstanding flavorings. Mouth-watering ice cream can be made from nearly any kind of nut—almond, pecan, walnut, cashew, peanut, pistachio, hazelnut (filbert), macadamia, and even chestnut.

The best ice cream is made with fresh nuts, available in the fall. If you wish to enjoy nut ice creams all year long, stock up when nuts are fresh. Shell and pack them in a sealed container and store it in the freezer. Nuts purchased out of season are often rancid or soggy, particularly when improperly wrapped. Look for the ones in vacuum sealed containers.

The most intense flavor comes from finely chopped nuts, but they can give ice cream a gritty feel. Most ice cream fans prefer nuts either coarsely chopped or ground into paste. Some nuts sold at natural food shops are pre-ground into nut butter, flour, or meal. For flavors like black walnut or praline pecan, most people prefer larger chunks.

Nut liqueurs, especially almond and hazelnut, are sometimes added to intensify nut flavors. Among the nut extracts and flavoring oils, almond is the most widely used. It is (surprise!) the primary flavoring in pistachio ice cream and is often added to bring out the fruity flavors of apricot, cherry, peach, and strawberry ice cream.

Preparation

Most recipes call for unsalted nuts, but many ice cream lovers feel that light salting brings out flavor. To salt, heat one tablespoon oil per one-half cup nuts in a large skillet over medium heat. Stir until the nuts turn slightly brown, about three minutes. Sprinkle with one-eighth teaspoon salt and toss lightly to coat evenly. For extra flavor, sprinkle on a little cinnamon, ginger, or other spice.

Unless they've been salted, nuts should be toasted so they won't absorb moisture as readily and thus stay crunchy longer in stored ice cream. Toasting also perks up stale, soggy nuts and brings out flavor intensity even in fresh ones.

Place the nuts in a single layer in a heavy skillet over low heat and stir until lightly brown. Don't overdo it—the nuts will continue to darken as they cool. You can also toast nuts in a 300° F (150° C) oven for fifteen minutes, shaking or stirring occasionally for even browning; or microwave them on high two to three minutes until they're lightly browned and fragrant, stirring every minute.

Fresh almonds and hazelnuts have dark, bitter skins you can remove either by blanching or by roasting. To blanch, cover nuts with boiling water and let stand five minutes. Drain in a colander and pinch off the skins while the nuts are still warm. Dry on a paper towel. Roasting has the advantage of skinning and toasting in one operation. Spread the nuts on a baking sheet and place it in a 350° F (180° C) oven fifteen minutes, shaking occasionally until the skins blister. Turn the nuts into a paper bag and shake until the skins loosen. Let them steam in the bag for ten minutes, then use a dish towel or paper towel to rub the skins away.

Praline pecans are scrumptious either stirred into ice cream or sprinkled on top. In a small saucepan, combine one-quarter cup light brown sugar with one tablespoon each butter and water. Bring to a boil and add one-half cup pecan pieces. Stir until the coating thickens and the nuts start sticking together (about five minutes). Turn the pecans onto a buttered baking sheet and separate them with a buttered fork. Store fully cooled praline pecans in an airtight container for up to one week.

Prepare nuts well in advance so they'll have time to cool fully before being added to your ice cream mix. Use them as the main flavoring or to enhance other flavorings. Toasted almonds, for example, combine readily with apricot, peach, cherry, or coffee. Walnuts are tasty with apple, prune, maple, or butterscotch. Pecans go well with chocolate, pineapple, coconut, or caramel.

Allow one-half cup per quart when nuts are the primary flavoring, one-quarter cup when they're combined with other flavors. To ensure even mixing and prevent slow freezing, toss nuts in after the ice cream is nearly frozen but before it's too stiff for good distribution.

POPULAR NUT ICE CREAMS	
Butter pecan	62.2%
Praline pecan	14.8%
Butter almond	9.4%
Black walnut	6.3%
Maple nut	4.8%
All others	2.5%
Source: The Latest Scoop, IICA, 1986	

Coloring

In an indirect way, color intensity affects flavor, since the appearance of ice cream influences your desire to taste it. Pale colors may give you the impression flavor is lacking, while unnaturally gaudy ones seem unappetizing.

Inherently colorful flavorings like strawberry, cranberry, blueberry, and apricot become more delicate when diluted by cream and other ingredients. Many flavorings contribute little or no natural color. Ice creams and sherbets made with lemon, banana, or pineapple, for example, all look like vanilla, creating false expectations that lead to confusion when you take a lick.

Even vanilla ice cream isn't always white, since milk from Jersey cows is yellower than milk from Holsteins, which in turn is yellower than milk from goats or sheep. In addition, dairy animals of the same kind don't produce milk of uniform color year-round. Most commercial vanilla ice cream is standardized with yellow coloring so it always looks like it's made with the richest summer cream. Although garish hues are normally shunned, around the holidays they are not only accepted but expected. At any time of year, you may choose to add green tint to flavors like pistachio, mint, and lime, or to use yellow to perk up lemon, banana, and pineapple. A mix should look a little darker than you want the ice cream to be, since it will lighten up during freezing.

Natural food dyes are not only expensive but come in a limited number of colors and are next to impossible to find. Most coloring contains artificial ingredients that many people are allergic to, and there's growing evidence they aren't healthy for the rest of us. One of the nice things about making your own ice cream is that you don't have to add food dyes if you don't want to. Besides, when you work with fresh ingredients, you soon learn to appreciate the refreshing appeal of their naturally delicate tones.

16

Smooth Texture

Ice cream consists of a combination of unfrozen solids, air cells, and ice crystals. The number and size of the ice crystals and the relative proportion of air and solids determine smoothness. In the next chapter, we'll see how stir freezing ensures small and numerous ice crystals. Here we'll look at the influence of air and solids.

Solids

In contrast to milk, which is eighty-seven percent water, an average ice cream is about sixty percent water. The rest is solids, supplied by milkfat, milk proteins, sugar, flavoring, and other ingredients. Because solids don't freeze into ice crystals, as water does, ice cream doesn't get as hard as plain milk when frozen. For this same reason, ice cream is smoother and more scoopable than ice milk.

About forty-three percent of the solids are emulsified fats and suspended proteins (milk proteins, gelatin, and so on) that do not dissolve. The remaining solids, primarily sugar, lactose, and milk salts, dissolve in the water portion of the mix. The more dissolved solids there are, the lower the temperature needed to freeze the mix.

When a mix is well-balanced, complete freezing requires a lower temperature than is possible in either an ice cream maker or a household freezer. A mix that doesn't freeze completely stays soft enough to scoop, even after hardening. Too many dissolved solids, on the other hand, keep the ice cream soft and sticky. Too many undissolved solids make it unpleasantly thick and chewy.

Besides influencing smoothness, solids also determine how readily ice cream cools you down. Cooling effect is related to the amount of heat needed to melt the ice portion. The fewer solids there are, the more ice, and the greater the cooling effect. Sherbet, sorbet, and ice all contain fewer solids than ice cream, which is why they make you feel cooler in warm weather. By the same token, low-fat ice cream seems colder than superpremium. To test this cooling effect, compare a sample of gourmet ice cream to a sample of El Cheapo brand. Notice how much colder the latter feels in your mouth.

Conversely, because ice cream is relatively high in solids, in cool weather it doesn't make your teeth chatter quite as much as a sherbet or sorbet. Not only is the immediate cooling effect less, but calories from the additional solids supply energy to keep you warm. So, although most of us eat more ice cream in summer than in winter, the opposite makes just as much sense.

Whipability

The more solids a mix contains, the thicker or more viscous it becomes. High viscosity favors smooth texture, resistance to melting, and greater whipping ability.

Whipping ability refers both to the rate at which air is incorporated into a mix during freezing and to the maximum amount of air the mix will absorb. Some ingredients, especially chocolate, inhibit whipping. Egg yolks, buttermilk, and other emulsifiers improve it. A little gelatin increases the whipability of ices and other fat-free mixes, but too much has the reverse effect.

Sherbet made from sugar, gelatin, and nonfat milk solids whips up light and airy. Add cream, and the whipability plummets, since air cells are weakened by milkfat. Milkfat by itself won't whip at all during freezing. Sugar, water, and emulsifiers must be added before it will retain air.

Whipping heavy cream is thus very different from whipping ice cream. When you whip cream, partially churned milkfat gets trapped along air cell walls. Whip long enough, and the milkfat churns completely into butter. Short of that, the combination of stiffening butterfat and trapped air gives cream its ability to stand in peaks.

Ice cream, in contrast, traps air not because the milkfat churns but because the cell structure of the mix gets increasingly more rigid as it freezes. Combine these two very different whipping properties by beating heavy cream into soft mounds and then folding it into a well-chilled mix, and you'll get extremely light, delicate ice cream.

Overrun

Without some air, ice cream would freeze into a dense mass you'd have a hard time scooping and not much fun eating. You can test this by pouring your favorite mix into a container and freezing it without stirring.

Ice cream freezers are designed to introduce air during freezing. The greater the surface area of the dasher blades, the more air they introduce. Speed of rotation is also important. A dasher turning at just the right speed carries an air pocket behind it. The mix closing in behind that pocket constantly entraps some of the air. If the dasher moves too slowly, the mix follows too closely behind it and doesn't trap any air. If the dasher turns too fast, it not only carries mix instead of air but it smashes any air cells in its path.

The increase in volume of a mix as it freezes is in part due to the expansion of water turned to ice, but is primarily due to the incorporation of air. The extra volume, called "overrun," increases smoothness. Excessive overrun creates unpleasantly snowy or fluffy texture, bland taste, and a relatively warm feel in your mouth. In short, the ice cream becomes too much like whipped cream or marshmallow fluff.

Overrun is expressed as the percent increase in volume. If you get two quarts of ice cream from one quart of mix, overrun is one-hundred percent. If you get one and one-quarter quarts of ice cream from one quart of mix, overrun is twenty-five percent. The accompanying chart gives you an idea of standard overrun for different freezes.

AVERAGE COMMERCIAL OVERRUN	
Freeze	**% Overrun**
Bulk ice cream (sold by the scoop)	90-100
Economy ice cream	90-100
Ice milk	80-100
Soft-serve soy ice cream	90
Trade brand ice cream	80-90
Premium ice cream	60-85
Frozen yogurt	50
Soy ice cream	50
Soft-serve ice cream	30-50
Sherbet	30-45
Sorbetto	30-40
Superpremium (gourmet) ice cream	20-40
Sorbet	20-35
Ice	15-20
Gelato	10

Controlling Overrun

Most home ice cream freezers incorporate less air than their commercial counterparts. Your ice cream will therefore likely be denser, nearly twice as heavy, and contain more calories serving for serving than a store-bought brand of similar composition. You can control overrun to some extent through your choice of ingredients affecting whipability, through the ice cream freezer you select, and through the way you operate it.

The slower a freezer works, the more time it has to promote overrun. Since ice cream makers designed to work inside your household freezer take longest, they make the fluffiest ice cream. To minimize overrun, fill the canister with either a little more or a little less mix than the manufacturer suggests. Overfilling makes it harder for the dasher to introduce air. Underfilling causes the mix to freeze faster, limiting the time it has to trap air.

The fastest working freezers are the internally cooled ones. Operated according to instruction, they introduce very little air, making ice cream as dense and smooth as the best superpremiums. Since cooling and agitation are on separate circuits, you can lighten texture by altering the operating procedure. A mix is most receptive to air after about one-third of its water portion has frozen, when it becomes thick enough to flow from a ladle in ribbons.

At that point, turn off the cooling mechanism and let the dasher continue turning until the ice cream reaches the consistency you desire. Take care not to run the freezer too long with the coolant off or your ice cream will melt and you'll have to start over. Don't be tempted to lengthen freezing time by pouring in your mix before the unit is sufficiently prechilled, or you may end up with dry, buttery ice cream.

Hand-crank freezers allow you to control overrun by regulating the speed of dasher rotation. For fine, smooth texture, begin cranking slowly—about 40 revolutions per minute (rpm). When you feel resistance, triple your speed to 120 rpm for about five minutes. Toss in any bits of flavoring you may wish to add and crank at 80 rpm a few more minutes until you achieve desired consistency. Varying the speed of rotation is simplified if your freezer has variable gear ratios, a highly uncommon feature.

Commercial manufacturers regulate overrun by independently controlling agitation and cooling, sometimes using a pump to force in additional air. To keep unscrupulous manufacturers from selling mostly air, store-bought ice cream must weigh at least 4.5 pounds per gallon (eighteen ounces per quart), sherbets and ices must weigh at least six pounds per gallon (1.5 pounds per quart).

Special ice cream scales are designed for measuring overrun, but you can check the relative amount of air with any ordinary scale. The closer ice cream is to the legal minimum weight, the more air it contains. This measurement works not only for homemade ice cream but for any you buy at the grocery, where the produce department scale can be used for a quick weight check.

Preparing the Mix

The order in which you mix ingredients and whether or not you heat them influences overrun as well as texture and taste. Unless a recipe specifies otherwise, combine all liquid and all dry ingredients separately. Then slowly sift dry ingredients into liquid ones, stirring to prevent lumpiness and encourage dissolving. This is especially important when adding cocoa, powdered milk, or flour.

Add flavoring last, after all other ingredients have been included. If ingredients are heated, include volatile extracts only after the mix has cooled. Hold back bits of solid flavoring such as chopped nuts, chocolate chips, cookie crumbs, and chunks of fruit until the ice cream is nearly frozen. Otherwise, they may not get evenly distributed or they may be whipped so much they lose their identity. Add alcoholic spirits toward the end as well, so they won't slow freezing.

Heating

Heating a mix improves its whipability and encourages better blending of ingredients. It's a necessary step when you use gelatin or flour or when you're making frozen custard. Heating also prevents sugar from settling into a sticky layer that has to be stirred back in before the mix is frozen.

To thoroughly dissolve sugar or honey, first heat the milk, cream, water, or juice either on the range or in a microwave set on high. Stir in the sweetener and continue stirring to ensure even warming and to keep solids in suspension until they're completely dissolved. Bring juice or water to a boil. Heat milk or cream just until bubbles form around the edges.

Commercial ice cream makers are required to pasteurize their mixes to destroy harmful bacteria, necessary because the ingredients are handled so much and because there's such a long storage period between manufacture and consumption. Heating a homemade mix to pasteurizing temperature is usually unnecessary.

Another commercial practice is to homogenize the mix while it's still hot. This process breaks up and evenly distributes milkfat, improving body and texture and keeping particles of fat from collecting and clumping on the dasher. The latter phenomenon, called "buttering" or "churning," is more likely to occur when butter or other cream substitutes are used. Homogenization also prevents the gradual rising of fat during storage. The lower overrun of homemade ice cream keeps this sort of thing from happening and, in any case, the homemade kind rarely sits around long enough for ingredients to separate out.

Chilling and Aging

Cool any mix containing dairy products as rapidly as possible, easily done by setting the saucepan or double boiler in a larger container of ice water. Some mixes, particularly those containing eggs, must be stirred during cooling to prevent lumping. Straining the cooled mix, or whirling it in a blender, removes any lumps of cream or egg solids that might otherwise detract from final texture.

After the mix has cooled, add any required extracts. Then chill the mix in the refrigerator for at least two hours—four if it contains gelatin or dairy products, twenty-four if it's high in fat. Chilling not only makes ice cream taste better but lets the freezer do its job more efficiently. A chilling period of longer than twenty-four hours is not beneficial and may actually cause the mix to deteriorate.

Proper aging, even of mixes you don't heat, results in smoother texture, mellower flavor, and greater resistance to melting. Custard based ice creams, as well as sherbets and ices containing gelatin, whip up to greater volume after aging. If you prefer denser consistency, refrigerate the mix just long enough to chill it completely.

No one is sure exactly what happens during aging. Either the gelatin absorbs water, swells, and sets up, or the fat particles start sticking together and solidifying. Both would result in a thickening of the mix, which especially benefits freezes that are low in solids.

Aging has another distinct advantage—it lets you prepare ice cream in two easy steps. Whip up the mix early in the day or a day ahead, then store it in the refrigerator until you're ready to freeze it. To speed up freezing, place the mix in the freezer compartment of your refrigerator for fifteen minutes before pouring it into your ice cream maker.

17

Stir Freezing

Ice cream is frozen in two distinct steps. The first occurs in an ice cream maker, where air is incorporated and large ice crystals are kept from forming. The second step involves hardening without agitation. Homemade ice cream is so irresistible it rarely survives this second step. For those with will power, hardening is discussed in the next chapter.

Preparing the Freezer

An ice cream maker works by removing heat from the mix and transferring it through the metal canister into the coolant. You can speed things along by prechilling the dasher and cream can, as well as the mix, thus reducing the amount of heat that must be transferred before freezing begins.

Canisters for sealed-in coolant freezers are automatically prechilled by virtue of being stored in the freezer. Cool a self-contained unit simply by pushing a button and waiting ten minutes or so. For any other ice cream maker, chill the dasher and canister in the refrigerator.

Freezers work most efficiently when the canister is filled at least halfway, but no more than two-thirds to allow for expansion as the ice cream freezes. Some canisters are marked to indicate how much they're designed to hold. Slight underfilling speeds up freezing but affects texture by reducing overrun. Slight overfilling also depresses overrun, but excessive filling may overload the motor of an electric unit, causing serious damage.

Freezing

Plain water freezes at 32° F (0° C). Sugar, lactose, and other dissolved ingredients push a mix's freezing point even lower. Some ingredients depress the freezing point more than others, so the exact temperature required to freeze a mix depends on its specific composition.

After enough heat has transferred into the coolant for the mix to reach its freezing point, some of the mix's water freezes into ice crystals. The sugar and other dissolved ingredients then become more concentrated in the remaining unfrozen water, further lowering its freezing point. The temperature of the mix must be lowered even more before additional ice crystals will form.

The freezing point keeps dropping in this manner until the unfrozen portion is so highly concentrated with sugars and other solutes that the mix simply can't freeze any more. Just how stiff ice cream actually gets depends on how much of its water freezes compared to how much remains unfrozen.

Between thirty and sixty percent of the water in a mix turns to ice during stir freezing. More is converted during hardening. Even after hardening, some ten percent of the water remains unfrozen. Less of the water freezes in sorbetto, since it's so high in sugar. Consequently, it remains soft and scoopable despite its otherwise low solids content.

Ice Crystals

The size of the ice crystals formed during freezing influences texture. At the extreme are very large crystals, such as those in coarse, still-frozen graniti. The smaller the crystals, the smoother the texture. In stir freezing, as soon as mix freezes against the canister wall, the dasher comes along and scrapes it away before ice crystals have a chance to grow large. Dasher action thus keeps ice crystals small and numerous for smooth texture.

Crystallographers like to study large, well-formed crystals. In contrast, those who make ice cream encourage all the things crystallographers abhor—strong agitation, rapid crystallization, and the introduction of numerous crystal centers.

A crystal center is any particle around which a crystal will form, including ice particles scraped by the dasher from the canister wall. The number of crystal centers, and their size, depends both on the condition of the canister and on the efficiency and speed of the dasher. Speed varies from one freezer to another, accounting in part for why some make smoother ice cream than others.

Dasher blades should fit against the canister so they just touch. Poorly designed or worn blades, or a scratched or dented canister, reduces scraping efficiency, causing coarse or lumpy texture by introducing larger chunks of frozen mix and fewer crystal centers.

In addition, if the blades skim rather than scrape, the thin film of frozen mix they leave against the canister wall acts as insulation and reduces the rate of heat exchange. This increases freezing time, slows crystallization, and causes larger crystals to form. If your freezer makes less smooth ice cream than it used to, maybe you need a new dasher, a new canister, or both.

Thawing and Refreezing

During stir freezing, a certain amount of melting and refreezing constantly takes place. Frozen mix scraped from the sides of the cream can thaws as it absorbs heat from unfrozen mix at the center, then refreezes when it comes back into contact with the cold metal wall.

The less thawing that takes place, the more rapidly the ice cream will freeze, the smaller will be its ice crystals, and the smoother will be its texture. Exactly how much freezing and thawing goes on depends on the volume of mix, the surface area of the canister, the design of the dasher blades, and the difference in temperature between mix and coolant.

Self-cooling freezer units are preset to control coolant temperature. A unit using the air inside your freezer as its coolant gets only as cold as your freezer setting, usually no less than 0° F (–18° C). Sealed-in coolants also rely on your freezer temperature, but their higher heat capacity lets them freeze mixes more rapidly.

The only ice cream freezers that let you control temperature are the old-fashioned kind requiring ice as a coolant. For this reason, die-hards still prefer these freezers, despite all the modern innovations.

Ice as Coolant

When ice is packed into the space between the cream can and the ice tub, it immediately begins to melt. The resulting cold water fills air spaces between the ice chunks, improving contact so heat can be more readily absorbed. Pouring a little cold water over the ice settles it and starts the melting, both shortening freezing time and preventing the ice from jamming up. Since in this case it's the canister, rather than the dasher, that rotates, jammed ice may stall your motor or wear out your cranking arm.

Some ice cream freezers are designed to use just a few trays of regular ice cubes, but even they work better if the ice is crushed. Other freezers call specifically for crushed ice, and plenty of it—from ten pounds (about seven quarts) for a two-quart freezer to twenty-five pounds (seventeen quarts) for a six-quart unit. The finer the ice is crushed, the better contact it makes with the cream can walls, the more evenly it melts, and the more quickly it absorbs heat from the mix. Snow works even better, but you'll need a prodigious amount.

In the old days, whole neighborhoods got together each winter to saw blocks of ice from frozen lakes, haul it by horse-drawn sled to a central ice house, and stack it between layers of insulating sawdust to keep it from melting until it was crushed for the annual mid-summer ice cream social. Our modern refrigerators come with automatic ice makers, but the cubes still have to be crushed.

Although you can buy crushed ice at the store, nostalgic ice cream buffs still enjoy crushing theirs the old-fashioned way, by stuffing cubes into an old pillow case or burlap sack and bashing it with a hammer—arduous work and tough on pillow slips. A little easier is to set a bottomless box on a concrete patio or basement floor, partially fill it with ice, repeatedly drop a sledgehammer into it, then lift the box away and scoop up the crushed ice with a dustpan. If you freeze ice cream often, a hand crank or electric ice crusher makes a wonderful investment.

Salt

Ice melts at 32° F (0° C), not nearly cold enough to freeze a mix. When salt is sprinkled on, atoms of salt and melted water unite and form chemical bonds that store heat as energy and drive the temperature down. Just how cold the brine will get depends on how well the mix and canister are chilled, the size of the salt and ice particles, the proportion of salt to ice, and the kind of salt used.

Theoretically, one pound of salt per three pounds of ice (about three-quarters cup per quart of ice) will push the temperature down to –58° F (–55° C) if the salt is calcium chloride, the kind used to thaw icy sidewalks. If you use sodium chloride, rock or table salt sold by grocers, the theoretical temperature will be –6° F (–21° C). Due to the heat contributed by surrounding air, however, you're unlikely to see temperatures much below 16° to 18° F (about –8° C).

Whether you use rock salt or table salt is a matter of choice. Rock salt is cheaper, especially purchased in bulk at a feed or hardware store, but table salt is usually on hand and therefore more convenient. Although table salt is a bit more expensive, it's ground finer so you'll need less of it.

The more salt you use, the colder the brine will get and the faster your mix will freeze. Too much salt, indicated when hand cranking becomes difficult or the electric motor stalls in less than twenty minutes, results in too rapid freezing, causing grainy, coarse, icy, hard, or lumpy texture. The same undesirable texture occurs if the ice isn't crushed fine enough, but you'll know the difference because, in this case, freezing will take considerably longer than twenty minutes.

If hand cranking is still easy after twenty minutes, or the motor shows no sign of slowing, more salt may be needed. Water absorbs salt only until it reaches the saturation point. After that, excess salt settles into an undissolved layer at the bottom of the tub. But the volume of water steadily increases as ice melts, constantly increasing its capacity for more salt.

It takes experience to learn just how much salt to use and how often to add it, which varies with the freezer and the mix. Ice cream, for example, requires one-half to two-thirds cup rock salt per quart of ice, while sherbet, sorbet, and frozen yogurt (with their lower freezing points) require three-quarters cup salt or more per quart of ice.

By freezing several batches in succession, you'll get more use from your crushed ice and salt, since leftover slush can be used to get the next batch started. Thrifty ice cream makers save briny slush in the freezer, although it won't freeze entirely solid, has to be thoroughly stirred before re-use, and must be packed in watertight containers to keep leaky brine from corroding metal freezer parts.

Since brine is so highly corrosive, carefully wipe down unwashed metal ice cream freezer parts after each use, including the bucket handle and motor housing. Besides corroding metal, brine kills plants. Dispose of it at curbside or in a drainage culvert, well away from landscape and garden. If you live in the country, avoid pouring it down the drain, since salt may upset the chemical balance in your septic tank.

Freezing Time

Large commercial continuous freezers work fast, freezing ice cream in as little as one minute. How fast your ice cream maker works depends on numerous factors, including the composition of your mix, how you prepare it, how well you chill it, condition of your dasher and canister, speed of dasher agitation, volume of mix relative to the canister's surface, volume and temperature of the coolant, rate of heat transfer from mix to coolant, and air temperature surrounding the freezer.

The more sugar a mix contains, the lower its freezing point and the longer it takes to freeze. This accounts for why sorbetto and frozen yogurt take longer than ice cream, and why chocolate and some fruit flavors take longer than vanilla.

A self-cooling ice cream maker freezes the same mix in about half the time it takes a unit using sealed-in coolant or salt and ice. The latter, in turn, freezes twice as fast as a machine that works inside your freezer. Aside from food processors, which make ice cream in seconds, the fastest ice cream freezer takes about ten minutes, the slowest, an hour and a half.

The colder ice cream gets during stir freezing, the less opportunity there will be for large ice crystals to develop during hardening. A well-frozen mix is approximately the consistency of mashed potatoes or commercial soft-serve ice cream. Many freezes taste best in this semi-frozen state, and they're less likely to make the inside of your mouth feel unpleasantly cold compared to ice cream that's been hardened. But take heed—because they're not as cold as they will be after hardening, you'll be inclined to eat much more.

18

Hardening and Storing

To be firm enough to hold its shape when scooped, ice cream must be hardened after it's been stir frozen. Since complex flavors continue to blend during this time, hardening is doubly important when you use flavorings in combination.

Ice cream is ready for hardening when it's stiff enough to heap into a mound yet soft enough to be shaken down in the container. If it's too cold and stiff, it will retain air pockets that collect ice crystals or develop freezer burn. If it's still soupy, it will take too long to harden, allowing tiny ice crystals to grow into larger ones that cause coarse texture. Each degree difference in temperature at the completion of stir freezing affects hardening time ten to fifteen percent.

Hardening Methods

If you use a cream can for hardening, remove the dasher and work out air pockets with a spatula. Some sealed-in coolant canisters retain enough freezing power for slight hardening, if wrapped in a towel and left no longer than half an hour. Other canisters may be placed in the household freezer for hardening.

Using a canister this way is quite common, even recommended by some manufacturers, but it isn't a very good idea. Scooping ice cream directly from the can leaves scratches that inhibit efficient freezing in the future. It's more sensible to repack ice cream into proper freezer containers. Repacking has additional advantages, including easier stacking for storage and freeing up your canister for the next batch. To avoid damage, empty the canister with a plastic or wooden utensil.

For smoothest texture, hardening should occur as rapidly as possible, preferably at a temperature below 0° F (–18° C). This can usually be achieved by storing containers in a household freezer, temporarily adjusted to its lowest setting. For winter fun, bury packed containers in a snow bank to harden, then let children search them out.

Brine Pack

The traditional hardening method calls for brine. A brine pack makes it possible to harden ice cream at picnics and other outings and offers the only satisfactory alternative

if your freezer doesn't get cold enough. Even a freezer that normally works well may be less efficient during hot weather. Once the ice cream has hardened, you can store it at a higher freezer temperature, as long as it remains frozen.

Brine-pack hardening may be accomplished in the ice tub of an ice cream maker or in an insulated picnic carrier. If you use ice for freezing, drain away the brine and pack the filled ice cream container in the leftover ice. Pack fresh ice over and around the container, taking care the lid is tight so brine won't seep in. Into the fresh ice, sprinkle one-half cup salt per quart, adding the salt only to the upper third so the brine can trickle down.

Cover the whole thing with newspaper, towels, or a blanket. A well-insulated pack shouldn't need additional ice before hardening is complete. If you have to add more, the temperature fluctuation may cause undesirable textural changes.

Hardening Time

Brine-pack hardening takes about two hours. Hardening in a freezer should never take longer than six hours. You can speed things up by distributing containers on coiled shelves or among packages of frozen food.

The longer ice cream takes to stir freeze, the longer it takes to harden. Gourmet ice cream hardens faster than ice cream that's lower in fat, which in turn hardens faster than sorbet or frozen yogurt. Overrun is another factor. The higher the overrun, the longer the hardening time.

Container size also influences how long hardening takes, which may be as little as half an hour for small containers or as long as twenty-four hours for ones that are too large. Pint-sized containers are ideal, quarts okay.

Containers

Smallish containers offer another advantage. Homemade ice cream is so low in overrun that it's fairly dense and difficult to scoop without a softening period. Small containers allow you to serve up the entire softened contents at once, leaving no partially melted leftovers to refreeze.

Whatever size or shape you choose, have the containers prechilled and fill them fast since partial melting damages texture. Leave a little space at the top to allow for expansion, and protect the ice cream's surface with a layer of waxed paper or plastic wrap before snapping on a tight-fitting lid.

Label containers with the date and kind of ice cream, especially if you make large batches so you can keep several flavors on hand. Labels help you locate what you're looking for before too much warm air gets into the freezer. Dated labels help guard against prolonged storage and the accompanying loss in quality.

Storage

The quality of most homemade ice cream peaks at some point between stir freezing and the completion of hardening. Nevertheless, many people like to freeze and store large batches so they'll always have plenty on hand. Under the best conditions, eventually ice structure breaks down and noticeable ice crystals begin to appear.

In general, high-fat ice creams keep longer than lower fat ones, and ice cream keeps longer than ice milk, sherbet, or sorbet. Heating a mix before freezing it improves keeping qualities. Like other frozen foods, ice cream keeps longer in a freezer unit than in a freezer compartment, and longer in a nonfrost-free freezer than in a frost-free one.

Ice cream may be stored for up to two months at a temperature of 0° F (–18° C). Longer storage requires around –20° F (–29° C), difficult to achieve in the best home freezer. In a refrigerator freezer compartment at the lowest setting, ice cream won't keep much longer than two to three weeks, even on the bottom shelf. If you've got both kinds of freezer, harden and store containers in the big one and move them to the other as you need them.

Heat Shock

Besides being colder, a freezer isn't opened as often as a freezer compartment. Every time the door opens, warm air enters and the temperature goes up, causing some of the water in ice cream to melt. This water invariably attaches itself to the nearest ice crystal, increasing its size when the temperature goes back down and the water refreezes.

This phenomenon, known as "heat shock," is a major headache for commercial ice cream makers, whose product rarely takes less than five days from freezing to marketing, then another three days on the grocer's shelf. Throughout this time, the ice cream is subjected to constant fluctuations in temperature.

When homemade ice cream is frozen, stored, and served with a minimum of handling, it's less likely to suffer heat shock, provided certain precautions are taken. Don't store it too long in a frost-free unit. Keep it off the door, which gets the first and longest blast of warm air when the freezer is opened. Don't refreeze partially melted ice cream. If heat shock does occur, whip the ice cream into a milkshake and no one will be the wiser.

Tempering

Most homemade ice cream is denser than the store-bought kind, making it harder to scoop unless it's been tempered. Because tempering raises the temperature, it not only eases scooping but increases depth of flavor. Tempering also helps prevent painful ice cream headache, caused by eating a frozen food too fast.

To temper a container of ice cream, set it out for a short time, just until it softens. Depending on how firm it is, softening may take ten minutes or longer at room temperature. On warm days, place the carton in the refrigerator for fifteen to thirty minutes. If you're in a big hurry, microwave on low for thirty seconds, turn, and microwave thirty seconds more. Use softened ice cream right away since refreezing causes heat shock.

Transporting

Properly packed ice cream can easily be brought along to potlucks and picnics as well as to ice cream socials and tastings. In an insulated picnic carrier, completely cover watertight containers with crushed ice and salt, mixed with one-half cup salt per quart of ice. Tamp down the ice as you go. Latch the lid and cover the carrier with a blanket or heavy towel. The ice cream will keep for about three hours.

If transporting takes longer or the day is very warm, you'll need dry ice. Its temperature is −220° F (−140° C), cold enough to "burn" your fingers, so wear gloves when you handle it. Unfortunately, dry ice isn't available in all areas. Check the yellow pages for your nearest dealer.

Dry ice is a clear, white, nearly odorless crystalline substance that evaporates into gaseous carbon dioxide as it melts, leaving no messy puddle like regular ice (the reason it's called "dry"). It weighs less than regular ice and usually comes in rectangular chunks wrapped in brown paper to slow evaporation. Leave on the wrapping when you tuck a piece into your insulated carrier.

How much dry ice you'll need depends on outside temperature, the amount of ice cream you transport, and how long you'll be in transit. In a well-insulated carrier, a quart-sized hunk should protect one gallon of ice cream for the better part of a day.

19

Socials and Tastings

"Ice cream is like wine," *New York* magazine commentator Gael Greene once wrote. "It ranges from the meanest *vin ordinaire* to the *grand cru* yield of the great chateaus." Just as wine tasting swept the country in the 1970s, ice cream tasting came into its own in the early 1990s, riding the coattails of the trend away from alcoholic beverages.

The idea wasn't anything new. For years tastings were attended by an elite corps of specialists, primarily at universities and within the ice cream industry, where professionals value their taste buds so highly they insure them for hundreds of thousands of dollars. When gourmet ice cream became popular, tasting techniques began filtering down to enthusiasts-at-large, thanks in part to pioneering ice cream appreciation experts like Baltimore's Bryan Soronson.

Today, tastings range from formal evaluations by ice cream manufacturers to informal gatherings where friends compare and critique each other's creations. No matter the purpose, the technique remains the same.

Flavor

The mouth perceives only four tastes, detected by receptors on different parts of the tongue:

Sweet — tip of tongue
Salty — tip and sides
Sour — sides, halfway back
Bitter — base

Only dissolved substances produce taste sensations. To prove this for yourself, place a small amount of sugar on your tongue. You won't taste anything until it dissolves, and then only if you roll your tongue so the dissolved sugar touches the tip.

You can't really taste ice cream before it melts in your mouth, which is why licking it is so much more satisfying than biting into it or spooning it from a dish. Because licking is done with the tip of the tongue, the first taste you experience is sweetness. As the ice cream slides back in your mouth, you may taste slight saltiness, sourness (in the case of fruit flavors), or bitterness (coffee or chocolate). All other nuances are the result of aroma, feel, and, to some extent, sight.

The first thing you notice about ice cream is its visual appeal—both the way it is served and its color. Appearance lets you decide whether you wish to taste at all, gives you advance notice what the flavor is likely to be, and influences how you react to that flavor.

Feel is the first sensation you experience when ice cream enters your mouth. Feel includes both your initial reaction as you take a lick or bite and your subsequent perception of the ice cream against your tongue. A smooth, velvety feel creates the impression of richness and contributes to your overall enjoyment of flavor.

Aroma is the bouquet released as the ice cream melts in your mouth. Ice cream tasting differs in this respect from wine tasting. You smell wine first, then taste it. Ice cream must melt before you smell it, and by then you've already tasted it. You experience aroma when the vapors of the volatile flavorings pass the olfactory nerves at the back of your palate. Since the vapors are inside your mouth, you have to exhale to smell them.

The combination of taste, feel, and aroma helps you identify the two characteristics of flavor—type and intensity. Type ranges from delicate to harsh. The more delicate the flavoring, the less quickly it tires your taste buds. Intensity varies from weak to strong. Ideal intensity is no greater than necessary for the intended flavor to be recognized. Because low temperature depresses intensity, ice cream tastes best when tempered sufficiently for a spoon to easily slide in.

OPTIMUM TASTING TEMPERATURES		
Ice cream	5° to 10° F	-15° to -12° C
Ice, sorbet	19° to 21° F	- 7° to - 6° C
Sherbet	19° to 21° F	- 7° to - 6° C
Soft-serve ice cream	20° to 22° F	- 6° to - 5° C

Tasting

Like wine, ice cream is variable, complex, and difficult to evaluate. Most people judge it by flavor, texture, body, and color. Connoisseurs examine each of these in great detail, noting such defects as flatness, staleness, excessive sweetness, and unusual aftertaste. They determine whether the texture is coarse or gummy, the body crumbly or weak. They watch for improper melting characteristics such as foaminess or slow melt-down.

Like a wine tasting, a formal ice cream tasting requires an educated palate, advance preparation, and a controlled environment. And, like a wine tasting, it may be organized as a social event, an educational experience, or both.

Procedure

Any evaluation requires a consensus on the part of the tasters regarding what constitutes perfection. This consensus gives everyone the same fixed point of comparison. Therefore, include in your tasting at least one ice cream, whether homemade or commercial, that all participants agree is excellent.

Your taste buds are most receptive first thing in the morning, a thoroughly impractical time for a tasting. You can help your taste buds along by eating lightly before the tasting so you'll be neither overly hungry nor uncomfortably full. Avoid heavy foods or strong-flavored ones that leave a lingering taste, onions and garlic included. Wash with mild soap and skip the perfume, aftershave, or other heavy scent.

Hold the tasting in a well-ventilated room where no strong odors prevail, and ask participants not to smoke. Have plenty of plain, lukewarm water on hand for mouth rinsing, and provide a platter of unsalted crackers as a palate neutralizer.

For every sixteen participants, allow one quart of each ice cream to be sampled. About a dozen samples are all most tasters can handle at one time. A professional tasting rarely includes ice cream of more than one flavor, most often vanilla. A just-for-fun tasting usually has greater variety. As wine tasters sample whites first, then rosés, and finally reds, ice cream tasters start with vanilla, work through fruit flavors, and end up with the strongest flavors, usually the chocolates.

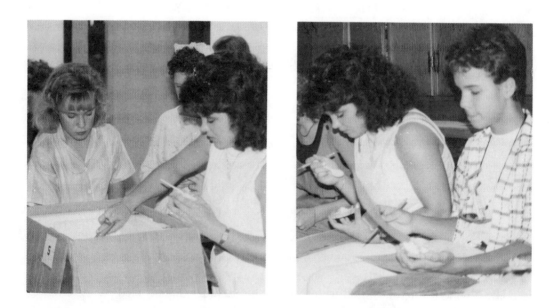

In a blind tasting, each sample is identified by code (left) and rated on a score card (right). (Photos by Allan Damerow.)

Blind Tasting

Blind tasting, where each sample is identified only by code, eliminates any preconceived notions tasters may have about a particular sample or its maker, especially when commercial brands are included. If possible, wrap all samples in identical cardboard or paper bags. Minimize melting by nestling containers either in cardboard boxes of dry ice or in styrofoam picnic carriers packed with salted ice, as described in Chapter 18.

Usually tasters scoop out their own samples, giving them a first impression of texture and body. At some tastings, participants taste directly from containers, taking a fresh disposable spoon for each sample. More often, each participant carries a little serving dish and a spoon. When a large group is involved, paper pill cups may be used and disposed of after each taste. Provide a separate small serving scoop for each sample. If everyone tastes each sample at the same time, you'll need only one scoop. Rinse and dry it before moving on to the next sample.

Evaluation

As each sample is taken, note whether its color is even and natural and whether bits of flavoring such as fruit, nuts, crushed candy or baked goods are evenly distributed. As you dip in, notice how the sample reacts to the scoop—an advance notice of heavy body or icy texture. If the sample contains very large ice crystals, you'll hear them scrape against the scoop.

Dip a small amount into your dish, then place a mere teaspoonful on your tongue and press it against the roof of your mouth. It should feel smooth. If it feels rough, the texture is coarse. If very rough, it's too icy. If roughness lingers after the sample melts, it's sandy.

Roll the melting sample over your tongue and let it come into contact with all your taste buds. Close your mouth and exhale, noticing any volatile essences reaching the organs of smell at the back of your mouth.

Concentration

Close your eyes and concentrate on the sample and your reactions to it, avoiding facial expressions that might influence other tasters. Hold each sample in your mouth an equal length of time, from five to ten seconds, while you evaluate without deliberately seeking defects.

As in wine tasting, it is considered improper to swallow the sample. Pros spit it into a receptacle provided for the purpose. Amateurs have been known to cheat.

After each sample, recondition your mouth by rinsing with plain, lukewarm water. If you crave ice water, follow it with a rinse of lukewarm water to thaw out your taste buds. If a sample was decidedly inferior or left an aftertaste, clear your palate with a bite of unsalted cracker.

Relax for two to five minutes. Then, before moving on, reevaluate the first sample to confirm your initial reaction. If you remain unsure, come back later for an out-of-sequence third taste. Remember, in the final analysis your own preferences and prejudices invariably influence your reaction, no matter how objective you try to be.

Score Cards

Score cards were originally designed for ice cream judging contests sponsored by 4-H groups and university dairy science departments and for evaluations by manufacturers developing new flavors. There is no standard or uniform card. To a greater or lesser extent, each is adapted to suit a specific purpose and varies in the characteristics rated and scoring system used.

In any system, the highest possible rating represents the ideal as established by the designers of the score sheet. Ratings assigned by tasters are based on their individual preferences and on their knowledge of the problems associated with making good ice cream.

In a professional evaluation, scoring is often divided so that forty-five percent of the points are for flavor, thirty percent for body and texture, fifteen percent for bacteria count, and five percent each for color and melting characteristics. Ratings for melting qualities and bacteria count (determined by laboratory analysis) are more important for commercial than for homemade ice cream. Except for melt-down and bacteria, all scores are subjective and depend on the experience of the taster. Pros may assign a perfect score to appearance, body, texture, and melt-down, but never to flavor. At professional tastings, therefore, no sample ever receives a perfect score.

At amateur tastings designed to help participants improve their ice cream making skills or judging abilities, scores are structured around individual defects, offering insight into areas needing improvement. A scoring range, say from one to ten, may be designated for each characteristic. Alternatively, specific scores may be assigned for slight, definite, pronounced, and unacceptable faults, and for no criticism. Slight defects are those noticed by experts but rarely by the average person. Definite defects are detectable by many people; pronounced ones recognized by everyone. An unacceptable fault prevents you from enjoying the sample.

At a tasting where participants bring ice cream for evaluation, tasters sometimes divide into teams of two or three to discuss and analyze each sample. Afterwards, those who contributed ice cream are given all the score sheets pertaining to their samples.

A simple scoring card, used at just-for-fun tastings, rates only the four main characteristics—taste, texture, body, and color. Greatest weight is given to flavor, least to color. Here, scores are more dependent on the tasters' likes and dislikes than on their ice cream making knowledge.

Samples of both a formal and an informal score sheet follow. You may wish to use a score sheet to evaluate new recipes or to distribute at your next tasting; or use the following examples to design your own scoring system, based on the kind of freeze to be evaluated and on your idea of perfection. Naturally, you won't be looking for the same traits in gourmet ice cream as in diet ice cream, for example, or in a sherbet or sorbet.

TASTER'S SCORE CARD		Sample No. _____					

Category		NO CRITICISM	SLIGHT	DEFINITE	PRONOUNCED	UNACCEPTABLE	SCORE
Color 8 – 0	uneven	4	3	2	1	0	____
	unnatural	4	3	2	1	0	____
Body & Texture 66 – 4	buttery	6	2	1	0	*	____
	coarse or icy	6	4	2	1	*	____
	crumbly	6	4	3	2	1	____
	dense or heavy	6	4	3	2	1	____
	fluffy, snowy, or flaky	6	3	2	1	0	____
	gummy or pasty	6	4	2	1	0	____
	hard	6	4	3	2	1	____
	lumpy	6	4	2	1	0	____
	sandy or gritty	6	2	1	0	*	____
	separated	6	5	3	2	1	____
	soft	6	4	2	1	0	____
Flavor 140 – 33	bitter	10	4	2	1	*	____
	cooked taste	10	9	7	5	3	____
	eggy	10	7	6	3	1	____
	flat (lacks sweetness)	10	8	7	6	5	____
	lacking fine flavor	10	9	8	7	6	____
	rancid or soapy	10	4	2	0	*	____
	salty	10	8	6	4	*	____
	sour or acidic	10	4	2	1	*	____
	stale or paper taste	10	7	6	5	3	____
	stale ingredient	10	6	4	2	*	____
	strong flavor	10	9	8	7	6	____
	too sweet or syrupy	10	9	8	6	4	____
	unnatural flavor	10	8	6	4	2	____
	weak	10	8	7	5	3	____

*unacceptable rating renders entire sample unacceptable

Key to scoring

excellent	147 – 214
good	108 – 146
fair	72 – 107
poor	38 – 71
unacceptable	37 or less

TOTAL SCORE: _____

TASTER'S SCORE CARD				Sample No._____	
Category	Excellent	Good	Fair	Poor	Unacceptable	Score
COLOR	5	4	3–2	1	0	
BODY & TEXTURE	6	5–4	3–2	1	0	
FLAVOR	10	9–8	7–4	3–1	0	
Total	21	18–16	13–8	5–3	0	

For the benefit of inexperienced tasters, consider inviting an ice cream appreciation expert to explain the characteristics under evaluation. Locate such a specialist through your county's extension home economist or your state's land-grant university dairy science department. Of course, you can also study the next chapter and become an expert yourself.

20

Trouble Shooting

Whether your goal is to create your own recipes, improve someone else's, or knowledgeably participate in ice cream tastings, it pays to familiarize yourself with possible defects and their causes. If you don't agree that all the characteristics described here are faults, take heart. Not long ago the density of today's superpremiums would have been considered a defect. Since no two ice cream lovers have the same taste, the final judgment call is entirely yours.

Color

The most appealing colors are delicate, natural, and appropriate to the flavor. Unevenness and unnatural appearance are the most common color defects.

Uneven—The color of such flavors as coffee or chocolate should be uniform. Unevenness may indicate that the mix wasn't thoroughly blended during freezing or that, after it was frozen, ingredients separated into layers due to thawing and refreezing.

Unevenness isn't always a defect. You may deliberately create a marbled or swirled effect; or you may find it charming to unevenly blend in fruit purée for a fresh-from-the-country look.

Unnatural—Any color that isn't coordinated with flavor seems unnatural, including an overly bright or gaudy hue. A grayish, unclean look, often associated with coarse texture, usually gets worse during storage. Grayness occurs when flavorings like vanilla extract, banana, or blackberry are added before a mix is heated, and then the mix gets too hot. Grayness also occurs when fresh bananas are added to a mix before it's aged, instead of just before it's frozen.

Bluish-gray color caused by cranberries can be prevented with a little lemon juice. Greenish-black splotches in chocolate ice cream stored in a metal canister are easily avoided by repacking the ice cream into a plastic container for hardening.

Texture and Body

Texture and body strongly influence how you feel about flavor. Texture refers to overall structure as determined by the size, shape, number, and distribution of solids, ice crystals, and air cells. It is subjectively measured by how smooth ice cream feels in your mouth. Body refers to weight and consistency as determined by the proportion of solids to air. It is subjectively measured by chewiness and degree of firmness.

Texture and body are the most variable characteristics and the most subject to disagreement. While aficionados agree that ice cream and frozen yogurt should be very smooth, some like denser body. Most like sherbet and ice milk to be as smooth as ice cream, others prefer them fluffy or snowy. Tastes in ices and sorbets vary the most. Preferences in texture range from light and snowy to coarse and grainy. In body they range from dry and crumbly to moist and sticky.

Defects in Texture

Buttery—Buttery lumps that stick to the roof of your mouth occur in high-fat ice cream in which some of the milkfat has churned into clumps of butterfat. The word "churning," sometimes improperly used to mean "stir freezing," refers to the process of stirring cream until it turns to butter, obviously highly undesirable in ice cream.

Churning is most likely to occur in mixes containing more than eighteen percent milkfat, due to their very low ratio of nonfat milk solids to fat particles. Churning may also be caused by acid ingredients or may result from using thawed cream that was frozen without sugar. Short of churning into lumps, excess fat may yield ice cream that feels unpleasantly buttery, pasty, or greasy.

Chilling a mix below 40° F (4.5° C) and fast freezing both help prevent churning. In still freezing, avoid it by whipping cream no stiffer than the soft peak stage.

Coarse/Icy—When ice crystals are large or uneven, and the surrounding air cells are much larger than the tiny, well distributed ones responsible for smoothness, texture is described as coarse or icy. You can easily identify this characteristic since your mouth will feel unusually cold and since your tongue can detect ice crystals larger than twenty microns or .0008 inch (.002 cm). If you bite into coarse ice cream, you'll hear the crystals crunch between your teeth.

Desirable in a granita, coarseness is the most common textural defect in other freezes because it has so many different causes. It may occur when a mix contains too little fat, too few solids, too little sugar or stabilizer, or ingredients that don't blend well. It may result if the mix is aged too long or not long enough, or the ice cream is packed too soon for hardening, is hardened at too high a temperature, or suffers heat shock.

The problem may be the fault of an ice cream machine that freezes too slowly or has poorly fitting, inefficient blades or a scratched or dented canister. If you use an old-fashioned freezer, iciness may mean you added too much salt in proportion to ice or you turned the crank too fast. Still-frozen desserts may be icy if not beaten thoroughly enough or often enough.

Coarseness is most likely to be a problem in diet ice cream, ice milk, frozen yogurt, sherbet, and sorbet, which lack oil or butterfat to coat ice crystals and retard their growth. Taking care to use neither too much nor too little sugar or stabilizer helps prevent it.

Rough, crusty, white crystalline splotches appearing on sherbets and ices after a portion has been removed from the container are caused by ice or sugar collecting on the disturbed surface. Minimize this problem by covering the surface with waxed paper or plastic wrap. Prevent it by substituting corn sugar for one-fourth of the granulated sugar in the mix.

Fluffy/Snowy/Flaky—Fluffy texture is very desirable in spooms, somewhat desirable in sorbetti, sometimes desirable in sherbets, but a defect in ice cream since it decreases the feeling of richness and causes too-rapid melting. It is related to a low proportion of solids, fat, or stabilizer (especially gelatin), or too much emulsifier. It is associated with high overrun or large air cells that produce open texture.

This defect may be caused by incorrect freezing techniques, including slow agitation, poorly designed blades that whip inefficiently, or prolonged freezing time. It is most likely to occur in sherbets and sorbets, making them more like spooms when they're not supposed to be. Snowiness is relatively rare in homemade ice cream, especially if milk or cream is warmed before the sugar is stirred in.

Gummy/Pasty—Instead of melting in your mouth, gummy ice cream sits on your tongue like a spoonful of rice pudding. In a dish, it retains its shape, even after melting. Associated with dense body, gumminess is most likely to occur in ice cream containing too much powdered sugar, cocoa, or fat. In diet ice cream, frozen yogurt, sherbet, or sorbet, it results from too much flour, cornstarch, or gelatin.

Lumpy—Lumps producing undesirable bursts of flavor in your mouth are due to ingredients that weren't thoroughly mixed prior to freezing. Lumps with no distinct flavor are caused by such rapid freezing that the dasher couldn't work fast enough to blend in frozen material smoothly. If you use an old-time ice cream maker, you may be salting the ice too heavily.

Sandy/Gritty—Among the worst defects is grittiness, feeling like sand on your tongue. You can readily distinguish this defect from iciness because the gritty feeling remains long after ice crystals would have melted. Sandy texture may be caused by using finely ground nuts, as opposed to coarsely chopped ones, or it may result from lactose crystallization.

Condensed milk in which the lactose settled to the bottom of the can may cause sandiness unless heated to dissolve the crystals. Fruit that wasn't stabilized with sugar, or nuts that weren't soaked in syrup or heated in butter, sometimes cause lactose precipitation. Using too much powdered milk in low-fat or diet ice cream also causes it. Homemade ice cream is unlikely to be sandy since it rarely contains the large amounts of nonfat milk solids required before lactose will crystallize.

Defects in Body

Crumbly—Crumbly ice cream, identifiable because it so easily falls apart when scooped, contains large air cells, making it also coarse in texture. Whether or not crumbliness is a defect depends on the freeze under evaluation. Many vegetable sorbets are unavoidably crumbly. In the extreme, still-frozen granite are *supposed* to be crumbly and coarse.

In sherbets and sorbets, crumbliness results from too few solids, too little sugar, not enough stabilizer, or so much overrun that the freeze disappears as soon as you spoon it into your mouth. Sorbet made without a stabilizer is more likely to suffer this defect than ice cream, since dairy products contain natural stabilizers. Dry body, similar to crumbly body but occurring only in ice cream, results from too much emulsifier, egg yolk, or stabilizer.

Dense/Heavy—Whether dense or heavy body is a defect is a matter of degree. It's desirable in gourmet and soy ice creams as an indication that they're loaded with solids and flavoring. Dense ice cream is moist in appearance and doesn't readily puddle as it melts.

When ice cream is too dense, it curls up in front of the scoop and leaves irregular waves behind it. In your mouth it feels doughy, pasty, or chewy. Excessive denseness results from too much powdered milk, cocoa, flour, or gelatin, usually combined with lots of sweetening and low overrun.

Hard—Excessive hardness may be caused by packing ice cream for hardening while it's still too soft. It also occurs in diet ice cream, ice milk, frozen yogurt, sherbet, and sorbet containing too few solids, especially sugar. Most still-frozen desserts freeze too hard unless occasionally beaten. Hardness is one of the greatest problems in homemade ice cream due to its characteristically low overrun.

Separated—Separation, also called "bleeding," "sticky bottom," or "pancake," occurs in sherbets and ices when highly concentrated, sugary syrup settles to the bottom of the container in a sticky, unfrozen goo, while air cells and ice crystals rise toward the top in a snowy, icy cloud. Separation is caused by too much sugar and too few solids, by high overrun, and by a too-high storage temperature. You can minimize the problem by adding a stabilizer to increase the viscosity of a mix.

A taffy-like deposit at the bottom of still-frozen ice cream means that new ingredients (such as whipped cream or whipped egg white) were added before freezing was far enough along or that the mix wasn't beaten often enough during freezing. In stir-frozen ice cream such a deposit means either the ice cream was hardened before freezing was complete or it wasn't stored at a low enough temperature. When the layer is coarse, hard, and unpalatable, the ice cream may have suffered serious heat shock.

Soft/Weak—In commercial ice cream, soft or weak body comes from too little fat, too few solids, and too little stabilizer, combined with very high overrun. The result is reduced richness and rapid melting.

Lack of firmness is less common in homemade ice cream than in homemade sherbet or sorbet. If it's soft and sticky, you've used too much sugar. If it's soft and pasty or gluey, you've added too much stabilizer. In ice cream, weak body can usually be traced to high overrun caused by a coolant consisting of either air inside a too-warm freezer or ice with too little salt sprinkled in.

Melting

The more natural ice cream is, the more readily it melts at room temperature, eventually looking just like the mix it was made from. Melting characteristics are more significant in the evaluation of commercial ice cream, since unnatural melt-down arouses consumer suspicion.

Homemade ice cream is less likely to contain ingredients you deem undesirable and, in any case, is gobbled up so quickly that its taste and texture are far more important than the way it melts. Melting qualities, evaluated by monitoring a sample left at room temperature for thirty minutes, serve primarily as a means of tracking down associated defects in body.

Defects in Melting

Foam—Although ice cream has been defined as frozen foam, there's such a thing as too much. Foam, froth, or bubbles on the surface of melting ice cream signals excess air or too-large air cells. Foaminess results from too much egg or gelatin in a mix that's otherwise low in solids.

Scum—Occasionally melting ice cream separates into a dull, wrinkled, scummy mess surrounded by a watery, wheylike liquid. This defect usually indicates acid, perhaps contributed by nonfresh milk or cream. Scum may also result from heat shock or from prolonged storage at a relatively high temperature.

Resistance to melting—Ice cream should neither retain its shape nor break into chunks as it melts. Melting resistance is often associated with foaminess, since foam on the surface serves as insulation and slows absorption of heat. Ice cream that continues to hold its shape as it melts may contain too much fat, gelatin, or total solids and therefore is likely to be dense or doughy in body.

Flavor

Few disagree that flavor is the most important feature of ice cream. Ideal flavor is fresh, sweet, delicate, pleasing, and typical for its type. Properly balanced ice cream neither tires your taste buds nor leaves an aftertaste. Variations from ideal may be caused by poor quality, stale or artificial ingredients, or by too much or too little sweetening or flavoring. Poor flavor may also result from combining ingredients that don't naturally blend well.

Flavor Defects

Bitter—A sharp or bitter taste, bitter aftertaste, or lingering harshness results from milk or cream that either wasn't fresh or was obtained from dairy animals fed weeds or strong feeds. Bitterness is also caused by inferior or artificial flavorings and by too much lemon or orange extract. When fresh citrus rind is used, bitterness occurs if even a little of the white flesh beneath the peel is inadvertently included. Commercially prepared citrus juices are often bitter because they're squeezed from whole fruit, peel and all.

A pungent, bitter taste on the surface of uncovered ice cream, particularly on frozen cakes or pies decked with whipped cream, was likely absorbed from stale freezer air. Prevent it by wrapping fancy desserts with plastic or foil as soon as they harden and by covering the surface of any ice cream left in the container after some has been scooped out.

Cooked flavor—When milk, cream, or any dairy-based mix is heated too long, milk proteins caramelize and develop a decidedly cooked flavor. Using too much evaporated milk or a poor quality powdered milk has the same effect. It is more noticeable in delicate flavors than in stronger ones like butterscotch, caramel, coffee, or chocolate.

Eggy—Egginess results from using too many eggs or combining eggs with ingredients of noncomplementary flavor. It's especially noticeable in low-fat frozen custard. A decidedly meringue taste in a spoom or sherbet means too many egg whites have overwhelmed the more delicate flavors.

Flat—Flatness in ice cream or any other dairy-based freeze means too little sweetening was used. In a fruit ice or sorbet, it indicates too much water in proportion to juice or purée. A flat vegetable sorbet probably needs salt.

Lacks fine flavor—Fine flavor is that elusive quality occurring when all ingredients blend in perfect harmony. It distinguishes excellent ice cream from merely good ice cream and is attributable to a flair for handling flavoring ingredients. The only way to educate your palate to recognize fine flavor is by tasting, tasting, and more tasting.

Rancid/Soapy—This defect is not easy to identify, especially in very sweet or strongly flavored ice cream. Rancidness or soapy flavor is caused by the chemical reaction occurring when milk or cream is improperly processed, raw and pasteurized milk are combined, a mix containing raw dairy products is aged too long, or ice cream made with raw milk or cream is stored too long. It is more likely to occur in homemade ice cream, since raw milk and cream are never used commercially. Soapy flavor also results when baking soda is used to neutralize old, soured cream, a trick few fans of homemade ice cream would care to copy from an unscrupulous few in the industry.

Salty—Saltiness comes from using too much salt or powdered milk. Since milk naturally contains sodium, additional salt is rarely needed except perhaps to enhance the flavor of low-fat, dairy-based freezes or vegetable sorbets.

Sour/Acidic—A quick, sharp, sour sensation on your tongue may be due to lactic acid from either nonfresh dairy products or improperly pasteurized, home-produced milk or cream. It may also occur when a dairy-based mix is cooled too slowly, aged too long, or aged at temperatures above 40° F (4.5° C).

An unpleasant sour edge to frozen yogurt means the yogurt was either too old or was incubated too long. A sour, yeasty taste in fruit flavors signals the presence of fermented fruit or fruit syrup. Any freeze flavored with a significant amount of reconstituted lemon juice will taste more sour than one made from fresh juice.

Stale/Papery—A stale or papery taste, reminiscent of wet cardboard, develops in dairy-based freezes containing fruit that was neither heated nor stabilized with sugar. Using too small an amount of an acidic fruit such as strawberries in a dairy-based mix may produce a cardboardy taste. Ice cream made with improperly pasteurized dairy products or old eggs may become papery tasting due to gradually decomposing fat.

If your canister (or milk separator) is due for re-tinning, or you store milk or a dairy-based mix too long in a metal container, a metallic, somewhat puckery taste will foreshadow the cardboardy flavor. This is less likely to occur in summer milk because summer dairy rations contain feedstuffs that guard against it, and because summer ice cream rarely lasts long.

Stale ingredient—A lingering aftertaste may indicate the use of old or stale ingredients such as rancid nuts or souring cream that imparts an unpleasantly strong, buttery flavor. If you have any doubt about the freshness of an ingredient, taste it before stirring it into your mix. Some foods, especially dairy products and nuts, begin spoiling even before you bring them home from the store.

Strong—A strong, sharp, sometimes bitter flavor results from using too much of an inferior or artificial flavoring. This defect rarely occurs when you use natural flavorings, which are usually quite delicate. In any case, never let the flavoring overpower the fresh taste of milk.

Sweet or syrupy—Cloying sweetness comes from using too much sugar, honey, or other sweetener. This defect is often associated with soft or separated body.

Unnatural—Unnatural flavor has any number of causes including inferior dairy products, poor quality gelatin, fermented fruits or syrups, and overly ripe or decomposing fruits. It may come from combining flavorings that don't blend well, especially where one flavor completely overpowers another, such as too much lemon in a fruit flavor or too much vanilla in chocolate or coffee.

Most often, unnatural flavor is caused by poorly imitating artificial flavorings, especially vanillin, which gives you a sharp, burning sensation at the sides of your tongue. Improper cleaning of ice cream equipment also causes off flavor.

Weak—Weak, barely discernable flavor may mean you used too little flavoring or a flavoring that was too mild. Stronger tasting ingredients may overpower the main flavoring, or perhaps the mix was heated after volatile extracts were added, causing flavoring essences to evaporate. Use only high-quality, fresh ingredients, and you'll rarely encounter this or any other flavor defect.

Part Three: Embellish It

Perhaps the most impressive thing about ice cream is its suitability for all occasions, no matter how formal or informal. A scoop atop a cone is a treat any time. The same scoop served in a fluted dish makes a glorious finale to the finest meal. This section explores ways to embellish that scoop, ranging from simple servings to simply elegant centerpieces. Scrumptious ice cream specialties are far easier to prepare than their lavish appearance suggests. They may be fashioned from either homemade or store-bought ice cream or a combination of the two. And they're easy to adapt to holidays and other events by combining colors or flavors traditionally associated with the anticipated festivity.

For Christmas and New Year's Day, include mincemeat, eggnog, or candied fruit flavors, or emphasize those associated with green and red—pistachio, avocado, or mint combined with cranberry, raspberry, or strawberry. Keep spring specialties on the light and fruity side—red raspberry or strawberry for St. Valentine's Day, lemon and purple plum for Easter, lime for St. Pat's.

Lighten up even more during warm summer months by switching to colorful sorbets and sherbets. Purée that traditional Fourth of July watermelon for a delightfully refreshing molded ice. Show your patriotic colors with a red, white, and blueberry layer cake or ice cream pie. For Halloween and Thanksgiving, turn your attention to orange, pumpkin, and spiced apple.

Let these and the following ideas, both traditional and innovative, become the spark that ignites your imagination, leading to customized combinations to suit your own unique style.

21

By The Scoop

The idea of molding and releasing ice cream by the scoop was the 1876 brainchild of George W. Clewell of Reading, Pennsylvania. Before then, it was dished up with an ordinary spoon. The first dipper designed specifically for serving ice cream had a conical bowl and two handles and required two hands to operate.

The round dipper came along in the early 1900s as an easier way to serve up single scoops. But interesting shapes and odd contraptions continued to appear until the stock exchange collapsed in 1929, putting a crimp on innovative designs.

Thereafter, the single biggest innovation was introduced in 1935 by Sherman Kelly of Toledo, Ohio, who devised a one-piece dipper with antifreeze sealed into its handle. Kelly's Zeroll self-defrosting dipper, warmed by the heat of your hand, slides easily into ice cream and just as easily releases the ball formed in its bowl. The Zeroll is now part of the Museum of Modern Art's permanent design collection, and those who've tried it consider it the perfect scoop. But watch out for inferior imitations.

Dippers

Scoops, dippers, dishers—whatever you choose to call them—come in several styles, most producing a perfectly round ball. Some have a spring-operated, thumb-release ejection mechanism. Unless your ice cream is fairly soft, the spring-release may be difficult to work, and too much pressure on the mechanism may eventually cause it to pop loose. Most thumb-release scoops are designed for right-handers, making them difficult for lefties to operate.

Squeeze-spring scoops can be worked with either hand but are somewhat awkward since you tend to squeeze the release while still trying to get the scoop full. The ice cream fanatic who has everything uses an electric or battery-operated dipper that relies on gentle heat rather than mechanical force.

None of these scoops is as easy to use or to clean as the one-piece Zeroll, which can be worked with equal ease in either hand and has no moving parts to break. You'll have to wash it by hand, though—the fluid sealed into its handle can't take high dishwasher temperatures.

Self-defrosting fluid in the handle of a Zeroll scoop or spade keeps ice cream from sticking. (Photo courtesy of the Zeroll Company, Fort Pierce, Florida.)

Ice Cream Spades

A specialized sort of one-piece dipper, the ice cream spade is a wide, flat, shovel-shaped spoon handy for getting into the corners of square containers, cutting into or repacking hard ice cream, or filling ice cream molds. Among its many advantages is the ease with which it scoops into homemade ice cream after a shorter tempering period than is required for a round scoop. A spade won't fit handily into small containers and can't be used to make cute, little round balls to fill a cone, but it does give you a relatively flat slab of ice cream, just the right shape to grace a slice of pie or cake without sliding or rolling off.

You can use a spade to heap hardened ice cream into a pie shell or to create spectacular two-tone swirls. For each swirled serving, form a base by placing a round scoop of ice cream in the center of a dish. Switching to the spade, skim off a layer of the same kind of ice cream and press it against the scoop. Skim a layer of contrasting color and press it against the first in an overlapping pattern, like the petals of a rose. Alternate one more layer of each so the last overlaps the first. The result is a heaping swirl of contrasting color and flavor. Attractive and tasty combinations include orange and vanilla, chocolate and coffee, avocado and strawberry.

Dipper Size

Whether or not you have an ice cream spade, you'll likely want to have a regular dipper as well. Round dippers come in nine sizes ranging from number six to a number forty. The lower the number, the larger the bowl. Different sizes have different purposes, but the main thing is to make sure the one you select fits easily into the containers you normally store your ice cream in.

Of the nine dipper sizes, five are used more often than the others—number twelve for sundaes and splits, number sixteen for sodas, floats, and single servings, number twenty for cake or pie a la mode, number twenty-four for cones, and number thirty for parfaits or sampler dishes containing several flavors. Numbers sixteen and twenty are considered all-purpose household sizes, with two dips offered per average serving. A melon scoop also makes a handy dipper for creating special effects with bite-sized balls of well-tempered ice cream.

Dipper size is supposed to correlate with the number of scoops dished out per quart. A number sixteen, for example, theoretically gives you sixteen scoops to the quart. How many you actually get depends in part on overrun. The more air ice cream contains, the easier it is to compress during dipping and the fewer scoops you'll get. The number of dips you get per quart also depends on your scooping technique.

Scooping

Although scooping may look like child's play, pros take lessons and study films to perfect their technique. For commercial dippers, much of the mystique involves creating scoops of uniform size so that each contains exactly the same amount. Commercial dippers try to maximize prof-

Traditional ice cream treats—sundae, cone, and ice cream soda. (Photo courtesy of the American Dairy Association, Rosemont, Illinois.)

its by getting the greatest number of servings per container. Some aren't above dipping out hollow scoops that look much bigger than they really are.

If you just want to get the ice cream into the dish, the trick is to let the scoop do the work. Ramming a dipper into the center of a carton, then dragging it to the side to pack the ice cream in is not only hard work but leaves a hollow well down the middle of the container, making it more difficult to scoop the next serving. The uneven surface is also more subject to ice crystals or freezer burn. When you finish scooping, the surface of the ice cream remaining in the carton should be horizontal and even.

Scooping is easier if you first temper the ice cream, as described in Chapter 18, "Hardening and Storing." If the dipper still doesn't slide in easily or won't let go of the scooped ice cream, keep a cup of warm water handy to heat the dipper between scoops. Using moderate pressure, dip the scoop's nose in at a forty-five degree angle. Draw the scoop toward you in an arc, skimming the surface until you get a smooth, round ball. Lift out the scoop by turning the handle.

To release the ice cream, gently touch it against the dish or cone (at the same time pressing the releasing mechanism, if there is one). When filling a cone, finish by gently pressing the back of the dipper against the ice cream to make it stick, taking care not to mash the ice cream or break the cone. A generous scoop will have a "skirt" of ice cream sticking out around the edges. Another way to make a scoop look opulent is to press a second, much smaller portion on top of the first.

Double-dipping results in an interesting marbled effect, with no two scoops turning out exactly alike. Half-fill your dipper with one flavor, then complete the scoop with another. Pair off cool fruit flavors such as orange and strawberry, raspberry and lemon, vanilla and lime; or combine rich flavors like chocolate and mocha almond or coffee and rocky road.

Pre-scooping

Serving ice cream to a crowd is fast and easy when you pre-scoop it well in advance. Place scoops on a chilled cookie sheet and cover with foil or plastic wrap to keep them from icing up or absorbing off-flavors. At serving time, transfer scoops to individual dishes and tuck in one or two fan-shaped cookies, rolled cookies, crisp sugar wafers, or waffled wafers. Alternatively, accompany each scoop with a fruit kebab made by skewering chunks of banana, kiwi, mandarin orange, mango, pineapple, and fresh strawberries on a cocktail pick; or, pop individual servings into one of the edible cups described in Chapter 22.

For added interest, roll scoops in toasted coconut, crushed cookies, candy shot, chocolate sprinkles, wheat germ, or finely chopped nuts, or candied fruit. The coating will stick better if scoops are allowed a short stint in the freezer before serving. Called "summer snowballs" or simply "snoballs," these treats look extra fancy when served in a pool of sundae sauce.

As an alternative to single servings, gently heap pre-formed scoops into a glass punch bowl and let guests help themselves. Mingle in fresh strawberries, long-stemmed cherries, chunks of tropical fruit, or pastel-hued sugared violets (see Chapter 28 for directions). Toss in some melon-ball-sized scoops of contrasting colors, or pre-shape only tiny scoops and combine them with a colorful mix of cantaloupe, honeydew, and watermelon balls.

Children and adults alike enjoy a do-it-yourself sundae session, created by surrounding a bowl of scoops with all the trappings, described in Chapter 24, "Sundaes, Parfaits, and

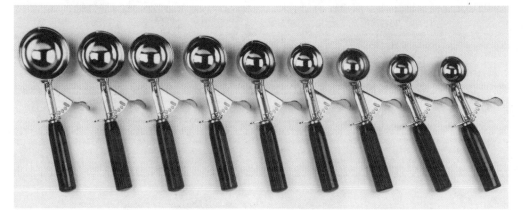

Dippers come in nine sizes, 6 through 40, numbered according to how many scoops of ice cream they'll dip from a quart. (Photo courtesy of Nasco, Fort Atkinson, Wisconsin.)

Scooping Technique: Grip the scoop near its bowl and, instead of digging a well down the center of the ice cream, draw the scoop toward you as you skim the surface.

When a well-shaped ball has formed in the scoop, turn and lit it away from the container, then release the ice cream by gently touching it against a cone or dish. (Photos courtesy of The Zeroll Company, Fort Pierce, Florida.)

Splits." Advance preparation is especially handy for children's parties, where everyone clamors to be served at once. Delight the kids with clowns made from pre-scooped ice cream cones, set upside-down and at a tilt on a chilled baking sheet, then frozen firm. Fashion clown faces with chocolate chip eyes, maraschino cherry noses, and cinnamon candy mouths. Chill until firm and serve your pointy-hatted clowns on lacy paper doilies that double as ruffled collars.

Chocolate Dip

The ultimate in pre-scooped ice cream is the chocolate dip, made by dunking firmly frozen scoops into melted chocolate coating. Ice cream dipped in chocolate was one of the many innovations of the Roaring Twenties, the heyday of such novelties as the Popsicle, Fudgsicle, Creamsicle, Drumstick. and Eskimo Pie.

The Eskimo Pie, which has nothing to do with Eskimos and isn't really a pie, was the first chocolate covered ice cream bar. It was invented in 1921 by Christian Nelson of Des Moines, Iowa. Since the original patent expired, imitations have continued popping up, but none has ever matched the popularity of the original.

Coming close was the Good Humor Bar, the first chocolate-coated ice cream on a stick. The invention, made by Harry Burt of Youngstown, Ohio, led to the institution known as the Good Humor Man and was responsible for the Yale riot of 1952, sparked when the Good Humor Man was denied his regular parking spot on campus.

Today's commercially coated bars (which don't seem to inspire the same sort of passion) are shaped and dipped by machine, but you can mold and coat your own using original hand-dipping methods. Ice cream coating is similar to chocolate candy coating, except that it has a lower melting temperature to keep the ice cream from melting. The lower temperature also keeps the coating from layering on too thickly and from freezing so brittle that it breaks off when you bite into it. This lower temperature is easily achieved simply by adding a little unsalted butter or cocoa butter to candy-dipping chocolate.

Chocolate Coating

Chocolate coating may be made with either chocolate or cocoa. Each of the following recipes makes enough for approximately eight number twenty scoops. For mocha-flavored coating, add one-half tablespoon instant coffee to either recipe.

For the chocolate version, melt six ounces semisweet chocolate bits and one-quarter cup unsalted butter in a double boiler. For the cocoa version, soften one-quarter cup unsalted butter and add one-half teaspoon vanilla. Blend two and a half tablespoons cocoa with one-third cup powdered sugar, and stir into the softened butter. Add a drop or two of liquid lecithin if necessary to improve adhesion. Stir smooth. Don't heat either coating more than necessary for the ingredients to blend.

Remove from heat but keep the pan over warm water. Have your ice cream pre-shaped and frozen firm. Working swiftly, flip or roll each portion in the warm coating until completely covered. Lift to drain. A sturdy candy-maker's fork comes in handy when working with round scoops.

While the coating is still soft, you may choose to roll or dip the scoop in chopped nuts or crushed toffee candy. Place each finished scoop on a chilled baking sheet lined with waxed paper, not touching, and freeze firm. Wrap individually after the coating has hardened, in about an hour. When working with a large number of scoops, dip and freeze them in small batches to prevent melting. Well-wrapped chocolate dips keep for about three weeks.

If you're in a hurry, instead of dipping the firmly frozen ice cream balls, drizzle them with chocolate shell coating from a squeeze bottle or roll them in grated dark or white chocolate, allowing one-half ounce per scoop.

Bars, Bonbons, and Truffles

Instead of dipping round balls, make bars by slicing ice cream hardened in the shape of a brick or loaf. If you add a Good Humor-style stick, do so before refreezing the bars prior to dipping. Alternatively, mold stir-frozen ice cream in three-ounce paper cups as you would for still-frozen ice pops, described in Chapter 1.

For smaller servings, cut ice cream into squares the size of petits fours, or pre-scoop it into tiny balls. Make bonbons by rolling scoops in finely chopped nuts before dipping. For frozen truffles, dip scoops of ginger, lemon, strawberry, raspberry, coffee, or rich chocolate ice cream, shaped with a number thirty or forty dipper or a melon-ball scoop.

Italian frozen truffles, or tartufi, consist of extra generous scoops of rich gelato with a little treat buried in the center. Possibilities include a soft mint, a maraschino cherry, or a small square of fudge. For a really special tartufo, press a chocolate covered cherry into the center of a scoop of softened chocolate gelato, freeze firm, and dip.

To make your own delicious tartufo nut filling, purée one-half cup toasted, skinned almonds or hazelnuts in a blender with two tablespoons almond or hazelnut liqueur and one-half cup vanilla or chocolate gelato. Freeze until firm enough to shape into eight tiny balls. Freeze balls firm and press them into the centers of eight scoops of soft chocolate or vanilla gelato (reversing the flavor of the filling). Freeze firm, dip, and refreeze. Serve tartufi at the table or eat them out-of-hand from muffin papers.

22

Edible Cups

Cones are the original edible ice cream containers, but no longer are they the only ones. Inventive ice cream fans enjoy devising a wide range of edible shells, nests, baskets, and boats. Although these alternatives can't be conveniently carried around like cones, they're equally appetizing and equally easy to make.

Cones

The origin of the edible ice cream cone is the subject of much debate. Most enthusiasts insist it's an American invention, but a few contend cones were popular in Europe and imported from England long before we learned to make our own.

One of the more colorful stories involves Italo Marchiony, who peddled lemon ice from a push-cart on Wall Street in the late 1800s. Washing dishes cut into his time and replacing broken ones cut into his profit. When he switched to paper cones, he found himself eternally picking up litter. Marchiony, it is said, developed the edible cone as an economical and ecologically sound way to serve ice cream.

The 1904 St. Louis World's Fair figures big in the history of the cone. There, as the story goes, a Syrian named Ernest Hamwi hawked a thin, crisp, waffle-like Persian pastry, zalabia, next door to an ice cream stand. Depending on who's telling the story, either (1) the ice cream vendor ran out of dishes and fast-thinking Hamwi developed an alternative; (2) on a whim Hamwi rolled one of his pastries and stepped over for a fill up; or, (3) Abe Doumar, a Lebanese souvenir salesman at the same fair, suggested that ice cream might be served in one of Hamwi's waffles folded to resemble middle-Eastern pita bread, whereupon Hamwi gave it a try. Whether the idea was Hamwi's or Doumar's, Marchiony beat them both to the punch, obtaining a patent on the cones he'd been making for at least eight years before the fair ever opened.

In any case, it wasn't until the fair that the idea really caught on. Cones were immediately dubbed "World's Fair cornucopias," and St. Louis became home to the first manufacturing plant, the Cornucopia Waffle Company, founded by Hamwi. Meantime, the wandering Doumar traveled up the East Coast vending his own version.

At first, cones were rolled by hand. Then a machine was invented to do the job. Later, molds were used to shape them from batter. During the wild and wonderful Roaring Twenties, weird designs were the norm. Cone-making was so competitive that companies were forced to tout newer and better models, including such oddities as double-headers, spirals, and dripless cones. As a result of the Depression and World War II, cones settled into the relatively unimaginative forms we know today.

Invented in the 1800s, cones are still the most popular way to serve ice cream. (Photo courtesy of the American Dairy Association, Rosemont, Illinois.)

Roll Your Own

No matter how the cone was invented, it has become our favorite way to enjoy ice cream. We eat billions of cones per year, making them a veritable American institution. As practical as they are crisp and tasty, cones come in two basic styles—flat-bottomed ones preferred by most adults, and pointy-ended cones favored by children.

Sadly, cones molded from batter are usually as tasteless as paper. Happily, the better ice cream shops have reverted to hand rolled ones containing such new-age ingredients as wheat, bran, malt, honey, finely ground nuts, carob, and various spices and extracts. Waffle cones are especially trendy, either imported from Europe or made in Euro-style waffle irons and rolled on a two-piece cone form. If you don't have a waffle-cone iron, you can still make cones on a cookie sheet or between the flat sides of a reversible teflon waffle iron, if it closes tightly enough.

Homemade cones, ranging from light and crisp to dense and chewy, require fast action to shape properly. Perhaps that's why baskets have become so fashionable. Baskets are baked the same as cones but are shaped over inverted dessert cups or between two bowls. Besides baskets, you can also gently fold cookies to resemble taco shells or cut them, while they're still warm, into six wedges like elegant, European fan-shaped cookies to be tucked, pointy end down, into a scoop of ice cream.

If you opt for rolling, your first few cones may look a bit crude, but don't despair— after two or three, you'll learn to work swiftly and smoothly, achieving near perfect cones time after time. For slower cooling cookies, gently stuff bits of crumpled waxed paper into the openings to keep them from collapsing until they firm up.

Your cones will be more uniform if you shape them over a cone form or metal cream horn, available at gourmet cookware shops. Three is a good number of horns to have, since that's how many cone cookies you can bake on an average-sized sheet. As soon as the cones cool enough to hold their shape, remove the horns for reuse on the next batch. Cones keep well for two to three days at room temperature or for several weeks in an airtight container in the freezer.

For a quick, nutritious after school snack, prefill cones with freshly frozen ice cream, slightly mounded at the top. Dip them, if desired, in sprinkles, miniature chocolate chips, or chopped nuts. Wrap each cone tightly in foil or plastic wrap and freeze firm. Prefilled frozen cones absorb moisture and lose their initial crispness, taking on the approximate consistency of the cookies flanking an ice cream sandwich. If you prefer crisp cones, fill them just before serving.

Bake crisp, tasty cones in a Euro-style waffle iron. (Photo courtesy of Maid of Scandinavia Company, Minneapolis, Minnesota.)

CRISP CONES

Vary the flavor of these delicate cones by adding a pinch of cinnamon or nutmeg, or by substituting almond, orange, lemon, or any other extract for the vanilla.

Beat at high speed until fluffy	$^3/_4$ **stick butter.**
Gradually add	$^1/_2$ **C sugar.**

Beat until fluffy, about 4 minutes.

Add	$^1/_8$ **t vanilla**
	$^1/_2$ **T water.**
Beat in, one at a time	**3 egg whites.**
Add and mix just until smooth	$^1/_2$ **C flour.**

Let batter set 2 hours at room temperature. Grease baking sheets. Outline three 6" circles on each sheet. Place $1^1/_2$ T batter in center of each. With back of spoon, spread batter to fill circle. Bake at 425° F (220° C) until lightly browned. Using wide pancake turner, remove from sheet and roll one at a time. If cookies cool and become too stiff to work, return to oven a few seconds to soften.

yield: 8 cones

COOKIE CONES

Make these hefty cones even tastier by sprinkling each with $^1/_2$ T sliced almonds before baking. For *chocolate* cones, stir in 1-oz melted semisweet chocolate.

Beat together	$^2/_3$ **C sugar**
	3 egg whites.
Add and beat smooth	**1 C flour.**
Melt and gradually beat in	$^1/_3$ **C butter**

Grease baking sheets well and sprinkle with flour. Using a paper cut-out or gently rotating an inverted 6" bowl, outline three 6" circles on each sheet. Place $2^1/_2$ T batter in center of each circle. With the back of a fork, spread batter to fill circle. Bake at 400° F (205° C), 8 to 10 minutes, until golden. Lift off one at a time, working fast so cookies don't have time to cool. Invert on paper towel. Using a second towel to protect fingers (or wearing clean cotton gloves), roll cookie into cone shape, keeping hold of tip for a sharp point. Pinch pointed end and place seam side down on counter top or wire rack to cool. Repeat for each cone. If cookies cool and become too stiff to work, return sheet to oven 1 to 2 minutes to soften.

yield: 8 cones.

SUGAR CONES

These slightly chewy cones develop an interesting textural pattern during baking. Use walnuts, pecans, or toasted almonds, or leave out the nuts for plain cones, but you'll get fewer of them.

Combine

1 egg
³/₄ t vanilla
3 T water
³/₄ C light brown sugar
1¹/₂ T melted butter.

Beat until sugar dissolves.

Add and beat smooth

¹/₂ C flour.

Stir in

³/₄ C finely chopped nuts.

Grease baking sheets well and sprinkle with flour. Outline three 6" diameter circles on each sheet. Place 2¹/₂ T batter in the center of each, spread evenly with a spatula or bottom of a measuring cup, taking care to leave no holes. Bake at 300° F (150° C) 15 minutes until firm. Remove from oven and loosen, then bake 3 minutes more, until lightly brown. Remove from oven, cool slightly, and roll one at a time. If cookies get too stiff to work, return sheet to oven and heat 1 minute.

yield: 8 cones

LACY CONES

Make these cones with lightly toasted pecans, hazelnuts, or walnuts. For delicate, fluted baskets, drape each cookie on an overturned glass until completely cooled and firm.

In small saucepan, combine

$^1/_4$ C **light brown sugar**
2 T light corn syrup
3 T unsalted butter
$^1/_4$ **t salt.**

Stirring, bring to boil.

Remove from heat and stir in

$^1/_4$ **C flour**
$^1/_4$ **C finely chopped nuts.**

Drop four 1 T mounds, 6" apart, onto two buttered baking sheets. Bake at 375° F (190° C) 8 to 10 minutes until golden. Cool on sheet until set but not firm, about 2 minutes. Remove with metal pancake turner and shape. If cookies cool too fast to work, soften in oven 1 or 2 minutes.

yield: 8 cones

WHOLE WHEAT HONEY CONES

These cones take a bit longer to firm up than most, giving you more time to get the shape right. For less sweet cones, use wheat germ in place of coconut. To make *malted* cones, substitute barley malt syrup for all or part of the honey.

In small saucepan over low heat combine

$^1/_2$ **C honey**
2 T butter
$^1/_8$ **t salt.**

Stir until butter dissolves.

Remove from heat and beat in

1 egg
$^1/_2$ **C whole wheat flour.**

Stir in

$^3/_4$ **C coconut.**

Grease baking sheets well and sprinkle with flour. Outline three 6" diameter circles on each sheet. Place 2$^1/_2$ T batter in the center of each, spread evenly with the back of a fork. Bake at 325° F (165° C) 15 minutes until edges brown.

WHOLE WHEAT HONEY CONES, cont'd.

Remove from oven, cool slightly, and roll one at a time. If cookies get too stiff to work, return sheet to oven for 1 minute.

yield: 8 cones

Chocolate Candy Cones

Chocolate clay tastes a bit like chocolate Tootsie Rolls and can be molded into any shape you dream up, including candy cones, fluted dishes, and cookie-based baskets. To make chocolate clay, place five and one-half squares of semisweet chocolate in a double boiler over hot water. Stir occasionally until the chocolate melts, then blend in three tablespoons light corn syrup. Spread the clay on waxed paper and let it stand until it's cool and stiff, which takes one hour or more. If you're in a hurry, cool the clay in the refrigerator a few minutes. Divide it into eight equal portions. Before shaping, knead each portion until it's pliable.

For candy cones, use a rolling pin to flatten each portion to a diameter of four and one-half inches. Shape as previously described for cookie cones, stuffing the opening with wadded waxed paper until the clay firms. To serve, wrap the base in waxed paper so the chocolate won't melt and stick to your hand.

For fluted dishes, flatten each portion of clay to a diameter of four inches. Press each against the bottom of a glass and, using the circular indentation as a guideline for the dish bottom, pinch sides for fluting.

To make baskets you'll need eight flat, two-inch diameter cookies. Roll each portion of clay into a twenty-inch rope. Using a cookie as the base, wrap a rope in three coils around the edge to form basket walls, pressing lightly to hold the clay in place. Fill baskets and other clay creations with orange chip, caramel nut, or any ice cream with a robust flavor.

Chocolate Shells

Although you can buy chocolate shells to serve ice cream in, it's still more rewarding to make your own. Solid cups are easy, lacy nests are only a bit trickier. In both cases, take care not to drip any water or other moisture into the melting chocolate or it will instantly solidify and become impossible to mold.

Until you're experienced enough to shape cups quickly before the chocolate hardens, make only three at a time. For each three cups, melt two squares of semisweet chocolate and two teaspoons of butter in a small saucepan over very low heat. Blend thoroughly. Prepare molds by stacking together three groups of three paper cupcake liners (for greater strength).

Divide melted chocolate among the molds and, working quickly, spread it to coat the bottom and insides evenly. Place molds in a muffin tin and refrigerate until hardened, about one hour. Remove one cup at a time from the refrigerator and gently peel back each layer of paper, taking care not to crack the cup.

Store cups in a cool place until you're ready to serve them, or fill them with freshly frozen ice cream or still-frozen mousse and harden it right in the cup. For extra flair, add a dab of whipped cream and serve cups in a pool of liqueur or sundae sauce; or, elegantly heap cups to the brim with melon-ball-sized scoops of assorted ice cream, sherbet, and sorbet, or tiny scoops of vanilla ice cream combined with fresh strawberries.

Two-Tone Cups

A variation of the all-chocolate cup is the two-tone chocolate/butterscotch cup—a super way to serve nut ice cream. For three cups, melt one ounce (two tablespoons) semisweet chocolate bits in a small saucepan over very low heat. In a second small saucepan over very low heat, melt one ounce (two tablespoons) butterscotch bits plus one-half teaspoon butter. Stir just to blend.

Prepare three molds as before. Divide melted chocolate among them and evenly coat bottom and walls on one side of each mold. Divide melted butterscotch and coat the other half of each mold. Chill, peel paper, and store as for chocolate cups. Of course, there's nothing to stop you from making butterscotch shells by omitting the chocolate and doubling the butterscotch.

Nests

To fashion chocolate nests, prepare molds by pressing squares of aluminum foil against a wide-rimmed, six-ounce glass or dessert dish. Trim away excess foil, leaving one inch extending around the edges and making a sharp fold where the glass meets the countertop—this is the nest rim. Slip the form from the glass and coat it with nonstick cooking spray. Prepare one form per nest.

You'll need six squares of semisweet chocolate for each four nests. Melt the first three squares in a small saucepan over low heat. Remove from heat and cool ten minutes. Spoon the chocolate into a pastry bag or a self-sealing plastic sandwich bag with a tiny portion of one corner snipped off. With the mold still upside down, pipe chocolate around the rim then crisscross it back and forth over the top. Refrigerate the first mold and continue on with the next.

When all four nests have been shaped, melt the remaining three squares of chocolate and pipe on a second layer for strength. Refrigerate nests until chocolate hardens, about one hour. Remove nests from the refrigerator one at a time and, working carefully to avoid cracking the chocolate, slowly peel away the foil. Return a nest to the refrigerator if it softens before the foil is off. Fill nests with soft ice cream or still-frozen mousse and harden.

Fruit Boats

Fruits and vegetables can be crafted into attractive, edible serving containers. The classic is half a cantaloupe or honeydew, seeded and filled with vanilla ice cream or fruit sherbet. A watermelon shell works nicely when serving pre-scooped ice cream to a crowd. Scoop the melon meat into little balls to mingle with the same size scoops of ice cream.

Fruit or vegetable shells are particularly suited for sherbets and sorbets since the scooped-out pulp can be used in the filling. Favorites are apple, papaya, pineapple, cucumber, and tomato. Don't feel compelled to refill hollowed-out shells with the same flavor. Try lemon sherbet in a cucumber boat, for example, or orange in a pineapple boat (cut in half lengthwise, leaves left on). For the California touch, arrange boats on a bed of grape leaves, curly kale, or other greens.

Citrus Shells

Orange, lemon, and grapefruit are available year-round and are easy to work with. Begin by cutting a thick slice off the stem end for a stable bottom. Turn and remove one-third from the top. If you wish, save the removed portion for a cap. Work pulp out with a serrated knife and a grapefruit spoon. For really smooth insides, and to remove the bitter white membrane, soak shells in hot water for ten minutes, then carefully turn them inside out and pull the membrane away from the skin. Turn them right-side around while they're still warm and soft.

Freeze shells and caps at least three hours before spooning in softened or freshly frozen ice cream or sherbet. Top with a little whipped cream and a sprig of mint. Add the cap; or, leave it off and sprinkle each serving with toasted slivered almonds or crown with a single berry or slice of fruit. Wrap shells individually in foil or plastic wrap and freeze until serving time.

Before serving, temper in the refrigerator fifteen to thirty minutes. When citrus shells are served as dessert after a light meal, arrange them into an attractive centerpiece just before you come to the table. They'll temper as the meal progresses.

Tulip Cups

With a little extra time and effort, you can turn your citrus shells into edible, candied tulip cups. Prepare eight medium-sized lemons, large limes, or small oranges as before, cutting off the base and cap and working out the pulp and membrane.

In a large saucepan, cover shells with cold water, bring to a boil, and simmer five minutes. Drain. Repeat twice more. Cover the shells with water and let them set in a covered container twenty-four hours. Drain. Cover shells once more with water and bring to a boil. Simmer fifteen minutes or until shells are tender. Drain well.

Combine and heat two cups water and four cups granulated sugar, stirring until the sugar dissolves. Bring to a boil. Gently drop in citrus shells and simmer ten minutes, stirring to ensure even absorption of syrup. Gently place shells upside down on a wire rack to drain.

While they're still warm but cool enough to work, stand shells upright on a tray. Using scissors, snip out four equally spaced zig-zags, no deeper than one-third down from the top, giving each cup a tuliplike appearance. Chill.

Into each shell, spoon freshly frozen fruit ice cream, sherbet, or sorbet and harden it in the freezer. Alternatively, fill shells with tempered ice cream just before serving.

Cookie Boxes

You can fashion cookie boxes from any rolled-out cookies shaped with a cutter, provided they don't spread while baking. For an unusual winter holiday treat, make gingerbread boxes to fill with rum-raisin, holiday ambrosia, or lemon ice cream. For quick, easy servers any time of year, use the same principle to make graham cracker boxes. Then try a new twist on traditional s'mores—fill graham boxes with vanilla ice cream and pour in the hot fudge.

To glue the boxes together you'll need a special kind of frosting that dries fast and stiff. In a small mixing bowl, combine one egg white with one and one-half cups sifted powdered sugar. Beat until fluffy, about five minutes. Spoon frosting into a pastry bag or self-locking sandwich bag with a tiny portion of one corner cut off.

For each graham cracker box, break one cracker in half and another into quarters, using perforations as a guide. Adding one side at a time and holding each in place until it stands by itself, arrange the quarters to form a square. Pipe frosting at the corners to hold them together. For the bottom, pipe frosting around the edges of the half cracker and press it on top of the square. Leave boxes upside down to dry. When the icing is dry, trim corners by adding a neat bead around all the edges. For a party touch, pipe names, initials, or any other decoration onto one or more sides of each box.

Construct gingerbread or any other cookie boxes the same way, making a cardboard pattern by cutting one square 2½" by 2½" and one rectangle 1½" by 2¼". For each box you'll need one square cookie and four rectangular ones.

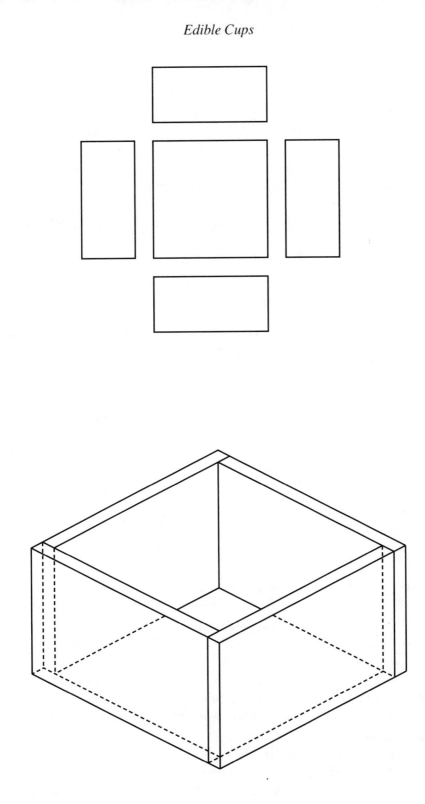

COOKIE BOX
Arrange sides of box first, overlapping corners as shown, then add bottom.

GINGERBREAD BOXES

This not-too-sweet cookie goes especially well with ice cream. Filled boxes make a great afternoon snack or hefty dessert.

In saucepan, combine	$^1/_3$ **C brown sugar**
	$^1/_3$ **C molasses**
	$^1/_2$ **t ginger**
	$^1/_2$ **t cinnamon**
	$^1/_4$ **t cloves.**

Bring just to a boil.

| Remove from heat and add | **1 t baking soda.** |

| Stir in until melted | $^1/_3$ **C butter.** |

| Thoroughly stir in | **1 egg** |
| | **2$^3/_4$ C flour.** |

Knead five minutes, then roll into a ball. Refrigerate 15 minutes or until firm enough to roll out. On level surface sprinkled with sifted powdered sugar, roll dough $^1/_8$" thick. Outline and cut required shapes. Carefully transfer cookies onto greased baking sheet, one-half inch apart. Bake at 325° F (165° C) 10 minutes. Cool on wire racks. Arrange rectangles in a square as shown in illustration, using frosting to glue corners as you work. Glue square on top. Leave boxes upside down until frosting is completely dry.

yield: 8 boxes

Ice Cream Puffs

Common ice cream puffs and elegant chocolate éclairs are made from the same pastry dough. The difference is in the shape—cream puffs are round, éclairs are elongated or finger-shaped. You can form less traditional shapes with a pastry tube or by working the dough with your hands. Whatever the shape, ice cream puffs are deceptively simple to make yet never fail to draw admiration.

Fill puffs with softened or freshly frozen ice cream, with or without replacing the cut-off top. Leaving the top off gives you room for more ice cream. You can then sprinkle on chopped nuts, top the whole thing off with whipped cream, or drizzle on a sundae sauce selected from among the recipes in Chapter 24.

If you elect to replace the cap after filling the puffs or éclairs, you can choose either to dust them with powdered sugar or to frost the tops with chocolate éclair glaze. To make the glaze, in a small saucepan combine two tablespoons water, three tablespoons sugar, and a dash of salt. Bring to a boil. Remove from heat and add one and one-half squares nonsweetened chocolate, stirring until the chocolate melts. Cool to spreading consistency.

ICE CREAM PUFFS

Fill pastries shortly before serving to keep them crisp. If you prefer to fill them ahead and store them in the freezer, you can perk them up in a hot oven for two minutes before serving, or deep-fry them as described in Chapter 29.

In saucepan, bring to boil	$\frac{1}{2}$ **C water** $\frac{1}{4}$ **C butter** $\frac{1}{8}$ **t salt.**
Reduce heat and stir in	$\frac{1}{2}$ **C sifted flour.**

Stir until mixture forms a ball.

Cool.

Add one at a time, beating smooth each time	**2 large eggs.**

Shape into 8 to 12 fingers or rounds and place on greased sheet. Bake at 400° F (205° C) 10 minutes, reduce heat to 350° F (175° C) and bake 25 minutes more, until puffs double in size and turn golden brown. Turn off heat, slit through crusts with a knife, and leave puffs in oven with door ajar 10 minutes to crisp. Cool on wire racks. Before filling, scoop out any excess dough.

yield: 12 small or 8 medium

Meringue Shells

Nothing beats crisp, delicate, melt-in-your-mouth meringue as an elegant way to serve ice cream. Made from egg whites and sugar, meringue dates back to 1720 when it was invented by an ingenious cook in the German village of Meyringen. Today, meringue shells filled with ice cream (sometimes called "*meringues glacés*," sometimes "ice cream on a cloud") remain a European favorite.

You can now find ready-made individual meringue shells and caps at better department stores and specialty food shops. But meringue shells aren't at all hard to make, provided you choose a dry day—humid weather keeps them from drying properly.

Begin with utensils totally free of oil or fat, which inhibits whipping. Separate egg whites into a large enough bowl to accommodate a four-fold expansion, taking care not to include the slightest bit of yolk, which contains natural fat. (Save the yolks to make French ice cream or gelato to fill the shells.) Warm the whites to room temperature so they'll accept more air—the key to light, crisp shells.

Procedure

Using an electric beater, whip whites foamy. Add cream of tartar to help them accept even more air. Whip until soft peaks form—they'll curl when you lift out the beater. To avoid inhibiting the incorporation of air, wait until this point to add the sugar. If you've beaten too long and the whites look stiff and dry, restore their texture by gently beating in one more room-temperature egg white.

Add sugar one tablespoon at a time, beating until it dissolves before adding more. You can tell the sugar has dissolved by rubbing a bit of raw meringue between your fingers to test for grittiness. Dissolving takes a bit longer with each addition. To speed things up, use extra fine sugar or powdered sugar.

Shape shells with the back of a large spoon, with a cookie press, with a pastry bag and large star tip, or with a self-sealing plastic bag, one corner nipped off. Pipe the bottom first, starting in the center and spiraling outward. Then build up the walls coil-on-coil. To prevent sagging, work slowly, taking care to keep the sides even and not let them get too high. Bake shells in a slow oven. When the time is up, turn off the oven and leave in the shells until they cool, thus ensuring they'll remain crisp and not turn sticky.

Finishing Touches

Fill shells with ice cream only after they've cooled completely. Place one large scoop in the center of individual shells or fill them with several smaller scoops (tiny scoops of pastel sherbet make attractive "eggs" in a meringue Easter basket). For larger shells, either pour in freshly made ice cream and then harden it or heap in hardened ice cream with a spade or small scoop at serving time. You'll need one quart of ice cream to fill eight individual shells or one large one.

Store filled shells in the freezer until ready to serve. Temper in the refrigerator fifteen minutes before serving. If desired, garnish with fresh berries or sliced sugared fruit and whipped cream, or top individual shells with sundae sauce and a meringue crown.

If you have meringue left over after shaping enough shells, pipe the remainder as cookies. Hard meringue cookies contain few calories and aren't filling because they're mostly air. Pipe bite-sized portions for satisfyingly crunchy cookies to accompany ice cream. Shape flattened rounds to fill as ice cream sandwiches. You can also pipe tiny dots onto the baking sheet and, when they cool, douse them with liqueur and stir them into softened ice cream for an exotic bisque.

HARD MERINGUE

Hard meringue is crunchy through and through. Stored in an airtight container, these shells keep well for three days.

Separate and warm to room temperature — **4 large egg whites.**

Beat whites foamy and add — **¹/₄ t salt**
1 t cream of tartar.

HARD MERINGUE, cont'd.   Beat into soft peaks.

Gradually beat in   **1¹/₄ C sugar.**

When all sugar has dissolved, add   **1 t vanilla.**

Variations:

Depending on what flavor you plan to fill shells with, you can flavor meringue according to one of the following variations. If you shape shells with a spoon instead of a piping tube, you can also include up to ¹/₂ cup minced candied fruit, nuts, coconut, or miniature chocolate chips.

almond—add ¹/₄ t almond extract and sprinkle shells with ¹/₂ C slivered almonds.

chocolate—beat in ¹/₂ C sifted cocoa.

chocolate mint—add ¹/₂ t mint extract and ¹/₂ C sifted cocoa.

citrus—add 2 T orange zest, ¹/₂ t lemon extract, and a few drops yellow food dye, if desired.

mint—add ¹/₂ t mint extract and a few drops green food dye, if desired.

rum—add 1 t rum extract.

INDIVIDUAL MERINGUE SHELLS

Grease two baking sheets. Pipe meringue into eight 3" circles, then build up a 1¹/₂" wall around the sides of each. Between shells, pipe eight peaked mounds or decorative rosettes for crowns. Bake 45 minutes at 275° F (135° C). Reduce heat to 250° F (120° C) and bake another 15 minutes or until shells are hard to the touch. Turn oven off and let shells cool for 1 hour before removing. Loosen with a pancake turner and transfer to individual serving plates.

yield: 8 shells and 8 caps

SINGLE MERINGUE SHELL

Grease baking sheet. Pipe meringue in a spiral wide enough to fit your serving platter. Continue building base until it's 2" high. Build up a 2" wall around the outside edge. Bake 1 hour at 275° F (135° C). Turn oven off and let ring cool 1 hour until firm and dry. Loosen with a pancake turner and transfer to serving platter.

yield: 8 servings

MERINGUE PIE SHELL

Grease a 9" pie plate and spread meringue just to the rim. Bake 1 hour at 275° F (135° C) until delicately brown and hard to the touch. Turn off oven and let shell cool 1 hour. (For pie filling ideas, see Chapter 29.)

yield: 8 servings

CRISP MERINGUE

In contrast to hard meringue, this one remains a bit chewy on the inside. It's also tan instead of pearly white. Store crisp meringue shells in an airtight container no longer than two weeks.

Beat stiff — **4 large egg whites.**

Gradually beat in — **1½ C powdered sugar.**

Blend together and add — **2 t vinegar**
2 t vanilla
2 t cornstarch.

Beat until stiff and glossy.

Pipe onto very well-greased sheets or use a spoon to spread in pie tin. Pre-heat oven to 300° F (150° C). Reduce to 250° F (120° C) and bake shells 40 minutes. Turn off oven and allow shells to cool 1 hour before removing from oven. Loosen with pancake turner and finish cooling on a wire rack.

yield: 8 servings

23

Soda Fountain Drinks

Earlier this century, the soda fountain was a place where families went for outings and teenagers met to socialize. In 1920, the London *Standard* printed this observation by one Sir John Frazer: "Young people do not go for country walks in America. They chiefly consort in the ice cream parlors." Not everyone agreed that such places were wholesome. The innocent young lady was publicly warned that the ice cream "saloon" was "likely to be a spider's web for her entanglement."

The demise of the soda fountain occurred not because it was such a dangerous place but because take-out packages appearing in the late 1940s allowed folks to enjoy ice cream in the comfort of their homes. Curbside service offered by 1950s drive-ins dealt the crowning blow.

But ice cream parlors made a comeback in the 1980s, thanks in part to neo-prohibitionism and in part to nostalgia. Commercial re-creations sprang up, and working models of soda fountains were constructed in such erudite establishments as Omaha's Western Heritage Museum and Chicago's Museum of Science and History. Collectors scrambled for authentic soda fountain memorabilia, and, in 1982, organized as the "Ice Screamers" to share information through an informal newsletter (see details in Appendix C).

Fountain Ware

Essential to the proper atmosphere of an ice cream parlor is traditional stemmed fountain ware, including soda glasses, ice cream and sherbet dishes, fluted sundae dishes, narrow parfait glasses, and long narrow banana boats. These old-timey dishes are manufactured by three major companies—Anchor Hocking, Lancaster Colony, and Libby.

If you don't have the correct dish for the occasion, you can easily improvise with fluted champagne glasses, goblets, tumblers, or other glassware of approximately the right shape and size.

Prechill any dish used for ice cream. Not only does the resulting frosted look enhance eye appeal, but a cold dish slows melting. Prechilling is especially important when serving sherbets and sorbets in warm weather. Chilled glasses keep ice cream sodas and other fountain drinks cold longer, giving you more time to sip and linger.

Nostalgia buffs enjoy re-creating mid-century soda fountains like this one. (Photo courtesy of Turnbull Bakeries, Chattanooga, Tennessee.)

Ice Cream Sodas

The original soda fountain drink was, naturally enough, the soda, made with flavored syrup, carbonated water, and cream. How ice cream got into the act is a hotly contested subject, with Philadelphia and Detroit both claiming credit. History favors Philadelphia, where soda jerk Robert Green was on hand to celebrate the fiftieth anniversary of the Franklin Institute in 1874. This hapless fellow either ran out of cream or discovered that his cream had soured. In desperation, he substituted vanilla ice cream, creating an instant hit with his new invention—the ice cream soda.

In the early days, syrups provided flavor, bland soda water contributed fizz, and the ice cream was usually vanilla. Later the flavor of the ice cream was matched with that of the syrup. A chocolate soda, for example, contained chocolate syrup and chocolate ice cream, a strawberry soda was made with strawberry syrup and strawberry ice cream. Now that both ice cream and carbonated beverages come in a range of flavors, syrup is not needed to flavor homemade ice cream sodas.

To make one, you do need a tall glass, preferably sixteen ounces, to accommodate the inevitable foam. Start with a scoop of ice cream. Stir in a little soft drink and, if desired, a bit of flavored syrup. Go easy on the syrup, though—more than a tablespoon or two can make the soda sickeningly sweet. Nearly fill the glass with additional soft drink, pouring it down the side to minimize foaming. Float a second scoop of ice cream on top. For a super-duper soda, add a gob of whipped cream and a maraschino cherry.

The classic ice cream soda, called a "black cow," is made with vanilla ice cream, one or two tablespoons of chocolate syrup, and root beer. The brown cow is similar but contains cola instead of root beer. Wonderfully thirst quenching during hot weather are light, fruity sodas made with orange or pineapple sherbet, perhaps combined with pineapple syrup or a little crushed pineapple, and ginger ale or similar soft drink. A soda made with sherbet instead of ice cream is often called a "cooler."

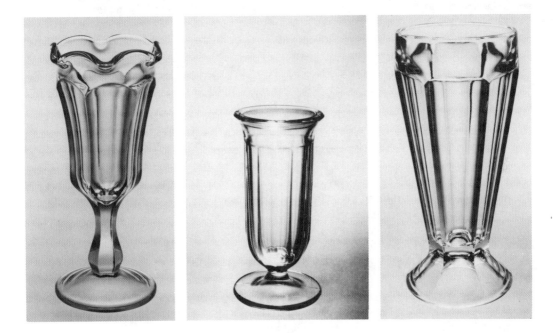

Traditional stemmed fountain ware includes sundae, parfait, and soda glasses. Stemmed ice cream dish and banana split boat complete the set. (Photos courtesy of Lancaster Colony Commercial Products, Columbus, Ohio.)

CHOCOLATE SODA

Vary this old-fashioned treat by co-ordinating different flavors of carbonated beverage with different kinds of ice cream. If desired, use milk for all or part of the initial soda water. For *chocolate mint* soda, add a drop of peppermint extract to this basic recipe.

In 16-oz glass, blend   **2 T chocolate syrup**
           1 scoop vanilla ice cream.

Stir in   **1 C carbonated water.**

Top with   **2 scoops chocolate ice cream.**

Add carbonated water to fill glass.

yield: 1 serving

PEPPERMINT SODA

The pretty pink hue of this minty drink comes from grenadine (pomegranate) syrup, which you can find in the mixed-drink section of any grocery store.

In 16-oz glass, blend   **1 C lemon-lime soda**
           1 T grenadine syrup.

Top with   **2 scoops pepper-mint stick ice cream.**

Add lemon-lime soda to fill glass.

yield: 1 serving

CITRUS COOLER

Top this refreshing drink with lemon or orange sherbet and garnish with a lemon twist. Invent your own cooling creations using other combinations of juice and sherbet.

In 16-oz glass, blend   **1 T orange-grapefruit juice concentrate**
           1 scoop lemon sherbet.

Stir in   **1 C ginger ale.**

Top with   **1-2 scoops sherbet.**

Add ginger ale to fill glass.

yield: 1 serving

Floats

A float is a simplified ice cream soda, made with neither syrup nor the initial muddling of ice cream and beverage. Instead, float one or two scoops of ice cream or sherbet in a glassful of carbonated beverage, fruit juice, or flavored milk. The root beer float, made with vanilla ice cream, is an enduring favorite.

Especially refreshing are fruity floats such as those containing vanilla ice cream and orange juice, orange ice cream and lemonade, or orange sherbet with orange juice and ginger ale. Other tasty combinations include sherbet with the same flavor soft drink, fruit ice cream with 7-Up, and frozen yogurt with fruit juice.

A popular upscale float, sometimes called a "coupe," consists of raspberry ice cream or sherbet swimming in a glass of bubbly champagne, stirred precisely once, with a twist of lemon, lime, or orange draped over the edge of the glass. Variations include lemon sherbet with sparkling wine or wine sorbet with ginger ale. As rule of thumb, select a rosé to combine with sweet, strongly flavored ice cream and a white wine to combine with sorbet.

Properly speaking, warm drinks capped with ice cream qualify as floats. Into this category fall Irish coffee topped with vanilla or coffee ice cream and hot cocoa topped with vanilla, coffee, or chocolate ice cream. Cool any hot drink to lukewarm to keep the ice cream from instantly melting.

Warm floats are sipped from the cup, alcoholic ones from a champagne glass. The proper etiquette for enjoying sodas or floats served in traditional fountain ware is another of the many things ice cream lovers can't agree on. Some provide only a straw so the drink may be sipped slowly as the ice cream melts. Others offer an iced-tea spoon in addition, so that bites of ice cream may be enjoyed between sips from the straw. The decision is yours.

RASPBERRY FLOAT

Substitute other strongly flavored fruits or berries here for *apricot*, *peach*, or *strawberry* floats. Top the floats with vanilla or coordinate ice cream and fruit flavors.

In 16-oz glass, blend

$^1/_3$ C raspberries
$^3/_4$ C milk
$^1/_8$ t almond
  extract.

Top with

2 scoops straw-
  berry ice cream.

Add milk to fill glass.

yield: 1 serving

CALIFORNIA FLOAT

Avocado lends its nutlike flavor and creamy texture to this West Coast original. Try it also with a couple of scoops of lemon sherbet, or substitute limeade for the orange juice and top with lime sherbet.

In 16-oz glass, blend

$^{1}/_{2}$ **mashed avocado**
$^{2}/_{3}$ **C orange juice**
2 T sugar.

Top with

2 scoops orange sherbet.

Add orange juice to fill glass.

yield: 1 serving

Milkshakes

All but gone is the charming ice cream parlor practice of leaving a second helping of milkshake in the mixing container for the customer to finish up. Happily, though, you can enjoy all the milkshakes you want at home, making them in an appliance designed for the purpose or using an electric mixer or blender.

Thick, frothy shakes, sometimes called "frosteds" and occasionally "frappes," are made with milk and at least an equal portion of ice cream. The more ice cream, the thicker the shake. Popular versions contain plain or chocolate milk combined with chocolate, vanilla, or coffee ice cream. A shake made with alternative ingredients, such as soy milk or sherbet and fruit juice, is called a "smoothie."

Syrups and other flavorings increase both richness and strength of flavor. To a chocolate shake, add up to one-quarter cup chocolate syrup or three tablespoons sifted cocoa. To a coffee shake, add one or two tablespoons instant coffee. If strawberry is your favorite, include one-quarter cup strawberry syrup or preserves, or one-half cup frozen strawberries per serving, beaten

Appliances are designed solely for the purpose of whipping up smooth, thick shakes. (Photo courtesy of Williams-Sonoma, San Francisco, California.)

into milk combined with vanilla or strawberry ice cream. Peach, banana, pineapple, and other fruit shakes are made similarly.

A malted milkshake, often called a "malted" or simply a "malt," has one or more tablespoons of malted milk powder added. The most popular malt is chocolate. Super thick malts may be nothing less than freshly frozen chocolate ice cream with one-quarter cup malted milk added per quart of mix, spooned into tall glasses right out of the ice cream maker. In addition to stir freezing a mix just until it's slushy, you can make thick shakes by softening hardened ice cream. A short stint in the microwave quickly turns any flavor into a shake.

Including an alcoholic spirit keeps ice cream the consistency of a shake, even after hardening. Make a combination dessert and after-dinner drink by blending two-thirds cup brandy with one quart rich vanilla, eggnog, or coffee ice cream. Freeze twenty-four hours to let flavors blend, stir smooth, and serve in large brandy snifters. One quart serves six to eight.

Scoopless Shake

Although milkshakes traditionally contain ice cream, with today's modern appliances they needn't. You can make terrific shakes using frozen fruit and milk, cream, or yogurt. For two tall shakes or three short ones, break up a couple of frozen bananas or a package of frozen fruit. Combine in a blender with just enough milk, cream, or yogurt (plain or flavored) to let the blades turn freely. For extra nutrition, toss in an egg or a tablespoon of wheat germ and whirl smooth. Sweeten to taste.

Iced coffee, once made by stirring vanilla ice cream into cooled, extra-strong coffee, can also now be blender-made. For two tall or three short drinks, whirl smooth in a blender two cups milk, one tablespoon instant coffee, one-quarter cup sugar (or to taste), one-quarter teaspoon vanilla, dash salt, and three cups ice cubes. Add more milk or cream as necessary until blades turn freely.

CHOCOLATE SHAKE

To make a *chocolate malted*, add 2 T malted milk powder to this chocolate shake. For a *mocha* shake, add ¹/₂ T instant coffee plus 1 t sugar. If you prefer a more subtle flavor, use vanilla ice cream instead of chocolate.

Whirl in blender

1 C cold milk
2 T chocolate
syrup
3 scoops chocolate
ice cream.

Serve in tall glass.

yield: 1 serving

STRAWBERRY SHAKE

To make a *raspberry* shake, substitute
¹/₂ C strained raspberries for the
strawberries. Try other fruits combined
with vanilla ice cream, or mix and
match flavors.

Whirl in blender

¹/₂ C strawberries
¹/₂ C milk
2 T sugar
2 scoops ice cream.

Serve in tall glass.

Top with

whipped cream

and

1 whole straw-
berry.

yield: 1 serving

SUNSHINE SHAKE

Make this shake with fruit and frozen
yogurt of the same flavor, or combine
flavors. Or, in place of fruit, try orange
juice, apricot nectar, or both.

Whirl in blender

1 C sliced fruit
3 scoops frozen
yogurt
2 T honey
2 T wheat germ
1 egg.

Serve in tall glass.

yield: 1 serving

PEACH SHAKE

With the appropriate substitutions, this
recipe also makes a good *banana* or
apricot shake.

Pit and cut into chunks

1 peach.

Whirl in blender with

¹/₂ C plain yogurt
3 scoops vanilla ice
cream
1 T honey
¹/₈ t almond extract
dash cinnamon.

Serve in tall glass.

yield: 1 serving

NUTTY SHAKE

For stronger chocolate flavor, use all chocolate ice cream in this shake. With pistachio, cashew, or other milder nut butters, use only vanilla ice cream.

Whirl in blender

1 C milk
2 scoops chocolate ice cream
1 scoop vanilla ice cream
2 T creamy peanut butter.

Pour into 16-oz glass.

Add milk to fill glass.

yield: 1 serving

TANGY MOCHA SHAKE

For a *spirited mocha* shake, substitute 2 T coffee liqueur for the instant coffee.

Whirl in blender

¹/₂ T instant coffee
¹/₂ C chocolate syrup
2 scoops vanilla frozen yogurt
1 C milk.

Serve in tall glass.

yield: 1 serving

BANANA MALTED

For a *chocolate banana malted*, either use chocolate ice cream instead of vanilla or add 2 T chocolate syrup.

Whirl in blender

1 C milk
1 ripe banana
1 T malted milk powder
2 scoops vanilla ice cream.

Serve in tall glass.

yield: 1 serving

ESPRESSO FROSTED

Mix up this treat before dinner and store it in the freezer until time for dessert. Garnish servings with a dollop of whipped cream and a single chocolate curl or a chocolate-coated coffee bean.

Whirl in blender

1 T instant espresso
1 C milk
²/₃ C coffee liqueur.

Add and blend smooth

1-qt coffee ice cream.

yield: 8 servings

24

Sundaes, Parfaits, and Splits

The first ice cream sundae was concocted some time between 1896 and 1900 in either Illinois or Virginia. Ice cream antiquarians can't seem to agree on the exact date and place or even on the original ingredients. Some believe the first sundaes were topped only with chocolate syrup. Since chocolate was very expensive, the treat was reserved for a special day of the week, hence the name "sunday" or "sundae."

Others credit the name "sundae" to religious restrictions prohibiting Sunday sales of such stimulating beverages as the carbonated water in an ice cream soda. An enterprising soda jerk left out the soda water, spooned flavored syrup over the ice cream, and labeled his creation with a deliberately misspelled tongue-in-cheek version of the day on which it was served.

According to the *Guinness Book of World Records,* the world's largest sundae was made in Edmonton, Alberta, in July 1988. It weighed fifty-five thousand pounds, forty-four thousand pounds of which was ice cream and the rest topping. The ultimate in twentieth-century sundaes comes in prefrozen packets. Pop one into the microwave for thirty seconds and you've got an instant hot fudge sundae.

Scrumptious Sundaes

Creating scrumptious sundaes is more art than science. It involves combining just the right topping with just the right flavor of ice cream or sherbet. Professionals attend sundae school, but some of the best homemade toppings are impromptu ones created by stirring in a little of this and a little of that until the taste is just right. Don't be afraid to try things that seem a bit on the wild side—the most improbable combination may turn out to be the taste treat of the century. On the other hand, you can't go far wrong sticking with one of the five all-time favorites—hot fudge, chocolate fudge, butterscotch, caramel, and strawberry.

Part of the artistry of making a sundae is deciding just how much topping to spoon on. You don't want so little that the sauce is gone before the ice cream, nor so much that a puddle remains after the ice cream is eaten up. The sweetness of the topping relative to the ice cream is an important factor. Too much of a very sweet sauce can be overwhelming. One of the advantages to making sundaes from scratch is that you can balance the sweetness of your syrups and sauces against that of your ice cream. As a general rule, to be broken on the merest whim, allow two tablespoons of sauce per scoop.

Syrups and Sauces

It doesn't take much time or effort to make toppings like chocolate, hot fudge, and butterscotch, but not everyone has the patience to stand over a stove stirring a bubbling pot nor the inclination to clean up afterwards. Commercially prepared toppings in a limited number of flavors are available at most supermarkets (a few mail-order sources for gourmet toppings are listed in Appendix C, "Supplies").

Pancake syrups, especially fruit flavored ones, expand the range of possibilities. So does maple syrup. Try some on coffee ice cream sprinkled with chopped hazelnuts. Grenadine—pomegranate syrup used to flavor mixed drinks—makes an interesting and decidedly different topping.

Fruit in season and freshly thawed frozen fruit both make luscious toppings, either puréed or chopped into bite-sized chunks. Fruit goes especially well with frozen yogurt, sorbet, and sherbet for a light-side sundae. Increase color interest by combining fruits such as peaches with blueberries, raspberries with sliced bananas, or strawberries with sliced kiwi. Among the easiest toppings is fruit sprinkled with brown or white sugar and refrigerated an hour or two, or overnight, to develop its own sweet syrup. For a smoother sauce, heat the fruit until the sugar dissolves, then cool thoroughly. To strengthen flavor, add fruit liqueur, brandy, or other spirits.

For fruity, fast sundae sauce, stir a jar of your favorite jam or preserves to spooning consistency. Thin down the jam, if necessary, with a little lemon juice or corn syrup. Try raspberry, strawberry, or kumquat preserves, perhaps tossed with chunks of fresh fruit or melon balls. Bits of candied ginger lend an exotic air to pineapple, peach, or apricot preserves, or go all out with ginger marmalade. Stir in a little brandy, rum, or fruit-flavored liqueur to bring out the flavor and tone down the sweetness of any jam.

Marshmallow cream, combined two to one with crushed fruit or berries, makes a sweet and satisfying sauce. Any topping is creamier with a little marshmallow blended in. For a marbled sauce, thin one cup marshmallow cream with one tablespoon milk or water and swirl with an equal portion of chocolate or caramel sauce. Or let the marshmallow itself be the sauce, served over peach, pineapple, or chocolate ice cream. For additional flavor, add a little extract, maple syrup, or liqueur.

Liqueurs and other spirits perk up just about any topping, flavors mixed or matched, or let the liqueur be the star attraction. An Irish coffee sundae, for example, is simply a scoop of coffee ice cream topped with Irish cream liqueur. A margarita sundae is lime sherbet splashed with tequila and garnished with a salted pretzel stick.

Heated Toppings

Warm toppings offer interesting contrast to an icy-cold scoop, but the ice cream must be fully hardened or it will melt too quickly. Microwave jams, preserves, marshmallow cream, or any sundae sauce for about a minute and a half or stand the jar in a pan of simmering water until it's fully warm. Avoid boiling, as some toppings separate or curdle and others easily scorch. If the sauce comes in a metal can, empty the contents into a dish or saucepan to warm.

Heated sauces open up a whole new world of sundae possibilities. Warm a can of cranberry sauce to top orange sherbet or poppy seed ice cream. Fold in an equal portion of marshmallow cream, and you've got berrymallow sauce. Heat spicy applesauce to spoon over French vanilla or cinnamon ice cream. Warm maple syrup and stir in a pat of butter, a bit of lemon zest, and a dash of ginger, cloves, or nutmeg or a splash of rum. Heat honey, stir in sesame purée (two tablespoons honey and one tablespoon purée per serving), and stir in some chopped pecans or dates. Spike warmed mincemeat with brandy or rum and pass the lemon ice cream.

Canned pie fillings may be spooned on cold, but make truly special toppings when heated. Serve warm cherry pie over chocolate chip ice cream. Spoon warm lemon filling over coffee ice cream. Top maple nut ice cream with steaming blueberry filling.

Cooked Toppings

Making toppings from scratch isn't all that tricky. For a hot, fruity topping, stew fresh or dried fruit until soft, purée in a blender or rub through a sieve, and cook until clear with an equal portion of sugar or honey. For a thick fruit sauce to serve cold, thaw a ten-ounce package of frozen fruit-in-syrup and heat with one tablespoon cornstarch, stirring until thickened, then chill. For a smooth, clear fruity sauce, blend two teaspoons cornstarch with two tablespoons lemon juice, stir in one cup jelly, bring to boil, stirring constantly, then cool.

To make a single serving of the easiest hot fudge sauce in the world, melt one ounce semisweet chocolate with one tablespoon evaporated milk or cream—delicious over vanilla or peppermint ice cream.

For a larger quantity of hot fudge, combine eight ounces semisweet chocolate (or six ounces chocolate chips) with one-half to one cup heavy cream, evaporated milk, or half and half. In a small saucepan, warm over low heat until the chocolate melts. Whisk smooth, adding just enough milk or cream to achieve desired consistency. Stir in one-half teaspoon vanilla.

Fudge sauce variations include adding one tablespoon instant coffee crystals; one-eighth teaspoon almond extract plus one-half cup slivered almonds; one-half cup crushed peppermint or toffee candy; one-eighth teaspoon orange or lemon extract plus the grated rind of one orange or lemon; or one-half cup marshmallow cream. You can also cool the fudge sauce and fold in one-half cup whipped cream.

Make an easy chocolate-mint sauce by melting chocolate-covered mint patties in a double boiler, stirring in a little cream to achieve spooning consistency. For easy creamy caramel sauce, melt one-half pound quality caramel candies in a double boiler and blend in up to one-half cup water, milk, or cream to desired consistency. Stir in two tablespoons instant coffee for coffee caramel. Serve warm.

One of the trickiest cooked toppings is caramel made from scratch. The intensity of the burnt sugar flavor is controlled by the amount of heat applied. The darker the sugar gets, the stronger the caramel flavor, almost to the point of bitterness, and the less sweet the sauce. Your full attention is needed to avoid underheating or overheating the sugar, or turning the sauce into a solid lump. But the whole thing goes quite fast, and it takes only a few tries to become an expert at caramelizing sugar.

Warm a large, heavy skillet over moderately high heat. Sprinkle the bottom with granulated sugar and stir with a fork until it melts to a rich golden brown. Remove the pan from the heat and stir a few minutes more to keep the sugar from darkening further. Add water, milk, or cream in an amount equal to the amount of sugar you melted, pouring the liquid down the side of the pan so rising steam won't burn your hand.

The melted sugar will instantly turn into a sticky lump. Return the pan to moderate heat and stir until the sugar redissolves. If the sauce foams up, be ready to lift the pan off the heat so it won't bubble onto the range. When the caramel is well blended, remove from heat and stir in a little vanilla. For caramel nut sauce, add chopped pecans or toasted slivered almonds.

Perhaps the most spectacular sundae is a flaming one. Just before coming to the table, douse sugar cubes with vanilla extract, brandy, or any liquor of at least seventy proof. Place one cube atop each sundae and light with a match. For a more dramatic effect, set the sauce itself afire. The trick to creating a successful flambé is to warm both the sauce and the spirits to be ignited. Although it's exciting to spoon flaming sauce onto ice cream from a chafing dish, you may feel safer stirring the sauce until the flames die down before serving.

Cherries jubilee is the classic flaming sundae, but you can use the same recipe to make cranberry, peach, or other fruit jubilee. For an easy version, heat and flambé fruit preserves or prepared pie filling. To enjoy the flavor without the flame, omit the final addition of spirits.

CHERRIES JUBILEE

This sauce is traditionally served over vanilla ice cream but it's equally delicious with chocolate, almond, or pecan.

In medium saucepan, combine | $^1/_4$ **C sugar**
$^1/_2$ **T cornstarch.**

Blend in | $^1/_2$ **C orange juice.**

Add | $^1/_2$# **pitted dark sweet cherries**
$^1/_2$ **t orange zest.**

Stirring constantly, heat until thickened.

Blend in | **2 T kirsch.**

Transfer to serving dish.

Top with | $^1/_4$ **C warmed brandy.**

Ignite immediately.

yield: about 1 cup

BANANA FLAMBÉ

Serve this sauce over French vanilla or strawberry ice cream, top with warmed rum, and ignite just before serving.

In skillet, melt | $^1/_4$ **C butter.**

Peel, halve, and add | **4 ripe bananas.**

Sprinkle with | **2 T brown sugar dash cinnamon.**

Heat until lightly browned.

Turn and sprinkle with | **2 T brown sugar dash cinnamon.**

Spoon 2 halves over each serving.

In small saucepan, warm | $^1/_2$ **C rum.**

Pour 2 T rum over each serving.

Ignite.

yield: 4 servings

MINCEMEAT FLAMBÉ

Serve this holiday treat over French vanilla, pumpkin, or walnut ice cream. For spirits, use either brandy or rum.

In small saucepan, warm   **1 C mincemeat.**

Stir in   **2 T spirits.**

Transfer to serving dish.

Top with   **2 T warmed spirits.**

Ignite immediately.

yield: about 1 cup

STRAWBERRY SAUCE

This sauce goes well with an assortment of flavors including chocolate, strawberry, avocado, peach, or almond.

Slice   **1¹/₂ C strawberries.**

In small saucepan, combine with   **¹/₄ C sugar
2 t lemon juice.**

Bring to boil.

Reduce heat and simmer 10 minutes.

Remove from heat and stir in   **¹/₄ t almond extract.**

Cool.

yield: about 1 cup

LEMON SAUCE

Serve this tangy lemon sauce, warm or chilled, with blueberry, coffee, chocolate, or banana ice cream.

In saucepan, combine   **2 t cornstarch
¹/₄ C sugar
¹/₄ t salt.**

Stir in   **¹/₂ C hot water.**

Stirring, heat until slightly thickened.

LEMON SAUCE, cont'd.

Beat	**2 eggs.**

Stir in cornstarch mixture.

Return to heat and cook until slightly thickened.

Stir in	**¹/₄ C lemon juice** **2 t lemon zest** **2 T butter.**

yield: about 1 cup

PEACHY SAUCE

Make peach sundaes with this sauce accompanied by slices of fresh peach, or spoon sauce over wedges of vanilla, strawberry, or peach ice cream pie (see Chapter 29).

In saucepan, combine	**2 C sliced peaches** **¹/₃ C orange juice.**

Cook over medium heat until tender.

In blender, whip smooth with	**2 T sugar** **¹/₈ t almond** ** extract.**

Chill.

yield: about 1 cup

BLUEBERRY SAUCE

Spoon this terrific sundae sauce over blueberry, lemon, or peach ice cream and garnish with a handful of whole berries.

In small saucepan, combine	**2 C blueberries** **¹/₂ C sugar** **1 T lemon juice** **dash nutmeg.**

Bring to boil.

Reduce heat and simmer 15 minutes.

Remove from heat and stir in	**¹/₂ t vanilla.**

Cool.

yield: about 1 cup

PINEAPPLE SAUCE

Pineapple sauce is perfect over peach or mango ice cream. Sprinkle chopped macadamia nuts on top.

In saucepan, combine	½ C crushed pineapple 6 T pineapple juice ¼ C sugar 2 T light corn syrup dash angostura bitters.
Chop and add	1 T candied ginger.
Simmer 15 minutes.	
Cool.	

yield: about 1 cup

HONEYED FRUIT SAUCE

Serve this sauce over frozen yogurt and garnish with strawberries or sliced kiwi. Try it also with pineapple chunks or a mango in place of a peach.

In skillet, melt	3 T butter.
Stir in	1 T lemon juice 1 T honey.
Chop into chunks and add	2 medium bananas 1 peach.
Stir gently until heated through, about 2 minutes.	
Serve warm.	

yield: about 1 cup

DATE NUT RUM SAUCE

Serve this sauce over coconut, pineapple, or banana ice cream, or any fruit-flavored frozen yogurt.

In small saucepan, combine	⅔ C heavy cream 3 T rum.

DATE NUT RUM SAUCE, cont'd.

Boil until reduced to ²/₃ cup, 10 to 15 minutes.

Stir in   **3 T chopped dates.**

Simmer uncovered 1 minute.

Stir in   **3 T toasted pecans.**

Serve warm.

yield: about 1 cup

BRANDY SAUCE

Serve this easy brandy sauce with fruit, nut, or bisque ice cream. Sherry, bourbon, or rum may be substituted for the brandy.

In saucepan, combine   **¹/₂ C milk**
                                       1 C sugar
                                       ¹/₄ C butter.

Stirring, bring to boil.

Remove from heat and add   **2 T brandy.**

Cool.

yield: about 1 cup

RUM SAUCE

Top any strong-flavored, rich ice cream with this foamy, spirited sauce. If you wish, substitute brandy, cognac, or bourbon for the rum.

In small saucepan, combine   **1 C powdered sugar**
                                         ¹/₂ C butter.

Beat and add   **2 egg yolks.**

Stirring, warm over low heat until thickened.

Beat to soft peaks and fold in   **2 egg whites.**

Fold in   **2 T light rum.**

Serve warm.

yield: about 1 cup

RICH VANILLA SAUCE

This old-time sauce is a natural with gingerbread ice cream, frozen fruit pudding, or rich gelato. Create new flavors by omitting the vanilla and substituting either ½ t almond or other extract, or 2 T coffee, chocolate, orange, or other liqueur.

In small saucepan, beat

5 egg yolks
2 T powdered
 sugar.

Blend in

¾ C heavy cream.

Stirring, heat 5 minutes.
Do not boil!

Stir in

1 t vanilla.

Chill.

yield: about 1 cup

MINTMALLOW SAUCE

Tint this mallow variation with a few drops of green food coloring, if you wish. Try it over chocolate or pineapple ice cream. ·

Whip fluffy

¼ C marshmallow
 cream
1½ T water.

Add and beat smooth

2 T mint jelly.

yield: about 1 cup

VANILLA SAUCE

Less rich than the previous vanilla sauce, this one, too, serves as the basis for new flavors with the addition of extracts or bits of chopped nuts or fruit.

In small saucepan, combine

6 T sugar
2 t cornstarch
dash salt.

Stir in

¾ C boiling water.

Heat until thickened,
about 5 minutes.

Stir in and blend well

2 T butter
1 t vanilla.

Serve warm.

yield: about 1 cup

MALLOW SAUCE

To make *fluffy mallow* sauce, beat one or two eggs into soft peaks, then whip them into stiff peaks while gradually pouring on hot mallow sauce. For interesting new flavors, add a drop of extract or use liqueur or fruit juice instead of water.

Combine

$^1/_4$ C water
$^1/_4$ C sugar.

Bring just to a boil.

Blend in

6 marshmallows.

Serve warm or chilled.

yield: about 1 cup

MOCHAMALLOW SAUCE

Serve this creamy sauce with any nut ice cream, or spoon it over vanilla and sprinkle with toasted almonds.

Combine

$^2/_3$ **C dark corn syrup**
$^1/_3$ **C cocoa**
12 marshmallows
3 T water
1 t instant coffee
dash salt.

Over medium heat, bring to boil.

Stirring occasionally, boil 3 minutes.

Stir in

1 T butter.

Cool and add

$^1/_4$ **t vanilla.**

yield: about 1 cup

BRANDIED BELGIAN SYRUP

Flavor this syrupy sauce with either brewed or instant coffee. Serve it over rich gelato or French ice cream.

In saucepan, combine

1 C brown sugar
1 C strong coffee.

Boil, uncovered, until thick, about 10 minutes.

Remove from heat and add

$^1/_4$ **t vanilla**
1 T brandy.

Cool.

yield: about 1 cup

COFFEE SAUCE

Caffe d'Oro flavored instant coffees make outstanding, not overly sweet sauces that go well with chocolate, coffee, or French vanilla ice cream. For continental flair, stir in an appropriately flavored liqueur.

Combine in small saucepan

1 C flavored coffee powder
³/₄ C water.

Boil 2 to 3 minutes until thick.

yield: about 1 cup

DUTCH CARAMEL SAUCE

European sundae sauces aren't nearly as syrupy sweet as American ones. This tasty but not-too-sweet caramel sauce is a perfect example. For *Dutch coffee caramel* sauce, add 1 t instant coffee crystals to the egg yolk mixture.

In heavy skillet, sprinkle

3 T sugar.

Heat until frothy,
shaking pan occasionally.

Remove from heat.

Without stirring,
pour down side of pan

¹/₂ C milk.

Beat together

¹/₂ C milk
1 egg yolk
1 t cornstarch.

Return skillet to low heat
(careful, it may foam up!).

Stir until sugar redissolves.

Stirring constantly,
slowly add egg mixture.

Heat until thickened,
about 10 minutes.

Stir in until dissolved

1 T sugar.

Cool.

yield: about 1 cup

EASY BUTTERSCOTCH SAUCE

To make chocolate and butterscotch sauce all rolled into one, melt in 4-oz semisweet chocolate. Cool sauce and stir in 1 t vanilla.

In saucepan, combine

1 C brown sugar
¹/₂ C evaporated milk
¹/₄ C butter.

Heat until thick, about 3 minutes.

Serve warm.

yield: about 1 cup

BUTTERSCOTCH SAUCE

For a spicy twist to this popular sauce, add ¹/₈ t nutmeg or mace. The firm ball stage occurs when a bit of syrup dripped into ice water forms a ball that doesn't flatten when lifted.

Combine

¹/₂ C light brown sugar
¹/₄ C evaporated milk
¹/₄ C corn syrup
1 T butter.

Bring to boil over medium heat.

Stirring, cook to firm ball stage, 246° F (120° C).

Add

¹/₄ C evaporated milk.

Heat 1 minute more.

Remove from heat and stir in

¹/₄ t vanilla.

Serve warm.

yield: about 1 cup

HONEY BUTTERSCOTCH
SAUCE

Keep this thick sauce warming in the double boiler until serving time, blending in more warm cream if necessary to maintain consistency. For a tropical treat, stir in ¹/₂ C shredded coconut, chopped dates, and/or chopped nuts.

In small saucepan, warm

In double boiler, melt

Stir in until melted

Add warm cream and

Stir until smooth.

Serve warm.

¹/₂ **C heavy cream.**

2 T unsalted butter
2 T honey.

6-oz butterscotch chips.

¹/₂ **t vanilla.**

yield: about 1 cup

CINNAMON NUTTY SAUCE

Serve this spicy sauce over chocolate, peach, rum raisin, or French vanilla ice cream. Vary it by substituting toasted almonds or pecans for the walnuts.

In small saucepan, combine

Boil 5 minutes.

Remove from heat and stir in

1 C dark brown sugar
¹/₂ **C water**
1 t ground cinnamon.

¹/₂ **C toasted walnuts.**

yield: about 1 cup

PRALINE SAUCE

This yummy Southern sauce goes great with vanilla, chocolate, coffee or avocado ice cream. Add Euro-flair by using hazelnuts instead of pecans.

In heavy saucepan, combine

Stirring, bring to boil over medium heat.

¹/₂ **C light corn syrup**
¹/₄ **C sugar**
3 T butter
1 beaten egg
dash salt.

PRALINE SAUCE, cont'd.

Without stirring, boil 2 minutes.

Remove from heat, stir in   **¹/₂ T vanilla**
¹/₂ C chopped
   pecans.

Serve warm or cooled.

yield: about 1 cup

WALNUT SAUCE

Serve this versatile, richly flavored nut sauce warm or chilled. It goes well with nearly any flavor ice cream.

In saucepan, combine   **1 C dark brown**
   sugar
¹/₄ C dark corn
   syrup
¹/₄ C water.

Stirring, boil 3 minutes.

Stir in until melted   **3 T butter.**

Remove from heat and add   **¹/₂ t vanilla**
¹/₂ C chopped
   walnuts.

yield: 1 cup

WALNUT TAFFY SYRUP

Like many recipes from bygone days, this one was designed for easy memorizing. Spoon it over French vanilla or Grape-Nuts ice cream.

In small saucepan, bring to boil   **¹/₄ C milk**
¹/₄ C molasses
¹/₄ C butter
¹/₄ C sugar.

Remove from heat and beat in   **¹/₄ t vanilla**
¹/₄ C chopped
   walnuts.

Serve warm or chilled.

yield: about 1 cup

PEANUT BUTTER SAUCE

Make this tasty sauce with chunky peanut butter, or use creamy style and top your sundae with chopped, salted peanuts.

In small saucepan, melt

²/₃ C miniature marshmallows

in

²/₃ C milk.

Stir in until blended

**¹/₂ C peanut butter
3 T corn syrup.**

Cool.

yield: about 1 cup

CHESTNUT GLACÉ

Make this wonderful European sauce with quality brandy and chopped *marrons glacés*. Or use chestnut liqueur and finely ground chestnuts (roasted fresh or purchased in jars at a specialty shop). Spoon over gelato or French ice cream.

Combine

**1 C chestnuts
¹/₄ C spirits.**

Marinate 30 minutes.

yield: about 1 cup

CHOCOLATE CRACKLE

As it flows over cold ice cream, crackle hardens into a crunchy crust with an underlying butter pecan flavor. Substitute white chocolate to make *white chocolate crumble*, which doesn't flow but instead settles in a crunchy crown.

In small saucepan over low heat, melt

2 T unsalted butter.

Stir in until lightly golden

¹/₂ C chopped pecans.

Grate and stir in until melted

4-oz semisweet chocolate.

Serve warm.

yield: about 1 cup

CHOCOLATE SAUCE

Unsalted butter lends finer flavor to chocolate sauces, but regular butter yields reasonable results. For *super chocolate* sauce, add 2 T crème de cacao or crème de menthe.

In small saucepan, heat	**6 T cream** **2 T sugar or honey.**
Stir in until melted	**2-oz nonsweetened chocolate** **2-oz semisweet chocolate** **2 t unsalted butter.**
Remove from heat and add	**$1/2$ t vanilla.**
Serve warm.	

yield: about 1 cup

HOT FUDGE SAUCE

Convert this delightfully chewy hot fudge sauce into *Mexican Hot Fudge* by omitting the vanilla and stirring in $1/8$ t cinnamon plus 2 T coffee liqueur.

Combine and bring to boil	**$1/3$ C evaporated milk** **3-oz nonsweetened chocolate** **$2/3$ C sugar.**
Stir until chocolate melts.	
Remove from heat and add	**$1/2$ t vanilla.**

yield: about 1 cup

WHITE HOT FUDGE SAUCE

Vary the flavor of this sauce by varying the spirits. For starters, try almond or hazelnut liqueur.

In saucepan, heat until bubbly	**$1/3$ C heavy cream.**
Over low heat, stir in	**6-oz white chocolate.**
Remove from heat and add	**1 T unsalted butter.**
Stir in	**2 T white crème de cacao.**

yield: about 1 cup

WHITE CHOCOLATE ALMOND SAUCE

In place of hard-to-find chocolate extract (a source is listed in Appendix C), vanilla or almond extract may be substituted.

In heavy saucepan over low heat, combine

$^1/_4$ **C light cream**
6-oz white chocolate.

Stir smooth.

Remove from heat and stir in

$^1/_2$ **t chocolate extract**
$^1/_2$ **C chopped almonds.**

Serve warm or cool.

yield: about 1 cup

HONEY FUDGE SAUCE

Here's a sweet and easy sauce that turns pleasantly chewy as it cools. For a little less chewiness, melt in as much as $^1/_4$ C butter.

In double boiler, combine

4-oz nonsweetened chocolate
1 C honey
$^1/_8$ **t salt.**

Heat, stirring, until blended.

Serve warm or cooled.

yield: about 1 cup

HAUTE FUDGE SAUCE

This robust hot fudge gets extra zip from instant espresso and a touch of brandy. You may substitute rum or other spirits for the brandy, or leave it out if you prefer.

In small saucepan, combine

3 T heavy cream
$^1/_4$ **C unsalted butter.**

Warm until bubbles form around edge.

Remove from heat and stir in

1 t instant espresso.

HAUTE FUDGE SAUCE, cont'd.   Grate and blend in   **5-oz semisweet chocolate.**

Whisk smooth.

Add   **1 T light corn syrup
1 T brandy.**

Serve warm or room temperature.

yield: 1 cup

Toppers

Garnishes, or toppers, give sundaes extra personality. Toppers include sliced fruit, whole berries, chopped toasted nuts, toasted wheat germ, shredded coconut, candied fruit or peel, sprinkles or nonpareils, crushed candy, crunchy cereal, shaved or chopped chocolate, chocolate curls, thin peppermint sticks, or any combination of these. If you make sundaes often, keep a variety of toppers on hand.

Mouth-watering hot fudge sundae with all the trimmings. (Photo courtesy of Ghirardelli Chocolate Company, San Leandro, California.)

PRALINE TOPPER

Praline powder, made with hazelnuts, pecans, or toasted almonds, is not only a fine topper but may also be stirred into ice cream or whipped cream as a flavoring. Store in an air-tight container for up to two weeks.

In small saucepan over low heat, combine

½ **C sugar**
2 T water.

Without stirring, increase heat until syrup boils and just begins to brown, about five minutes.

Coarsely chop and add   ½ **C nuts.**

Heat until syrup turns golden, about three minutes.

Pour onto a lightly buttered baking sheet to cool. Break into pieces and whirl in a food processor until finely ground.

yield: about 1 cup

Whipped Cream

Sweetened whipped cream is the most extravagantly voluptuous of all sundae toppings. Keep sweetening to a minimum and let the cream balance the sweetness of ice cream and sauce. Allow at least one tablespoon per sundae.

To prepare whipped cream up to twenty-four hours in advance, in a glass or cup soften one-half teaspoon plain gelatin in one tablespoon cold water. Set the glass in simmering water and stir until the gelatin dissolves. Cool. Whip one cup heavy cream into soft peaks, add gelatin and one tablespoon sugar, and whip until stiff. Lightly whisk the cream just before serving.

To keep peaked caps on hand for spur-of-the-moment sundaes, heap mounds of whipped cream onto a chilled baking sheet and freeze firm. Seal in an air-tight container.

For festive sundaes with a minimum of calories, skip the sauce and let a dab of whipped cream be your sole topping. You won't miss the sauce if you flavor the cream, based on the following ideas. For starters, try a luscious lemon sundae, made with lemon sherbet and whipped cream flavored with lemon zest. Sprinkle on a little grated, semisweet chocolate and dig in.

FLAVORED WHIPPED CREAM

For each 1 C whipped cream, sweetened with 1 T sifted powdered sugar,
add one of the following (to combine
two flavorings, add half the amount
listed for each):

$^1\!/_4$ t cinnamon

$^1\!/_4$ t almond, rum, or other extract

$^1\!/_2$ t nutmeg

$^1\!/_2$ t vanilla

1 T instant coffee dissolved in 1 t water

1 T orange or lemon zest

1 T chocolate syrup

1 T rum, sherry, brandy, cognac, or other spirits

2 T liqueur or kirsch

2 T chocolate sprinkles or grated semisweet chocolate

2 T plain or flavored cocoa plus 2 T sifted powdered
  sugar

2 T nut butter

2 T plain or toasted coconut

2 T Kool-Aid powder

$^1\!/_4$ C fruit purée

$^1\!/_4$ C chopped or ground nuts

$^1\!/_4$ C currants or chopped raisins

$^1\!/_4$ C finely crushed brittle, peppermint, or other candy

$^1\!/_4$ C cookie crumbs

$^1\!/_4$ C jelly, jam, or preserves

yield: about 1 cup

SOUR CREAM TOPPING

Sour cream topping complements any
tangy-sweet ice. Try this variation over
lemon sorbetto.

Combine

1 C sour cream
2 T powdered
  sugar
2 T orange liqueur
$^1\!/_2$ t lemon zest.

Cover and chill.

yield: about 1 cup

STRAWBERRY WHIPPED CREAM

Use any juicy, flavorful fruit or berry in this recipe. Strawberries create the prettiest pink hue.

In small saucepan, combine

¼ **C strawberries**
2 t sugar.

Bring to boil.

Purée, strain and chill.

Whip into soft peaks

⅓ **C heavy cream.**

Fold in chilled strawberry sauce.

yield: about 1 cup

Parfaits

A parfait is essentially a sundae built up in layers in a tall, slender glass large enough to hold at least three scoops. The artistry of creating tantalizing parfaits lies in combining flavors, textures, and colors to maximize both visual appeal and taste sensation. Many parfaits can be made ahead and stored in the freezer until serving time.

Perhaps the simplest parfait consists of alternating scoops of contrasting ice cream such as vanilla and strawberry, chocolate and coffee, or cherry and pistachio. For textural appeal, combine different freezes of the same flavor—an ice cream and a sherbet, for example, or a sherbet and a still-frozen mousse. Granita makes a terrific parfait, layered with whipped cream or French vanilla. For greater variety, alternate granita flavors such as coffee and lemon, lemon and strawberry, strawberry and chocolate, or chocolate and coffee.

Some of the best parfaits are made with sugared fresh or frozen fruit. Tried and true combinations include strawberries with chocolate and vanilla ice cream, peaches or raspberries with strawberry and vanilla ice cream, blueberries with vanilla ice cream and orange sherbet, and pineapple bits with vanilla and cherry or strawberry ice cream. Spoon a small amount of fruit into the bottom of a chilled glass and add a scoop of ice cream. Spoon in more fruit and add another scoop of the same or different flavor ice cream. Continue alternating fruit and ice cream to the top.

Parfaits may be layered with any sundae sauce, liqueur, or crushed cookies in an endless variety of combinations. Consider chocolate sauce with lemon, mint, coffee, or raspberry ice cream; coffee sauce with lemon, strawberry, avocado, orange, or ginger ice cream; strawberry sauce with pineapple, orange, lemon, or peach ice cream.

Top off the whole thing with a gob of whipped cream and a slice of fruit, a whole berry, or any of the toppers you'd use to trim a sundae.

Banana Splits

A proper banana split is practically a meal in itself. The grandest one ever constructed was four and one-half miles long, created in Selinsgrove, Pennsylvania, in April 1988.

To make a deluxe split for only one ravenous mortal, start with a banana, sliced in half lengthwise. Open a small can of pineapple rings and dip the banana into the pineapple juice to keep it from browning. (If you omit the pineapple, coat the banana with lemon juice.) Lay one pineapple ring in the center of a banana boat or other long, narrow dish and place a banana half on either side. Although experts claim it's correct to face the cut sides outward, many veteran split-makers prefer to face the cut sides inward.

Place a scoop of vanilla ice cream on top of the pineapple slice. On one side, place a scoop of strawberry or other fruit ice cream or sherbet. On the other side, drop a scoop of chocolate or coffee. Slice a second pineapple ring in half and tuck the halves, cut side down, between scoops.

Ladle butterscotch, strawberry, or raspberry sauce over the vanilla ice cream. Spoon chocolate or hot fudge sauce over the fruit flavor, and marshmallow, white chocolate, pineapple, or strawberry sauce over the chocolate ice cream. Heap a generous cloud of whipped cream down the ridge, sprinkle the whole thing with chopped nuts, and top each scoop with a maraschino cherry or whole fresh strawberry. For a calorie-conscious version, substitute sliced strawberries, kiwi, or other fruit for all that lavish topping.

There you have it—pure decadence of the most delectable kind!

SODA FOUNTAIN BASICS (per average serving)	
Scoop with wafer	2 scoops; 1 cookie (rolled, fan-shaped, or waffled wafer).
Scoop with fruit	2 scoops; 1/4 C fresh, sliced sugared fruit.
Soda	3 T flavored syrup in 16-oz glass, 1 scoop stirred in; fill 3/4 full with carbonated beverage; top with 2 scoops and 1 T whipped cream.
Shake	2 scoops, 3 T flavored syrup, 2/3 C milk, well blended.
Sundae	2 scoops; 2 T sauce or 1/4 C sliced fruit; 1 T whipped cream, chopped nuts, maraschino cherry, strawberry, or single slice of fruit on top.
Parfait	1 T crushed fruit or sauce plus 1 scoop, alternated at least 3 times; 1 T crushed fruit or sauce, 1 T whipped cream, maraschino cherry, strawberry, single slice of fruit, or nut half on top.
Split	1 split banana; 3 scoops; 2 T each of 3 kinds of topping; 2 pineapple rings; 3 T whipped cream; chopped nuts; 3 maraschino cherries, whole strawberries, or slices of fruit.

25

Ripples

The idea of combining two or more colors to create variegated ice cream came into its own during the 1930s. Variations include rainbow, marble, and aufait. Perhaps best known is ripple, ice cream ribboned through with colorful, flavorful syrup. Ripples make attractive scooped ice cream and fanciful filling for any of the pie shells described in Chapter 29.

A proper ripple has even veins of color with no large erratic globs. Swirl in syrup while the ice cream is still soft, yet firm enough to prevent the syrup from settling out. Consistency is usually just right in freshly frozen ice cream, ready to pack for hardening. But, depending on the mix and on the specific freezer, ice cream may be ripe for rippling before you would otherwise remove it from the ice cream maker, or it may need to be hardened a bit first.

Choose a syrup with a bright color that contrasts with the color of the ice cream and one with a complementary flavor. The syrup should be thin enough to pour but not so thin that it easily blends in and loses its identity. Most syrups work best at room temperature or slightly chilled. Warm ones melt the surrounding ice cream to spoil the effect; cold ones tend to clump on contact. Fudge syrups are usually thicker than others, making the ribboning less even.

An effective ripple contains ten to twenty percent syrup, or one-half to one cup per quart of ice cream. Less syrup loses the effect. Too much syrup not only drastically alters texture, but makes the whole thing unpleasantly sweet.

Easy Ripples

Syrups used for rippling invariably contain lots of sugar to keep them from getting hard or gathering ice crystals in the freezer. Many sundae sauces double as ripples, thinned to consistency as necessary with water, milk, or cream. A sauce that's slightly on the thin side may be thickened by chilling. Popular ripples are chocolate, fudge, caramel, marshmallow, and various fruit flavors including raspberry, strawberry, and pineapple.

For an easy chocolate ripple, use ordinary chocolate syrup straight from the can. Another option is to melt chocolate chips in a saucepan over low heat with one-third cup sugar and one-third cup milk per cup chips. Stir until the ingredients blend and cool before swirling into one quart of ice cream. Chocolate goes well with every flavor, but especially sets off vanilla, coffee and cherry. Substitute butterscotch chips for butterscotch ripple to swirl into chocolate or nut ice cream, or use peanut butter chips to ripple into strawberry or banana.

One of the best ripples is caramel. In a small saucepan, combine one-half pound quality caramel candies and one-half cup milk. Heat, stirring, until the caramels melt and the syrup is blended smooth. Cool before swirling into mocha or butter pecan ice cream.

For marshmallow swirl, thin one cup marshmallow cream with two or more tablespoons milk. To make a chewier version, blend one-third cup marshmallow cream and two teaspoons milk and fold in one-half cup miniature marshmallows. Marshmallow ripple goes well with apricot, peach, or peppermint ice cream.

Any well-stirred jelly makes a dandy ripple. Grape jelly swirled into peanut butter ice cream is a classic hit. Jams and preserves may need thinning with a little corn syrup, lemon juice, kirsch, brandy, or orange liqueur. Swirl strawberry jam into pineapple or strawberry ice cream, raspberry jam into chocolate or French vanilla.

Canned fruit in heavy syrup, well-drained and puréed with corn syrup (three tablespoons syrup per one pound can for each quart of ice cream), then chilled, makes a fine ripple. Go for pineapple in banana ice cream, purple plum in lemon, fig in walnut or pecan.

Fresh fruit ripples need added sugar to keep them from turning icy when hardened, but if the ice cream will be served after only a brief hardening period, sweet, well-ripened fruit or berries can be puréed and rippled without sugar. Here you can use up to three times the usual amount, as much as three cups per quart. Successful combinations include blueberries in maple or lemon ice cream, raspberries in peach or vanilla, stewed dates or prunes (cooled and puréed) in any nut flavor.

Technique

Ice cream manufacturers pump in streams of syrup along with ice cream as it's packed into cartons, causing a rippling effect hard to duplicate any other way. Techniques for homemade ripples yield a different effect that's no less attractive. The trick is not to stir the ice cream after adding syrup but rather cut through it to swirl it in.

Instructions for ice cream freezers with add-ingredient openings in the lid sometimes suggest pouring syrup through the opening in a steady stream and letting the dasher ripple it in as freezing reaches completion. Success here depends largely on the design of the dasher. Unless ice cream moves steadily downward, the syrup will blend into the upper portion of the ice cream to make a new flavor. In any case, the dasher must be stopped after only one or two revolutions, or the syrup will be thoroughly incorporated into the ice cream.

A second rippling method is to remove the dasher and poke a hole down the center of the finished ice cream with the handle of a wooden spoon. Fill the opening with syrup, then cut through the ice cream a few times with a plastic spatula or wooden spoon. This technique works best with canisters having a capacity of two quarts or less. In a larger canister, poke the hole only halfway down and ripple half the ice cream, then finish the remainder after packing the top half for hardening. In a smaller canister, or one that's wider than it is tall, remove the dasher, smooth out the surface, then cut a circular groove in it. Pour in syrup and immediately scoop the ice cream into containers, letting it ripple as it will.

 If your canister design isn't suitable for these techniques, or you're making still-frozen ice cream, you still have two other options. You can combine syrup and ice cream as you pack the freezer containers, although the rippling won't be very even since the syrup tends to settle into lower spots. Fudge ripples work best for this, since they don't run as readily as thinner ones. Half fill the container with ice cream, pour in half the sauce, swirl with the tip of a knife. Repeat with the ramaining ice cream and sauce. Finally, you might spread soft ice cream in a prechilled cake pan or other wide, flat container. Cut deep parallel grooves in the surface and drizzle syrup into them. Harden for about an hour then cross hatch by cutting through the ice cream perpendicular to the grooves, causing the syrup to streak.

FUDGE RIPPLE

Fudge variations include adding 1 T instant coffee; $^{1}/_{4}$ t almond extract plus $^{1}/_{2}$ C chopped toasted almonds; $^{1}/_{4}$ t orange extract plus zest from one orange; $^{1}/_{2}$ t cinnamon; $^{1}/_{2}$ C chopped peanuts and/or miniature marshmallows.

In small saucepan over low heat, combine

  3-oz semisweet chocolate
  $^{1}/_{2}$ C evaporated milk
  8 marshmallows.

Stirring, heat until blended.

Remove from heat and stir in **$^{1}/_{8}$ t vanilla.**

yield: about 1 cup

SPIRITED FUDGE RIPPLE

Swirl this spunky ripple into vanilla, chocolate, strawberry, pistachio, or lemon ice cream. For other ice cream flavors, vary the syrup by substituting other liqueurs—orange for orange ice cream, coffee for coffee ice cream, almond for toasted almond ice cream.

In small saucepan, melt

  2-oz semisweet chocolate
  $^{1}/_{4}$ C light cream

Stir in until smooth

  1 C sifted powdered sugar
  2 T butter
  $^{1}/_{4}$ t salt
  2 T crème de cacao.

Cool to room temperature.

yield: about 1 cup

FRESH FRUIT RIPPLE

Fully ripened peaches, apricots, strawberries, or strained raspberries make the best fresh fruit ripples. Swirl this ripple into contrasting ice cream or combine it with ice cream of the same flavor for an attractive two-tone effect.

Combine

$^3/_4$ **C fruit purée**
$^1/_2$ **T lemon juice**
6 T sugar.

Chill 30 minutes.

yield: about 1 cup

PURPLE PLUM RIPPLE

Purple plums create a sweet-tart, richly colored ripple that goes nicely with many fruit and nut ice creams especially lemon, pecan, or French vanilla.

Pit and slice

6 medium fresh plums.

In small saucepan, combine with

$^1/_2$ **C sugar.**

Heat until soft.

Purée in blender.

Return to saucepan.

Heat until reduced to 1 cup.

Chill.

yield: about 1 cup

CANDIED APPLE RIPPLE

Swirl this gently tinted fruit ripple into cinnamon or coffee ice cream. For a fast version, dissolve 2 T cinnamon candies in $^1/_4$ C heated corn syrup and stir in enough prepared apple sauce to make one cup. For a less spicy variation, substitute currant jelly for the cinnamon candies.

Peel, core, and cut into chunks

1 large, tart cooking apple.

In saucepan, combine with

2 T red cinnamon candies
2 T water
$^1/_4$ **C light corn syrup.**

Stirring, heat until candies melt and apples are tender.

Purée and cool.

yield: about 1 cup

CHERRY CHEESECAKE RIPPLE

Swirl this decidedly different ripple into lemon, chocolate or vanilla ice cream. For a change of pace, try blueberry, strawberry, or peach preserves in place of cherry.

In mixing bowl, beat smooth

1¹/₂ T cream cheese
¹/₄ C cream or
yogurt.

Blend in

¹/₂ C cherry
preserves.

yield: about 1 cup

Aufait

An aufait is similar to a ripple, differing primarily in being layered rather than swirled. It's the French version of an English trifle without the cake. Create one by alternating ice cream with thin layers of fruit in the form of jam, preserves, sheets of fruit leather, minced candied fruit or peel, or fruit-flavored gelatin (made with only half the called-for amount of water). Keep fruit layers thin so they won't freeze hard and make slicing difficult.

Add any number of layers or combinations of fruit and ice cream, with an eye toward appetizing color and flavor combinations. Don't overlook frozen yogurt and buttermilk sherbet, which make especially tasty aufaits. Freeze each layer firm before adding the next, and firmly freeze the finished aufait before slicing and serving it.

Mold aufait in a loaf pan and serve it in half-inch slices, freeze it in a round cake pan and serve in wedges, or incorporate one into your next bombe (Chapter 26), cake (Chapter 27), or ice cream pie (Chapter 29).

Marble

Marbling involves swirling together two or more different colors of ice cream or sherbet so that interesting patterns appear during scooping. Manufacturers use pumps and filters to achieve a wavy look that can't be duplicated at home. You'll come close by alternating layers of ice cream or sherbet and stirring once or twice to mingle the colors. Work gently to avoid blurring.

Combine any two ice creams whose colors and flavors go well together, such as chocolate and mint, blueberry and lemon, pineapple and strawberry, avocado and pecan, vanilla and anything. Ice cream combined with a sherbet makes a particularly fine marble. Both orange and raspberry sherbet are set off nicely by a creamy rich vanilla ice cream. Lemon and strawberry sherbet go well with a strong, rich chocolate.

Rainbow

A rainbow is a marble without the swirl. Three or more different colors are layered so that stripes or bands appear on slicing or scooping. To prevent waving, harden each layer before adding the next. Slice or scoop a rainbow immediately before serving—melting makes the bands blend together and look muddy.

Neapolitan—equal layers of chocolate, vanilla, and strawberry or orange—is a classic rainbow. Since fruit sherbets come in so many pretty pastel shades, they are used in rainbows more often than ice cream. At least one layer is usually a citrus flavor, enhancing the fruity taste of the others. Sherbet rainbows make dazzling ice cream molds, constructed according to directions coming up in the next chapter.

26

Bombes and Other Molds

In the eighteenth century, ices were sculpted into fantastic and ornately decorated centerpieces. Today, few of us have time for such painstaking endeavors. Luckily, there's an easy way out—freezing ice cream in simple decorative molds to be sliced at the table.

Earlier this century you could buy molds designed expressly for the purpose. Now they're found primarily at flea markets and garage sales, where competition is fierce among serious collectors. As a result, reproductions in a limited number of sizes and shapes are now available (for a source, see Appendix C, "Supplies"). The old-time molds come in two halves for shaping three-dimensional geometric designs, fruits, flowers, statues, and even animals.

Molds intended for gelatin or fancy cakes may also be used for ice cream. Perhaps best known of all ice cream molds is the melon mold, or bombe, the more sinister designation supplied by the French in honor of its bomblike shape. You needn't run out and buy a bona fide bombe mold. Any round-bottomed metal mixing bowl will do. So will a loaf pan or a tubular cake pan.

Harmony

A three-dimensional mold usually contains only one flavor—it's the shape that counts. The appeal of plainer forms like the bombe, on the other hand, is in their combination of two or more different flavors, either layered in bands or spread to conform to the mold's contours. A typical two-flavor mold might contain strawberry and vanilla ice cream, or chocolate and peppermint. Traditional three-flavor combinations are chocolate, vanilla, and strawberry (Neapolitan) or pistachio, vanilla, and raspberry or strawberry.

Choose whatever combinations appeal to you, as long as colors and flavors blend harmoniously. For textural, visual, and taste variety, combine ice cream with sherbet, frozen yogurt, or fruit sorbetto. Many traditional recipes call for an outer layer or two of ice cream and a center of still-frozen mousse.

To heighten contrast, stir colorful candied fruit or bakery bits into one or more of the layers. The classic example here is spumoni, consisting of a layer of vanilla ice cream, one of macaroon or chocolate mousse, and a core of tutti-frutti. An alternative to incorporating crushed candy, chopped nuts, or candied fruit into one of the ice cream layers is to sprinkle it between layers, but sparsely, so it won't cause the layers to separate on unmolding.

Procedure

Prepare a mold well in advance of serving so each layer has plenty of time to harden. Exactly how long you'll need depends on the size of the mold and the number of layers. A large mold may require two or three days for total preparation. To speed things up, or if your freezer doesn't get cold enough for firm freezing, seek out a local source of dry ice. If you wish to mold ices and sorbets, or to create one of the intricate shapes like a strawberry with all its little dimples, dry ice is the only way you can get the temperature low enough. Be sure to wear gloves when working with dry ice, to keep your fingers from "burning."

Begin by washing your mold and drying it thoroughly to keep frozen water from spoiling the shape. Chill the mold to the temperature of the ice cream or colder. You'll get best results with an intricate mold if you chill it on dry ice for ten minutes. Just before filling, coat the mold lightly with oil or nonstick cooking spray.

If you use a loaf pan, bowl, or other smooth-sided form, line it with plastic wrap, buttered brown paper, waxed paper, or heavy foil to facilitate unmolding. Let at least an inch of paper stick out around the rim to help pull the ice cream loose. Using a liner has one disadvantage—the surface of the ice cream will show wrinkles you'll later have to smooth out or cover up.

As you fill the mold, try not to press the ice cream down, which releases air and makes the finished shape harder to cut. Packing isn't a problem when you use soft, freshly frozen ice cream. If you're adding several layers, you'll have plenty of time while each one hardens to make the next. Homemade or store bought ice cream already frozen firm may need to be softened slightly, care taken to minimize heat shock. The ideal molding temperature is 10° F (−12° C).

If the first layer slips in the mold, either the ice cream is too soft or the mold is too warm. Place both in the freezer for up to half an hour, or set them on dry ice a few minutes. After spreading each layer, freeze it one to two hours (ten to fifteen minutes on dry ice), or until it's firm enough for the shape to hold when you spread the next layer. Continue adding and freezing layers to fill the mold. For a bottom pastry layer, finish off a pan or bowl by patting on a crumb crust (recipes in Chapter 29, "Ice Cream Pies").

Seal the mold with foil or plastic wrap, using freezer tape if necessary to hold it down. If you're working with a two-part mold, simply fill both sides at the same time, press them together, and freeze until firm.

The ice cream must be fully hardened if it's to hold its shape on unmolding. The larger the mold, the longer hardening takes. Adjust your freezer to its coldest setting and allow at least four hours for a one and one-half quart mold, six hours for a two-quart mold, and eight hours for a full-sized, two-part mold. To ensure even freezing, rest the mold on packages of frozen foods, never on a coiled shelf. If you use dry ice, you can unmold in just fifteen to twenty minutes. Don't wait too long or the ice cream may shatter when you unmold it.

Unmolding

If you use dry ice and a mold specifically designed for ice cream, unmolding simply involves dipping the whole thing in cold water, prying the mold open, and releasing the ice cream. To avoid losing delicate surface features, return the ice cream to the freezer as quickly as possible and let it harden before serving.

If you're molding in a bowl or pan, run a spatula or knife around the edge and invert the ice cream onto a chilled platter. Dip a towel into hot water, wring dry, and wrap the mold for a few minutes. Warm odd corners by rubbing them with the warm towel. Depending on the thickness of the mold and on the firmness of the ice cream, you may need to rewarm the towel a time or two. If the ice cream still doesn't come loose, lift the plate and mold together and shake gently. Here's where a paper or foil liner comes in handy—tug the edges after briefly wrapping the mold in a warm towel and the ice cream will slip right out. Smooth wrinkles with a knife or stiff spatula or cover them with whipped cream.

A springform cake pan with a fitted liner at the bottom is among the easiest shapes to unmold. Invert the pan over a chilled serving dish and wrap the outside with a hot towel to loosen the edge so you can undo the buckle. Then simply lift off the bottom and peel away the paper.

Occasionally you'll see instructions telling you to run hot water over the bottom of a mold or to dip the whole thing into hot water. This can quickly melt the outer layer of ice cream, spoiling the appearance of a mold you don't intend to trim.

If you do decide to trim your ice cream mold, you might frost it with flavored whipped cream or coat it with chocolate (directions are in Chapter 28). Bombes and square shapes may be encased in baked Alaska (Chapter 30). A reviving art is air-brushing three-dimensional molds with food dye to bring them alive (one source for a home-video is listed in Appendix C).

Unnmolded creations to be stored longer than two hours should be covered tightly with foil or plastic wrap to prevent off-flavors, ice crystals, and freezer burn. If you allow approximately one cup of ice cream per person, a standard two-quart mold will serve eight to ten.

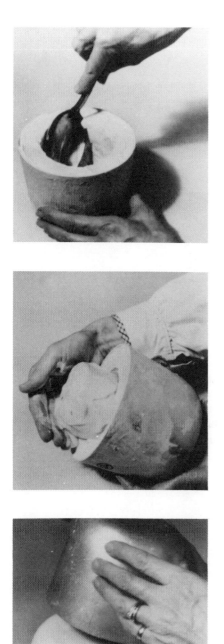

Molding a two-flavor bombe:

1. Spread soft ice cream in chilled mold, leaving center open, and freeze firm.

2. Fill center with second flavor and freeze firm.

3. Unmold on serving plate and either smooth out surface or decorate bombe.

(Photos courtesy of Maid of Scandinavia Company, Minneapolis, Minnesota.)

SICILIAN SPUMONI

Spumoni has an endless number of variations, attesting to the enduring popularity of this traditional mold. Nearly every version contains fruit, nuts, spirits, chocolate, and a center of still-frozen mousse. This Sicilian spumoni is traditionally served with ground almonds sprinkled on top.

Mince	**¹/₂ C candied fruit.**
Add and set aside	**2 T cognac.**
Spread 2-quart bombe with	**3 C vanilla ice cream.**
Freeze firm.	
Spread with	**3 C chocolate ice cream.**
Freeze firm.	
Whip	**³/₄ C heavy cream.**
Fold in	**¹/₄ C powdered sugar.**
Stir in marinated fruit.	
Whip stiff	**1 egg white.**
Combine with whipped cream and fill center of mold.	
Cover and freeze firm, about 4 hours.	

yield: 8-10 servings

SPECTACULAR SPUMONI

Instead of spumoni's usual three layers, this version has four. Raspberry ice cream or sherbet may be substituted for the center mousse.

Spread 2¹/₂-quart bombe with	**3 C pistachio ice cream.**
Freeze firm.	
Blend together	**3 C vanilla ice cream** **¹/₄ C rum, or** **1 t rum flavoring.**
Spread over pistachio and stud with	**30 maraschino cherries.**

**SPECTACULAR SPUMONI,
cont'd.**

Freeze firm.	
Spread with	**2 C chocolate ice cream.**
Freeze firm.	
Whip	**³/₄ C heavy cream.**
Combine and fold in	**1 C fresh raspberries ¹/₄ C sugar.**
Cover and freeze firm, about 6 hours.	

yield: 10-12 servings

MOCHA MOLD

Drizzle mocha mold with ¹/₄ C caramel sauce and pass more in a serving dish, or omit pecans and garnish with chocolate curls (directions in Chapter 28).

In large skillet, melt	**1 T butter.**
Toss until well coated	**36 pecan halves.**
Cool.	
In 2-quart bombe spread	**2 C coffee ice cream.**
Freeze firm.	
Spread with	**1-qt chocolate ice cream.**
Freeze firm.	
Fill center with	**2 C coffee ice cream.**
Cover and freeze firm, about 6 hours.	
Unmold on serving plate and garnish with pecans.	

yield: 8-10 servings

DELMONICO BOMBE

Delmonico's New York restaurant (1827-1923) was famous for its ice cream concoctions. This variation on aufait recreates one of them. For a modernized version, use crushed chocolate sandwich cookies instead of macaroons, omit the spirits, and substitute raspberry jelly for currant.

Crush	**9 small macaroons.**
Sprinkle with	**2 T amaretto.**
Set aside.	
In 2-quart bombe, spread	**2 C French vanilla ice cream.**
Freeze firm.	
Spread with	**¼ C currant jelly.**
Sprinkle with half the macaroons.	
Spread with	**2 C French vanilla ice cream.**
Freeze firm.	
Spread with	**¼ C currant jelly.**
Sprinkle with remaining macaroons.	
Spread with	**2 C French vanilla ice cream.**
Cover and freeze firm, about 6 hours.	

yield: 6-8 servings

ALL-OUT LEMON AUFAIT

By attractively arranging candied fruit and nut halves on top, you can trim this mold to look like a holiday fruitcake. For extra flavor, substitute orange frozen yogurt for one or two layers of lemon.

Mince	**1 C candied fruit.**
Combine with	**³/₄ C strawberry preserves** **¹/₂ C crushed pineapple** **1 T rum.**

Marinate at room temperature several hours.

Divide into three portions.

In 2-quart mold spread	**1¹/₂ C lemon frozen yogurt.**

Freeze firm.

Spread with ¹/₃ fruit mixture and	**1¹/₂ C lemon frozen yogurt.**

Freeze firm.

Spread with ¹/₃ fruit mixture and	**1¹/₂ C lemon frozen yogurt.**

Freeze firm.

Spread with remaining fruit and	**1¹/₂ C lemon frozen yogurt.**

Cover and freeze firm, about 6 hours.

yield: 8-10 servings

RAINBOW MOLD

Let your imagination run rampant in combining fruit sherbet, frozen yogurt, ice cream, or sorbet for attractive and tasty rainbow molds. Possibilities include strawberry, lemon, and blueberry; pineapple, cherry, and peach; raspberry, lemon, and avocado; cantaloupe, watermelon, and lime.

Beat foamy	**2 C heavy cream.**
Add and beat into soft peaks	**¼ C powdered sugar**
Coarsely grate and fold in	**4-oz semisweet chocolate.**
Spread half into 2½-quart mold.	
Freeze firm.	
Spread with	**2 C orange sherbet.**
Freeze firm.	
Spread with	**2 C lime sherbet.**
Freeze firm.	
Spread with	**2 C raspberry sherbet.**
Freeze firm.	
Combine with remaining cream	**½ C chopped pecans.**
Spread in mold.	
Cover and freeze firm, about 6 hours.	

yield: 10-12 servings

TROPICAL BOMBE

This rainbow mold is fairly bursting with tropical flavors. For an *Oriental* bombe, substitute preserved ginger for orange marmalade, toasted almonds for the buttered macadamias, and 2 T kumquat preserves for the pineapple.

Combine	**3 C lemon sherbet** **2 T orange marmalade.**
Spread in 2-quart mold.	
Freeze firm.	

TROPICAL BOMBE, cont'd.

Chop fine and sauté	**2 T macadamia nuts**
in	**2 t butter.**
Cool.	
Combine with	**2 C vanilla ice cream.**
Spread in mold and freeze firm.	
Combine	**3 C orange sherbet** **¹/₂ C drained crushed pineapple.**
Spread in mold.	
Cover and freeze firm, about 4 hours.	

yield: 8-10 servings

NEAPOLITAN RAINBOW

Raspberry or orange ice cream or sherbet may be substituted for the middle layer of this variation on a rainbow classic. Garnish slices with raspberries, strawberries, or fresh peaches.

In 8-inch springform, spread	**1-qt vanilla ice cream.**
Freeze firm.	
Drain	**9-oz crushed pineapple.**
Combine with	**1-qt strawberry ice cream.**
Spread in springform and freeze firm.	
Spread with	**1-qt chocolate ice cream.**
Cover and freeze firm, about 6 hours.	

yield: 12-14 servings

Molded Soufflé

No discussion of molding would be complete without directions for soufflé. Begin by fitting a regular soufflé dish with a collar: Cut a strip of foil nine inches wide and long enough to fit around the top of the dish. Fold the foil in half lengthwise, wrap it around the dish for a three-inch collar, secure it with a large rubber band, and fasten the ends with a paper clip.

Fill the dish to the top of the collar and pop it into the freezer for hardening. To serve, remove the collar and trim the exposed sides with walnut or pecan halves, or with toasted almond slices. Trim the top with puffs of whipped cream and maraschino cherries, pineapple chunks, or whole strawberries. Spoon the soufflé into serving dishes at the table.

Mold stir-frozen soufflé or spoom (Chapter 3), or fluffy still-frozen mousse (Chapter 1); or, whip egg whites left over from making frozen custard and fold them into any freshly frozen ice cream to mold as a soufflé. The following recipe shows how it works.

STRAWBERRY SOUFFLÉ

To make pineapple soufflé, substitute drained crushed pineapple for the strawberries. For banana soufflé, use well-ripened mashed bananas. For peach or apricot soufflé, add amaretto instead of orange liqueur. You know you've reached the thread stage when you drop some syrup from a spoon and it spins a 2-inch thread.

In small saucepan, combine	**1 C sugar** **¹⁄₃ C orange juice.**
Stirring, heat until sugar dissolves.	
Without stirring, cook to thread stage (232-234° F or 112° C).	
Beat until very stiff	**6 egg whites.**
Beating, drizzle in hot syrup.	
Cool.	
Wash, hull, and purée	**1-qt strawberries** **¹⁄₂ C orange** **liqueur.**
Fold into	**1¹⁄₂-qt French** **vanilla ice cream.**
Fold in cooled meringue.	

**STRAWBERRY SOUFFLÉ,
cont'd.**

Turn into collared 2-quart soufflé
dish and freeze firm, about 8 hours.

Remove collar, press onto sides   **1 C toasted sliced
                                      almonds.**

yield: 10-12 servings

Mini-Molds

In contrast to a large mold brought to the table for slicing, miniature molds hold individual servings of ice cream. You can use antique molds, reproductions, or single-serving gelatin molds. Fill, freeze, and unmold them as you would a larger form.

For an easy version, layer different flavors in muffin cups and freeze firm, then peel away the paper; or, mold the ice cream directly in the muffin pan, then run a knife around the edges and gently heat the bottom with a warm towel to loosen. Serve mini-molds on chilled plates in a pool of sundae sauce or surrounded by sliced fruit or a few fresh berries.

To eliminate the need for unmolding, freeze ice cream directly in attractive custard cups or other small dessert bowls. Make a mini-spumoni, for example, by spreading vanilla ice cream over the sides and bottom of each chilled dish. Freeze firm. Half fill the remaining space with chocolate ice cream and freeze firm. Finish filling with sweetened whipped cream combined with well-drained mixed fruit and freeze firm. Temper just until spoonable before serving. Another attractive way to mold individual servings is to layer ice cream in parfait glasses held at a tilt so the stripes look a bit tipsy.

Make mini-molds even more fun by hiding a treat at the center in the manner of tartufi (described in Chapter 21). Serve topped with chocolate crackle (recipe in Chapter 24).

To broaden the range of possibilities, shape ice cream with extra thick cookie cutters selected to suit the occasion. Line a prechilled baking sheet with plastic wrap, spread soft ice cream over it, and top with a second sheet of plastic. With the palms of your hands or a rolling pin, press the ice cream to a thickness of one inch. Freeze firm, about one hour. Dip cookie cutters into hot water before cutting each shape. Use a pancake turner to lift shapes onto prechilled individual serving dishes. Freeze firm. Decorate according to the occasion. One pint of ice cream and a two-inch diameter cutter will give you four servings.

If you wish to get a bit colorful, cut one flavor with a round cutter (or slice hardened ice cream into squares or rounds) and freeze firm. Cut a smaller shape of contrasting color and press it on top. Freeze firm before serving. This technique imitates the "center mold" of bygone days, in which one flavor was molded inside another, the contrasting center shaped according to the occasion—a red heart for Valentine's Day, a green shamrock for St. Patrick's Day, a golden star for Christmas. The design at the center was revealed when the ice cream was sliced for serving.

27

Cakes and Sandwiches

Ice cream cakes come in many styles and sizes, ranging from shortcakes to multilevel layer cakes. Sometimes the cake isn't layered but rolled into ice cream logs or folded into crepes. Sometimes the ice cream is pressed between two cookies for an individual, hand-held serving, or sandwich.

Ice Cream Sandwiches

With the same cookie cutters used to create the mini-molds in Chapter 26, you can make ice cream sandwiches in any shape or size. Simply press one firmly frozen ice cream cut-out between two cooled cookies of the same shape. If desired, trim one or both sides with frosting, or dip the edges into grated chocolate, chopped toasted nuts, crushed candies, or sprinkles. Wrap the sandwiches individually in foil or plastic wrap and freeze. One quart of ice cream and sixteen two-inch cookies make eight sandwiches.

For neat little sandwiches, mold ice cream in twelve-ounce orange juice containers, freeze firm, then peel away the paper. Cut the ice cream into rounds and sandwich them between chocolate wafers or other small cookies. Give these little sandwiches an air of elegance by dipping one edge into chocolate coating (recipe in Chapter 21).

Instead of using hardened, preshaped ice cream, with care you can fill sandwiches with soft ice cream without having it all squish out. Place a heaping spoonful between two cookies. Gently press them together until the ice cream spreads evenly to the edges. Freeze firm on a baking sheet lined with waxed paper. Wrap individually when hardened.

Variations

Vanilla ice cream combined with chocolate cookies is *the* ice cream sandwich, but don't hesitate to try chocolate cookies with lemon, orange, raspberry, or mint-chip filling. Consider, too, branching out in the cookie department. How about ginger snaps with pistachio ice cream, edges rolled in chopped toasted almonds or pistachios? Or oatmeal cookies filled with rum-raisin ice cream; chocolate chip cookies with chocolate or mint-chip ice cream; peanut butter cookies with strawberry or raspberry ice cream?

Of course, ice cream sandwiches don't necessarily have to be made with cookies. Fashion round, flat wafers of hard or crisp meringue (recipe in Chapter 22), or buy meringue wafers ready-made. Dense cake such as brownies, moist gingerbread, sponge cake, pound cake, or sliced jelly roll all make great sandwiches. Cut larger sheets into sandwich-sized pieces to fill, or fill and freeze it as one large slab before dividing it into individual sandwiches. If you want to get fancy, spread layers of sponge or pound cake with jelly or preserves before filling them with ice cream.

For a more substantial snack, sandwich ice cream slices between packaged, frozen waffles. Serve out-of-hand or lay on a plate and garnish with whipped cream and sundae sauce.

SANDWICH COOKIES

Here's the classic ice cream sandwich cookie. If you wish, stir in ¹/₂ C finely chopped pecans or walnuts just before baking.

In large bowl, cream

¹/₂ C butter
1 C sugar.

Blend in

1 egg
1 t vanilla.

Melt and add

1-oz nonsweetened
   chocolate.

Combine and stir in

1 C flour
¹/₃ C cocoa
¹/₂ t baking soda
¹/₄ t salt.

Drop by spoonfuls 2" apart onto nongreased sheet.

Bake 10 minutes at 350° F (177° C).

Cool before removing from sheet to fill.

yield: 18 servings

MINI-WICH

You can whip up these miniature ice cream sandwiches in a jiffy. Combine any flavor pudding you like with chocolate wafers, vanilla wafers, or any little cookie of your choice. Allow two sandwiches per serving.

Combine

1¼ C cold milk
1 pkg instant
  pudding mix.

Beat at low speed 2 minutes.

Chill until partially set.

Whip and fold in **1 C heavy cream.**

Spread 1 T filling on each of **24 wafer cookies.**

Top with **24 wafer cookies.**

Wrap individually and freeze until firm.

yield: 12 servings

S'mores

It was inevitable that someone would come up with an ice cream version of campfire s'mores, and then equally inevitable that a myriad of variations would follow. For starters, sandwich one-half cup chocolate chip ice cream between two graham crackers. Seal the edges with dipping chocolate (recipe in Chapter 21), or drizzle six sandwiches with three ounces of melted semisweet chocolate. For a slightly spicy touch, fill cinnamon grahams with vanilla ice cream and press the edges into grated chocolate. How about peanutty s'mores? Spread crackers thinly with peanut butter and fill them with strawberry or chocolate ice cream, or a little of each.

To make lots of s'mores at once, cover a baking sheet with a single layer of graham crackers, spread with chocolate ice cream and marshmallow cream, or vanilla ice cream and thick, creamy fudge sauce. Top with a second layer of crackers. Freeze firm. Separate servings by cutting between crackers. Mmmm . . . so good, you'll want s'more!

Ice Cream Cakes

An ice cream cake is essentially a gigantic ice cream sandwich served in slices or wedges. From another point of view, it's ice cream molded together with one or more layers of bakery goods. As with any mold, the ice cream must be soft and spreadable, either used straight out of the ice cream freezer or tempered to spreading consistency.

Forms designed expressly for fashioning cakes have a little hole in the bottom, about the size of a dime, so you can poke in your finger or a spoon handle to push out the finished product. You really don't need a special pan, though. You can construct cakes in a springform, in a square, round, or rectangular cake pan, or on a baking sheet or serving platter.

One of the easiest ways to prepare an ice cream cake is to spread soft ice cream evenly onto one cooled layer of cake, freeze firm (about two hours), then press a second cake layer on top. You'll get somewhat neater results if you shape the ice cream by freezing it in a waxed paper lined springform. Release the form, peel away the paper, and press the ice cream between two cooled layers of cake. Frost with soft ice cream and freeze firm. An average-sized cake with one and one-half quarts of ice cream serves twelve.

Sponge cake and angel food both go well with ice cream because they're light and airy and don't turn hard when frozen. Most are tall enough to slice into three layers for a truly sumptuous dessert. Spread a quart of ice cream between each layer and another on top.

Vary your cakes by varying the number and composition of the layers. Instead of one layer of ice cream between two layers of cake, sandwich one layer of cake between two of ice cream; or, start with a single cake layer and stack it with an ice cream or sherbet rainbow, perhaps including preserves, aufait style (see Chapter 25). You might also alternate large rounds of hard meringue (Chapter 22) with layers of colorful flavors like strawberry, chocolate, and pistachio, or coffee, lemon, and avocado, starting and ending with meringue.

The bakery layers might consist of whole or crushed cookies. It's easy to construct a log-shaped cake with French vanilla ice cream and thin chocolate wafers. Press two tablespoons of ice cream between each, arranging cookies side by side and skewed at a slight angle. Freeze firm, about three hours. Frost with more ice cream or sweetened whipped cream and freeze firm, about one hour. Slice and pass the hot fudge or strawberry sauce.

The pie crust recipes in Chapter 29 offer more tasty alternatives. Press a layer of crushed cookie, nut, or coconut crust into a springform or other cake pan lined with foil. Spread one quart of ice cream on top and freeze firm. Add another crust layer and another quart of ice cream. Freeze firm. Continue alternating to the desired height, allowing one quart of ice cream for every four servings. If your pan is too shallow for many layers, freeze the layers separately before assembling them.

Unmold an ice cream cake as you would any mold, following directions in Chapter 26, "Bombes and other Molds." Frost, if desired, with whipped cream or butter cream and trim according to directions in Chapter 28, "Decorating Ice Cream Creations."

STRAWBERRY ALMOND LOAF

For delicious variations of this scrumptious cake, substitute amaretto for orange liqueur and chocolate ice cream for strawberry, or try coffee ice cream and coffee liqueur.

Thaw and purée	**1 pkg frozen strawberries.**
Combine in saucepan with	**4 t cornstarch** $^1/_2$ **C water.**
Boil 2 minutes.	
Chill and set aside.	
Line loaf pan with plastic wrap.	
Slice into 4 layers	**10$^3/_4$-oz pound cake.**
Brush layers with	**$^1/_4$ C orange liqueur.**
Blend smooth	**1$^1/_2$ C vanilla ice cream** **1 C coarsely chopped toasted almonds.**
Place bottom layer in pan and spread with half the ice cream.	
Top with second cake layer.	
Spread with	**1 C strawberry ice cream.**
Top with third cake layer.	
Spread with remaining vanilla ice cream.	
Top with fourth cake layer and spread with strawberry glaze.	
Cover and freeze firm, about 4 hours.	

yield: 14-16 servings

MOCHA HAZELNUT TORTE

If the ice cream gets too soft before the torte is assembled, chill both ice cream and cake in the freezer for half an hour or until firm enough to work. For easy cutting at serving time, temper torte 15 minutes.

Beat stiff	**6 egg whites.**
Beat until light yellow	**6 egg yolks.**
Add and beat until creamy	**½ C sugar.**
Stir in	**1 C (¼#) finely ground hazelnuts** **1 T dried bread crumbs.**

Fold in egg whites.

Pour into nongreased 10" springform.

Bake 30 minutes at 350° F (177° C).

Cool and slice into three layers.

Combine	**1½-qt coffee ice cream** **2-oz melted nonsweetened chocolate** **2 T coffee liqueur.**

Spread 2 C ice cream between each layer, frost with remaining ice cream.

Freeze firm, then wrap well.

yield: 16-18 servings

FROZEN TRIFLE

Garnish trifle with heaps of sweetened whipped cream, toasted sliced almonds, and sugared strawberries. Or accompany it with fruit or fudge sauce (recipes in Chapter 24).

Split in half and use to line bottom and sides of 10" springform

20 ladyfingers.

Blend together

1-qt vanilla ice cream
$^1/_4$ C chopped toasted almonds
$^1/_2$ t almond extract.

Spread over ladyfingers.

Freeze firm.

Purée

18-oz crushed pineapple.

Combine with

2 C raspberry sherbet.

Spread over vanilla layer.

Freeze firm.

Combine

1-qt vanilla ice cream
$^1/_4$ C orange liqueur.

Spread over raspberry layer.

Cover and freeze firm.

yield: 14-16 servings

CHOCOLATE PEANUT CAKE

For extra chocolate flavor, substitute chocolate chip ice cream for one or both layers of vanilla. To save time, instead of baking brownies, combine 1½ C crushed chocolate wafers with ⅓ C melted butter, press into form, and chill.

Bake in 10" springform or cut and arrange to line bottom	**1 batch brownies.**
Combine and stir until crumbly	**1½ C chunky peanut butter** **2¼ C powdered sugar.**
Divide into thirds.	
Spread over the brownie layer	**1-qt vanilla ice cream.**
Sprinkle with ⅓ peanut butter mixture and freeze firm.	
Spread with	**1-qt chocolate ice cream.**
Sprinkle with ⅓ peanut butter mixture and freeze firm.	
Spread with	**1-qt vanilla ice cream.**
Gently press remaining peanut butter mixture onto surface.	
Cover and freeze firm, 3 to 4 hours.	

yield: 14-16 servings

BLACK FOREST LAYER CAKE

For *snappy layer cake*, substitute ginger snaps for vanilla wafers, any fruit or nut ice cream for chocolate, and thinly spread preserves for the cherries. For a more formal garnish, pipe whipped cream on top and trim with pecan halves and chocolate curls (directions in Chapter 28).

Combine	**2 C crushed chocolate wafers** **$^2/_3$ C melted butter.**
Press into springform.	
Chill until firm.	
Spread with	**3 C French vanilla ice cream.**
Freeze firm.	
Drain and pat dry	**16-oz dark pitted cherries.**
Layer in springform and freeze firm.	
Spread with	**2 C chocolate fudge ice cream.**
Freeze firm.	
Drain and pat dry	**16-oz dark pitted cherries.**
Layer in springform and freeze firm.	
Spread with	**3 C French vanilla ice cream.**
Combine and sprinkle on top	**$^3/_4$ C chopped pecans** **$^1/_2$ C grated semi-sweet chocolate.**
Cover and freeze firm.	

yield: 10-12 servings

RAINBOW CAKE

This colorful cake may be built up with any of the rainbow molds described in Chapter 26, or your own creation. Garnish with mandarin orange sections or arrange rosettes of sliced maraschino or candied cherries on top.

In medium bowl, combine

**³/₄ C crushed vanilla wafers
¹/₂ C finely chopped almonds
¹/₂ C flaked coconut
6 T melted butter.**

Press into bottom of 10" springform.

Bake 15 minutes at 375° F (190° C) until lightly browned.

Cool, then chill.

Spread with

1-qt orange sherbet.

Freeze firm.

Strain

1 pkg puréed raspberries.

Combine with

1-qt raspberry sherbet.

Spread in springform and freeze firm.

Spread with

1-qt lemon sherbet.

Cover and freeze firm.

yield: 12-14 servings

Shortcake

Shortcake counts among the few truly native American desserts. When heaped with ice cream, it's about as all-American as you can get. The original version is strawberry, but you can make shortcake with any sweetened fruit, from fresh blueberries and peaches to chilled stewed rhubarb. Unlike other ice cream cakes, shortcake is assembled just before serving.

For cake, use sweetened biscuits, still warm from the oven, or slices of sponge cake toasted in the broiler until golden (about five minutes). During strawberry season, prepared shortcake shells are on display at every grocery store, or bake your own fresh, bowl-shaped maryannes from the recipes that come with maryanne baking forms.

Spoon the crushed, sweetened fruit over individual servings of cake, letting plenty of sweet juice soak in. Add a generous scoop of vanilla or fruit ice cream, and spoon on more fruit. Top the whole thing off with a gob of sweetened whipped cream and garnish with more sliced fruit or whole berries.

OLD-FASHIONED SHORTCAKE

Old-timey shortcakes are split and packed with fruit and ice cream while they're still warm from the oven. These dropped shortcakes have a homey appearance. If you prefer a formal look, knead dough on a floured board until smooth, about ¹/₂ minute. Divide into 8 equal portions, roll each into a ball, and flatten to 2¹/₂" round on baking sheet. Bake as usual.

Combine	**1 C flour**
	¹/₂ T baking powder
	¹/₄ t salt
	2 T sugar.
Cut in until crumbly	**3 T softened butter.**
Stir in	**6 T milk.**

Drop in 8 equal portions onto greased sheet. Bake 10 minutes at 400° F (205° C). Split while biscuits are still warm.

yield: 8 servings

Ice Cream Rolls

Ice cream rolls are made with the same half-inch-thick, springy sheet cake used for jelly rolls. While the cake is in the oven, lay out a linen tea towel or cotton (non-terry) dish towel sprinkled with sifted powdered sugar.

As soon as the cake is done, invert it onto the towel, roll it lengthwise, and cool thirty minutes, seam side down. Carefully unroll, trim hard or crusty edges, and spread one pint to one quart of ice cream or sherbet to within one inch of the edge. Reroll, wrap tightly in foil or plastic wrap, and freeze firm.

Plain cake goes well with any flavor filling. For extra flair, spread the cake with currant, raspberry, cherry, or strawberry jam before filling with vanilla or fruit ice cream. Lemon cake enhances fruit flavors, especially strawberry and lemon ice cream, or lemon and raspberry sherbet. Fill chocolate cake with coffee ice cream for a mocha roll, or try it with French vanilla, strawberry, extra rich chocolate, pistachio, mint, maple nut, or butter pecan.

To keep the cake from rolling off the serving platter, cut a triangular slice from each end to wedge against each side of the roll. Sprinkle finished cake with powdered sugar and serve it with strawberries or other fresh fruit; or, frost the roll with additional ice cream,

VANILLA ROLL

For *lemon* roll, substitute ¹/₂ t lemon extract for vanilla and add 2 t lemon zest. Use orange extract and zest for an *orange* roll. To make a *chocolate* roll, combine ¹/₄ C cocoa with sugar. For *chocolate mint* roll, substitute ¹/₂ t mint extract for the vanilla in a chocolate roll.

Beat together

4 egg yolks
³/₄ t baking powder
¹/₄ t salt.

Gradually beat in

¹/₂ C sugar.

Beat until thick and light yellow.

Stir in

³/₄ C sifted cake flour
1 t vanilla.

Beat into soft peaks

4 egg whites.

Add and beat until stiff

¹/₄ C sugar.

Fold into yolk mixture.

Spread in greased 15" x 10" x 1" jelly roll pan lined with greased and floured waxed paper. Bake at 400° F (204° C) 13 minutes. Gently peel away waxed paper, roll, and cool. Unroll, spread with ice cream, reroll, and freeze firm, 4 to 5 hours.

yield: 10-12 servings

Crepes

Whether you call them "frozen crepes," "frozen enchiladas," or "ice cream blintzes," the treat's the same—tissue-thin pancakes enfolding strips of ice cream. You can buy crepes prepackaged or make them yourself.

To make your own, you'll need a crepe pan or a heavy six- or eight-inch skillet and any dessert crepe recipe. For especially light crepes, use half water and half milk for the liquid. To increase flavor, substitute brandy, rum, or cognac for one or two tablespoons of liquid. Pour just enough batter into the hot pan to coat the bottom when you tilt it from side to side. One heaping tablespoon is about right for a six-inch pan, two tablespoons for an eight incher. Since crepes are rolled to show only one side, you needn't brown both sides. Stack crepes, browned side down, between slips of waxed paper and chill before filling.

To assemble, spoon soft ice cream down the center, wrap, place crepes side by side in a rectangular baking pan, seam side down, cover, and freeze firm. If you're wrapping hardened ice cream, slice it into narrow strips resembling sticks of butter halved lengthwise. For additional flavor, arrange thinly sliced fruit down the center of each crepe, spread crepes with jam or jelly, or dip ice cream sticks in sundae sauce and roll them in ground nuts and/ or coconut.

Instead of using sundae sauce on the inside, spoon some over the top or ladle spoonfuls onto individual plates to lay the crepes in. Warm sauces go nicely with crepes prepared and frozen ahead of time. You might skip the sauce and heap on whipped cream, chopped nuts, and strawberry slices or pineapple chunks. A tablespoon of liqueur spooned over each finished crepe is another tasty alternative. Orange liqueur goes well with strawberry, banana, pineapple, or cherry filling. Coffee liqueur goes with chocolate-filled crepes and chocolate crepes filled with coffee ice cream.

For the ice cream version of blintzes, wrap lemon frozen yogurt, buttermilk sherbet, or sour cream ice cream (see Chapter 7) sprinkled with cinnamon. Garnish crepes with sour cream topping (Chapter 24) or sweetened, flavored yogurt.

Instead of rolling crepes, use them to line individual dessert cups. Fill cups with ice cream or sherbet, fold excess crepe over the top, and pop into the freezer until serving time. Add a dab of whipped cream and garnish as desired. To make a crepe banana split, drape a crepe over the cut banana before piling on ice cream and other goodies (see Chapter 24 for split-building ideas).

As a dazzling finale to any meal, arrange well-frozen crepes side by side in a chafing dish, pour on one of the flaming sauces described in Chapter 24, and ignite. Bring to the table and serve immediately.

FROZEN CREPES

For crepes to be filled with fruit ice cream or sherbet, substitute orange or lemon zest for vanilla. To make *chocolate* crepes, combine 3 T cocoa with the sugar. For *tangy chocolate* crepes, use 1 C buttermilk in place of milk and water.	Sift	**³/₄ C flour.**
	Blend in	**¹/₂ C milk** **¹/₂ C water.**
	Add and beat smooth	**1 egg.**

FROZEN CREPES, cont'd.

Add

> 1 T melted butter
> 2 t sugar
> ¹/₂ t vanilla
> ¹/₈ t salt.

Let batter stand 1 hour. Heat 8" crepe pan until a drop of cold water skips across the surface. Brush with vegetable oil. Remove pan from heat and pour in 2 T batter, tilting pan to thinly coat bottom. Return to medium-high heat and cook just until top of crepe loses sheen and bottom browns lightly, about 15 seconds. Loosen edge with pancake turner, remove crepe, and repeat for next one. If batter becomes too thick, thin with a little cold water.

yield: 12 crepes

SPIRITED CHOCOLATE CREPES

For *mocha* crepes, dissolve 1 T instant coffee in the milk. To make *chocolate orange* crepes, add ¹/₂ t orange zest. For *spicy chocolate* crepes, add ¹/₄ t cinnamon.

Blend together

> 1 C flour
> ¹/₂ C milk
> ¹/₂ C water.

Add and beat smooth

> 2 eggs
> 2 T sugar
> 1 T brandy
> ¹/₄ t salt.

In small pan over low heat, melt

> 2-oz semisweet
>   chocolate
> 1 t butter.

Blend in until smooth.

Let batter stand one hour. Heat 8" crepe pan until a drop of cold water skips across the surface. Brush with vegetable oil. Remove pan from heat and pour in 2 T batter, tilting pan to thinly coat bottom. Return to medium-high heat and cook just until top of crepe loses sheen and bottom browns lightly, about 15 seconds. Loosen edge with pancake turner, remove crepe, and repeat for next one. If batter becomes too thick, thin with a little cold water.

yield: 12 crepes

28

Decorating Ice Cream Creations

Ice cream cakes and molds look fine served just as they are, but they also lend themselves to being frosted with fluffy whipped cream or butter cream, encased in sheets of chocolate, garnished with glazed strawberries, or decked out with a variety of other tasty trims.

Whipped Cream

Sweetened whipped cream is the most popular frosting for ice cream creations. Use a prepared topping such as Cool Whip or whip your own fresh cream.

Cream with forty percent milkfat or more holds up best under freezing. If the cream is skimmed from home-produced milk, age it for forty-eight hours. At whipping time, the cream should be neither warm nor icy cold, but around 45° F (7° C). Simply remove it from the refrigerator a few minutes before beating begins. Since the cream will double in volume, allow one-half cup for each cup of frosting you need.

Using a chilled bowl and beaters, beat the cream stiff, taking care not to whip it too long or it will become buttery and feel grainy when frozen. To guard against overwhipping, beat at medium-high speed just until thickening begins, then switch to low and continue until the consistency is right for spreading or piping. You can easily identify this point since the cream will begin to lose its sheen, signaling that it's on the brink of churning into butter. If it suddenly turns stiff, gently beat in one or two tablespoons of light cream or evaporated milk.

After the cream has been whipped, add one to three tablespoons sifted powdered sugar and one-half teaspoon vanilla per cup. Depending on the flavor of the cake or mold, you may wish to include other flavorings as well (for ideas, see Chapter 24). To whipped cream used as frosting, you may also add up to one-half cup coconut or finely ground nuts.

For minted frosting, add one cup finely crushed small white dinner mints per cup cream. To make chocolate whipped cream, from each cup of cream reserve two tablespoons to heat with one-quarter cup sugar, one ounce grated semisweet chocolate, and one-eighth teaspoon salt. Stir until well blended, cool, and fold into remaining whipped cream.

Spread plain or flavored whipped cream with a flexible-bladed spatula or table knife. Use the back of a spoon to finish off the surface with light swirls.

Piping Cream

You'll get a more formal look if you pipe whipped cream through a pastry bag. Stabilized cream holds its shape better for piping. For each cup of cream, soften one-half teaspoon plain gelatin in one tablespoon cold water, then heat until the gelatin dissolves. Add the gelatin when the cream has been beaten just enough to begin thickening. Marshmallow cream, which contains gelatin, also serves as a stabilizer. Added at the rate of two-thirds cup per cup cream, marshmallow doubles as a sweetener.

Pipe ornamental patterns using a pastry bag fitted with a decorative metal tip. Basic tips are the piping tip used for writing and the small and large star tips used to make rosettes and scalloped borders. The latter tip works best with whipped cream. Pastry bags come in a variety of sizes and are typically thrown away after one use.

For plain piping or ribbons of cream, use a self-locking plastic bag with one corner nipped off. Place the empty bag in one hand, edges folded back over your fingers. Spoon in the whipped cream, fold the edges forward, press out the air, and seal the bag shut. Squeeze gently from the top to force out a steady stream of cream.

Cake-decorating classes are offered almost everywhere, but you can easily learn the basics on your own by experimenting with smoothly whipped mashed potatoes as a stand-in for whipped cream and a paper plate as the cake. No matter if you use professional or make-do equipment, it won't take long before you get the hang of it. For the finest professional appearance, use a lazy susan to rotate your ice cream cake or mold smoothly while you work.

You can lay a decorating foundation right from the start by spreading a thin layer of whipped cream in your form before filling it with ice cream. Alternatively, after unmolding the ice cream, smoothly spread on a bit of whipped cream with a knife or spatula, freeze firm, then pipe on ornamental patterns.

Instead of piping designs directly on the ice cream, you can pipe rosettes and other designs onto a foil-lined sheet, freeze them firm, then arrange them on the ice cream with a dab of unfrozen whipped cream to hold them in place. Whenever you have cream left over, pipe and freeze rosettes to trim individual cake or pie slices, or pipe the cream into small, frozen serving shells, shaped like the individual meringue cups described in Chapter 22.

Butter Cream

Butter has more than twice the fat of heavy cream and therefore whips into a richer, denser frosting. Spread or pipe butter cream just as you would whipped cream. Vary its flavor similarly, by substituting extracts or liqueurs for vanilla or by stirring in coconut or finely ground nuts.

The simplest butter cream consists of butter whipped with just enough powdered sugar for stiff but spreadable consistency. One-half cup butter plus just under one cup powdered sugar, flavored with one-half teaspoon vanilla or other extract, will give you around one cup of butter cream.

Continental butter cream freezes exceptionally well and has a finer texture because it's stabilized with sugar-water syrup, boiled to the soft ball stage—indicated when a drop of hot syrup in cold water forms a soft ball that flattens when you try to lift it.

CONTINENTAL CHOCOLATE BUTTER CREAM

For *Continental mocha* butter cream, add ¼ C espresso or other strong coffee along with the cognac. Although the latter is the Continental spirit of choice, bourbon, brandy, or rum yield a more typically American flavor.

In small saucepan, combine	**⅔ C sugar** **¼ C water** **⅛ t cream of tartar.**
Bring to boil over medium heat.	
Without stirring, boil to soft ball stage, 234° F (112° C).	
In small bowl, beat until fluffy	**2 egg yolks.**
Gradually beat in hot syrup.	
Beat on high until cool and fluffy, about 3 minutes.	
Melt and beat in	**5-oz semisweet chocolate.**
Beat	**1 C unsalted butter.**
Whip into yolk mixture.	
Beat in	**3 T cognac.**

yield: about 1½ cups

EASY BUTTER CREAM

For *easy chocolate* butter cream, add 1-oz melted nonsweetened chocolate. To make *easy mocha* butter cream, substitute ¹/₂ T instant coffee dissolved in 1¹/₂ T cold water for the liqueur in chocolate butter cream. You may use any spirits in place of the liqueur, or substitute cold milk or water.

Whip until fluffy	¹/₂ C softened butter
	1¹/₂ C powdered sugar.
Beat in	¹/₂ T vanilla
	1¹/₂ T liqueur.

yield: about 1¹/₂ cups

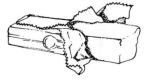

CONTINENTAL BUTTER CREAM

Vary the flavor of this frosting by using other extracts in place of vanilla or by substituting 1 T any flavor liqueur. For *Continental white chocolate* butter cream, substitute 1 T white crème de cacao for vanilla, melt 4-oz white chocolate with 2 T water, and beat it into the yolks.

In small saucepan, combine	²/₃ C sugar
	¹/₄ C water
	¹/₈ t cream of tartar.
Bring to boil over medium heat.	
Without stirring, boil to soft ball stage, 234° F (112° C).	
In small bowl, beat until fluffy	**2 egg yolks.**
Gradually beat in hot syrup.	
Beat on high until cool and fluffy, about 3 minutes.	
Soften and whip smooth	**1 C unsalted butter.**
Beat into yolk mixture.	
Add in	**1 t vanilla.**

yield: about 1¹/₂ cups

FROSTING GUIDE		
Cake or mold size	**Whipped Cream**	**Butter Cream**
	(approximate amount in cups)	
8" round, short	2	$1^1/_4$
9" round, short	$2^1/_2$	$1^1/_2$
10" round, short	3	2
8" round, stacked	$2^3/_4$	$1^3/_4$
9" round, stacked	$3^1/_4$	2
10" round, stacked	$3^3/_4$	$2^1/_2$
8" square, short	$2^1/_2$	$1^1/_2$
9" square, short	$3^3/_4$	2
9"x13" rectangle, short	$4^1/_4$	$2^1/_2$
9" tube	3	$2^1/_2$
10" tube	$3^1/_2$	3
loaf	$2^1/_2$	$1^1/_2$
12 individual molds	$5^1/_2$	3

Strawberry Garnish

Nothing has more refreshing appeal than ice cream garnished with strawberries. Wash and drain well-formed, bright red berries and halve them or leave them whole. For strawberry fans, slice large strawberries lengthwise and fan out the pointy end. At serving time, arrange berries on frosted cake or mold, fixing them in place with dabs of frosting.

For a special touch, brush berries with strawberry glaze. To make enough for one quart of berries, in a small saucepan combine one-quarter cup strawberry jam with one tablespoon water. Stirring, heat just until bubbly. Press through a sieve and stir in two tablespoons brandy or kirsch. Arrange berry halves over cake or mold, using whipped cream to hold them in place. Brush berries with warm glaze.

Instead of glazing halved strawberries, you might dip whole ones in chocolate. Select well-shaped berries with their stems intact. Rinse and drain dry. Nearly melt eight ounces semisweet chocolate in a double boiler over low heat. Remove from heat and stir until chocolate is fully melted but still thick enough to hold its shape.

Grasping each berry by its stem, dip lower half into chocolate, if necessary using a spoon to coat the bottom. Set berries on a chilled sheet lined with waxed paper or plastic wrap and refrigerate until firm, or freeze for just a few minutes. At serving time, arrange chocolate-dipped berries on puffs of whipped cream or butter cream.

Chocolate Casing

Instead of trimming an ice cream cake or mold with frosting, encase it in chocolate. Then, if desired, sprinkle the top with coconut or chopped nuts, or garnish with strawberries or nut halves set in dabs of whipped or butter cream. Perhaps the easiest coating to use is chocolate shell coating in a squeeze bottle. Gently squeeze the bottle to spread coating

These whole, fresh strawberries dipped in chocolate are ready to garnish an ice cream cake or mold. (Photo courtesy of Ghirardelli Chocolate Company, San Leandro, California.)

evenly over the ice cream's surface. If you use a wire cake rack with waxed paper underneath, you can collect and reuse any chocolate that drips down.

For milk chocolate coating made from scratch, in a double boiler combine five ounces milk chocolate with one-quarter cup butter. Stir just until blended, cool slightly and spread over top and sides of cake, working quickly so the chocolate won't firm up too fast.

To make an elegant dark chocolate casing for a straight-sided cake or mold, measure the circumference of the finished mold, divide that number by two, and add one-quarter inch. Cut two strips of waxed paper that length, as wide as the cake is high. Paper strips for a stacked eight-inch cake, for example, would measure thirteen by three inches, for a ten-inch cake, sixteen by three inches. In a double boiler melt six ounces bittersweet or semisweet chocolate and evenly spread half over each strip. Cool until firm but still pliable. Press one strip against side of firmly frozen cake, holding the end down with a knife while you carefully peel away the paper. Overlap the second strip, and continue around to complete the casing. Freeze until firm. Trim the top with whipped cream or chocolate curls.

Chocolate Whimsies

Instead of frosting, or in addition to it, deck out your creations with chocolate whimsies. In a double boiler, melt bittersweet or semisweet chocolate and spread it in a thin layer over a waxed paper-lined sheet and chill until firm. Using petite cookie cutters, cut chocolate into decorative shapes to arrange around the sides and top of a firmly frozen cake or mold.

Chocolate spider webs look terrific but don't require much time or skill. In a small saucepan over low heat, melt two ounces semisweet chocolate and two teaspoons butter, stirring until smooth. From the tip of a spoon, drizzle chocolate over the surface in web-thin lines or loops. Freeze until serving time.

Chocolate Curls

Chocolate curls are nothing more than a chic version of grated chocolate. Ordinarily, chocolate is grated by rubbing a square against the shredder side of a grater, or by shaving it with a paring knife or potato peeler, using short strokes. Grated chocolate may be sprinkled over the top layer of ice cream or the frosted surface of a cake before it's hardened.

For making curls, milk chocolate works best. Slightly soften the chocolate either by holding the paper-wrapped square in your hand for a few moments or by setting it in a warm place for fifteen minutes. Unwrap and shave the bottom with a sharp paring knife or swivel-bladed potato peeler, using long, slow strokes for loose curls, long, fast strokes for tight ones. Lift and arrange curls with a toothpick to avoid breaking them.

For larger, rosebud-like curls, melt six ounces bittersweet or semisweet chocolate in a double boiler and spread it on a nongreased baking sheet. Refrigerate until the chocolate is firm but not brittle. Using a metal pancake turner, smoothly scrape the sheet lengthwise. Arrange curls over soft ice cream or frosting. Freeze firm.

Chocolate Leaves

Chocolate leaves are incredibly impressive yet deceptively easy to make. Collect, wash, and thoroughly dry a dozen small, well-formed, nonpoisonous leaves. Those from mint, rose, and ivy have particularly nice patterns. Camellia and lemon leaves are easiest to work with.

In a double boiler, melt three ounces bittersweet or semisweet chocolate and one teaspoon shortening. Stir smooth, and cool slightly. If desired, add a drop or two of peppermint extract. With a brush or small spatula, spread a one-sixteenth- to one-eighth-inch-thick layer on the back of each leaf, not quite to the edges to simplify their removal. Place leaves on a tray, chocolate side up, and refrigerate until firm, about thirty minutes.

Starting at the stem end, carefully peel away and discard real leaves. Place chocolate leaves, vein side up, on a plate and refrigerate until ready to use. Since leaves are somewhat delicate, keep them in the refrigerator and arrange them on your cake or mold at the last moment.

Flowers, Ribbons, and Bows

For a springtime look, combine chocolate leaves with sugared flowers. Uncomplicated blossoms with few petals are easiest to sugar. Pastel ones such as pansies, violets, and sweet peas are most appealing, especially on a sherbet mold. Obtain flowers from a safe source—any purchased from a florist are likely to have been sprayed with toxins.

Just before sugaring, cut off all but one inch of each stem. Lightly beat one egg white and use it to thoroughly coat both sides of each blossom with a small brush. Holding the flower over a dish or a sheet of waxed paper, sprinkle both sides with granulated sugar. Dry flowers on a wire rack and store them in an airtight container until ready to use.

For festive occasions, wrap a cake or bombe with marzipan ribbons tied with marzipan bows. Trim a chocolate frosted cake with white marzipan. Add a few drops of food dye for a colorful ribbon against white frosting. Combine one seven-ounce can of almond paste with two tablespoons powdered sugar. Knead until smooth and pliable, about five minutes. Roll to one-eighth-inch thick and cut into inch-wide strips. Arrange strips so ice cream appears to be wrapped with a ribbon and tied with a bow. Return to freezer until serving time.

You can also make ribbons and bows from chocolate clay (recipe in Chapter 22). Simply flatten clay ropes with a rolling pin and cut them into strips to arrange the same as marzipan.

Coconut

Coconut makes an attractive and appetizing trim, sprinkled over frosted or nonfrosted ice cream. The coconut may be flavored with one-half teaspoon extract, one teaspoon cocoa, two tablespoons fruit juice, or one-quarter cup fruit juice concentrate. It may be left white, tinted any color, or coated with chocolate.

To make one cup of colored coconut, dilute a few drops of food dye with one teaspoon milk or water. Combine with coconut and toss until evenly tinted, or shake in a quart jar. To make one cup of chocolate-covered coconut, heat two ounces semisweet chocolate in a double boiler until it's nearly melted. Remove from heat and stir until melting is complete. Toss with two-thirds cup shredded coconut. Spread coconut on a baking sheet, separating shreds with a fork. Chill until set. Plain, tinted, or coated with chocolate, coconut makes great feathers or fur for cut-ups.

Cut-Ups

Make ice cream cut-ups by arranging sections of a round, square, or rectangular molded ice cream on a platter to depict a bird or animal. Highlight eyes, nose, whiskers, and other parts with gum drops, flattened on a sugar-covered surface with a rolling pin and cut into desired shapes. To brighten a child's party, a baby shower or any other festive event, follow one of the patterns included here or create your own fun designs.

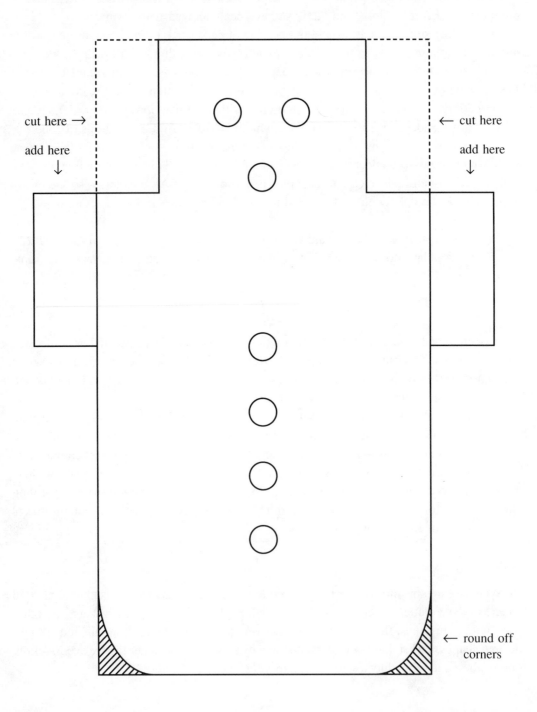

cut here →

← cut here

add here
↓

add here
↓

← round off
corners

SNOW MAN (one rectangle)

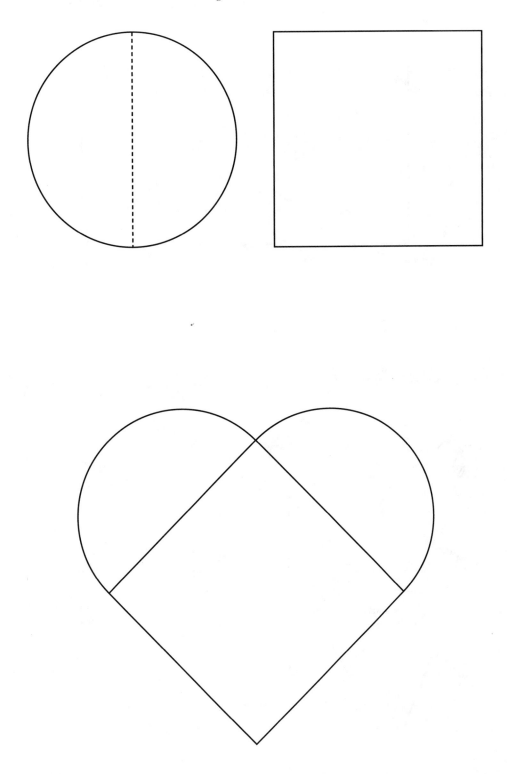

HEART (one round and one square)

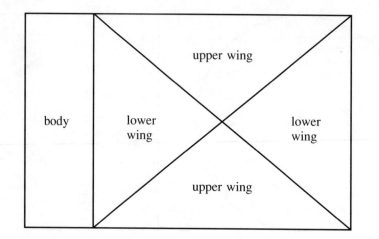

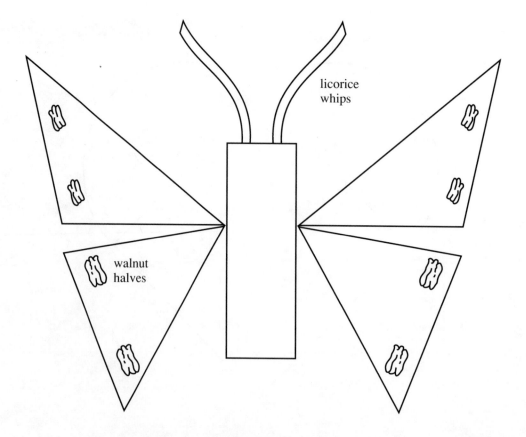

BUTTERFLY (one rectangle)

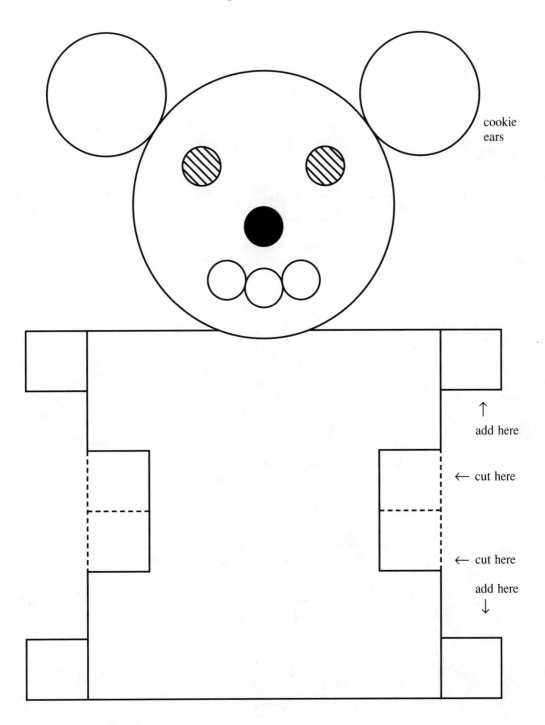

cookie
ears

↑
add here

← cut here

← cut here

add here
↓

TEDDY BEAR (one round and one square)

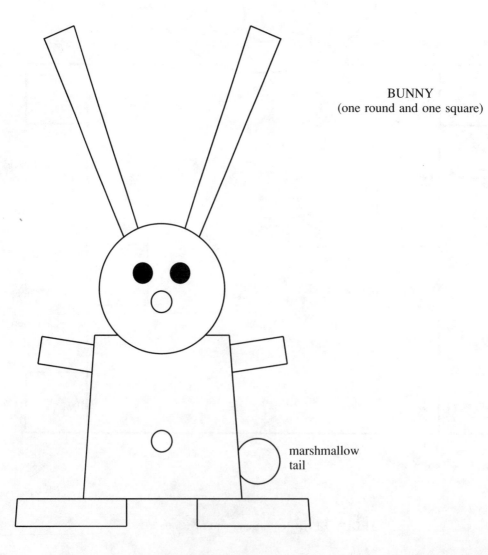

BUNNY
(one round and one square)

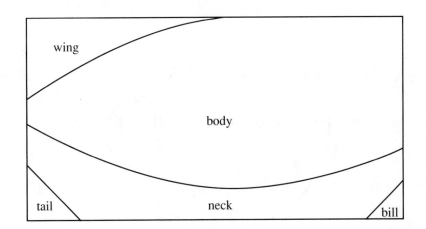

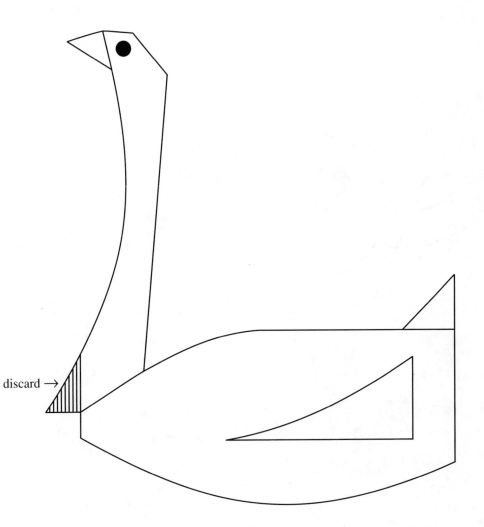

SWAN (one rectangle)

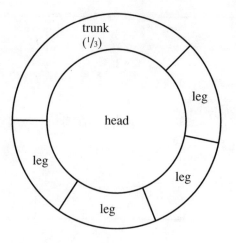

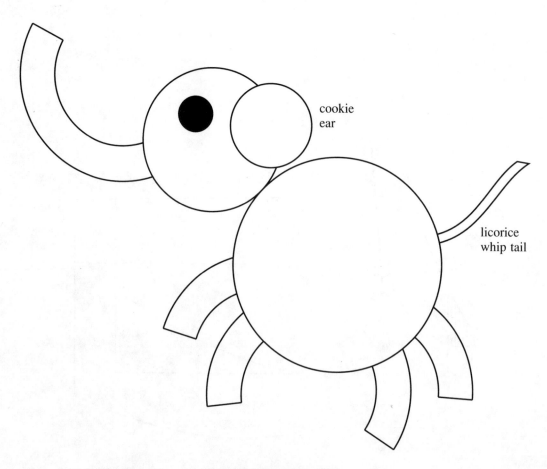

ELEPHANT (two rounds)

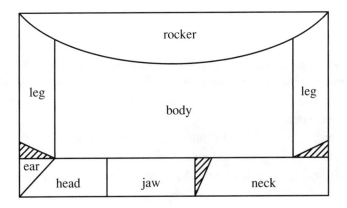

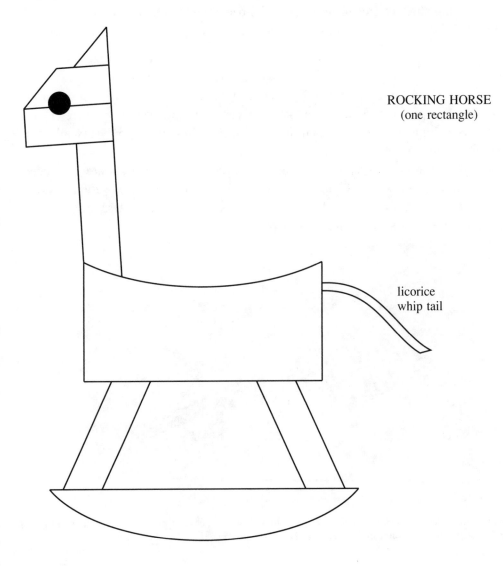

ROCKING HORSE
(one rectangle)

licorice
whip tail

Easy Way Out

If you haven't time to get fancy, here are a few decorating tips that are as easy as they are attractive. For starters, run a clean, ten- or twelve-inch comb with widely spaced tines over the top and sides of nonfrosted ice cream to create decorative ridges. Add extra color by drizzling on melted chocolate or flavorful syrup in parallel lines and drawing the comb through them for perpendicular streaks.

For spring festivities including Easter or baby and bridal showers, freeze ice cream in a tubular springform. Just before serving, unmold on a platter and set a tall glass of fresh flowers in the center. For birthday parties or winter celebrations, fill the center opening with a large, lit candle.

To suit any occasion or season, from major holidays to minor sporting events, you can't beat rice paper wafers. Printed in intricate designs with tinted sugar solutions and placed directly on a smoothed ice cream surface, the rice paper melts right in to become soft and cuttable. Mail-order sources for edible rice paper are listed in Appendix C, "Supplies."

Storing and Serving

When your ice cream creation is fully decorated and firmly frozen, wrap it in plastic wrap, then foil, to preserve its flavor and keep its surface from developing an ice-crystal crust. At serving time, temper ice cream in the refrigerator for fifteen to twenty minutes, sherbet for five to ten minutes.

Slice cakes or molds into half-inch slabs or wedges with an electric knife, a serrated bread knife, or any long knife dipped in hot water. For neatly corrugated servings, use a tined cake breaker. Chill plates in advance so servings won't slide off. Use high-rimmed dessert plates for slices served with fruit, berries, or sundae sauce.

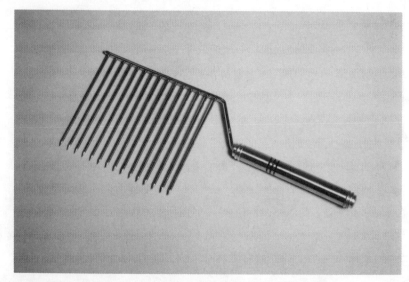

Cake-cutting fork slices neatly corrugated servings from an ice cream cake or mold. (Photo courtesy of Maid of Scandinavia Company, Minneapolis, Minnesota.)

29

Ice Cream Pies

Ice cream pies are easy to make and fun to serve. They can be all ice cream, the "crust" made by spreading one-half inch soft ice cream in a pie tin with a second tin placed on top for shaping. Freeze firm, then rub a warm, damp towel over the top tin to remove it. As a filling, use soft ice cream of contrasting color. Freeze firm. For a two-crust pie, spread another layer of the first flavor on top and harden.

You can make ice cream pies with conventional pastry shells, purchased or homemade, or you can line a pie tin with sponge cake or lady fingers. Chill the shaped pastry before filling it with soft ice cream or still-frozen mousse, and allow plenty of time for the pie to freeze firm before cutting it. Hardened ice cream may be shaped into melon ball-sized scoops and heaped into a shell at serving time.

A nine-inch tin holds up to three pints of ice cream, enough to serve eight. Trim pies with whipped cream, chopped nuts, chocolate curls, sundae sauce, or bits of fruit; or, seal the top with meringue, browned according to directions in Chapter 30. Another idea is to serve pie a la mode in reverse, topping wedges of creamy cold ice cream pie with warmed fruit-pie filling.

Variations

Chocolate, strawberry, and banana are the most popular flavors in ice cream pie, but you can successfully use any ice cream, frozen yogurt, sherbet, or sorbet. For a double treat, layer two or more contrasting flavors, perhaps combining different kinds of freeze. To make an "ice and cream" pie, for example, spread fruit ice in a prepared shell, freeze firm, and top with French vanilla ice cream, mousse, or sweetened whipped cream.

For ribbon pie, a variation of aufait (Chapter 25), spread one pint of ice cream in a chilled shell, freeze firm, spread one cup of thick sundae sauce, freeze firm. Repeat both layers. If you like nut pies, fill any pastry shell with coffee or chocolate ice cream and top with one and one-half cups chopped toasted almonds, buttered pecans, macadamias, Brazil nuts, or hazelnuts.

The ice cream version of banana cream pie is always a hit. Line a ginger snap or vanilla wafer shell with banana slices coated with lemon juice. Fill the shell with banana ice cream (or chocolate or lemon) and top with sweetened whipped cream or soft meringue. Garnish with additional banana slices.

For an easy way to serve gooey banana splits to a crowd, pack all the makings into a pie shell. Coat banana slices with lemon juice and arrange them in a coconut, chocolate, or graham cracker crust. Spread one pint each chocolate, vanilla, and strawberry ice cream in layers, or scoop the ice cream into tiny balls to fill the shell. Top pie wedges with whipped cream, sprinkle with chopped nuts, and garnish with a slice of banana, a chunk of pineapple, and a maraschino cherry skewered together on a toothpick. Drizzle with chocolate, caramel, or fruit sauce, or set out a variety of sauces and let guests help themselves.

For a new twist on a traditional holiday pie, fill a walnut or pecan shell with pumpkin ice cream. Another holiday idea is a mincemeat shell—one cup drained mincemeat mixed with one-half cup chopped toasted almonds—filled with creamy eggnog ice cream.

On the Fourth of July or other patriotic occasion, serve a red, white, and blue pie. Layer one pint each raspberry sherbet or strawberry ice cream and vanilla ice cream. Add a third layer of blueberry or blackberry ice or ice cream. For the blue layer, you might instead garnish each wedge with fresh blueberries or blueberry sauce.

How about an ice cream pizza? Cover a pizza tray (or the bottom of a springform) with a thin round of cake. Ideal here is the kind of cake used for ice cream rolls (see recipes in Chapter 27), trimmed to fit. Divide the cake into wedges, leaving it on the tray. Arrange small scoops of ice cream and slices of fruit on top. Bring the pizza to the table for serving and pass the hot fudge or strawberry sauce.

Black-bottom pie is an old Southern favorite. For an ice cream version, spread one pint chocolate gelato in a vanilla wafer or graham cracker crust. Top with one pint French vanilla ice cream, flavored with two tablespoons white rum. Garnish wedges with whipped cream and grated chocolate.

Perhaps best known of all ice cream pies is the mud pie, called "Mississippi mud pie" in the South, "Sacramento mud pie" in the West, and "cappuccino" pie in the Northeast. Heap soft coffee ice cream into a chocolate or graham cracker shell and freeze firm. Drizzle wedges with hot fudge or top them with whipped cream flavored with coffee liqueur. Garnish with chocolate curls (directions in Chapter 28).

COOKIE CRUMB SHELL

Use vanilla or chocolate wafers, ginger snaps, graham crackers, or zwiebacks for this shell. To make *spicy cookie* shell, add $^1/_4$ t cinnamon. For *crumb nut* shell, add $^1/_4$ C finely chopped nuts. For *no-bake crumb* shell, simply press crumbs into a pie tin and chill. When using sandwich cookies, such as Oreo, decrease butter to $^1/_4$ C and chill without baking.

Thoroughly mix   **$1^1/_2$ C cookie crumbs
$^1/_3$ C melted butter.**

Press evenly in 9" pie pan.

Bake 5 minutes at 350° F (180° C).

Chill before filling with ice cream.

yield: 9" shell

CHOCOLATE CRUMB SHELL

Make this no-bake cookie crumb shell with graham crackers, vanilla wafers, ginger snaps, or zwiebacks. This shell goes nicely with banana or lemon ice cream or frozen yogurt.

Thoroughly mix   **$1^1/_2$ C cookie crumbs
$^1/_3$ C melted butter
$^1/_4$ C light brown sugar
$^1/_8$ t nutmeg.**

Melt and blend in   **1-oz nonsweetened chocolate.**

Press evenly in 9" pie pan.

Chill before filling with ice cream.

yield: 9" shell

COCONUT SHELL

This shell is especially nice with fruit or nut flavors. For the no-bake version, stir coconut and butter in a warm skillet until golden, press into pie pan, and cool.

Combine   **2 C flaked coconut
$^1/_4$ C melted butter.**

Press evenly in 9" pie pan.

Bake 25 minutes at 300° F (150° C).

Chill before filling with ice cream.

yield: 9" shell

CHOCOLATE COCONUT SHELL

Fill this shell with pineapple, orange, banana, chocolate fudge, or vanilla fudge ripple ice cream. Sprinkle additional toasted coconut over the top.

Spread on baking sheet **1³/₄ C flaked coconut.**

Toast at 375° F (190° C) 8 minutes until golden.

Melt and stir in **4-oz semisweet chocolate ¹/₄ C butter.**

Press evenly in buttered 9" pie pan.

Chill before filling with ice cream.

yield: 9" shell

NUT SHELL

Make this shell with almonds, Brazil nuts, hazelnuts, macadamias, pecans, walnuts, or a combination of any two. For *sugarless nut* shell, beat in 2 egg whites in place of sugar. To make *no-bake nut* shell, omit butter and press sugared nuts in pan, reserving ¹/₄ C to sprinkle on top.

Spread in 9" pie pan **3 T softened butter.**

Combine **1¹/₂ C finely ground nuts 3 T sugar.**

Press evenly in pie pan.

Bake 10 minutes at 400° F (205° C) until golden.

Chill before filling with ice cream.

yield: 9" shell

COOKIE SHELL

This shell tastes great with any kind of filling. It tends to slide down during baking, so press plenty of dough up along the sides. For *chocolate* cookie crust, add one square melted semisweet chocolate and increase flour by 2 T flour.

Combine   **3 T sugar**
                           ³/₄ C flour.

Soften and cut in   **6 T butter.**

Press evenly into greased tin.

Bake 10 minutes at 350° F (180° C).

Chill before filling with ice cream.

yield: 9" shell

BROWNIE SHELL

This shell is equally good made with pecans or walnuts. If you prefer toasted almonds, substitute almond extract for the vanilla. To make a chocolate ice cream pizza crust, spread and bake this pastry in a buttered 9" spring-form.

In saucepan over low heat, melt   **¹/₄ C butter**
                                   2-oz semisweet chocolate
                                   1-oz nonsweetened chocolate.

Blend until smooth.

Remove from heat and add   **1 egg**
                            ¹/₂ C sugar
                            ¹/₂ t vanilla.

Beat in until shiny   **2 T flour.**

Fold in   **1 C chopped nuts.**

Spread evenly in buttered 9" pie pan.

Bake 30 minutes at 325° F (165° C).

Chill before filling with ice cream.

yield: 9" shell

OAT BRAN SHELL

This shell contains no dairy products and so is ideal for soy ice cream or any other nondairy filling. If you wish, use amaranth graham crackers instead of oat bran crackers. For a baked shell, heat in a 350° F (180° C) oven five minutes.

Crush **15 small oat bran crackers.**

Combine with **3 T melted soy margarine**
$^{1}/_{2}$ t cinnamon (optional).

Press evenly into pie tin.

Chill before filling with ice cream.

yield: 9" shell

Tarts

For no-fuss tarts, fill pre-made miniature pastry tarts or "cuplets" with soft ice cream and freeze firm. If you prefer to bake your own, just mix up your favorite flaky pie crust; or, try this time-tested recipe: Combine two cups flour with one teaspoon salt, cut in two-thirds cup shortening, and stir in five to six tablespoons apple juice or water, just enough to moisten the dough without making it sticky. Roll out dough, cut into large rounds with the end of a coffee can dipped in flour, and press onto the *backs* of muffin cups. Bake at 450° F (230° C) for eight to ten minutes until lightly browned. Cool fully before removing. Fill with any ice cream or sherbet and top with a pyramid of whipped cream, a strawberry, a stemmed cherry, a fresh peach slice, or a half walnut or pecan.

Using a muffin tin as a form, you can make sponge cake baskets. Cut a one-inch sheet of warm sponge cake into six-inch squares. Round off the corners and generously coat each square with powdered sugar. Press into the cups of a large muffin tin, cool, then chill. Heap baskets with soft ice cream and freeze firm, or fill them with scooped ice cream at serving time and top with fruit or sundae sauce.

A popular Continental ice cream tart of sorts is the coffee cup, an all-in-one coffee and dessert. Drop macaroons into the requisite number of chilled coffee cups, douse each with rum, and fill cups with coffee ice cream topped with sweetened whipped cream.

For thumbprint tarts, cut a one-quart brick or loaf of vanilla ice cream into eight slices. Cut each slice in half diagonally, creating sixteen triangles. With the back of a spoon, make a dent in the center of one triangle and fill it with preserves, puréed stewed fruit, or the tartufo nut filling described in Chapter 21. Fit the second triangle over the first and smooth out the edges. Thoroughly coat each tart with chopped toasted almonds, buttered pecans, toasted coconut, or cookie crumbs. Freeze firm.

Serve tarts on individual plates, or pass the platter for guests to help themselves, combining different flavors for greatest appeal. Tarts make nifty snacks, wrapped individually and stashed in the freezer.

Fried Pies

It's a well-known secret that Southerners enjoy frying just about anything. Ice cream is no exception. As early as 1802, a southern gentleman from Virginia, Thomas Jefferson, reportedly treated his guests to ice cream encased in warm pastry. Northerners interpret this description as an early version of baked Alaska, but Southerners know better—surely Jefferson must have served fried ice cream pies. Southerners are in good company with their mania for frying things. The Japanese also dip ice cream in batter and deep-fry it, in the manner of tempura.

Fried ice cream pies aren't really pies, but they really are deep fried. The trick is to get the fat hot enough to quickly crisp the coating without melting the ice cream. For an upscale variation, fill cream puff or éclair shells (recipe in Chapter 22) with soft ice cream, stick on the cap, wrap, and freeze firm, then deep fry at 350° F (180° C) for thirty seconds until crisply golden. Drain and serve with any fruit or fudge sauce to complement the filling.

A down-home fried pie is encrusted with cookie crumbs—crushed vanilla wafers, sugar cookies, ginger snaps, coconut cookies, shortbread, graham crackers, or cinnamon grahams. Wheat germ, corn flakes, or Grape-Nuts are sometimes also used.

Dip ice cream with a number eight scoop, or divide into one-half cup portions and shape with your hands. Roll balls in coconut or chopped nuts, if desired, and freeze firm. Dip scoops into one beaten egg, flavored with $1/4$ t vanilla or other extract, then roll in cookie crumbs until thoroughly coated. Once again, freeze firm. For a super thick crust, repeat egg dip and crumb coating. Freeze firm. For each quart of ice cream, or eight servings, you'll need one egg and two cups of crumbs per layer.

The ice cream must be fully frozen before frying, so prepare scoops well in advance. Fry them at 375° F (190° C) for thirty seconds, just until the coating turns crisp. The ice cream inside may soften slightly, but it shouldn't melt. Drain fried ice cream pies and serve them immediately, with or without sundae sauce.

30

Baked Alaska

Baked Alaska is a wonderful combination of cake and ice cream topped with sweet, warm meringue. It was invented at the once-famous Wall Street restaurant, Delmonico's, where it was first served to commemorate Seward's purchase of the Territory of Alaska in 1867. The amazing thing about baked Alaska is that it's served straight out of a hot oven, where the meringue is toasted golden but the ice cream doesn't melt.

Procedure

The ice cream core of a baked Alaska is insulated by cake at the bottom and by meringue at the top and sides. For maximum insulating value, warm the egg whites to room temperature so they'll accept lots of air during whipping.

This meringue is the soft sort, in contrast to hard or crisp meringue used to make the shells described in Chapter 22, "Edible Cups." Soft meringue contains less sugar and is baked for a much shorter time in a very hot oven. For interesting contrast, use a hard meringue shell in place of the usual cake base.

Although there are pans designed specifically for creating this dessert, a baking sheet works perfectly fine. Begin with a base of one-half- to one-inch-thick angel food, yellow, or sponge cake. The cake should not be fresh, but slightly dry so it will readily absorb moisture without turning soggy. For extra flavor, sprinkle a few tablespoons of rum, brandy, sherry, or other spirits over the cake. A batch of brownies—chocolate or butterscotch— also makes a dandy base.

Top the cake with a loaf-shaped ice cream mold or a bombe, either of single flavor or a combination molded according to directions in Chapter 26, "Bombes and other Molds." Dairy- and soy-based ice creams are more successful than lighter sorbets or sherbets, which melt far too readily. The ice cream must be firmly frozen before the meringue is spread. For best results, unmold the ice cream onto the base and return it to the freezer for an hour or two before coating with meringue.

Ideally, the base should extend about one-quarter inch out from the unmolded ice cream, all around. To prevent heat from leaking in and melting the ice cream, the meringue must completely cover the ice cream and form a good seal at the base. If no skirt of cake extends beyond the ice cream, be sure to spread the meringue to fully overlap the cake.

For most versions, meringue goes directly on the ice cream. A heftier, so-called Norwegian-style baked Alaska has additional strips of cake laid over the ice cream to cover it completely before meringue is applied. After the meringue has been smoothed, it may be embellished with swirls created with the back of a spoon or with curlicues piped through a cake-decorating tube.

Most recipes call for spreading meringue just before browning and serving, but you can apply it as much as six hours in advance, store it in the freezer, and bake just before serving. Leftovers can be returned to the freezer and served later. A round, eight-inch cake topped with two and one-half quarts of ice cream serves ten to twelve.

Variations

No less spectacular than a large baked Alaska brought to the table for slicing are individual servings, variously called "igloos" or "baked Nebraskas." Here, the cake is cut into squares and topped with ice cream sliced from a loaf, or the base can be shaped into rounds with a large cookie cutter and topped with generous scoops of ice cream molded with a number eight scoop or shaped in your hands. For added flavor, roll scoops in coconut, chopped nuts, crushed candy, or shaved chocolate.

Alternative igloo bases include individual hard meringue shells (Chapter 22), maryannes or store-bought shortcakes, large slices of brownie, or big, thick oatmeal, chocolate chip, or sugar cookies. Spread meringue over each igloo, completely overlapping the base, and brown in a hot oven for three minutes (two minutes shorter than the larger version). If you wish, serve igloos in a pool of sundae sauce.

An unusual version of individual baked Alaskas invented for the Neiman-Marcus Zodiac Room calls for one small clay flower pot per serving. Scrub new pots and dry them thoroughly. Line the bottom of each with a round of sponge cake. Top with several scoops of ice cream, heap with meringue, and brown for three minutes. Poke in two or three soda straws and slip a long-stemmed flower into each.

Although baked Alaska usually begins with cake, there's no reason it can't be a pie. Firmly freeze any of the pies described in Chapter 29, top with half a batch of meringue, and brown for three minutes. Be sure to try the baked Alaska version of lemon meringue pie, made with a vanilla wafer or cookie shell and lemon ice cream.

You can also build a super baked Alaska pie using any fruit pie as a base. Cool a single-crust, nine-inch pie baked in a deep pan. Slice firmly frozen ice cream one-inch thick and cover the top of the pie. Immediately coat the ice cream with half a batch of meringue, and brown three minutes. Try toasted almond or chocolate fudge ice cream with cherry pie, cinnamon or nutmeg ice cream with apple pie, vanilla ice cream with mincemeat or pumpkin pie.

For a baked Alaska at the other end of the calorie scale, skip the pastry and substitute a scooped out orange or grapefruit half (described in Chapter 22). Arrange two to four citrus segments in the bottom of each chilled half, pack with ice cream to within one-quarter inch of the top, and freeze firm. Heap with meringue flavored with orange or lemon zest, allowing half a batch per eight servings. Brown for three minutes.

For convenience as well as safety (read about the use of partially cooked eggs in Chapter 13), you can make soft meringue from pasteurized powdered egg whites. Tins of egg white powder are sold by cake decorating suppliers, including the mail-order sources listed in Appendix C.

BASIC SOFT MERINGUE

For added appeal, sprinkle unbaked meringue with granulated sugar, slivered almonds, or shredded coconut. To make *peppermint* meringue, stir in $^1/_2$ C finely crushed peppermint candies or candy canes, reserving 2 T to sprinkle on top.

Beat until foamy	**6 large egg whites.**
Add and beat into soft peaks	**$^1/_4$ t salt** **1 t cream of** ** tartar.**
Gradually beat in	**$^3/_4$ C sugar.**
Add	**$1^1/_2$ t vanilla.**

Beat into stiff peaks.

Thoroughly cover ice cream.

Bake 5 minutes at 500° F (260° C).

yield: 1 Alaska or 8 igloos

SPICY MERINGUE

This spicy version goes well with pumpkin, butter pecan, or French vanilla ice cream. Or try it over a molded Neapolitan of chocolate, vanilla, and butter pecan.

Beat until foamy	**6 large egg whites.**
Add and beat into soft peaks	**$^1/_4$ t salt** **1 t cream of** ** tartar.**
Combine and gradually beat in	**$^3/_4$ C brown sugar** **$^3/_4$ t pumpkin pie** ** spice.**

Beat into stiff peaks.

Thoroughly cover ice cream.

Bake 5 minutes at 500° F (260° C).

yield: 1 Alaska or 8 igloos

MARSHMALLOW MERINGUE

Flavor this meringue with any jam, jelly, or preserves. For an unusual touch, use the same flavor preserves to mold an aufait for the center, as described in Chapter 26. This meringue can be quite touchy—watch it doesn't burn!

In double boiler, combine	**¹/₂# (38) marsh-mallows** **¹/₄ C preserves.**
As soon as marshmallows begin melting, remove from heat and beat smooth.	
Beat until foamy	**4 egg whites** **¹/₄ t salt.**
Gradually beat in	**¹/₂ C sugar.**
Beat into stiff peaks.	
Fold in marshmallow mixture.	
Thoroughly cover ice cream.	
Bake 2 minutes at 500° F (260° C) until lightly browned.	

yield: 1 Alaska or 8 igloos

BAKED ALASKA TRIFLE

Serve this dessert with a matching or contrasting sundae sauce from Chapter 24—strawberry or fudge sauce with strawberry ice cream; blueberry sauce with blueberry or lemon ice cream; Belgian coffee syrup with coffee or chocolate ice cream.

Line a 9" round cake pan with	**12 ladyfingers.**
Cut in half	**12 ladyfingers.**
Arrange to stand around edges.	
Fill with	**1¹/₂-qt ice cream.**
Freeze firm.	
Thoroughly cover with	**one-half batch meringue.**
Bake 3 minutes at 500° F (260° C).	

yield: 10-12 servings

ALASKA FLAMBÉ

Following directions in Chapter 26, mold the center of this festive dessert from gingerbread and lemon ice cream, pumpkin and maple nut ice cream, nesselrode and chocolate or coffee ice cream, or any combination of your choice. There couldn't be a more sensational grande finale!

Sprinkle	**8" yellow or sponge cake**
with	**2 T brandy or rum.**
Unmold and top with	**1½-quart bombe.**
Thoroughly cover with	**one batch meringue.**

Bake 5 minutes at 500° F (260° C).

Meanwhile, heat	**2 T rum or brandy.**

Immediately pour over meringue.

Ignite and serve at once.

yield: 10-12 servings

Appendix A

Mix-Ins

Ice cream flavors are so numerous there's no way this or any book could list them all. New flavors and combinations are dreamed up every day. If you make ice cream often enough, sooner or later you'll start inventing new ones of your own. The following list is offered as a jumping-off point to get you started on the high road to ice cream adventure.

Most flavorings are simply added to a vanilla ice cream base in which vanilla extract is either reduced or eliminated. Adding bulky ingredients may significantly increase the volume of a mix. If the capacity of your ice cream maker is exceeded, either reduce the recipe or divide the mix and freeze it in two parts.

When fast-paced living doesn't give you time to make ice cream from scratch, purchase a quality ready-made brand to personalize with your flavoring favorites. Just temper the ice cream, stir in one of the following flavoring formulas, and quickly repack for hardening (perhaps as a pie, cake, or bombe).

These formulas provide enough flavoring to satisfy most tastes. If you favor bare-minimum flavorings or ones that come on a bit stronger, adjust quantities to suit yourself.

Almond—reduce vanilla by half and add 1 t almond extract plus up to 1 C chopped toasted almonds per quart vanilla ice cream.

Almond coconut—$^1/_2$ C cream of coconut plus $^1/_4$ t almond extract plus $^1/_4$ C chopped toasted almonds per quart vanilla ice cream.

Almond fudge—$^1/_4$ C chopped toasted almonds plus $^1/_2$ C crumbled fudge candy per quart coffee ice cream.

Almond mocha—$^1/_2$ C chopped blanched almonds plus $^1/_2$ C grated semisweet chocolate per quart coffee ice cream.

Almond, toasted—1 C chopped almonds browned golden in 2 T butter per quart ice cream.

Almond toffee—$1/4$ C crushed toffee candy plus $1/4$ C chopped toasted almonds per quart vanilla ice cream.

Apple—1 C sliced cooked apples plus 2 T sugar, *or* 1 C apple pie filling, *or* $3/4$ C applesauce plus 2 T lemon juice per quart vanilla ice cream or frozen yogurt.

Apple cinnamon—1 t cinnamon per quart apple ice cream or frozen yogurt.

Apricot—1 C puréed apricots plus $1/4$ C sugar, boiled 5 minutes, cooled and added to 1 quart vanilla ice cream or frozen yogurt with vanilla extract omitted; $1^1/4$ C apricot purée or 2 C apricot nectar per quart sherbet or ice.

Avocado—2 large puréed Hass avocados plus $1/4$ C sugar plus 2 T lemon juice per quart vanilla ice cream or frozen yogurt.

Banana—2 well-ripened, mashed bananas (1 C) plus 1 T lemon juice plus 2 T orange liqueur (optional) per quart vanilla ice cream or frozen yogurt.

Banana nut—$1/4$ C chopped almonds, pecans, walnuts, or macadamias per quart banana ice cream or frozen yogurt.

Banana orange—$1/2$ t orange extract or orange zest per quart banana ice cream.

Banana rocky road—2 well-ripened, mashed bananas (1 C) plus 1 T lemon juice plus 1 C miniature marshmallows plus $1/2$ C chopped walnuts per quart chocolate ice cream.

Beech nut—$1/2$ cup beech nuts per quart vanilla or caramel ice cream.

Berry berry—$1/3$ cup each raspberries, strawberries, and blueberries per quart vanilla ice cream; $2/3$ cup each per quart sherbet or sorbet.

Biscuit tortoni—$1/2$ C crushed macaroons soaked in $1/4$ C sherry, brandy, or rum per quart rich vanilla ice cream, *or* 2 to 4 T sherry, brandy, or rum per quart macaroon bisque.

Bisque—up to 1 C crushed coconut or almond macaroons, cake, cookies, brownies, miniature marshmallows, Grape-Nuts, or other crisp cereal per quart any flavor ice cream or frozen yogurt.

Blackberry—1 C blackberries plus $1/4$ C sugar, boiled 3 minutes and rubbed through a sieve to remove seeds, per quart vanilla ice cream or frozen yogurt; 2 C berries plus $1/2$ C sugar per quart sherbet or ice.

Black walnut—$^1/_3$ C chopped black walnuts per quart vanilla, caramel or maple ice cream.

Blueberries 'n' cream—3 C mashed or puréed blueberries plus $^3/_4$ C sugar swirled into 1 quart French vanilla ice cream.

Blueberry—1 C puréed or whole blueberries plus $^1/_4$ C sugar per quart lemon or vanilla ice cream, lemon sherbet, or frozen yogurt.

Blueberry maple—1 C blueberries plus $^1/_4$ C sugar per quart maple ice cream.

Brandy Alexander—3 T white crème de cacao plus 2 T brandy plus $^1/_8$ t nutmeg per quart French vanilla ice cream.

Bubble gum—4 sticks bubble gum, broken into small pieces, per quart vanilla, banana, or chocolate ice cream.

Burnt almond—$^2/_3$ to 1 C chopped toasted almonds per quart caramel ice cream.

Butter crisp—$^1/_2$ C Grape-Nuts or wheat flakes plus 1 T brown sugar plus 1 T chopped nuts plus $^1/_2$ T butter, tossed in a heated pan 3 minutes or until sugar caramelizes, cooled and crumbled, per quart vanilla ice cream.

Butter crunch—$^1/_2$ C crushed butter crunch candy per quart vanilla or caramel ice cream.

Butter pecan—$^1/_2$ C crushed butter crunch candy plus $^1/_4$ C chopped pecans, *or* $^3/_4$ to 1 C chopped pecans tossed with 2 T melted butter, *or* $^3/_4$ to 1 C chopped pecans plus $^1/_2$ T butter flavoring per quart vanilla ice cream made with brown instead of granulated sugar (optional).

Butterscotch—$^1/_2$ to $^3/_4$ C butterscotch syrup per quart vanilla ice cream.

Candy (candy bar)—$^1/_2$ C crushed candy (butter crunch, nut brittle, molasses taffy, toffee, mint chips, or any flavor candy bar) per quart vanilla ice cream.

Cantaloupe—one very ripe cantaloupe, puréed, plus $^1/_3$ C sugar per quart rich vanilla ice cream or frozen yogurt.

Cappuccino—$^1/_4$ t cinnamon plus $^1/_8$ t nutmeg per quart coffee ice cream or espresso gelato.

Caramel—$^1/_4$ to $^1/_2$ C burnt sugar or up to $^3/_4$ C prepared caramel topping per quart vanilla ice cream.

Caramel nut—$^1/_4$ C chopped nuts per quart caramel ice cream.

Carob—$^1/_3$ C carob powder per quart vanilla ice cream or frozen yogurt.

Carob honey—carob ice cream sweetened with honey instead of sugar.

Cashew—$^1/_2$ to $^2/_3$ C cashew butter plus $^1/_4$ cup sugar plus $^1/_3$ C chopped cashews (optional) per quart vanilla ice cream or frozen yogurt.

Cashew honey—cashew ice cream sweetened with honey instead of sugar.

Cheesecake—1 C cottage cheese substituted for 1 C milk or cream plus $^1/_3$ C lemon juice plus 1 t lemon zest per quart vanilla ice cream.

Cherry—1 C chopped maraschino or sour cherries plus $^1/_2$ t cherry or almond extract per quart vanilla ice cream or frozen yogurt; 2 C (1#) black or sour red cherries plus $^2/_3$ C sugar, boiled 4 minutes, strained well, per quart sherbet, ice, or sorbet.

Cherry nut—$^1/_2$ C chopped toasted almonds or pecans plus $^1/_2$ t almond extract per quart cherry ice cream or frozen yogurt.

Chestnut—15-oz chestnut purée plus $^1/_4$ C dark rum per quart French vanilla ice cream.

Chocolanilla—2-oz semisweet chocolate per quart Philadelphia ice cream.

Chocolate—reduce vanilla by half and add $^1/_2$ to $^3/_4$ C chocolate syrup, *or* 2-oz melted semisweet chocolate, *or* $^1/_4$ C nonsweetened Dutched cocoa plus $^1/_4$ C sugar, *or* 1- to 2-oz nonsweetened chocolate plus $^1/_4$ C sugar per quart vanilla ice cream or frozen yogurt.

Chocolate almond—$^1/_3$ C chopped toasted almonds plus 1 t almond extract per quart chocolate ice cream or frozen yogurt.

Chocolate almond, whiskied—$^1/_4$ C bourbon per quart chocolate almond ice cream.

Chocolate amaretto—$^1/_4$ C amaretto per quart rich chocolate ice cream.

Chocolate banana (monkey's uncle)—1 to 2 mashed ripe bananas per quart chocolate ice cream or frozen yogurt.

Chocolate, bittersweet—reduce vanilla by half and add 1- to 2-oz bittersweet or nonsweetened chocolate per quart vanilla ice cream.

Chocolate cherry (Black Forest)—1 C pitted, drained, and halved Bing cherries or $^1/_2$ C chopped maraschino cherries per quart chocolate ice cream.

Chocolate chestnut—8-oz chestnut purée per quart rich chocolate ice cream.

Chocolate chip—$^1/_2$ C miniature chocolate chips per quart any flavor ice cream.

Chocolate chocolate chip (double chocolate)—$^1/_2$ C miniature chocolate chips per quart chocolate ice cream.

Chocolate coconut—$^1/_2$ C shredded or flaked coconut per quart chocolate ice cream.

Chocolate cookie—$^1/_2$ C crushed chocolate cookies (about 8) per quart any flavor ice cream.

Chocolate hazelnut (Belgian chocolate)—$^1/_2$ C chopped hazelnuts plus 2 T hazelnut liqueur or $^1/_4$ C rum or 1 t rum extract per quart rich chocolate ice cream.

Chocolate malted (frosted malted)—$^1/_4$ C instant malted milk or 2 T barley malt syrup per quart chocolate ice cream.

Chocolate, mandarin—1 T orange zest plus 2 T orange liqueur or $^1/_2$ t orange extract per quart rich chocolate ice cream or frozen yogurt.

Chocolate, Mexican—$^1/_8$ t cinnamon plus $^1/_2$ C chopped, toasted almonds per quart chocolate ice cream or frozen yogurt.

Chocolate peppermint—$^1/_4$ C crushed peppermint candies or $^1/_2$ t peppermint extract per quart chocolate ice cream.

Chocolate, white—see *White chocolate.*

Choco-loco—$^1/_2$ C grated white chocolate or chopped white chocolate chips per quart chocolate ice cream.

Cinnamon—$^1/_2$ t ground cinnamon per quart French vanilla ice cream or frozen yogurt.

Cinnamon nut—$^1/_8$ t cinnamon plus $^1/_3$ C chopped walnuts per quart vanilla or French vanilla ice cream.

Cocoa mocha—$^1/_4$ C crème de cacao per quart coffee ice cream or frozen yogurt.

Coco-loco—2 oz grated milk chocolate plus $^1/_2$ C flaked coconut per quart rich vanilla ice cream.

Coconut—$^1/_2$ C fresh or nonsweetened shredded coconut per quart French vanilla ice cream or frozen yogurt. For extra flavor, substitute coconut milk for a portion of the milk or cream—whirl equal amounts coconut and milk or cream 30 minutes in blender at high speed, strain.

Coconut tortoni—1 C toasted coconut plus $^1/_4$ C coconut cream per quart vanilla ice cream. (Serve fresh—toasted coconut loses its crunch during hardening.)

Coffee—1 to 3 T instant coffee (or $^1/_2$ C very strong brewed coffee substituted for $^1/_2$ C milk) plus $^1/_4$ C sugar per quart vanilla ice cream or frozen yogurt.

Coffee chip—$^1/_2$ C miniature chocolate chips per quart coffee ice cream.

Coffee coconut (Hawaiian coffee)—1 T instant coffee powder per quart coconut ice cream, *or* $^1/_2$ C grated coconut per quart coffee ice cream or coffee ice cream with coconut milk substituted for a portion of the milk.

Coffee, flavored—reduce vanilla to 1 t and add $^1/_2$ C flavored instant coffee powder per quart vanilla or French vanilla ice cream.

Coffee nut—$^1/_4$ C chopped almonds, pecans, hazelnuts, or macadamias per quart coffee ice cream or frozen yogurt.

Coffee nutmeg—$^1/_2$ t ground nutmeg per quart white coffee ice cream.

Coffee, spiked—2 T coffee liqueur or $^1/_4$ C brandy, whisky, rum, or kirsch per quart coffee ice cream.

Coffee sunseed—$^1/_2$ C toasted sunflower seeds per quart coffee ice cream.

Coffee, white—$^1/_4$# coarsely ground roasted coffee beans, heated (not boiled) 30 minutes with 1 C milk, strained, substituted for 1 C milk per quart French vanilla ice cream. (To roast beans, spread in shallow pan, place in 350° F(180° C) oven for 5 minutes, cool.)

Cookies 'n' cream—$^1/_2$ C (about 8) crushed chocolate sandwich cookies per quart vanilla ice cream.

'Cots 'n' cream—1 C puréed apricots plus $^1/_4$ C sugar swirled into softened vanilla ice cream.

Cranberry—³/₄ C jellied cranberry sauce or 2 C whole cranberry sauce per quart vanilla ice cream.

Curaçao—¹/₄ C curaçao plus juice of 2 oranges (²/₃ C) plus 3 T sugar per quart French vanilla ice cream or frozen yogurt.

Currant—¹/₂# fresh currants plus ¹/₂ C sugar, boiled 3 minutes and rubbed through a sieve to remove seeds, per quart sherbet, ice, or sorbet.

Daiquiri—¹/₄ C light rum per quart lime ice or sorbet.

Daiquiri, banana—1 mashed ripe banana per quart daiquiri ice or sorbet, *or* ¹/₄ C rum per quart banana ice or sorbet.

Daiquiri, strawberry—¹/₂ C puréed strawberries per quart daiquiri ice or sorbet, *or* ¹/₄ C rum per quart strawberry ice or sorbet.

Date—²/₃ C chopped dates per quart vanilla, lemon, or caramel ice cream or frozen yogurt.

Date nut—¹/₃ C chopped walnuts, pecans, or toasted almonds plus ¹/₂ t orange or lemon zest per quart date ice cream or frozen yogurt.

Date nut pudding—2 T brandy per quart date nut ice cream.

Eggnog—2 T bourbon or brandy plus 2 T rum plus ¹/₈ t nutmeg per quart French vanilla ice cream, *or* freeze one quart of prepared eggnog drink.

English toffee—¹/₂ to 1 C crushed English toffee per quart vanilla, caramel, or chocolate ice cream.

Fig—¹/₂ C puréed canned figs *or* ¹/₂ C fresh figs, stemmed and puréed, plus 2 T sugar, boiled 4 minutes then cooled, per quart vanilla ice cream.

Fig nut—¹/₄ C chopped walnuts per quart fig ice cream.

Filbert—see *Hazelnut*.

French nougat—¹/₂ C drained crushed pineapple plus ¹/₂ C miniature marshmallows per quart French vanilla ice cream.

Fruit—¹/₂ to 1 C sugared puréed fruit substituted for 1 C milk per quart vanilla ice cream or frozen yogurt. Reduce vanilla by half for peaches, apricots, and cherries and add $1/4$ t almond extract.

Ginger—$1/3$ C minced preserved ginger root or 2 T syrup from preserved ginger, or both, per quart vanilla ice cream; 1 C minced candied ginger per quart orange ice or sorbet.

Ginger apricot—$1/2$ to 1 C minced candied ginger per quart apricot ice cream, sherbet, or sorbet.

Ginger honey—ginger ice cream sweetened with honey instead of sugar.

Ginger honey rum raisin—$1/4$ C chopped raisins soaked in 2 T rum per quart ginger honey ice cream.

Ginger, spiked—$1/4$ C ginger brandy or ginger wine per quart ginger ice cream, sherbet, or sorbet.

Granola—1 C crunchy granola per quart vanilla ice cream or frozen yogurt.

Granola banana—1 C crunchy granola per quart banana ice cream or frozen yogurt.

Grape—$1/2$ C grape juice concentrate per quart vanilla ice cream; $1^1/2$ C grape juice concentrate per quart sherbet or sorbet.

Grapefruit—omit vanilla and add 1 C grapefruit juice plus $1/4$ C sugar per quart very rich vanilla ice cream.

Grape-Nuts—omit vanilla and add $1/2$ t maple extract or $1/4$ C maple sugar plus $1/2$ C Grape-Nuts per quart vanilla ice cream or frozen yogurt.

Grape-Nuts, chocolate—$1/2$ C Grape-Nuts per quart chocolate ice cream.

Grape-Nuts, malted—$1/2$ C Grape-Nuts plus $1/4$ C instant malted milk powder per quart chocolate or vanilla ice cream.

Grasshopper—2 T crème de menthe plus 2 T white crème de cacao (or 1 t each mint and brandy extract) plus 1 t vanilla per quart lime ice cream or sherbet, *or* 1 t mint extract plus $1/2$ C crushed chocolate sandwich cookies per quart vanilla ice cream.

Hazelnut (filbert)—$1/2$ C chopped, blanched hazelnuts plus 2 T hazelnut liqueur (optional) per quart French vanilla ice cream.

Honey—substitute honey for all or part of the sugar in any ice cream or frozen yogurt, selecting a mild-flavored honey for bisque or fruit flavors.

Jam 'n' cream—$^1/_2$ C any flavor jam or preserves stirred smooth and swirled into one quart rich vanilla ice cream.

Jelly bean—$^1/_2$ C chopped jelly beans per quart vanilla or fruit ice cream.

Kahlua 'n' cream—$^1/_4$ C Kahlua per quart rich vanilla or coffee ice cream.

Kiwi—3 ripe kiwis puréed with $^1/_2$ C orange juice per quart vanilla ice cream.

Lemon—juice of 2 lemons ($^1/_4$ C) plus juice of 1 orange ($^1/_3$ C), *or* juice of 2 lemons plus 2 t lemon zest, *or* 3 oz thawed, undiluted lemonade per quart vanilla ice cream or frozen yogurt; juice of 2 lemons plus juice of 1 orange plus $^2/_3$ C sugar per quart sherbet or ice. For stronger flavor, add $^1/_8$ t lemon extract or oil. (To prevent curdling of dairy based mix, add juice just before freezing.)

Lemon anise—$^3/_4$ t crushed anise seed per quart lemon ice cream.

Lemon chip—$^1/_2$ C crushed hard lemon candies per quart lemon ice cream.

Lemon pineapple—$^1/_2$ C crushed pineapple per quart lemon ice cream, *or* $^1/_2$ C crushed pineapple plus $^1/_2$ t lemon extract per quart vanilla ice cream.

Lemon pistachio—$^1/_2$ C chopped pistachio nuts per quart lemon ice cream.

Lemon vodka—$^1/_4$ C vodka per quart lemon sherbet.

Licorice—omit vanilla and add 1 t anise extract per quart vanilla ice cream.

Liqueur—2 T to $^1/_4$ C liqueur of similar or contrasting flavor per quart any flavor ice cream or frozen yogurt.

Loganberry—$1^1/_4$ C loganberry juice plus $^1/_2$ C sugar per quart sherbet or ice.

Macaroon—$^1/_2$ to 1 C crushed macaroons per quart any flavor ice cream.

Mallow—12 to 18 melted marshmallows or $^1/_2$ C marshmallow cream per quart vanilla ice cream.

Malt—$^1/_4$ C malted milk powder or 2 T barley malt syrup per quart any flavor ice cream. (In nondairy ice cream use barley malt syrup.)

Mandarin chocolate—substitute $^3/_4$ C orange juice for 1 C milk or add $^1/_2$ t orange extract per quart chocolate ice cream.

Mango—1$^1/_2$ C mango purée plus $^1/_3$ C sugar per quart vanilla ice cream.

Maple—omit vanilla and add $^1/_2$ t maple flavoring or $^1/_4$ C maple syrup per quart vanilla ice cream.

Maple blueberry—1 C blueberries plus $^1/_4$ C sugar per quart maple ice cream.

Maple nut—$^1/_2$ C chopped walnuts, black walnuts, or pecans per quart maple ice cream.

Margarita—$^1/_3$ C tequila per quart lime ice or sorbet.

Margarita, mango—$^1/_3$ C tequila plus 2 T lime juice per quart mango ice or sorbet.

Margarita, melon—$^1/_3$ C tequila plus 2 T lime juice per quart cantaloupe or honeydew ice or sorbet.

Marshmallow—1 C miniature marshmallows per quart any flavor ice cream. Dry marshmallows in slow oven for chewy texture.

Marshmallow divinity—$^2/_3$ C marshmallow cream plus $^1/_2$ C chopped maraschino cherries plus $^1/_2$ C drained, crushed pineapple plus $^1/_4$ C chopped nuts per quart rich vanilla ice cream.

Melon—$^1/_2$# peeled, puréed muskmelon or cantaloupe plus $^1/_3$ C sugar per quart vanilla ice cream or frozen yogurt.

Mincemeat—1 C mincemeat per quart French vanilla ice cream or frozen yogurt.

Mincemeat nut—$^1/_2$ C slivered toasted, blanched almonds plus 1 t orange zest per quart mincemeat ice cream.

Mint—1 t mint extract or 2 T crème de menthe per quart rich vanilla ice cream or frozen yogurt.

Mint chip—$^1/_2$ C chopped mint chocolate chips, *or* $^1/_2$ C miniature chocolate chips plus 1 t mint extract or 2 T crème de menthe per quart vanilla ice cream.

Mint chocolate—$^1/_2$ C chopped mint chocolate chips, *or* $^1/_2$ C miniature chocolate chips plus 1 t mint extract or 2 T crème de menthe per quart chocolate ice cream.

Mint grapefruit—$^1/_4$ t mint extract or mint oil per quart grapefruit ice or ice cream.

Mint julep—$^1/_3$ C bourbon per quart mint ice or sorbet.

Mocha—$^1/_4$ C chocolate syrup per quart coffee ice cream, *or* 2 T instant coffee crystals per quart chocolate ice cream, *or* 1 T instant coffee plus 2-oz melted nonsweetened chocolate plus $^1/_4$ C sugar per quart French vanilla ice cream.

Mocha almond fudge—$^1/_3$ C chopped almonds per quart coffee ice cream rippled with $^1/_2$ C chocolate syrup or fudge sauce.

Mocha chip—$^1/_2$ C miniature chocolate chips per quart mocha ice cream.

Molasses taffy—$^1/_2$ C chopped molasses taffy per quart vanilla or caramel ice cream.

Nectarine—1 C nectarine purée plus $^1/_4$ C sugar per quart vanilla ice cream or frozen yogurt; $1^1/_2$ C purée plus $^1/_3$ C sugar per quart sherbet, ice, or sorbet.

Nesselrode—$^3/_4$ C chopped mixed fruit and nuts (crushed pineapple, maraschino cherries, candied cherries, candied orange rind, raisins, roasted chestnuts, walnuts, almonds, and pecans) per quart French vanilla or chocolate ice cream.

Nut—1 C chopped or grated almonds, black walnuts, Brazil nuts, chestnuts, hazelnuts, macadamias, peanuts, pecans, pistachios, or walnuts, *or* $^1/_2$ C nut butter plus $^1/_4$ C sugar per quart any flavor ice cream.

Nut, toasted—up to 1 C chopped toasted nuts per quart any flavor ice cream.

Nut brittle—1 C crushed nut brittle per quart vanilla or caramel ice cream.

Orange—juice of 2 Valencia oranges ($^2/_3$ C) plus juice of $^1/_2$ lemon ($^1/_2$ T) plus $^1/_3$ C sugar, *or* 3-oz frozen orange juice concentrate per quart vanilla ice cream or frozen yogurt; juice of 2 Valencia oranges plus juice of $^1/_2$ lemon plus $^2/_3$ C sugar per quart sherbet. For stronger flavor, add $^1/_8$ t orange extract or oil or 2 t orange zest. (To prevent curdling of dairy based mix, add juice just before freezing.)

Orange chocolate chip—1 t orange extract plus $^1/_2$ C miniature chocolate chips per quart vanilla ice cream.

Orange pineapple—¹/₄ C drained crushed pineapple per quart orange ice cream or frozen yogurt.

Peach—1 C puréed peaches plus ¹/₄ C sugar plus ¹/₄ t almond extract per quart vanilla ice cream or frozen yogurt; 1¹/₄ C purée, rubbed through sieve to remove skin, per quart sherbet or ice. For strongest flavor, include some nectarines or apricots and substitute mild honey for a portion of the sugar.

Peach mallow—1# (22) melted marshmallows plus ³/₄ C peach nectar per quart rich vanilla ice cream.

Peanut—1 C chopped peanuts per quart vanilla, chocolate, or peanut butter ice cream.

Peanut brittle—¹/₂ C crushed peanut brittle candy per quart vanilla or caramel ice cream.

Peanut butter—¹/₂ to ²/₃ C smooth or crunchy peanut butter plus ¹/₄ C sugar per quart vanilla or chocolate ice cream.

Peanut butter 'n' jelly—¹/₂ C grape (or any flavor) jelly swirled into peanut butter ice cream.

Pear—1 C puréed Bartlett pears plus ¹/₄ C sugar per quart vanilla ice cream.

Pecan crunch—¹/₂ C crushed pecan crunch candy per quart vanilla or caramel ice cream.

Peppermint crunch—¹/₂ to 1 C crushed peppermint candy cane or hard candies per quart vanilla ice cream.

Persimmon—1 C puréed persimmon plus ¹/₄ C sugar plus 1 T grated orange rind per quart vanilla ice cream or frozen yogurt.

Piña colada—1 C cream of coconut plus ¹/₃ C dark rum per quart pineapple ice cream or sherbet, *or* 1 C drained crushed pineapple plus ¹/₃ C dark rum per quart coconut ice cream or sherbet.

Pineapple—²/₃ C drained crushed pineapple or up to ³/₄ C prepared pineapple topping per quart vanilla ice cream or frozen yogurt; 1 C drained crushed pineapple plus ¹/₄ C lemon juice per quart sherbet, ice, or sorbet.

Pineapple coconut—¹/₄ to ¹/₂ C grated coconut per quart pineapple ice cream or frozen yogurt.

Pineapple grapefruit—substitute pineapple-grapefruit juice for juice in any pineapple or grapefruit ice or ice cream, *or* substitute crushed pineapple or pineapple juice for half the juice in grapefruit ice, *or* substitute grapefruit juice for half the pineapple or pineapple juice in pineapple ice.

Pineapple nut—$^1/_2$ C chopped walnuts or pecans per quart pineapple ice cream or frozen yogurt.

Pine nut—$^1/_2$ C pine nuts per quart vanilla, coffee, caramel, or mint ice cream.

Pistachio—$^1/_2$ C chopped pistachio nuts plus $^1/_2$ t pistachio or almond extract per quart vanilla ice cream.

Plum—1# dark plums, crushed with $1^1/_2$ C water, boiled 5 minutes, strained, and added to $^3/_4$ C sugar—add 1 C per quart vanilla ice cream, $1^1/_4$ C per quart ice or sorbet.

Plum pudding—$^3/_4$ C chopped mixed fruit (dates, figs, mincemeat, candied fruit, or rind), nuts, and mixed spices per quart French vanilla ice cream.

Prune—$^3/_4$ to 1 C mashed stewed prunes per quart vanilla ice cream or frozen yogurt.

Prune nut—$^1/_2$ C chopped walnuts per quart prune ice cream.

Pumpkin—1 C cooked pumpkin purée plus $1^1/_2$ T orange zest or minced candied orange rind per quart vanilla ice cream or frozen yogurt.

Pumpkin bourbon raisin—$^1/_2$ C raisins steeped in $^1/_4$ C bourbon, cooled, per quart pumpkin ice cream.

Pumpkin bourbon raisin nut—$^1/_3$ C chopped walnuts or pecans per quart pumpkin bourbon raisin ice cream.

Pumpkin, New England—1 t maple flavoring per quart pumpkin ice cream.

Pumpkin nut—$^1/_3$ C chopped walnuts or pecans per quart pumpkin, New England pumpkin, or western pumpkin ice cream.

Pumpkin spice—1 t pumpkin pie spice per quart pumpkin ice cream.

Pumpkin, western—2 T to $^1/_4$ C rum per quart pumpkin or pumpkin spice ice cream.

Raisin—$^1/_2$ to $^3/_4$ C seedless raisins, half chopped and half whole (or puréed), per quart vanilla or other flavor ice cream or frozen yogurt.

Raspberries 'n' cream—$1^1/_2$ C red or black raspberries, rubbed through a sieve to remove seeds, plus $^1/_4$ C sugar plus 2 t lemon juice swirled into 1 quart rich vanilla ice cream.

Raspberry—1 to $1^1/_2$ C red or black raspberries, rubbed through a sieve to remove seeds, plus $^1/_4$ C sugar plus 2 t lemon juice per quart vanilla ice cream or frozen yogurt; 2 C ripe raspberries, rubbed through sieve, plus $^1/_3$ C sugar per quart sherbet, ice, or sorbet.

Rhubarb—$^1/_2$ C stewed rhubarb plus $^1/_4$ C sugar plus $1^1/_2$ T orange zest or minced candied orange peel plus $^1/_8$ t mace per quart vanilla ice cream; 2 C (1#) stewed rhubarb per quart sherbet.

Rhubarb nut—$^1/_4$ C chopped pecans per quart rhubarb ice cream.

Ripple—$^3/_4$ to 1 C room temperature syrup, sundae sauce or sweetened fruit purée swirled into one quart soft ice cream, any flavor.

Rocky road—1 C miniature marshmallows plus $^1/_2$ C chopped walnuts per quart chocolate ice cream.

Roman punch—$^1/_3$ C dark rum per quart lemon ice or sorbet.

Rose—1 t rose water, adjusted according to strength, per quart French vanilla ice cream.

Rum coconut—$^1/_4$ C rum per quart coconut ice cream.

Rum raisin—$^1/_4$ C dark rum or $1^1/_2$ t rum extract per quart raisin ice cream. For fullest flavor, soak chopped raisins in rum at least $^1/_2$ hour or bring to simmer, then cool.

Rum raisin, chocolate—2-oz melted semisweet chocolate per quart rum raisin ice cream, *or* $1^1/_2$ t rum extract or $^1/_2$ C raisins soaked in $^1/_4$ C dark rum per quart chocolate ice cream.

Saffron—omit vanilla and add $^1/_4$ t powdered saffron per quart rich vanilla ice cream.

Saffron honey—substitute mild-flavored honey for the sugar in saffron ice cream.

Scarlet O'Hara—$^1/_4$ C Southern Comfort plus juice of $^1/_2$ lime per quart cranberry ice or sorbet.

Sesame (tahini)—$^1/_4$ to $^1/_2$ C sesame seed purée (tahini) plus $^1/_4$ C sugar per quart vanilla or honey ice cream or frozen yogurt.

Sesame almond—$^1/_3$ C chopped toasted almonds per quart sesame ice cream.

Spumoni—$^1/_2$ C chopped, mixed candied fruit plus 2 T rum or 2 t rum flavoring per quart vanilla ice cream.

Strawberries 'n' cream—1 to 1$^1/_2$ C red, ripe mashed strawberries combined with $^1/_4$ C sugar swirled into softened vanilla ice cream.

Strawberry—1 to 1$^1/_2$ C red, ripe mashed strawberries and $^1/_4$ C sugar, *or* up to $^3/_4$ C prepared strawberry topping per quart vanilla ice cream or frozen yogurt; 1$^1/_2$ C strawberries plus $^1/_3$ C sugar per quart sherbet, ice, or sorbet.

Strawberry banana—1 large mashed banana per quart strawberry ice cream.

Strawberry banana nut—$^1/_3$ C chopped pecans per quart strawberry banana ice cream.

Strawberry pineapple—$^1/_2$ C crushed pineapple per quart strawberry ice cream, *or* $^1/_2$ C crushed strawberries per quart pineapple ice cream.

Sunseed (sunflower seed)—$^1/_2$ C salted or unsalted toasted sunflower seeds per quart vanilla or coffee ice cream.

Sweet potato—1$^1/_2$ C sweet potato purée plus $^1/_4$ C granulated or brown sugar plus 1$^1/_2$ T lemon zest (or minced candied rind or crushed lemon hard candies) per quart vanilla ice cream.

Sweet potato, candied—1 C miniature marshmallows per quart sweet potato ice cream.

Tahini—see *Sesame.*

Tea—steep $^1/_4$ C any flavor tea in 1 C hot milk for 5 minutes, strain, substitute for 1 C milk per quart vanilla ice cream.

Toffee—$^1/_2$ to 1 C crushed toffee per quart vanilla, chocolate, or coffee ice cream.

Torroncino—steep one broken-up cinnamon stick in heated mix, reduce vanilla by half and add 1 t almond extract per quart vanilla gelato.

Tutti-frutti—$^1/_2$ to 1 C mixed candied fruits and peels plus $^1/_2$ C chopped raisins plus 2 T rum (optional), *or* $^1/_2$ C chopped, mixed fresh or frozen fruit, *or* $^1/_4$ C each chopped maraschino cherries, drained crushed pineapple, chopped raisins and nuts per quart vanilla ice cream.

Tutti-frutti rum—$^1/_4$ C rum per quart tutti-frutti ice cream.

Two-tone—3-oz fruit flavored gelatin prepared with half the required water, set up in a $^1/_2$"-thick slab and shredded or cut into cubes per quart any flavor ice cream or sherbet.

Vanilla—up to 1 T vanilla extract or seeds from a 3" piece of vanilla bean per quart ice cream or frozen yogurt.

Vanilla honey—substitute honey for sugar in vanilla ice cream.

White chocolate—omit vanilla extract and add 8-oz melted white chocolate (plus 2 T almond liqueur or white crème de cacao, optional) per quart rich vanilla ice cream.

White chocolate almond—$^1/_2$ chopped toasted almonds per quart white chocolate ice cream, *or* $^1/_2$ t almond extract plus two chopped Nestle Alpine White bars per quart vanilla ice cream.

White chocolate chip—$^1/_2$ C chopped white chocolate chips per quart coffee or chocolate ice cream.

White chocolate 'cot—$^1/_2$ C chopped dried apricots per quart white chocolate ice cream.

White chocolate frutti—$^1/_2$ C minced candied fruit per quart white chocolate ice cream.

White chocolate nut—$^1/_4$ C chopped almonds or hazelnuts plus 2 T almond or hazelnut liqueur (optional) per quart white chocolate ice cream.

White chocolate rum raisin—$^1/_4$ C chopped golden raisins soaked in 2 T light rum per quart white chocolate ice cream.

White chocolate violet—$^1/_2$ C candied violets per quart white chocolate ice cream.

Zabaione—$^1/_2$ C Marsala, Madeira, port, sherry, or quality brandy per quart French vanilla ice cream or gelato.

Appendix B

Conversions

Temperature conversions from Fahrenheit to Celsius have already been given as they came up throughout this book. Where baking is involved, as in preparing ice cream cakes, temperatures have been rounded to the nearest five degrees to provide practical, realistic oven settings.

In measuring most ingredients, whether liquid or dry, American cooks usually go by volume rather than by weight, using standardized teaspoons, tablespoons, and cups. Occasionally, liquids are measured in fluid ounces, and fruit and canned goods are measured in pounds and (avoirdupois) ounces. The following chart is offered to help overseas readers comprehend our quirky American system.

U.S. TO METRIC CONVERSIONS	
American	**Metric**
$^1/_4$ teaspoon	1.25 ml
$^1/_2$ teaspoon	2.5 ml
1 teaspoon	5 ml
$^1/_2$ tablespoon (1$^1/_2$ teaspoon)	7.5 ml
1 tablespoon (3 teaspoons)	15 ml
$^1/_8$ cup (2 tablespoons)	30 ml
$^1/_4$ cup (4 tablespoons)	60 ml
$^1/_3$ cup (5 tablespoons + 1 teaspoon)	80 ml
$^1/_2$ cup (8 tablespoons)	120 ml
1 cup (16 tablespoons)	240 ml
1 quart (4 cups)	950 ml
1 fluid ounce (2 tablespoons)	30 ml
8 fluid ounces (1 cup)	240 ml
1 ounce	28.4 g
1 pound (16 ounces)	454 g

Appendix C

Supplies

Ice cream freezers and the companies making them constantly come and go. The following models are available as this book goes to press. Since products change rapidly, look into what else is currently on the market before making up your mind. Prices shown here are list prices suggested by manufacturers or distributors. You can often do considerably better at a discount store.

ICE CREAM FREEZERS		
	Hand-Crank	**Electric**
CRUSHED ICE AND ROCK SALT		
Richmond Cedar Works	X	X
Rival		X
White Mountain	X	X
ICE CUBES AND TABLE SALT		
Oster		X
Rival		X
Waring		X
SEALED-IN COOLANT		
Donvier	X	
M.A.S.		X
Nordic	X	
Presto		X
Salton	X	
Simac		X
Waring	X	X

ICE CREAM FREEZERS, cont'd.		
	Hand-Crank	**Electric**
HOUSEHOLD FREEZER		
none available as of this writing		
SELF-COOLING		
Gaggia		X
SaniServ (commercial)		X
Simac		X
Taylor (commercial)		X
MIX IS COOLANT*		
Vita-Mix		X
Cuisinart		X
(*any quality food processor fitted with a steel blade)		

Cuisinart food processors come in 5 sizes ranging in capacity from 3 to 20 cups and in price from $115 to $625. See-through canister has add-ingredient opening in lid. Some ice cream recipes included. Made in Japan (except "Classic" model, which is made in U.S.A.). Three-year limited warranty. Cuisinarts, Inc., 77 Havemeyer Lane, Stamford, CT 06902, 203-975-4600, 800-726-0190.

Donvier "Chillfast" hand-crank ice cream makers with sealed-in coolant range from "Half-Pint" ($15), through 16-ounce children's models ($25), to 1-quart Euro-designed "Premier" ($35). All have see-through lids. Recipe booklet. Made in Japan. One year limited warranty. Krups North America, 7 Reuten Drive, Closter, NJ 07624, 201-767-5500.

Gaggia "Gelatiera" $1^1/_2$-quart, internally cooled electric freezer retails for $450. Built-in stainless steel bowls plus two removable aluminum bowls. See-through lid. Automatic timer. Recipe booklet in five languages including English, requires conversion. Made in Italy. One year limited warranty. Liberty/Richter Inc., 400 Commerce Boulevard, Carlstadt, NJ 07072, 201-935-4500.

M.A.S. "Cream 'n Serve" electric sealed-in coolant freezer dispenses $1^1/_2$ quarts of soft-serve through a built-in nozzle. Additional freezing cylinders available for back-to-back freezing. Recipe booklet included. Frozen yogurt mix available. Full one year warranty. Made in Hong Kong. M.A.S. of America, Inc., 7165 S. W. 47th Street #314, Miami, FL 33155, 305-662-9244, 800-433-8412.

Nordic "Supremer Ice Creamer" comes in 1¹/₂-pint ($35) and 1¹/₂-quart ($40) models, both with sealed-in coolant. Variable gear ratio adjusts dasher speed without altering hand-cranking rhythm. Gear and cover take dexterity to assemble. Dishwasher safe, see-through lid. Made in U.S.A. Three year limited warranty. Nordic Ware, Division Northland Aluminum Products, Highway 7 at 100, Minneapolis, MN 55416, 612-920-2888.

Oster "Quick Freeze" ($54) holds 2 quarts, uses salt and small-sized ice cubes. See-through lid has add-ingredient opening. Also available as a $30 accessory for the Oster "Kitchen Center." Recipe sheet included. Made in U.S.A. One year limited warranty. Oster Housewares, 5055 N. Lydell Avenue, Milwaukee, WI 53217, 414-332-8300.

Presto 1-quart "IceCreamNow" electric freezer with sealed-in coolant retails for $76. Recipes included. Made in China. One year limited warranty. National Presto Industries, Inc., Eau Claire, WI 54703, 715-839-2121.

Richmond Cedar Works, ice-and-salt units range from 2 to 6 quarts, $20 to $55. Hand-crank and electric (with automatic shut-off). Tongue-and-groove wood or plastic buckets. Some units have see-through lids. Recipes included. Ice cream mix available. Made in U.S.A. One year limited warranty. Richmond Cedar Works, PO Box 3388, Danville, VA 24543, 804-797-4444.

Rival "Dolly Madison" electric ice-and-salt freezers come in 3 plastic models ranging from 2-quart ($32) to 6-quart ($34), and one wood and brass model ($53), all with see-through lids. Recipe booklet. Made in U.S.A. Full one year warranty. Rival Manufacturing Company, 3601 Bennington, Kansas City, MO 64129, 861-861-1000.

Salton "Big Chill" hand-crank freezer makes 1¹/₂ quarts, retails for $40. See-through lid has large add-ingredient opening. Recipe booklet. Aluminum canister made in Italy, plastic parts made in U.S.A. One year limited warranty. Salton, 550 Business Center Drive, Mount Prospect, IL 60056, 708-803-4600, 800-233-9054.

SaniServ commercial stainless steel countertop batch freezers come in 4 and 6 quart capacities, air or water cooled. Both must be wired directly. Prices start at $5,200. Made in U.S.A. One year limited warranty. SaniServ, 2020 Production Drive, Indianapolis, IN 46241, 317-247-0460, 800-733-8073.

Simac "Il Gelataio" electric ice cream freezers come in both self-cooling and sealed-in coolant models. One-quart sealed-in coolant unit ($90) has see-through lid with add-ingredient opening. A few recipes included. "Duet" ($125) makes two flavors at once, 1 pint each. Four-language instruction booklet requires recipe conversion. "Il Gelataio Super" ($625) self-cooling freezer holds 1 quart in removable stainless steel bowl, with extra bowls available. Nice recipe booklet. All units made in Italy. One year limited warranty. Lello Appliances Corporation, 355 Murray Hill Parkway, East Rutherford, NJ 07073, 201-939-2555, 800-527-4336.

Taylor commercial countertop 3-quart batch freezers are air or water cooled. Both models plug into heavy-appliance outlet (similar to clothes dryer outlet). Price is established by individual distributors. Made in U.S.A. One year limited warranty. Taylor Company, 750 North Blackhawk Boulevard, Rockton, IL 61072, 815-624-8333, 800-255-0626.

Vita-Mix, with or without pressurized spigot for dispensing soft-serve, retails for $425. Rapid blade reversal makes ice cream from frozen ingredients, heats toppings without scorching. See-through lid has large add-ingredient opening. Stainless steel canister, heavy duty power unit. Ice cream recipes included. Made in U.S.A. Five year limited warranty. Vita-Mix Corporation, 8615 Usher Road, Cleveland, OH 44138, 216-235-4840, 800-848-2649.

Waring "Ice Cream Parlor" 3-pint sealed-in coolant model comes in electric ($60) or combination hand crank and electric ($68). Two-quart model ($44) works on ice cubes and salt. All have see-through lids with add-ingredient openings. Two-quart model has optional juicer attachment for super-fresh citrus freezes, convenient stow-away cord. Recipe booklet. Made in U.S.A. One year warranty. Waring Products Division, Dynamics Corporation of America, New Hartford, CT 06057, 203-379-0731.

White Mountain, makes 11 ice-and-salt models, hand-crank and electric, 2 to 20 quarts, $75 to $890. Large handles on hand-operated units reduce cranking fatigue. Universal non-stalling motor is a bit noisy but works until the job is done. Handcrafted tongue-and-groove pine buckets. Extra tall, tin-plated steel canisters for extra-fast freezing. Cast iron dasher with wooden blades is designed to last. Recipes included. Ice cream mix available. Made in U.S.A. Canisters warranted five years; other parts, one year limited warranty. White Mountain, Lincoln Avenue, Winchendon, MA 01475, 617-297-0015.

Ice Cream Resources

The following festivals, organizations and mail-order sources for hard-to-find ingredients and supplies are listed here only as an aid to readers. No pretext is made that this list is comprehensive.

Astor Chocolates Corp., 48-25 Metropolitan Avenue, Glendale, NY 11385, 718-386-7400—Chocolate shells.

Cake-D-Cor, PO Box 402, Lebanon, NJ 08833, 201-236-9484—Edible rice paper wafers.

Caffe D'Oro Enterprises, Brad Barry Company, Ltd., 751 East Kingshill Place, Carson, CA 90746, 213-532-4102, 800-421-1158—Instant espresso, quality flavored coffees.

Cook Flavoring Company, 1103 A Street, Suite 352, Tacoma, WA 98402, 206-627-5499—Natural extracts in hard-to-find flavors such as chocolate, fruit, nut, and spice.

DDP Corporation, 21 Taft Woods Way, Media, PA 19063, 215-565-9066—Lead-free reproductions of antique molds in 3-ounce and 3-pint sizes, home video shows how to mold and air brush.

Finnigan's, Museum of Science and Industry, 57th Street & Lake Shore Drive, Chicago, IL 60637, 312-684-1414—Working old-time ice cream parlor.

Hawaiice Ice Shaver, Back to Basics Products, Inc., 11660 S. State Street, Sandy, UT 84070, 801-571-7349, 800-688-1989—Hand-crank appliance shaves ice soft and fluffy or coarse and grainy, children's model has blade safety feature.

The Ice Screamers, PO Box 5387, Lancaster, PA 17601, 717-569-1866, 717-569-5663—Devotees of ice cream parlor and soda fountain collectibles, bi-monthly newsletter, annual meeting.

Kitchen Krafts, Box 805, Mt. Laurel, New Jersey 08054, 800-776-0575—Air brush materials and other decorating supplies.

Jackson-Mitchell Meyenburg Goat Milk Products, PO Box 5425, Santa Barbara, CA 93150, 805-565-1538—Fresh, evaporated, and powdered goat milk.

Lactaid, Inc., PO Box 111, Pleasantville, NJ 08232, 609-653-6100, 800-257-8650—Lactase enzyme.

Loma Linda Foods, 11503 Pierce Street, Riverside, CA 92505, 714-687-7800, 800-932-5525—Evaporated and powdered soy milk.

Maid of Scandinavia, 3244 Raleigh Avenue, Minneapolis, MN 55416, 612-925-9256, 800-328-6722 (800-851-1121 from Minnesota)—Decorating supplies, rice paper wafers, egg white powder, liquid lecithin, flavorings, dyes, molds, cone irons, chocolate dessert cups, etc.

Miss Martha's Old Fashioned Sunday Social and Ice Cream Crankin', Trinity Presbyterian Church, 3201 Hillsboro Road, Nashville, TN 37201, 615-297-6514—August homemade ice cream contest and all-you-can-eat social.

Mountain Ark Trading Company, 120 S. East Avenue, Fayetteville, AR 72701, 501-442-7191, 800-643-8909—Kudzu, koji, sweet brown rice, etc.

Nasco, 901 Janesville Avenue, PO Box 901, Fort Atkinson, WI 53538, 414-563-2446, 800-558-9595—Ice cream freezers, scoops, molds, cone iron.

New England Cheesemaking Supply Company, PO Box 85, Ashfield, MA 01330, 413-628-3808—Ice cream freezers, yogurt makers, goat milk yogurt culture.

Old Fashioned Ice Cream Festival, Rockwood Museum, 610 Shipley Road, Wilmington, DE 19809, 302-571-7776—July ice cream social, antiques display.

The Soda Fountain, Western Heritage Museum, 801 S. Tenth Street, Omaha, NE 68108, 402-444-5071/5072—Restored soda fountain serving old-fashioned ice cream sodas.

Soft Twirl Ice Cream Server, G & S Metal Products Company, Inc., 3330 E. 79th Street, Cleveland, OH 44127, 216-441-0700—Hand-crank appliance whips 2 1/2 cups hardened ice cream to soft-serve consistency, blends flavorings in.

Soronson Ice Cream Specialties, PO Box 30062, Baltimore, MD 21270, 301-635-2952—Ice cream related gifts, ice cream theme parties, ice cream appreciation workshops by Bryan Soronson.

Technodyne Corporation, 380 Linden Street, Reno, NV 89502, 702-829-1199, 800-468-3477—"Hot Scoop" electric, battery operated and rechargeable dippers.

Williams-Sonoma, Mail Order Department, PO Box 7456, San Francisco, CA 94120, 415-421-7900—Ice cream freezer, cone iron, shake mixer, fountain ware, fudge sauce, fan wafers.

Wilton Enterprises, 2240 West 75th Street, Woodridge, IL 60517, 708-963-7100—Decorating supplies, egg white powder.

Worthington Foods, 900 Proprietors Road, Worthington, OH 43085, 614-885-9511, 800-628-3663—Powdered soy milk sweetened either with sugar or with corn syrup.

The Zeroll Company, 3405 Industrial 31st Street, Fort Pierce, FL 34946, 800-872-5000—Dippers in sizes 10, 12, 16, 20, 24; ice cream spades, fountain ware, gift sets.

Glossary

Age—to refrigerate a mix 4 to 24 hours to improve its flavor and viscosity before freezing

Aqutaq—see *Eskimo ice cream*; variations include "ackutuk," "agutuk," "aqutuq," "akutaq"

Aufait—molded ice cream, often brick shaped, with thin, alternating layers of fruit gelatin or preserves; named according to the fruit used, such as "raspberry aufait"; also, ice cream rippled with fruit sauce

Banana split sundae—banana or other ice cream topped with fudge or fruit sauce and garnished with banana slices

Bisque—ice cream flavored with bits of baked goods such as cake, cookies, or cereal; also, a confection

Black and white—a twin sundae consisting of vanilla ice cream topped with fudge sauce and chocolate ice cream topped with marshmallow sauce or whipped cream

Black cow—an ice cream soda made with root beer, chocolate syrup, and vanilla ice cream

Bleed—tendency of ices and sherbets to develop a syrupy layer at the bottom of the container during storage

Body—the group of characteristics determining the weight and firmness of ice cream

Bombe—ice cream molded in the shape of a bowl (or bomb); also called a "melon mold"

Bon-bon—a bite-sized scoop of ice cream coated with chocolate; also, a sundae garnished with candied fruit

Brick—a rectangular or loaf-shaped ice cream mold

Brown cow—an ice cream soda made with cola, chocolate syrup, and vanilla ice cream

Canister—the part of an ice cream freezer into which mix is poured for freezing

Carbonated beverage—soft drink; also called "soda," "soda pop," "pop"

Center mold—an ice cream molded in two or more contrasting colors so that an emblem (heart, shamrock, star, etc.) appears when the ice cream is sliced for serving

Churn—to whip cream until it turns to butter, undesirable in making ice cream; sometimes erroneously used as a synonym for stir freezing

Composite ice cream—ice cream flavored with fruit, nuts, or baked goods, in contrast to plain ice cream

Confection—ice cream flavored with bits of crushed candy

Coolant—a substance, such as ice or antifreeze, that allows a mix to freeze by absorbing its heat

Cooler—a drink made with fruit juice, carbonated beverage and sherbet, sometimes served in a punch bowl; also, a soda made with sherbet instead of ice cream

Coupe—French for "cup" or "goblet," a rounded champagne glass roughly the shape of a sherbet dish; ice cream served in such a container; in Britain, a serving of ice cream, usually garnished with fruit and sometimes sundae sauce, liqueur, or champagne, served in a cup-shaped dish

Cream can—see *Canister*

Cup—see *Coupe*

Cylinder—the canister for a sealed-in coolant ice cream freezer

Cylinder-type freezer—sealed-in coolant ice cream maker

Designer ice cream—very rich ice cream named after a known personality or a made-up Scandinavian sounding word

Dip—to scoop ice cream; a single scoop of ice cream

Dipper—the tool used to scoop ice cream; a scoop

Double sundae—a scoop of ice cream topped with sauce of the same flavor

Emulsifier—an ingredient that allows the blending of other ingredients that don't normally mix

Emulsion—one liquid evenly dispersed within another, such as globules of milkfat in milk

Eskimo ice cream—a snack made from whipped fat and fresh or dried berries, frozen or not; also called "aqutaq"

Eskimo pie—patented, chocolate-coated ice cream bar commercially manufactured under license

Flambé—flaming

Float—a carbonated beverage, fruit juice, or milk served in a tall glass and topped with one or more scoops of ice cream or sherbet

Frappe—a northeastern milkshake

Frappé—a slushy drink made with a combination of fruit juices; also, liqueur served over shaved ice

Freeze—a frozen food such as ice cream, sherbet, sorbet, frozen yogurt, etc.; also, a slushy fruit drink made with crushed ice

French ice cream—a smooth, rich ice cream containing cooked egg yolks; also called "French custard," "frozen custard," "New York ice cream," "parfait," "Neapolitan"

French pot—old-time ice cream freezer consisting of two metal bowls, one packed with ice and salt and the other filled with mix that's worked by hand; also called an "ice cream pot"

Frogurt—frozen yogurt, now registered as a trade name

Frosted—a milkshake

Frosty—a shake made with sherbet, sorbet, soy ice cream, or anything other than regular ice cream; also sometimes called a "smoothy"

Frozen custard—legally, ice cream containing a specified minimum of egg yolk solids; in practice, ice cream made from a custard base; see also *French ice cream* and *Gelato*

Fruit salad—a frozen mousse flavored with mayonnaise and fruit, often served on lettuce or other greens; also, equal portions of mayonnaise and fruit ice cream used as a dressing for fresh fruit

Gelateria—Italian ice cream shop

Gelato—intensely flavored, very dense Italian frozen custard containing lots of egg yolks and little or no cream; also, any freeze sold at an Italian ice cream shop or gelateria

Glacé—French for frozen or iced, refers to any frozen treat; also, a sundae made with glazed fruits or nuts

Going all the way—chocolate ice cream with chocolate cake

Granita—a flavorful, still-frozen ice of very crumbly texture (plural: granite)

Harden—to finish stir-frozen ice cream by storing it in the freezer until firm

Heat shock—undesirable textural change resulting from variable temperature during storage

Hokey-pokey—obsolete word for cheap ice cream sold by a street vendor or hokey-pokey man

House boat—a banana split

Ice—a tart freeze consisting primarily of sugar-water syrup and fruit juice, fruit purée, or coffee

Ice cream—a dairy-based freeze containing cream; also, imitation ice cream; also, a standardized frozen dessert manufactured under the specifications set forth in the Federal Food and Drug Administration Code of Federal Regulations Title 21, Part 35

Ice cream gâteau—French for ice cream cake (plural: gâteaux)

Ice cream headache—a pounding sensation at the top or sides of the head as a result of eating ice cream too fast

Ice cream soda—carbonated beverage muddled with a little ice cream and sometimes flavorful syrup and served with a scoop of ice cream floating on top

Ice cream stomach ache—a painful condition prevalent in the early 1800s due to poor sanitation, occurs today only in one case out of 36 billion according to Cornell University

Ice milk—a very low fat ice cream

Imitation ice cream—any freeze that resembles ice cream but contains no dairy products

Italian ice cream—see *Gelato*

Jerk—to dispense ice cream sodas; also, the person who does the dispensing (see *Soda jerk*)

Lacto—obsolete word for ice cream made with a cultured dairy product such as yogurt or buttermilk

Lactose—a natural sugar occurring in milk

Lecithin—a natural emulsifier usually derived from soy beans

Lover's sundae—twin sundae served with two spoons

Mallow—any ice cream or sundae sauce containing marshmallow; also called "marlow"

Malted—a milkshake flavored with malt; also called a "malt" or "malted milkshake"

Marlow—see *Mallow*

Mellorine—ice cream made with vegetable oil instead of cream

Mellow—to temper

Melon mold—see *Bombe*

Meringue glacé—a hard meringue shell filled with ice cream

Milkshake—a thick, frothy, smoothly blended drink containing milk, flavoring, and ice cream or sherbet

Milkstone—chalky deposit on the surface of a metal canister due to improper cleaning

Mold—any form, such as a metal bowl or loaf pan, in which ice cream is shaped and hardened before serving; also, shaped and hardened ice cream from which individual servings are cut

Mousse—a frozen dessert made from sweetened whipped cream, traditionally still frozen but now sometimes stir frozen; also, a frozen dessert made by combining sweetened whipped cream with an equal amount of softened ice cream

Neapolitan—an ice cream mold, usually in brick form, consisting of layers of three different flavors, often chocolate, strawberry, and vanilla; also, frozen custard

Nonfat milk solids—the combination of protein, lactose, and minerals left after all the milkfat and water have been removed from milk; also called "milk-solids-not-fat (MSNF)," "serum solids," "nonfat dry milk"

Nonpareils—tiny bits of chocolate or colored candy sprinkled on ice cream, primarily in the East; also called "sprinkles"

Novelty—a single-serving ice cream snack such as a sandwich, bar, or prefilled cone

Overrun—the amount of air accounting for the increase in volume between a freeze and its original liquid mix

Parfait—French for "perfect," refers to alternating layers of ice cream and fruit, nuts, whipped cream, or sundae sauce served in a tall glass; also, an especially rich frozen custard

Parvine—kosher nondairy ice cream, combined from the word "pareve" (a nondairy food) and "margarine"

Pasteurize—to heat milk or a mix to a specific temperature for a specific length of time (temperature and time vary according to the method used) to destroy bacteria without causing major chemical changes

Philadelphia ice cream—ice cream containing only cream, sugar, and flavoring; also, vanilla ice cream flavored with visible vanilla seeds or crushed vanilla pods

Plain ice cream—a smooth-textured ice cream such as vanilla or chocolate, in contrast to a composite ice cream such as strawberry or maple nut

Popsicle—registered trade name for a specific kind of frozen sucker

Pudding—a frozen custard containing a generous amount of mixed fruit, nuts, or raisins, sometimes flavored with spices or liquor

Punch—a fruit ice flavored with an alcoholic beverage, extract, or flavoring, usually rum

Purée—to whirl smooth in a blender or food processor, rub through a fine sieve, or mash thoroughly with a fork

Purple cow—an ice cream soda made with grape juice and vanilla ice cream

Quiescent freezing—freezing without agitation; also called "still freezing"

Rainbow—different colored freezes, often six or more, layered or swirled together

Raw—unpasteurized milk or cream; also, uncooked fruit

"Real"—a promotional designation sponsored by dairy organizations; when printed on a commercial ice cream carton within a seal that looks like a drop of milk, indicates a product conforming to federal and state standards of identity

Refrigerant—a coolant

Ripen—to age; sometimes erroneously used as a synonym for harden

Ripple—ice cream containing ribbons of sundae sauce, fruit syrup, or sweetened fruit purée

Rock salt—particles of sodium chloride or calcium chloride used to lower the temperature of ice used as a coolant

Royal—sundae garnished with sliced fruit, nuts, and sundae sauce

Sandy—a textural defect of ice cream resulting from the crystallization of lactose or from adding finely chopped nuts

Sanitizer—a substance used to destroy bacteria on dairy equipment including ice cream freezers

Scoop—a round serving of ice cream shaped in a spoon designed for the purpose; also, to create such a serving

Scotch Highball—a butterscotch-flavored ice cream soda

Semi-freddo—an Italian soft-serve ice cream containing whipped cream or whipped egg white (plural: semi-freddi)

Serum solids—Nonfat dry milk

Shake—a milkshake

Sherbet—similar to ice cream except that it contains more fruit juice or purée and less milk or cream; also, a standardized frozen dessert manufactured under the specifications set forth in the Federal Food and Drug Administration Code of Federal Regulations Title 21, Part 35

Skirt—the ring of ice cream sticking out around the edges of a scoop on a cone

Slush—a soft sorbet or ice served in a tall glass; also, a drink made from fruit purée or juice and finely crushed ice

Smoothy—a milkshake, usually nondairy

Soda—ice cream soda; also, a carbonated beverage or soft drink

Soda fountain—originally a refreshment bar serving carbonated water flavored with syrups, now any ice cream shop or parlor

Soda jerk—someone who dispenses ice cream sodas, so-called after the dramatic practice of jerking the lever of an old-fashioned soda dispenser to make the soda spray out

Soft-serve—to dispense a freeze before it's hardened; also, a freeze so served

Sorbet—French for sherbet or ice; also, any freeze containing no eggs or dairy products

Sorbetto—a strongly flavored Italian ice (plural: sorbetti)

Soufflé—a sherbet or ice made with whole eggs or egg yolks

Specialty—a mold, bombe, ice cream pie or cake, rippled or marbled ice cream, novelty, or any fancy frozen dessert

Spoom—a sorbet or sherbet fluffed up with whipped egg whites, often shaped in a mold or piped into fancy designs from a pastry tube

Sprinkles—see *Nonpareils*

Spumoni—an Italian molded dessert consisting of two or three flavors of ice cream and/or mousse, usually including chocolate and vanilla, one of which contains candied fruit

Stabilizer—any ingredient added to a mix to prevent changes in taste, color, or texture

Still frozen—frozen without agitation

Stir frozen—frozen under agitation so that air is incorporated and ice crystals are kept small for smooth texture

Sultana roll—a tubular mold with tutti-frutti ice cream in the center and pistachio mousse around the outside

Sundae—a scoop of ice cream, sherbet, or other freeze topped with flavored syrup or sauce and fruit, nuts, and/or whipping cream

Superpremium—a high-fat, low-overrun ice cream made with top-quality, usually natural, ingredients; also called "gourmet" ice cream

Tartufo—an Italian-style frozen truffle consisting of a generous scoop of gelato filled with nut purée or fruit and coated with dark chocolate (plural: tartufi)

Temper—to warm ice cream until it's soft enough to scoop

Texture—the overall structure of ice cream as determined by the size, shape, number, and arrangement of its finer particles

Tin roof—ice cream rippled with fudge sauce combined with chopped salted peanuts

Tofu glacé—upscale term for soy ice cream

Tofutti—registered trade name for a specific kind of soy ice cream

Topper—garnish for a sundae, parfait, or banana split

Topping—sweet sauce or whipped cream served on ice cream

Touchdown—a sundae, once popular during football season, in which a (football shaped) Brazil nut is hidden

Tutti-frutti—ice cream containing bits of mixed fruit

Twin sundae—a two-scoop sundae

Vanillin—the primary flavoring component of pure vanilla; more often, a compound having the same chemical composition as natural vanillin but derived from alternative sources and lacking the same depth of flavor

Variegated—a combination of two or more flavors or kinds of freeze, or a single flavor with syrup or sauce swirled through; variations include marble, ripple, and rainbow

Water ice—obsolete term (still used in government publications) for an ice, coined in the days when sherbet was called "milk ice" and ice cream was "cream ice"

White cow—a vanilla milkshake

Selected Bibliography

Arbuckle, W.W. *Ice Cream*. Westport, Connecticut: AVI Publishing Company, Inc., 1986.

American Diabetes Association, Inc., and The American Dietetic Association. *Exchange Lists for Meal Planning*. Chicago, Illinois: American Dietetic Association, 1986.

Dickson, Paul. *The Great American Ice Cream Book*. New York: Atheneum, 1978.

Frandsen, J.H. and D. Horace Nelson. *Ice Creams and other Frozen Desserts*. Amherst, Massachusetts: J.H. Frandsen, 1950.

International Association of Ice Cream Manufacturers (now called "International Ice Cream Association"). *The History of Ice Cream*. Washington, D.C., 1986.

International Ice Cream Association. *The Latest Scoop*. Washington, D.C., 1984-1989.

Shurtleff, William and Akiko Aoyagi. *Tofutti & Other Soy Ice Creams*. Lafayette, California: The Soyfoods Center, 1985.

Smith, Wayne. *Ice Cream Dippers, An Illustrated History and Collector's Guide to Antique Ice Cream Scoops*. Walkersville, Maryland: Wayne Smith, 1986.

United States Department of Agriculture. *Code of Federal Regulations Title 21: Parts 100-169*. Washington, D.C.: United States Government Printing Office, 1989.

Wheaton, Barbara Ketcham. *Victorian Ices and Ice Cream: One Hundred and Seventeen Delicious and Unusual Recipes Updated for the Modern Kitchen*. New York: The Metropolitan Museum of Art, 1985 (reissue of *Victorian Ices and Ice Cream* by Mrs. A.B. Marshall, London, 1885).

Index